Suzie Lane

Oct 1997

D0024964

THERAPEUTIC RECREATION

Processes and Techniques

Third Edition

DAVID R. AUSTIN
INDIANA UNIVERSITY

SAGAMORE PUBLISHING
Champaign, IL 61820

© 1997 Sagamore Publishing
All rights reserved.

Production Manager: Susan M. McKinney
Production Coordinator: Michelle Summers
Cover design: Michelle R. Dressen
Editor: Susan M. McKinney
Proofreader: Phyllis L. Bannon

ISBN: 1-57164-032-7

Printed in the United States.

To Ron, Dorothy, Joan, and Janet

Contents

PREFACE

This book is a revision of the second edition published in 1991. The original material has been updated and new information has been included to expand the depth and breadth of the topics covered. My goal was to produce a text that would add to the knowledge and enhance the technical abilities of therapeutic recreation students and clinicians. Ultimately, the purpose of this book is to improve the quality of therapeutic recreation services available to clients.

I wrote the original edition because there was a need for a book that explained how to practice therapeutic recreation. Instead of providing information about therapeutic recreation services and client characteristics, I wrote a book that emphasized substantive concerns involved in the actual practice of therapeutic recreation. As in the first edition, many practical guidelines, exercises, and examples are provided throughout the book. In this text I have discussed not only theory, but the implications of theories for the practice of therapeutic recreation.

This text was written to go beyond the common-sense approach that utilizes knowledge gained primarily through personal experience. The content of this book includes literature from psychiatry, education, nursing, and counseling as well as academic disciplines representing the behavioral sciences. This broad-based foundation provides a scholarly basis for understanding therapeutic recreation processes and techniques.

Finally, I wished to provide a book that is readable and easy to follow. Each chapter adheres to a set format that includes objectives to guide the reader's learning and a set of reading comprehension questions. This structure is explained in detail in Chapter One.

There have been several changes in this edition. A segment on cognitive-behavioral therapy has been added to the coverage of major theoretical bases of practice in Chapter Two. Chapter Three, Facilitation Techniques, has been enlarged to include aromatherapy, aquatic therapy, cognitive rehabilitation and validation therapy. Throughout the book, sections have been expanded, including those dealing with assessment, activity analysis, and challenges that confront group leaders. Over 100 new references appear in this third edition. Unique elements found in the second edition of the book have been updated. These include health and safety considerations, therapeutic communication skills, social psychological phenomena, and clinical supervision.

A word about the choice of terms in this book is in order. The term "client" has been used because it is widely accepted in the world of therapeutic recreation today and is a more universal term than patient, student, or resident. Also, the term "therapeutic recreation specialist" has been consistently applied when referring to therapeutic recreation professionals.

I am indebted to many individuals and institutions for assistance in the preparation of this book. I am particularly grateful for the work of my wife, Joan; in addition to co-authoring Chapter Ten, she made many suggestions and edited drafts of the manuscript.

—*David R. Austin*

— *Chapter One* —

BASIC CONCEPTS

CHAPTER PURPOSE

Therapeutic recreation accomplishes its goals through the actions of specialists who, as helping professionals, serve clients. To become a competent helping professional, the therapeutic recreation specialist must gain both the theoretical and the technical knowledge necessary for successful practice. An introduction to helping others and to the content and format of the book is presented within this chapter.

KEY TERMS

- Helping relationships
- Objectives
- Theory

OBJECTIVES

- Comprehend the nature of the content contained within this book.
- Grasp what makes the therapeutic recreation specialist different from the layperson.
- Know the major topics to be covered in this book.
- Understand the format followed in each chapter.

- Recognize that the approach taken within this book is to make the student the focus of instruction.

Since there are other books on therapeutic recreation, one might ask, "Why add another one to the collection?" One reason might be that an improved version of prior works is needed. However, there are already several well-prepared works among the current therapeutic recreation textbooks. I have written this book because I believe there is a great deal of information regarding therapeutic recreation that has not been covered in previously published textbooks.

Introductory therapeutic recreation textbooks necessarily provide information about therapeutic recreation services and client characteristics but do not deal extensively with the actual delivery of direct client service. This book marks a departure from the survey type of textbooks that have served the profession well as literature for introductory courses in therapeutic recreation. This book will examine the methods of therapeutic recreation. It is aimed toward the *how* of therapeutic recreation. Although it is based largely on theory, the book covers basic helping skills required in the practice of therapeutic recreation.

ON HELPING OTHERS

We in therapeutic recreation require literature that will expand our knowledge of the processes and techniques central to the delivery of direct client services. In successful **helping relationships** we assist the client to meet a problem or need. If we are able to do this better than the client can alone or with family or friends, we must possess more than good intentions. The difference between a layperson's approach to the client and that of the trained practitioner is that the practitioner bases his or her service on processes and techniques drawn from the theoretical, scientific, and experiential knowledge of his or her profession. People rely on therapeutic recreation practitioners to have the theory and skills that will enable them to do things they could not otherwise accomplish alone.

It is therefore critical that basic processes and techniques of therapeutic recreation be thoroughly understood and skillfully applied by those practicing in the profession. This book provides professional information to assist those developing themselves for careers in therapeutic recreation to gain competencies necessary for the provision of quality therapeutic recreation services.

MAJOR TOPICS COVERED

Chapter 1: Basic Concepts

A brief overview and discussion of this book's major concepts, purposes, and its organization.

Chapter 2: Theories and Therapies

One distinction between the layperson and the professional is that the professional draws on **theory** as a basis for action. Differentiating among psychoanalytic, behavioristic, cognitive-behavioral, growth psychology, and other theories—and therapeutic approaches related to these orientations—provides a fundamental level of knowledge for the therapeutic recreation specialist.

Chapter 3: Facilitation Techniques

Facilitation techniques such as values clarification, horticulture therapy, therapeutic touch, social skills training, progressive relaxation training, animal-facilitated therapy, reality orientation and reminiscing are less comprehensive in their development than the major theories and therapies presented in Chapter 2. Nevertheless, many facilitation techniques can be used as interventions by therapeutic recreation specialists.

Chapter 4: The Therapeutic Recreation Process

The therapeutic recreation process is a systematic method of problem solving applied in therapeutic recreation. Through a progression of steps involving assessment, planning, implementation, and evaluation, the therapeutic recreation process is utilized to bring about changes in the client and the client's environment.

Chapter 5: Helping Others

Therapeutic recreation takes place through interpersonal relations. Helping people is a complex act requiring an understanding of both human behavior and what constitutes an effective helper and a helping relationship. This understanding is an essential ingredient for the therapeutic recreation specialist in order to bring about the therapeutic use of self.   The development of self-awareness is vital to therapeutic recreation specialists because knowing one's self is a basic competency necessary for helping others.

Chapter 6: Communication Skills

All interpersonal relationships depend on communication. Without communication, no relationship can exist because relationships depend on a two-way sharing of ideas and experiences (Sundeen, Stuart, Rankin & Cohen, 1985). This is unquestionably true in therapeutic recreation; good interpersonal communication is necessary for effective relating with clients in clinical practice.

Chapter 7: Being a Leader

One of the most critical elements in therapeutic recreation is leadership. The interactions that occur between the leader and the client, and among clients, are central to the success of therapeutic recreation programs. Skills in leadership help the therapeutic recreation specialist use therapeutic interventions or facilitate client growth. Leadership in therapeutic recreation calls for competencies in dealing with both individuals and groups.

Chapter 8: Specific Leadership Tasks and Concerns

Leadership in therapeutic recreation requires knowledge of a number of specific tasks and concerns. Among these tasks and concerns are: (1) client documentation, (2) teaching/learning principles, (3) leisure counseling, and (4) understanding transactions with clients. Areas covered within the section on understanding transactions are self-concept, learned helplessness, the self-fulfilling prophecy, labeling, loneliness, self-efficacy, and attributional processes.

Chapter 9: Clinical Supervision
      Clinical supervision is a cooperative process between a supervisor and an individual who has direct responsibility for carrying out the agency's clinical program through work with clients. The supervisor helps the supervisee to improve his or her clinical abilities and to achieve the goals sought for the clinical program. The clinical supervision process is beginning to be recognized as a key to successful clinical practice of therapeutic recreation.

Chapter 10: Health and Safety Considerations
      Theory forms the underpinnings for professional practice; however, therapeutic recreation professionals also must possess certain technical knowledge and skills. Among the areas of technical knowledge that may be required in therapeutic recreation are the use of first aid and safety procedures with members of specific client groups, the proper use of mechanical aids, procedures for transfers and assistive techniques, and information on the effects of commonly used psychotropic and anticonvulsant drugs.

THIS BOOK'S FORMAT

      Each chapter begins with a brief statement of purpose and key terms, which are followed by a listing of the major objectives for the chapter. At the conclusion of the chapter, reading comprehension questions are provided to guide your reading. They also serve the instructor and students as questions for class discussion.
      Within the chapter you will find questions or statements heading each section. These questions or statements are often designed to further break down the objectives for the chapter into smaller, more digestible parts.

The Focus of Instruction
      You, the reader, are the central point of focus for this book. The focus is on *you* and the **objectives** you must achieve to possess competencies necessary to meet the personal and professional demands that will be made on you as a therapeutic

recreation specialist. Your mastery of the skills, attitudes, and knowledge required for professional service in therapeutic recreation is critical to your personal success and that of your profession.

The Objectives

The objectives at the beginning of each chapter form a road map for learning. Making the purpose clear by the listing of major objectives enhances learning and removes the mystique that sometimes accompanies, and plagues, instructions.

READING COMPREHENSION QUESTIONS

1. How does this book claim to differ from the traditional "survey" textbooks often used in therapeutic recreation courses?
2. Why does a therapeutic recreation practitioner need more than "good intentions" in order to practice successfully?
3. What makes the therapeutic recreation specialist, or any professional helper, different from the layperson?
4. Outline the parts or items found in each chapter.
5. Where is the focus of the book directed?

Chapter Two

THEORIES AND THERAPIES

CHAPTER PURPOSE

There is no one preferred therapeutic approach found in therapeutic recreation. Instead, a great variety of methods are applied in the clinical, rehabilitative, continued care, educational and recreational environments in which therapeutic recreation takes place. Understandably, emerging therapeutic specialists may be confused by the diversity of approaches in practice today. This chapter will help the reader to grasp a fundamental understanding of major therapeutic approaches that apply to intervention and counseling programs in the wide range of settings in which therapeutic recreation services are delivered.

KEY TERMS

- Eclecticism
- Behavior therapy
- Classical conditioning
- Psychoanalytic approach
- Positive reinforcement
- Extinction
- Chaining
- Premack principle
- Gestalt therapy
- Cognitive-Behavioral Therapy
- Family therapy
- Multimodal therapy

- Ego defense mechanisms
- Behavior modification
- Operant conditioning
- Principle of reinforcement
- Negative reinforcement
- Shaping
- Modeling
- Person-centered therapy
- Rational-emotive therapy
- Reality therapy
- Transactional analysis
- Psychodrama

OBJECTIVES

- Appreciate the role of theory in influencing the practice of therapeutic recreation.
- Know what is meant by eclectic approach.
- Differentiate among psychoanalytic, behavioristic, cognitive-behavioral and growth psychology theories of human nature.
- Assess selected therapeutic approaches to understand implications for practice in therapeutic recreation.
- Define basic terminology and concepts of therapeutic approaches related to therapeutic recreation.
- Accept responsibility to begin to formulate personal theoretical notions in harmony with abilities, beliefs, and interests.

Theory is a unifying focus for the assumptions that underlie therapeutic approaches. A case can be made for the necessity of theory to direct methods of practice. Following this reasoning, theory furnishes a basis for action, because it provides beliefs, concepts, and assumptions that directly bear on the selection of specific therapeutic techniques. Even without formally studying the theories related to helping, each of us form personal beliefs and assumptions that operate to guide our everyday actions (Okun, 1992). No doubt you have already begun to develop your own theory for practice, although you may not have systematically analyzed your theory to determine if it consistently and comprehensively integrates the beliefs, concepts, and assumptions from which it is comprised.

THE ECLECTIC APPROACH

Therapeutic recreation is characterized by **eclecticism**, or the utilization of approaches and techniques drawn from several sources. The rationale for this eclectic approach is that even though each of the widely accepted therapeutic approaches has strong points, no single one has all the answers. Therefore, instead of imposing a specific approach on all clients, methods are dictated by the nature of client needs. By gaining familiarity with major theories and approaches, the therapeutic recreation specialist can select and combine the most appropriate techniques from a variety of sources. Of course, techniques chosen for actual practice should be in harmony with the personal abilities, beliefs, and interests of the therapeutic recreation specialist, as well as with the policies and practices of the agency in which he or she is employed.

A bewildering number of therapeutic approaches exist. I have, therefore, organized the material within this chapter into several sections in an attempt to present the approaches in digestible portions. I first discuss the four major theoretical approaches to human behavior and the techniques that relate to them. Then, in a separate section titled *Developed Therapies*, I deal with the most fully developed therapeutic approaches, and discuss therapies such as multimodal therapy, family therapy, and transactional analysis. Facilitation techniques and less fully developed therapeutic approaches are covered in Chapter 3. There coverage is given to approaches such as values clarification, relaxation techniques, adventure/challenge therapy, animal-facilitated therapy and reminiscence.

The four major theories of human behavior related to helping are the psychoanalytic, behavioristic, cognitive-behavioral and growth psychology theories. In this section each of these major theoretical orientations will be briefly described.

PSYCHOANALYTIC APPROACH

Sigmund Freud's work represents a great contribution to the world of psychiatry, clinical psychology, and psychological theory. As a physician who proposed a psychological view of mental disorders in contrast to the then traditional organic view, Freud was not accepted by his medical colleagues. For the greater part of his career, he was viewed by the medical community as an extremist obsessed by sex (Maddi, 1996). Yet no other individual had the profound influence on psychological theory and treatment that Freud ultimately produced through the development of his **psychoanalytic approach**.

Freud proposed that there are basic instincts common to all people. These instincts have biological origin, but they are at the core of personality because of the powerful influence they have on thought and behavior. When an instinct is felt, it is an indication that the person is in a state of deprivation. This state of deprivation produces tension that the individual must somehow handle. Therefore the goal of instincts is to relieve tension produced by biologically induced deprivation. These instinctual drives energize humans into action (Maddi, 1996).

Central to Freud's view is the assumption that there exists within each person a basic tendency to allow the maximum gratification of the primitive instincts, while giving minimum attention to the demands of society. This clash between maximizing instinctual desires and minimizing punishment and guilt resulting from society's social controls is the source of all goal-directed behavior. Adjustments in life center around the ability to meet this conflict by working out a compromise among self-centered, selfish, instinctual demand and the requirements of society (Maddi, 1996; Alderman, 1974).

Freud proposed a balance model in order to conceptualize the dynamics underlying this basic conflict. Under his model he identified three divisions of personality: the id, superego, and ego. All goal-directed behavior results from the interaction of these three systems.

The *id* is the primitive part of us. It is propelled by three major instinctual, biological drives. The first, the *self-preservation instinct*, preserves biological life. It deals with our basic needs for food, water, and oxygen. The other two major forces are the *sexual instinct* and the *aggression instinct* (which Freud later developed into the death instinct).

Freud gave much attention to the sexual instinct, which played an integral part in his theory. He termed the energy for sexual urges the *libido*. The libido induces action when sexual expression has been deprived. According to Freud's early writings, complete gratification of the sexual instinct was produced only by having intercourse with a person of the opposite sex. Other sexual activity was seen to lead to only partial fulfillment (Maddi, 1996). Later, however, Freud broadened his view of the sexual instinct to include pleasurable sensation from the erogenous zones and unidentified "inner" responses that produce pleasurable sensations (Ford & Urban, 1963). Therefore it may be noted that Freud eventually broadly defined the term sex to refer to almost anything pleasurable. The sexual instinct was perceived by Freud to develop to an adult level of maturity through five psychosexual stages (see Table 2-1). However if the child was overindulged or too greatly restricted during any stage, a partial fixation with that stage could develop. Such a fixation would later be revealed in adult life (Borden & Stone, 1976).

TABLE 2-1
FREUD'S STAGES OF
PSYCHOSEXUAL DEVELOPMENT

Oral Stage

The oral stage lasts from birth until about 18 months and is characterized by preoccupation with feeding. The mouth is the primary erogenous zone, thus giving the stage its name. The main source of pleasure is through sucking during the early part of the oral stage. Once teeth are developed, pleasure is obtained through biting. Weaning is a critical experience during this period in which the developmental task is the establishment of trusting dependence.

If the child receives either too much or too little oral gratification, he or she may become fixated at the oral level and is likely to develop dependent relationships in adulthood. If fixated at the early part of the oral stage, the individual may be gullible and may exhibit behavior centered around oral experiences such as smoking, obesity, substance abuse, and difficulty with trust. The person fixated at the later aggressive (biting) phase may be pessimistic, envious, and highly aggressive as an adult. In general, those who become fixated at the oral stage have lifelong feelings of overdependence and inadequacy.

Anal Stage

The anal stage lasts from approximately 18 months to three years of age, and is marked by a shift of erotic activity from the mouth to the anus. As the child becomes capable of voluntary control over defecation, he or she begins to express feelings of autonomy through pleasing or annoying parenting adults by retaining or expelling feces. The critical experience at this stage is, of course, toilet training.

Adult fixations may develop around either excretory process, the retentive (holding back) or expulsive (forcing out). The individual with an anal-retentive personality is likely to be compulsive, perfectionistic, stubborn, stingy, and have an inability to control impulses and emotions. The anal-expulsive personality may display a generous, outgoing nature and may be highly creative.

The oral and anal stages are together termed the *narcissistic phase*. This is because the child's libido is satisfied within his or her own body.

Phallic Stage

The phallic stage extends from the end of the third year through the fifth year, during which time the libido is centered in the genital region. During this stage, the questioning of adults about sex, masturbation, and interest in the genitals of the opposite sex are common. The stage is termed *phallic* because, according to Freud, the penis is the object of main interest. Young girls supposedly develop *penis envy*, while young boys fear castration. The *Oedipus Complex* occurs when the child falls in love with the parent of the opposite sex and develops feelings of rivalry and aggression toward the same sex parent. The resolution of this conflict occurs with identification with the parent of the same sex. The developmental task of sexual identity takes place as the child begins the socialization process by adopting characteristics of adults of the same sex.

Fixation at the phallic stage may involve problems in the resolution of the Oedipus conflict. Men may engage in sexual conquests with little depth of affection. Women's behaviors may become extremely flirtatious and seductive. Other behavioral manifestations may be faulty sexual identity, sexual deviations, problems with authorities, phobic reactions, and conversion reactions.

Latency Stage

Latency is the stage from about age six to puberty in which the child's sexual urges remain dormant. The primary developmental task is identification with groups of peers at school and in recreation activities. During this stage, there is increased intellectual activity and a weakening of home ties. Problems can develop with self-motivation, in relationships with persons of the same sex, with inability to accept social roles, and with behavioral disorders such as stealing and lying.

Genital Stage

The genital stage begins with puberty when the adolescent becomes sexually mature with the capacity for orgasm. The libido is once again centered on the genital area. The early phase of the stage is characterized by selfish interests. After this, there is for many teens a temporary homosexual phase when adolescents desire to meet with those of the same sex. Finally, attraction of the opposite sex asserts itself and most individuals enter into heterosexual relationships. Persons also strive for independence as they begin to assume adult roles.

The major developmental task of this stage is the resolution of the dependence-independence conflict. Manifestations of the failure to accomplish this task are sexual acting out, hostile attitudes toward authority figures, excessive dependence, unsatisfactory heterosexual relationships, and problems with frigidity and impotence.

Sources: Beck, Rawlins, & Williams (1992); Murry & Huelskoetter (1991); Okun (1992); Rowe & Mink (1993).

The aggressive instinct leads to free-floating aggressive energy that builds up to the point that aggression must be expressed. Even though it may be displaced or sublimated, the aggressive urge will rebuild and once again, must be released. The release of aggression is therefore a continual process (Austin, 1971).

The sexual and aggressive urges and emotions of the id are extremely selfish and self-centered. The id is propelled by raw forces of biological necessity, without accompanying social refinement. The process of seeking immediate gratification without concern for reality or moral constraint was termed by Freud as *pleasure principle functioning*.

The second system of personality is the *superego*. The superego is the person's social conscience. Its crucial role is to incorporate societal values that balance the impulsiveness of the id. Through the superego we take in, or internalize, socializing forces. Not surprisingly, much of the content for internalization comes from our parents or parent figures. Other prime teachers of societal values and beliefs are family members, peer group members, and other significant people in our lives. Once the roles of society are internalized, individuals are no longer controlled primarily by threat of punishment but by the guilt they experience if they transgress against their personal moral codes. Young people commonly have not formed their own value systems. Having not yet learned the rules of society, they are more likely to function at the level of the pleasure principle; and, therefore, must be controlled by threat from parents, police, and other authority figures who have the power to levy punishment. At the other extreme, "mental illness" may occur when the superego has become too strict or unrealistic, and the person cannot cope with the resulting conflict.

The final system of personality is the *ego*. The ego is the moderator between the id and superego. It balances the primitive forces of the id with the structures that the superego attempts to impose. Two functions are thus performed by the ego. The first is to aid in the satisfaction of instincts within the reality demands of the external world. The second function is to allow the expression of instinctual urges consistent with the demands of the superego. In carrying out these functions, the ego is guided by *reality principle functioning*, which leads to the realistic integration of the id's urges by arriving at a compromise that will meet the requirements of society. Thus the ego is the socialized unit of personality that allows people to make intelligent choices, taking into consideration the demands of the id, superego, and the environment. It is the part of the mind that controls higher cognitive powers and engages in realistic thinking based on accumulated experiences and perceptions of the environment.

Ego Defense Mechanisms

In order to meet the instinctual demands of the id while defending against the moral structures of the superego, the ego may turn to the use of **defense mechanisms**. Defense mechanisms function unconsciously to protect us when we feel a threat to the integrity of our ego, or sense of self-concept. They put up a protective shield against psychic pain (i.e., guilt, anxiety, shame) by displacing the energy of instinctive urges of the id toward objects or actions other than those from which they originated

(Alderman, 1974; Tamparo & Lindh, 1992). Among the commonly employed defenses are denial, repression, displacement, projection, sublimation, rationalization, and intellectualization. These defense mechanisms are outlined in Table 2-2. All the defenses are covered in most textbooks dealing with abnormal psychology. For example, Carson's (1996) abnormal psychology textbook lists 17 defense mechanisms, while Murry and Huelskoetter's (1991) psychiatric nursing textbook lists 19 defense mechanisms.

TABLE 2-2
COMMON DEFENSES

- *Denial*. The source of distress is not acknowledged or perceived because it is too threatening. The person refuses to admit being frightened by an event or action of another individual.

- *Repression*. Unacceptable or anxiety-provoking thoughts or feelings are blotted out of consciousness. People forget threatening occurrences.

- *Displacement*. Emotions are transferred from the original person or object to a less formidable, or safer, target. It is the "kick the cat" defense.

- *Sublimation*. Directing a socially unacceptable desire or activity into a socially acceptable one. For example, releasing sexual urges through dance.

- *Projection*. Rejecting an unacceptable thought or feeling by blaming it on another person. By attributing it to someone else, the unacceptable thought or feeling is removed from the person.

- *Intellectualization*. Painful emotions or feelings associated with an event are explained away by the use of a rational explanation.

- *Rationalization*. A socially acceptable reason is given to avoid having to face a non-acceptable belief about oneself.

Psychoanalysis

Before turning to psychoanalytic views directly related to play and recreation, it may be appropriate to discuss briefly the distinction between *psychoanalysis* and treatment based on psychoanalytic principles. Psychoanalysis is a long-term therapy based primarily on exploring the unconscious to make it conscious. In orthodox psychoanalysis, the patient is encouraged to transfer unknowingly to the therapist (psychoanalyst) attitudes and feelings the patient has held toward significant others. Through this expression of attitudes and feelings, the therapist can examine the patient's reactions. This process of identifying the therapist with a person from the patient's past is called **transference**. Supposedly the awareness gained by the patient through transference allows him or her to become free from past confusion and conflict. The term *countertransference* is used to describe the process when the therapist responds to the client as though he or she were someone from the therapist's past. Countertransference is not sought and must be guarded against by the therapist so that the client is responded to genuinely and not like another person from the therapist's past (Corey, 1995).

Psychoanalytic Psychotherapy

Psychoanalytic psychotherapy, on the other hand, does not deal with extensive probing of the unconscious but employs psychoanalytic principles in dealing with specific problems in living (Kovel, 1976; Blackham, 1977). Play therapy, as discussed in the next paragraph, is a type of psychoanalytic psychotherapy for children.

Play Therapy

Children's play was seen by Freud as a partial means to master painful or tension-producing experiences by acting them out over and over again. The purpose of repetitious play, in which children portray events they have experienced, is to absorb and incorporate unpleasant experiences or excessive stimuli into the ego, according to Freud's theory. Through play, children grasp the situation and feel mastery, or control, over reality (Ellis, 1973). Play therapy, as developed by psychoanalytic theorists, is based on this basic idea that symbolic play offers a means for the child to bring real life problems to the surface in order to be able to deal with them and establish control over them. In play therapy children are allowed to play out traumatic experiences under the direction of a therapist schooled in psychoanalytic theory. This therapy applies psychoanalytic principles during play sessions to help the child to understand the meaning behind these play activities.

In recent years, play therapy has broadened from its original psychoanalytic basis that primarily emphasized the unconscious "to include the child's conscious cognition, observable behaviors, recent experiences, family interactions, and peer and social interactions" (Critchley, 1995, p. 335). Nondirective and behavioral approaches have joined the psychoanalytic approach as theoretical bases for play therapy (Critchley, 1995).

Recreation and Psychoanalytic Theory

Psychoanalytic theorists have presented the positive effects of play and recreation in helping people to lead happier lives. Among these theorists have been the eminent psychiatrists Karl and William Menninger, who have suggested recreation activities as a means to discharging sexual and aggressive impulses in a socially acceptable manner (Menninger, 1960; Gussen, 1957). The influence of psychoanalytic theory has also found its way into therapeutic recreation literature. In a paper titled, "The Rationale of Recreation as Therapy," Meyer discussed the strengthening of defense mechanisms through recreation activities (Meyer, 1962). Included was information on the substitution of acceptable activities for aggressive impulses, the sublimation of sexual urges through dance and other art forms, and the development of skills to compensate for real or imagined inadequacies. O'Morrow (1971) in an article entitled "The Whys of Recreation Activities for Psychiatric Patients," suggested that therapeutic recreation activities provide approved outlets for aggression and other emotions by facilitating sublimation and permitting unconscious conflicts to be expressed.

The idea that recreation can provide outlets for pent-up aggressive urges has been widely accepted. Ventilating aggression supposedly provides a safe opportunity to rid the individual of aggressive energy. Sports and competitive games have been seen as proper outlets through which to express aggression in order to bring about what has been termed a cathartic effect. Freud is credited with developing the cathartic notion although, from the days of Aristotle, people have felt that venting an emotion can free a person from that emotion. Two ideas underlie the cathartic notion. One is that the expression of aggression can provide relief from the tension or make a person feel better. The second is that the person who expresses aggression will have a tendency to be less aggressive (Austin, 1971).

Social psychologists Quanty (1976) and Berkowitz (1978) have completed extensive reviews of the research evidence regarding the cathartic notion. These reviews indicate that viewing aggressive sports does not drain aggression, but actually increases it. Likewise, both reported similar findings in regard to actual participation in aggressive activities. This participation in aggressive activities only made people more aggressive. There is, therefore, a great deal of evidence to suggest that although aggressive responses may have temporary tension-reduction properties and make people feel better, they may lead to increased aggression. Recent reviews by contemporary social psychologists also have found fault with the cathartic notion. Following their review of the research evidence, Baron and Byrne (1994) wrote that: "Contrary to popular belief, then, catharsis does not appear to be as effective a means for reducing aggression as is widely assumed" (p. 471). Similarly, Feldman (1995) stated: "the idea of catharsis is appealing, because it suggests that permitting people to 'let off steam' can reduce their subsequent penchant for violence. Despite its appeal, though, results of experiments investigating catharsis do little to buttress the claims of theorists (who favor the cathartic notion)" (p. 293). It now seems clear that aggression when rewarded, or at least condoned, simply brings about further aggression. If children and adults are encouraged to behave aggressively during recreation participation, it would be expected that they will become more aggressive, not less aggressive, as once hypothesized.

Quanty (1976) has pointed out that the social learning model (i.e., behavior can be socially reinforced) contains the implication that prosocial responses to frustration can be just as effectively reinforced as aggressive responses. Therefore nonaggressive responses to anger can produce tension reduction and lead to more healthy interpersonal relationships.

Although the cathartic notion that aggression may be reduced through participation in aggressive recreation activities has been brought to question by the authorities previously cited and others (e.g., Martens, 1975; Parke & Sawin, 1975), the general influence of psychoanalytic theory may be felt in the practice of therapeutic recreation today.

The Neoanalytic Theorists
Well-known neoanalytic theorists, such as Alfred Adler, Carl Jung, Karen Horney, Harry Stack Sullivan, and Erik Erickson, have brought about many modifications in psychoanalytic theory over the years. Adler developed the concept of the inferiority complex. Jung brought a more optimistic view of human beings that emphasized that maladaptive behaviors arise largely from social and environmental factors. Sullivan's interpersonal theory of personality focused on understandings gained from knowledge of clients' interpersonal histories (Brammer, Abrego & Shostrom, 1993; Murry & Huelskoetter, 1991; Rowe, 1980). Erickson formulated a model of psychosocial development containing eight stages, the first five of which roughly parallel Freud's psychosexual stages (Beck, Rawlins & Williams, 1988).

Summary
Within this section, Freud's psychoanalytic theory has been presented as a conflict model involving three systems of personality (id, ego, and superego) and two primary instinctual drives (sex and aggression). His theory attached a great deal of significance to unconscious factors operating in the id and superego and to the mediating role of the ego. Freud's classic psychoanalytic theory also placed great emphasis on the biological determinism reflected in the instinctual urges that supposedly propel behavior (although neo-Freudians have placed greater emphasis on social and cultural aspects as determinants of behavior). Although it is no longer the sole form of psychotherapy as it once was, the psychoanalytic approach is usually what comes to mind when the average person thinks of therapy (Kovel, 1976), and it continues to represent an influence on therapeutic recreation.

Implications for Therapeutic Recreation
Therapeutic recreation specialists will not conduct psychoanalytically-oriented psychotherapy, but the theoretical ideas represented by the psychoanalytic viewpoint will likely pervade the practice of therapeutic recreation specialists. Therapeutic recreation specialists must recognize that

unconscious motivational factors may affect behavior, the use of defense mechanisms in protecting against threats to self-concept, and the effects the developmental years have on adult behavior (Okun, 1992). Therapeutic recreation specialists must review the evidence for themselves to determine if it is appropriate to encourage clients to discharge aggressive impulses through socially acceptable recreation activities, because previously accepted psychoanalytic principles have been refuted by numerous researchers and theorists. Ideas concerning the releasing of aggressive urges have common sense appeal, but current evidence strongly suggests that these concepts may lack the validity once afforded them by therapeutic recreation specialists.

BEHAVIORISTIC APPROACH

In the 1960s, there emerged a new form of intervention that became known as behavior therapy or behavior modification. Many use the terms interchangeably; however, the term **behavior therapy** seems to be employed mostly in psychiatric practice, while **behavior modification** is associated with other client groups, such as persons who are mentally retarded. No matter what terminology is used to describe the behavioristic approach, it is concerned with bringing about changes in behavior. The theory and techniques used to bring about behavioral changes are based on the psychological theory of behaviorism.

Behaviorism arose as a protest to the psychoanalytic model. In contrast to the psychoanalytic approach, where emphasis is on hidden, unconscious forces that underlie behavior, the basis for behaviorism comes from academic learning theory. John B. Watson is noted as the founder of behaviorism. In 1913 he wrote the paper "Psychology as The Behaviorist Sees It," in which he set down basic positions of behaviorism. Watson attacked subjectivity, saying that psychology should not be concerned with subjective experiences but with overtly observable behavior.

Followers of this new school of psychology also rejected the concept of mental illness. Instead, they assumed that abnormal behavior was not a disease, but rather that it was learned. The behavioral assumption is that all maladaptive behaviors are learned and that they can be modified through learning. Some behaviorists, therefore, contend that the term *therapy* is not appropriate for their approach because change occurs by means of an educational experience that involves a teaching/learning process (Corey, 1985).

Pavlov and Thorndike

The basic concepts of behaviorism spring from the early work of Pavlov and Thorndike. Pavlov emphasized the simple association of events that become linked when they repeatedly occur together. This theory, which became known as **classical conditioning,** or *respondent conditioning*, involves substituting one stimulus-evoking response for another. In Pavlov's famous dog study there was the pairing of one stimulus to which there was already a set response (salivation to food) with a neutral stimulus (the sound of a bell). After a number of pairings, the neutral stimulus (in this case, the bell) begins to take on the characteristics of the first stimulus (food-bringing on salivation). The *unconditioned stimulus* (food) and the *conditioned stimulus* (bell) become connected to bring about the *response* (saliva).

Thorndike emphasized that behavior is controlled by its consequences. That is, rewards function to reinforce certain behaviors, whereas negative outcomes tend to eliminate the occurrence of behavior. A reinforcer is basically anything that reinforces behavior. Commonly employed reinforcers include food, money, attention, affection, and approval or praise. The potency of a reinforcer depends on the need state of the person. For example, food would be a poor reinforcer after dinner. Candy would not be a good reinforcer for someone on a diet. B.F. Skinner has more recently been associated with this line of thought, which has been termed **operant conditioning** or *instrumental conditioning*. The terms come from the idea that it involves voluntary actions that operate on the environment instead of just responding to the environment as in respondent conditioning.

Pavlov's classical or respondent conditioning theory involves the **principle of association,** while Thorndike's theory (operant or instrumental conditioning) involves the **principle of reinforcement.** These two basic principles help to form the foundation for techniques of the behavioral approach (McDavid & Harari, 1968; Berkowitz, 1972).

What specific intervention techniques have resulted from the behavioral approach? Terms such as positive reinforcement, negative reinforcement, extinction, modeling, shaping, chaining, prompting, fading, time-out, token economies, behavioral contracts, and the Premack principle may be familiar as techniques that have a basis in the behavioral approach. The following section will briefly review each of these techniques based on information drawn from Crawford and Mendell (1987), Dattilo and Murphy (1987), Diebert and Harmon (1977), Fine and Fine (1988), Hunter and Carlson (1971), Hussian and Davis (1985), Kanfer and Goldstein (1991), and Vernon (1972).

Positive and Negative Reinforcement

The idea of **positive reinforcement** is that people tend to repeat behaviors that provide rewards. Any behavior that is followed by a positive reinforcer (reward) is likely to be repeated. Teaching new behaviors or increasing the occurrence of existing behaviors therefore depends on the participants finding the behaviors rewarding. Following this train of thought logically, even frequently repeated behaviors that seem to be inappropriate or unproductive must somehow be rewarding for those who perform them.

Negative reinforcement involves the removal of an aversive stimulus in order to increase the future occurrence of a desired behavior. The rationale behind negative reinforcement is that if an individual is subjected to unpleasant or painful stimulation, any behavior that results in the withdrawal of the stimulus is reinforced. Negative reinforcement is sometimes confused with punishment, a procedure used to decrease the future occurrence of an undesired behavior. The two are different, as Kanfer and Goldstein (1991) have noted. They state: "With negative reinforcement, an ongoing aversive stimulus is removed or terminated following the desired behavior in order to *increase* the probability of the response, while with punishment, an aversive stimulus is added or *applied* following an undesired behavior in order to *decrease* its probability of occurrence " (p.128). Because negative reinforcement is rarely employed in therapeutic recreation, the focus of this section will be on positive reinforcement.

Kinds of Reinforcement

While we may first think of M&M™ candies as a reinforcer, people find many things to be rewarding. As previously mentioned, rewards include food and money as well as social reinforcers such as attention, affection, and approval. More subtle are rewards gained from discovery or learning that people may gain as outcomes of educational or recreational experiences (Vernon, 1972). According to Vernon, children are least affected by subtle reinforcers. Therefore food is often initially used as a reinforcer in programs serving children. After a short while, praise is given along with the food and, occasionally, praise is given alone. Gradually, praise is used more and more by itself as a reinforcer.

Attention can be a potent reinforcer whether provided in the form of praise or approval or just paying attention to the person. As a matter of fact, the leader must be on guard not to give too much attention to those who act out or behave inappropriately. People who feel neglected may cause problems just to draw attention to themselves. Positive outlets must be found for these persons so that they can receive rewards for appropriate behaviors.

If desirable behavior exists it has been reinforced. It follows that the simplest way to get rid of a behavior is to stop reinforcing it and it will go away. Each time a behavior is emitted without being reinforced, the strength or frequency of that behavior is diminished. This process of withholding reinforcement is termed **extinction**.

Reinforcement Techniques

The timing of the delivery of reinforcers is critical to their success. To have the greatest effect, they should come immediately after the behavior occurs. For this reason, athletes in Special Olympics competitions are rewarded immediately following completion of their events. The frequency of reinforcers is likewise important. During the time when behaviors are first being established, a continuous schedule of reinforcement seems to be best. The reward should occur every time the person performs the behavior if at all practical. Once the behavior has been established, it is possible to change to a partial schedule of rewarding the person only once in a while. This should be done slowly by gradually reducing the frequency of giving reinforcement. Diebert and Harmon (1977) suggest first decreasing reinforcement patterns to reinforce 80 percent of the time, then 50 percent, then 30 percent and, finally, only once in a while.

Shaping is another technique in reinforcement or operant conditioning. It is the process by which reinforcement is differentially applied to the responses that are made toward approximating a desired behavior. Reinforcement is delivered only when a particular standard is reached. Once reached, the standard is continually raised until the person being rewarded makes a closer and closer approximation of the behavior that is being conditioned. Eventually, the final form of desired behavior is reached. **Chaining** is an associated concept that involves linking one learned response with another to build to a more complex response.

Modeling is a form of social learning that may employ reinforcement. Through modeling, new responses can be acquired more quickly if the learner can see a model demonstrate the desired behavior, especially if this is combined with positive reinforcement. Responses can be learned through modeling combined with either seeing the model rewarded or the learner directly receiving a reward. Rawson (1978) has reported success in the use of modeling and reinforcement to alter the behavior of children with behavioral disorders in a camping program. Reynolds and Arthur (1982) used modeling as a technique to alter the social play of children with emotional problems.

Wehman and Rettie (1975) have used modeling and social reinforcement in developing play behaviors with young women who were severely retarded. Wehman (1977) has also reported using various other behavior modification techniques to help severely and profoundly retarded children develop play patterns. Among the techniques employed were *prompting* and *fading*. In prompting, the leader physically guides the child through the desired play skill. For instance, the child is manually guided to pull a wagon or roll a ball. Successes are followed by praise and affection. Fading involves gradually removing the physical guidance of the prompts when the play skill has become learned.

A procedure often employed in behavior modification programs for children is time-out. Time-out is a type of negative reinforcement because it involves the removing of a reinforcer or time away from positive reinforcement (Johnson, 1995). Time-out is used as an alternative to punishment when the behavior of an individual is disruptive or may be harmful to himself or herself or to the group. It involves simply removing the person for a short time from the setting in which others are able to gain positive reinforcement. This is done matter of factly without berating the person. Typically, the time-out room is a small, plain room devoid of stimuli so that there is nothing for the child to do. Therefore, time-out involves stimulus removal in contrast to punishment's stimulus delivery.

Token economies are found in residential settings. Tokens are given by staff members to the residents as rewards for performing selected behaviors that have been determined to be desirable. The tokens are made of plastic or some other inexpensive material and have no value in themselves, but they can be redeemed for items or privileges that have value to the residents. Recreation participation has been used in some facilities as a privilege that may be earned with tokens. Woods (1971) has described one such token economy program, called PAYREC, in a residential school for children with mental retardation.

Behavioral contracts are written agreements, typically between client and therapist, in which the consequences of specified client behaviors are set in advance. The contract usually specifies reinforcers to be received by the client upon completing certain behaviors within a given time period. Therapists should encourage clients to become involved in the writing of the contract so they may help decide on the behaviors to be specified, the accepted length of time, and appropriate reinforcers. It is generally agreed that clients who cooperate in formulating contracts will be motivated to fulfill them. Elements that need to be considered in a contract are:

- The client behavior must be stated in clear and detailed terms;
- Time limits need to be specified;
- Positive reinforcements need to be specified;
- The timing for delivery of the reinforcers needs to follow the response as quickly as possible. It may be that for individuals who have difficulty with delaying reinforcement, both short- and long-term behaviors will need to be reinforced;

- Means to observe, measure and record progress need to be included;
- Spaces for the signatures of the client and therapist should appear.

In addition, a bonus clause may be used to indicate additional reinforcers if the client exceeds the minimal behavior stipulated and provisions may be made for aversive consequences should the contract not be fulfilled.

Premack Principle

The final behavior modification procedure to be discussed is the widely accepted **Premack principle**. Premack introduced the idea that naturally highly-preferred behavior can be used to reinforce a less-preferred behavior. For example, quiet activity of children (the less-preferred behavior) might be reinforced by allowing the children to have outside play on the playground (a naturally highly-preferred activity). This procedure has two obvious advantages. One is that highly-preferred behaviors are easily observed, so appropriate reinforcers can be predicted relatively simply for a given individual. Second, because activities are used as reinforcers, a behavior can be increased without depending on outside rewards such as candy or other food.

Schmokel (1980), in an unpublished student research project, has called to question the validity of the Premack principle alone to predict behavioral outcomes adequately. According to Schmokel, a better explanation is the *response deprivation hypothesis* proposed by Timberlake and Allison (1974). Under this hypothesis either a highly-preferred behavior or a less-preferred (low-rate) behavior can serve as a reinforcer. The key is that the individual is deprived of his or her normal level of activity until he or she increases the sought behavior above its accustomed level. Even a relatively low-rate behavior can be used as a reinforcer if the person is deprived from participating in it at the accustomed level. On the other hand, a high-preference activity will not serve as a reinforcer unless the individual feels deprived of participation at the normal level of activity. Thus the Premack principle, by itself, does not seem to explain reinforcement patterns sufficiently.

Implications for Therapeutic Recreation

The focus of the behavioristic approach is clearly on the objective observation of overt behavior and the learning of new behaviors. This approach emphasizes the need to make precise behavioral observations and consider conditions that may alter behavior. Therapeutic recreation specialists must be accountable by providing outcome measures resulting from designated plans and continually examining reward systems that surround and influence client behavior (Okun, 1992). Specific behavior modification procedures may prove useful in diverse therapeutic recreation settings ranging from institutions to camps. Behavior modification is a particularly effective approach in therapeutic recreation programs serving institutionalized residents with mental retardation (Wehman, 1977; Wehman & Rettie, 1975; Woods, 1971) and children with behavior disorders (Rawson, 1978) and emotional disturbances (Reynolds & Arthur, 1982).

Three therapeutic approaches, that have come to be viewed as entities unto themselves, are related to the behavioral approach. Assertiveness training and progressive relaxation training rest upon behavioristic theory. Social skills training has been influenced by several theoretical perspectives including behaviorism. These approaches and their implications for therapeutic recreation are covered later in the following chapter under "Facilitation Techniques."

COGNITIVE-BEHAVIORAL APPROACHES

Albert Ellis, William Glasser, and Aaron Beck have provided leadership for cognitive-behavioral approaches that focus on helping clients to examine thinking processes and the effects of those processes on behaviors and emotions. Cognitive-behavioral approaches assist clients to identify thoughts and beliefs they hold about themselves and the world, to examine the validity and usefulness of these cognitions, and if deemed necessary, to change the way they think about themselves and their environments. Clients then are assisted in acting on their cognitions in their daily lives. In sum, cognitive-behavioral theorists hold there is an interdependence of thoughts, behaviors and emotions (Craighead, Craighead, Kazdin & Mahoney, 1994; Okun, 1992).

Ellis developed rational-emotive therapy (RET), Glasser brought about reality therapy (RT) and Beck produced cognitive-behavioral therapy. These three major approaches are covered in the material that follows.

Rational-emotive Therapy

Rational-emotive therapy (RET) is a system of philosophy, a theory of personality, and a psychological treatment approach (Ellis, 1976). Albert Ellis' rational-emotive therapy relies heavily on the cognitive processes, or people's thinking processes. Its philosophical origins go back to a notion first put forth by Epictelus, an early philosopher, who wrote: "Men are disturbed not by things, but by the view which they make of them." Later this same thought was expressed by Shakespeare in *Hamlet* when he wrote: "There's nothing either good or bad but thinking makes it so" (Ellis, 1984).

Ellis (1976, 1984) uses an A-B-C theory. The A is the activating experience (or what the person irrationally believes causes C). C stands for the consequences (e.g., feel upset, worthless, depressed). B represents beliefs about A. B is the critical intervening variable that influences the way we look at what happens to us. Ellis holds that we value, perceive, or conceptualize first; then we feel. Therefore it is what we bring to each experience in the way of our beliefs, concepts, and attitudes (or our way of thinking) that influences our feelings.

According to RET, we have a predisposition to expand ourselves, to be creative and to experience enjoyment in the here and now. Ellis (1976) has written:

> RET clearly defines appropriate feelings and rational beliefs as those aiding human survival and happiness—particularly those enabling you to accept objective reality, live amicably in a social group, relate intimately to a few members of this group, engage in productive work, and enjoy selectively chosen recreational pursuits (p.21).

However, we can also engage in irrational thinking involving absolutes ("I must") or perfection ("I should") or other irrational beliefs leading to inappropriate feelings. In short, we can be rigid and intolerant of ourselves to the point of destroying our health and happiness (Ellis, 1984). By entering into self-defeating thinking, we may become the creators of our own psychological disturbances. It is the task of RET to assist in changing basic self-defeating beliefs and attitudes in order to correct irrational thinking. Once this is done, we are rid of the emotional blockages that have prevented us from reaching our true potentials. Thus the basic goal of RET is not helping the client to solve a particular problem but to develop a new philosophy of life.

During therapy, RET therapists help the client identify irrational beliefs: they attack these beliefs, show the client they cannot be validated, and ultimately teach the client to change his or her irrational belief system (Ellis, 1976, 1984). In addition to therapy sessions, homework assignments utilizing behavioral techniques are also employed with RET clients.

Implications for Therapeutic Recreation

The most obvious implications of RET for the therapeutic recreation specialist are: the strong relationship between cognitive processes (beliefs and attitudes) and feelings, and the need for people to discard irrational thinking that prevents enjoyment in the here and now. It is particularly important that those doing leisure counseling be aware that beliefs and attitudes may block leisure enjoyment for many persons. For example, some people cannot escape work, and feel guilty about having free time. Such persons might profit by examining the thinking that prevents them from enjoying leisure.

Reality Therapy

The focus of the **reality therapy** of William Glasser is on present behavior, facing reality and taking responsibility for one's own needs. Responsibility and reality are central to Glasser's approach. Responsibility deals with achieving personal needs without depriving others from fulfilling their needs. Reality has to do with facing instead of denying the world around us (Glasser, 1965).

According to Glasser, the basic human needs are to find love and worth—or relatedness and respect. Those who fail to meet these psychological needs (those who feel lonely and worthless) escape hurt and pain by denying the world of reality. Psychotic persons who cannot make it in the real world cope with loneliness and worthlessness by withdrawing and creating their own worlds of reality. Some deny the laws of society and engage in crime or antisocial acts. Others may become physically ill and seek help for backaches, headaches, or other illnesses. Still others drink to escape feelings of inadequacy. Anyone of these and other denying responses are seen by Glasser to be irresponsible coping behaviors that have been learned throughout life (Glasser, 1965).

Reality therapy does not dwell on feelings, but instead helps clients to examine their present behavior, confront irresponsible actions, and establish commitment to change. Once a client makes a plan, the therapist does not accept any excuses from the client. No matter what has occurred in the past, no excuse is accepted for irresponsible behavior in the present. Therefore, unlike conventional therapy, reality therapy emphasizes the present, not the past. Even though personal insights may be interesting, the therapist's interest lies in the actual behavior of the client, not the unconscious motivations that may be offered as an excuse for irresponsible behavior (Glasser, 1984).

Because clients have the need to love and be loved and to feel worthwhile to themselves and others, it is necessary that the therapist build a firm relationship with the client. Involvement on the part of the therapist begins immediately to reduce the client's loneliness and worthlessness. Therefore a warm, caring attitude is mandated on the part of the therapist. Nevertheless, cautions Glasser (1976), the helping professional must be careful never to promise more involvement than he or she plans to provide.

Reality therapy has been used in a number of settings, including homes for delinquent children, outpatient mental health services, psychiatric hospitals, and public schools. Exhaustive training is not necessary in order to apply the principles of reality therapy. Parents, teachers, ministers, and work supervisors have successfully employed Glasser's approach (Glasser, 1976).

Implications for Therapeutic Recreation

Perhaps the major implication of reality therapy for therapeutic recreation specialists is that all helping relationships demand an accepting and understanding attitude and that positive involvement by the helper may immediately reduce client feelings of loneliness and worthlessness. Through his or her personal relationship with the client, the therapeutic recreation specialist can provide a feeling of involvement and being cared for. The client can then become actively involved with others through participation in therapeutic recreation groups, ultimately leading to expanded involvements within ongoing recreation groups. Without such involvements people cannot help themselves to fulfill their needs to feel cared for and to care for others.

A second implication is that clients can take responsibility to alter irresponsible behavior. Therapeutic recreation specialists must provide opportunities for clients to learn and try out social behaviors that will lead to new relationships and more satisfying involvements. The climate created in therapeutic recreation should provide an accepting atmosphere that encourages positive social interaction.

The final implication from reality therapy is to help clients to live in the present. Therapeutic recreation, like reality therapy, is geared primarily toward helping people function in the here and now. Robert Wubbolding, author of the book, *Using Reality Therapy* (1988), has encouraged therapeutic recreation specialists to employ reality therapy principles in his article (1988), "Reality Therapy: A Method for the Recreation Therapist."

COGNITIVE-BEHAVIORAL THERAPY

The central feature of Aaron Beck's **cognitive-behavioral therapy** is the concept that people's cognitions influence the way they react to life situations. Cognitive-behavioral therapy was first used by Beck (1976) to treat clients with major depressions. His approach has more recently been extended to successfully treat individuals with anxiety disorders, personality disorders, eating disorders and substance abuse (Hales & Hales, 1995; Ivey, Ivey & Simek-Morgan, 1993).

The basis for cognitive-behavioral therapy is that maladaptive assumptions underlie individuals' thoughts and beliefs. Distorted thought patterns (irrational ideas or faulty reasoning) then cause problems for individuals as they deal with life situations, particularly in times of stress. The purpose of therapy is to help these troubled individuals to acknowledge and change their distorted thinking. In order to learn to think differently, clients first have to identify inappropriate or distorted ways of thinking. The therapist elicits the client's thoughts and self-talk and how these are interpreted by the client. Discussion then turns to the validity of the client's interpretations and, finally, to testing the client's interpretations (perhaps through homework assignments) which, in turn, provides for further discussion (Okun, 1992).

Examples of irrational ideas or faulty reasoning that produce distorted thought patterns have been delineated by Hales and Hales (1995). They include *overgeneralizing* (making global conclusions from a single negative event), *arbitrary inference* (drawing a mistaken conclusion from an event or experience), *selective abstractions* (focusing on a single negative detail taken out of context), *dichotomous thinking* (all-or-nothing thinking or seeing only in terms of extremes), *magnifying* or *minimizing* (overstating the worst aspects of an event or underestimating the importance of an event), *personalization* (taking events that have nothing to do with the individual and personalizing them) and *automatic thoughts* (spontaneously thinking negative ideas such as "You're stupid" or "You can't do anything right.").

In cognitive-behavioral therapy, the therapist helps the client to identify irrational thoughts, such as those listed in the previous paragraph, and to take steps to establish new thought patterns. One specific strategy to develop new thought patterns is the use of cognitive rehearsal. During cognitive rehearsal, the client envisions a situation that in the past has been disconcerting and imagines just how he or she would overcome it by breaking it down into manageable steps that he or she rehearses mentally (Hales & Hales, 1995). Other strategies include the use of a number of techniques drawn from various sources. Role-playing, exposure therapy, homework assignments, relaxation training and social skills training are all psychoeducational techniques employed by therapists in cognitive-behavioral therapy (Ivey, Ivey & Simek-Morgan, 1993). No matter what strategy is selected, the focus of cognitive-behavioral therapy remains on problem-solving in the here and now (Hales & Hales, 1995).

Implications for Therapeutic Recreation

Cognitive-behavioral therapists recognize the complex interdependence of thoughts and behaviors. Therapeutic recreation specialists must be aware of the interrelation of thoughts, feelings and behaviors as they plan and conduct interventions with their clients. Cognitive-behavioral therapists also stress the notion that clients have the capacity to examine themselves and to develop insights into themselves. The focus of cognitive-behavioral therapy on helping clients to identify their assumptions, beliefs and expectations, and the effects of these on behaviors and emotions, can be easily transferred to leisure counseling. In leisure counseling, counselors are helping clients to appraise leisure beliefs, values and attitudes and to understand how these affect leisure feelings and behaviors. Additionally, cognitive-behavioral therapists readily draw on strategies and techniques from other theories. Therapeutic recreation specialists doing leisure counseling or using other interventions need to understand there are a wide variety of strategies and techniques upon which to draw from the various theories of helping. Finally, like cognitive-behavioral therapists, therapeutic recreation specialists largely assist clients to deal with the here and now.

THE GROWTH PSYCHOLOGY APPROACH

The term growth psychology is taken from Schultz's (1977) book *Growth Psychology: Models of the Healthy Personality*, in which he presents the nontraditional views of figures such as Maslow, Allport, Fromm, Jung, Rogers, and Perls (most of whom would be considered to be humanistic psychologists). It is a way of looking at human nature that rejects what many consider to be the negative and deterministic views presented by the psychoanalytic and behavioristic approaches. Growth psychologists do not see people as being primarily driven by instinctual urges or conditioned by the environment in a robotic manner. Growth psychology recognizes biological drives and the influence of past learning, but it goes beyond previous theories to see people as being self-aware, capable of accepting or rejecting environmental influences, and generally in conscious control of their own destiny. Furthermore, under the growth model the emphasis is not so much on past failures and conflicts, but on tapping previously unused creative talents and energies. In short, growth psychology takes a positive view of human nature in contrast to the relatively pessimistic picture offered by psychoanalytic theory and behaviorism.

Critical Review

Humanistic psychologists have been critical of the psychoanalytic and behavioristic approaches. A number of these criticisms have been presented by Borden and Stone (1976) in their book on human communication. The discussion that follows highlights an extensive review of the subject by these authors.

First, the orthodox Freudians emphasize biological determinism and the behaviorists follow an environmental determinism. Neither assume that people have the intellectual and emotional capacity to be aware of their self-concepts and to be in control of their own destiny, so that they may engage in self-determination. Second, the traditional theories view humans as passive organisms who do not possess the will and ability to pursue actively their potentials for growth in a self-directed way. Third, psychoanalytic theory sees people as being driven by sexual and aggressive instincts; behavioristic theory views people as being motivated to seek pleasure and avoid pain. In contrast, humanistic theorists see people as being motivated to attain self-fulfillment, yet being able to transcend their personal needs for the betterment of others. A fourth point of criticism is in regard to the ability to enter into meaningful relationships with others. Of primary concern to psychoanalytic theory is the self-gratification of instinctual drives, while behavioristic theory focuses on doing things for rewards, instead of for altruistic reasons. Humanistic theory views humans as being capable of enduring relationships and foregoing personal needs out of the love for another. Finally, neither psychoanalytically oriented theorists nor behaviorists believe people are truly responsible for their own behavior. Psychoanalytically oriented theorists believe behaviors result from unconscious drives. Behaviorists perceive people to be controlled by the environment. In contrast, humanistic theorists see people as being responsible for their behavior. Since people have freedom of choice, they must assume responsibility for their actions. All of these notions are central to growth psychology, which views people as having to strive toward self-fulfillment in a self-aware, self-directed manner.

Schultz (1977) has referred to growth psychology as *health psychology*, since it is concerned with wellness. Growth psychologists view mental health as more than the mere absence of neurosis or psychosis. Healthy persons are self-aware. They realize their strengths and weaknesses, and they do not pretend to be something they are not. They live in the present instead of dwelling on the past or fantasizing about the future. They are not satisfied to maintain the status quo but seek challenges and experiences in life. Person-Centered and Gestalt Therapy are therapeutic approaches that come from growth psychology traditions.

Person-centered Therapy

One of the most widely accepted growth-oriented therapeutic approaches is the **person-centered therapy** of Carl Rogers. To Rogers, people have the capacity to be rational thinkers who can assume responsibility for themselves and whose behavior will be constructive when given the freedom to set directions in life. People are seen as motivated by a basic tendency to seek growth (to actualize potentials) and self-enhancement (to feel positive regard).

As each person grows up, a sense of self begins to form. A positive concept of self is developed when a person receives love (positive regard) from others. If parents and significant others freely give love (unconditional positive regard) there is no need for defensive behavior or to feel guilty or unworthy. The person will feel good about himself or herself and will experience congruence between positive self-concept and life experiences with others.

When incongruence between the concepts of self and life experiences occurs, it is disturbing and poses a threat to established self-perception. Anxiety results and defense mechanisms become aroused. Through defense mechanisms experiences are distorted or denied in order to bring them in line with self-perceptions. Therefore psychological problems arise when incongruences exist between life experience and self-concepts. Intervention through person-centered therapy allows the person to reestablish congruence and once again begin to pursue self-actualization.

The role of the helping professional in person-centered therapy is to display unconditional positive regard (complete acceptance) for the client. The basic hypothesis on which person-centered therapy rests is that the support of an empathetic, genuine, accepting helper will enable the client to change.

Techniques are secondary to attitude, since the helper is not an expert with insight who can condition the client but someone to strengthen and support the client in efforts to become responsible for his or her own life. The helper is nonjudgmental and nondirective, providing an accepting atmosphere that will allow the client to assume the same positive self-regard the helper has shown the client. Since the client is obviously valued and cared for by the helper, the client begins to feel he or she is a person worth being cared for. In such a nurturing climate feelings are brought into awareness, and the client learns to revise his or her concepts of self to bring them into congruence with life experiences. Once this process is complete, the client no longer feels threatened and is open to new experiences (Meador & Rogers, 1984; Okun, 1992; Schultz, 1977).

Gestalt Therapy

A second well-known growth-oriented approach is **Gestalt therapy**. Frederick (Fritz) Perls conceived Gestalt therapy after he became disenchanted with Freud and psychoanalysis. The term "Gestalt" is a German word that implies an organized whole or sense of wholeness.

Perls felt that many people repress impulses and wishes so that they become aware of only parts of themselves instead of knowing the whole self. Preconceived perfectionistic ideas cause these people to inhibit their feelings and impulses and to become afraid to express them. They live as they believe others expect them to behave. Instead of following natural and spontaneous responses guided by a true awareness of self and the world, external controls move them in stereotyped, predetermined ways. In short, they are directed by their environment rather than being self-directed.

Because they are unable to accept their own impulses and feelings, they project these onto others. By distorting the situation, they do not have to own up to their feelings. They may also deny that parts of themselves exist. Nevertheless, their hidden impulses and feelings will seek release in some indirect form such as a nervous tic or an ulcer.

The goal of Gestalt therapy is to restore the personality to wholeness. This is done by helping the client to gain a full awareness of what is really happening to him or her so that the person may recognize that he or she can be free of external regulations (including those that have become internalized). Without such awareness the person will be unable to be himself or herself and will continue to assume roles that he or she feels others expect.

Techniques of Gestalt therapy are aimed at opening up direct, immediate experiences so that the client can become aware of what he or she is feeling, thinking, and doing. The emphasis is always on present behavior (the "here and now") and on the direct expression of impulses, thoughts, and feelings instead of on following stereotyped social roles that keep people from becoming aware of their needs and feelings. The critical aspect of Gestalt therapy is, therefore, opening the person's awareness of real needs and feelings (which avoidance mechanisms have excluded from awareness) and having the person assume the responsibility to act directly to express his or her impulses and feelings.

In addition to awareness of the self, Perls presented two other levels of awareness: awareness of the world, and awareness of intervening fantasy between the self and the world. Gestalt therapy helps persons to become aware of the aspects of the personality that contain fantasy and irrational prejudices and to discontinue them so that they are no longer barriers between the self and the real world. In becoming aware of intervening fantasy, people see things as they really exist. They can then experience the world in the present instead of consuming energy dealing with prejudices and fantasies.

The methods of Gestalt therapy revolve around training people to observe themselves by bringing experiences into awareness so they can be examined. Techniques such as role playing and group awareness exercises are used to help clients get in touch with what they are experiencing so that they may become more deeply aware of themselves. The therapist remains active during therapy in order to redirect the client when he or she tries to avoid problems. Thus the therapist must remain alert to signals in tone of voice, posture, or other nonverbal cues that indicate true feelings are being denied so that the client's attention may be drawn to them.

The facilitation of client awareness is seen as the therapist's main responsibility. Once healthy awareness of the self and the world are established, unhealthy processes that substitute for growth and block self-actualization are removed. The healthy person can then actualize his or her potentials by responding spontaneously and naturally to needs and feelings (Kaplan & Sadock, 1995; Okun, 1992; Matson, 1977; Schultz, 1977).

Implications for Therapeutic Recreation

As will be discussed in Chapter 4, the general humanistic orientation reflected in growth psychology has been felt in the philosophy and practice of therapeutic recreation. Many implications of the humanistic view of human nature are highlighted in that discussion and, therefore, are not covered here. Implications for the two specific therapies covered under growth psychology are briefly reviewed in the following paragraph.

Many of the skills of person-centered therapy may be applied in the daily practice of therapeutic recreation. Healthy interpersonal relationships, empathetic listening without levying judgment, and a warm, accepting climate are elements basic to the practice of therapeutic recreation. Like Gestalt therapists, therapeutic recreation specialists are interested in clients talking but also gaining personal awareness through experiences—including trying out new expressions of impulses and feelings. While certain skills of Gestalt therapy may be helpful in the practice of therapeutic recreation (such as Gestalt awareness exercises in leisure counseling), the emerging therapeutic recreation specialist should be warned that Gestalt techniques tend to take on a gimmicky quality in the hands of persons who have not had training in their use.

DEVELOPED THEORIES

Some therapeutic approaches have more fully evolved than others. These approaches have generally existed longer than less complete therapies and, therefore, have undergone testing and revision over time. Developed approaches include transactional analysis, family therapy, psychodrama and multimodal therapy.

Transactional Analysis

Transactional analysis (TA) is a theory of personality and social interaction conceived by Eric Berne. It is most commonly used as a basis for group therapy. Along with rational-emotive therapy and reality therapy, transaction analysis emerged in the 1950s. It was not, however, until Berne's book, *Games People Play* (1964), became a best-seller in the middle of the 1960s that transactional analysis gained popularity.

According to Berne's theory, there are four primary methods used to understand human behavior: structural analysis (to understand ego states within a given individual); transactional analysis (to understand interactions between two people's ego states); racket and game analysis (to understand repetitive transactions that are useless and of a devious nature); and script analysis (to understand life plans formed in childhood on which adults base choices on how their lives should be lived) (Harris, 1976; Woollams et al., 1976). Following Berne's death in 1970, another element of transaction analysis emerged, the egogram (to symbolize the amount of time and energy the individual exudes in each egostate) (Dusay & Dusay, 1984).

Structural Analysis

People have the capacity to store recordings, or "tapes," of past experiences in the brain. From these, they can recall both information and feelings related to specific events, the most significant of which occur during the preschool years. Different tapes play back depending on which of three ego states a person is operating in—the Parent, Child, or Adult (Harris, 1976). Through structural analysis, the ego state that is operating in a given individual at a particular time is identified.

The source of the *Parent ego state* is a massive tape of external experiences absorbed during the most formative years (birth to age 6). An enormous store of attitudes, beliefs, values, and rules for living learned primarily from parents (or parent substitutes) direct patterns of behavior of the Parent. A person's Parent can be nurturing or controlling and critical. In either case, these attitudes can be expressed directly in the individual's words, demeanor, voice tone, and expressions or gestures—or indirectly as an effect on the Adult or Child.

Associated with the Critical Parent would be words such as bad, should, ought, and always; a stern and judgmental demeanor; a critical or condescending tone of voice, and gestures such as pointing the index finger. The Nurturing Parent would use words such as good, nice, cute, and I love you, a caring demeanor;

a warm tone of voice; and expressions and gestures such as smiling and open arms.

The *Child ego state* is based on another tape that has been made simultaneously with the Parent tape. This tape has recorded the internal reactions or feelings of the child to external events (Harris, 1976). Thus the Child ego state is made up of all the emotions that spring from early experiences in addition to natural or innate feelings. As with the Parent, the Child can be divided into two major parts: the Adapted child and the Natural child (or Free child). The Adapted child responds in ways that gain acceptance from "big people." The Natural child is spontaneous and free from worry about pleasing others (Woollams et al., 1976).

The *Adult ego state* is the rational part of the person that weighs facts before making decisions. It begins to develop late in the first year of life. Through exploration and testing, the infant begins to take in and respond to information (as the Parent and Child) and to gain control over the environment. The Adult ego state is the computerlike data processor that makes decisions based on information from the Parent, the Child and from data the Adult has collected and continues to gather (Harris, 1976). By the time the person has reached 12 years of age, the Adult has matured to the point of becoming fully functional (Woollams et al., 1976).

The emotionally healthy individual can function appropriately from the ego state of his or her choosing, whether it is serving as a Nurturing Parent to a youngster, the Adult making a decision, or the Natural Child enjoying recreation (Woollams, et al., 1976). Problems develop when a person is unable to work from the appropriate ego state in a particular situation. For example, the person who lets the Critical Parent pattern his or her behavior during leisure deprives himself or herself of a true recreational experience and may be a disruptive force in the recreational enjoyment of others.

Transactional Analysis

Transactions are interactions between two people's ego states. For example, two mature persons might interact on an Adult-to-Adult level. Through transactional analysis, such interactions are examined. In the example given a parallel transaction exists. In such parallel transactions the response comes from the ego state at which it was directed, and the returned response is aimed at the original ego state that initiated the transaction. In parallel transactions the flow of communication continues.

In contrast, nonparallel (crossed) transactions always cause a breakdown in communication. For example, one person may ask from the Adult, "Where are the cards?" Another person responds, "Why can't you take care of things?" The second person responded from his or her Parent to the Child of the first. It is easy to see how this transaction could lead to a communication breakdown.

Both parallel and crossed transactions are diagrammed in Figure 2-1. In the first transaction the Adult-to-Adult parallel transaction is shown. In the second diagram a parallel transaction exists between parent and child. The crossed transaction discussed in the preceding paragraph is shown in the third diagram. Finally, a Parent-to-Child transaction is responded to with an Adult-to-Adult reply, creating a crossed transaction in the fourth diagram.

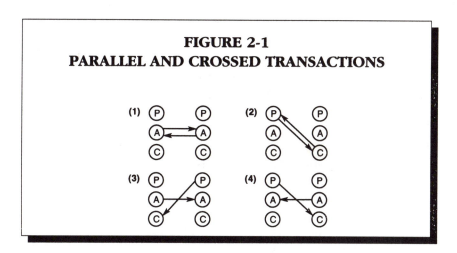

FIGURE 2-1
PARALLEL AND CROSSED TRANSACTIONS

Rackets and Games Analysis

The phrase "collecting stamps" is used to describe the process by which people collect feelings, much as shoppers might collect trading stamps. These stamps (feelings) are later cashed in to justify some behavior. People cash in their stamps toward any number of things, from getting drunk to attempting suicide. Their logic is that they deserve whatever "prize" they desire (Woollams et al., 1976).

Healthy persons do not collect stamps. Instead, they deal with feelings as they occur. Unhealthy persons save up stamps in order to justify acts that fit into their life position of feeling they are no good. The actual act of pursuing and saving stamps is the person's *racket*. Different rackets exist, including anger rackets and depression rackets in which people collect anger stamps or depression stamps depending on their particular racket.

Games substitute for intimate relations. Essentially they are a series of dishonest transactions people repeat over and over in order to accomplish ulterior motives. Games follow set formats, so that those who play them may reach the payoff they seek in terms of collecting bad feelings or stamps.

Script Analysis

Early in life most people determine a life plan by which they live their lives. This plan, or script, preordains the roles they will assume in later life (Steiner, 1974). If the script results mostly in positive strokes (recognition), it is a winner's script. If the strokes are generally negative it is a loser's script. Routine, boring scripts that look good superficially but in which people actually do not take chances and avoid emotionally charged situations are termed nonwinning or banal scripts. An example of a banal script is the hardworking businessman who relies on his Adult but does not seek intimacy or release his Natural Child (Woollams et al., 1976). Since scripts are self-determined, they may be altered. Once understood, a person can focus on his or her script and change it.

Scripts are closely related to *life positions* because scripts are formed out of the vantage point of one of four life positions.

- I'm OK-You're OK
- I'm OK-You're not OK
- I'm not OK-You're OK
- I'm not OK-You're not OK

When an infant enters the world, he or she naturally assumes the healthy I'm OK-You're OK position. This position is maintained as long as the person receives positive strokes (recognition). These can be nonverbal (a pat on the back) or verbal ("You're beautiful"). When a person's stroke bank is full, a stroke reserve is built to draw on and the person feels OK. When the reserve is depleted, the person feels not OK (Campos & McCormick, 1980).

The need for people to gain strokes is called stimulus-hunger. Structure-hunger (the need to structure time) is an extension of exchanging or avoiding strokes (Woollams et al, 1976). There are six ways of structuring time:

- withdrawal
- rituals
- pastimes
- games
- activities
- intimacy

Withdrawal is removing oneself from others. By withdrawal, people avoid strokes. *Rituals* are predictable exchanges of strokes. *Pastimes* are goal-directed communications. Both are superficial and result in minimum stroking. *Games* are useless time fillers that substitute for intimate relations. They result only in negative strokes. *Activities* have to do with accomplishing things people want to do or have to do. *Intimacy* is represented in genuine caring relationships that are totally free from games or exploitation. Activities and intimacy provide positive strokes that reinforce OK feelings (James & Jongward, 1971).

Egograms

The egogram is used to symbolize, in bar form, the amount of energy in each of the five functional ego states of any person. An individual's distinctive personality may be charted showing the different levels of psychological energy in the Critical Parent (CP), Nurturing Parent (NP), Adult (A), Free Child (FC), and Adapted Child (AC). CP represents the part of the Parent ego state that is controlling and critical, in contrast to NP, the Nurturing Parent ego state. A represents the rational Adult ego state. FC represents the Free or Natural Child and AC stands for the Adapted Child functions that are compliant or rebellious. An example of an egogram appears in Figure 2-2.

As may be seen in Figure 2-2, the egogram is a bar graph constructed of the five functional ego states, CP, NP, A, FC, and AC. The higher the column, the more time and energy is expended in the ego state. A balanced personality is represented in Figure 2-2 with the Adult (A) being the primary ego state. In contrast, were the column representing AC the highest, the individual's personality would be shaped largely by what others thought about him or her. If the FC column was highest, the person would be natural, playful and uninhibited, and so forth.

An individual's egogram does not change until the person consciously decides to take steps to alter his or her ego states. It is hypothesized that once a change is made in one of the five functional ego states, however, this change will alter another ego state. If the energy level in one is heightened, another must be reduced. For example, were the energy level of the Adapted Child to be lowered, the Free Child could show increased energy as the person became more natural and uninhibited.

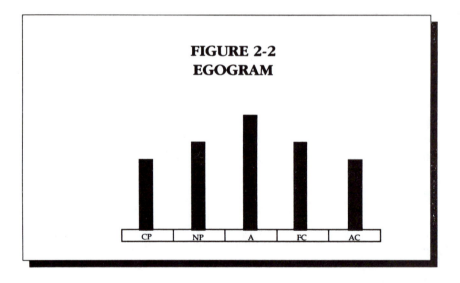

FIGURE 2-2
EGOGRAM

Practitioners using transaction analysis employ a variety of techniques to raise the energy levels of the five functional ego states. For example, to enhance the energy level of the Nurturing Parent the therapist might use a group exercise involving hugging or group members making positive comments about one another. To increase the energy level of the Free Child, the therapist might encourage the client to be more spontaneous in creative activities (Dusay & Dusay, 1984).

Implications for Therapeutic Recreation

Every person needs positive stroking. Positive stroking encourages young persons to grow into the winner roles they were born to assume. Ignoring individuals or giving negative strokes pushes young persons toward losers' scripts and reinforces losers' scripts for older people (James & Jongward, 1971). By structuring opportunities for activities and intimacy, therapeutic recreation specialists will lead people to give and obtain positive strokes. Leaders following TA traditions create a safe, protective climate where clients feel free to be themselves and to experiment in developing new cognitions and behaviors (Corey, 1995; Okun 1992). Therapeutic recreation specialists can likewise provide protective atmospheres in which clients will feel comfortable and risk change. Therapeutic recreation specialists can also help people release the script-free Natural Child in order to be able to experience the freedom and joy found in play and recreation. Transaction analysis also can be used to help clients improve interpersonal communications. Since transaction analysis is not the private domain of any single professional group, it can be employed by therapeutic recreation specialists who have studied its theories and processes. Transaction analysis offers the leisure counselor a common sense, understandable approach through which clients can gain insights and make choices to change leisure behavior. James and Jongward (1971), in their best selling book on transactional analysis, *Born to Win*, have presented exercises related both to people's childhood and current play that are appropriate for use in leisure counseling. Gunn (1977) has written of using transaction analysis approaches in a major work on leisure counseling edited by Epperson, Witt, and Hitzhusen.

Family Therapy

The foundation for **family therapy** is that the family is the basic unit in our society and, as such, has a tremendous impact on its members. Therefore, each client needs to be considered within the context of his or her family group. Friedman (1992) has underscored the crucial role the family plays in the life of each individual. She has written:

> The family serves as the critical intervening variable (or as some authors term it, "buffer" or "bargaining agent") between society and the individual. In other words, the basic purpose of the family is *mediation*—taking the basic societal expectations and obligations and molding and modifying them to some extent to fit the needs and interests of its individual family members (p.4).

She goes on to say:

> Although a number of groups have a mediating function, the family is of central importance in that it is the primary group for the individual. Each family member belongs to a number of groups, but usually only the family is concerned with the total individual and all facets of his or her life. The highest priority of the family is usually the welfare of its family members. Other groups such as co-workers, church, school, and friends do not have this concern for the complete individual, but usually limit themselves to one facet of the individual's life: for example, cooperation and friendliness at work, sincerity and involvement in church affairs, or productivity and achievement at school (p. 4).

Jones and Dimond (1982) have emphasized the critical nature of the family to the health of the individual. They have stated: "The family is the most important social unit to an individual. As such, the family constitutes the most important social context within which illness occurs and resolves. The family serves as the primary unit in health and illness" (p.12).

Family therapy arose in the United States due to observed inadequacies of prevailing individual-based treatment approaches. It has evolved out of group therapy over the last quarter-century, gaining increasing popularity within mental health circles within the past decade. In fact, it may be categorized as a type of group therapy done with the family, a natural, preformed group. There is no one accepted theoretical basis for family therapy, but, instead, eclectic approaches are commonly employed by practitioners (Epstein & Loos, 1989; Harré & Lamb, 1986; Nicholi, 1988).

Kovel (1976) has termed family therapy as "the most pragmatic of all therapies" (p.196), largely because it "enables a person to focus more directly on the real behaviors that affect life with those closest to him" (p.196). He goes on to say: "Certain aspects of the emotional world that appear right away in family treatment may remain inaccessible to any form of individual therapy, or even other group therapy" (p.196).

Belkin's (1988) description of family therapy provides helpful understandings. He writes:

> In practice, family counseling involves the joint participation of several family members. It is used descriptively for all settings in which family members are working together to solve common problems. However, most writers also emphasize the conceptualization of personality or psychopathology from a family systems point of view (p.342).

Greiner and Demi (1995) offer another helpful description of family therapy. They write:

> Family therapy is more than a mode of treatment. It is a way of thinking. Philosophically, it differs greatly from an individual approach or a group approach. The aim of family therapy is to see the family from a comprehensive perspective. Because family therapy conceptualizes emotional and behavioral problems broadly, multiple ways of intervening are appropriate (p.358).

Typical of such conceptualization is the work of Kovel (1976) who has written:

> Family treatment is useful for schizophrenia, where people in the family are not well individuated; for all those instances where the family unit itself is jeopardized and people are more concerned about its security than about their separate development; for families where a host of social and economic problems complicate psychological ones; and for many types of intergenerational conflicts, including a wide range of emotional disturbances in children (p.19).

General goals for family therapy are the development of cohesion and adaptability in the family unit, within the context of developmental issues that affect the family. Effective families allow members to become enmeshed into the family but still permit them to be alone at times. Cohesion exists when there is neither total enmeshment or disengagement. Effective families also allow for flexibility in the face of stressful circumstances. Leadership within the adaptable family is neither authoritarian or chaotic. Understanding family developmental issues is important to helping families. Developmental transitions are marked by events such as the birth of a child, the child leaving home, or events such as illness or relocations (Brammer, Abrego, & Shostrom, 1993; Ivey, Ivey, and Simek-Morgan, 1993).

Even though family programming in therapeutic recreation has been relatively limited to date, the general goals of pioneering programs have been congruent with the overall philosophy and purposes of family therapy. Monroe (1987), in describing the program at the Portsmouth Psychiatric Center, has stipulated the purpose of the program is: "to enhance family relationships through participation in structured family leisure activities" (p.47). Objectives of the program are to: (a) develop communication or cooperative skills; (b) improve leisure attitudes, skills and abilities; (c) learn to make family decisions; (d) develop parenting skills; and (e) develop family self-esteem (p.47).

DeSalvatore, with Rosenman (1986), and writing alone (DeSalvatore, 1989), has described the family therapy program on the children's psychiatric unit at the New England Memorial Hospital. The goals of the program are to assess and treat families in terms of family process and family structure. Under family process are objectives related to:

- communication skills and patterns;
- the effectiveness and the styles employed in parent-parent and parent-child interactions;
- task performance skills;
- ability to use therapeutic interventions; and
- parent understandings of the developmental needs of children.

Under family structure are objectives related to the family's:

- hierarchy,
- rules,
- boundaries, and
- roles (DeSalvatore & Rosenman, 1986, p. 214).

Areas covered in *The Parent-Child Activity Group Manual* (Ayers, Colman & DeSalvatore, n.d.) prepared by staff of the New England Memorial Hospital include: parenting, communication, discipline and limit setting, positive reinforcement, playing with children, feelings, and self-esteem.

Monroe (1987) has detailed the Portsmouth program that is a multifamily group limited to no more than four families. Each session contains three parts: an introduction, an activity portion, and a discussion. The introductory phase consists of the therapist covering the purpose of the particular session, which for example, might be the enhancement of family communication. During this time, families are invited to discuss any problems they have encountered in the area of focus. The second phase of the session involves participation in an activity. An activity that encourages communication would be chosen by the therapist for a session on family communication. During the activity, the therapist observes the communication patterns within each family. The third and last phase of the session deals with the issue during a group discussion. For example, problems the families encountered in communicating would be discussed. At the conclusion of the session, the therapist summarizes for the group.

The New England Memorial Hospital program described by DeSalvatore (1989) is structured much differently than the Portsmouth program. Parents come onto the unit to spend the entire day with their child, attending all the activities in which the child normally participates (including activity groups). A staff member is assigned to "coach" the family during this time. The staff member processes with the family to evaluate how the parents did and if the family was able to achieve its goals.

Implications for Therapeutic Recreation

Perhaps because most therapeutic recreation has transpired in hospitals instead of in clients' homes and communities, family treatment has been limited within the therapeutic recreation profession. With more and more therapeutic recreation occurring in the community, it would appear a natural consequence may be an enlarging role for family-centered programs. Obviously, therapeutic recreation specialists may wish to consider establishing family therapy programs similar to those described by Monroe (1987) and DeSalvatore (1989).

Therapeutic recreation specialists need to have adequate preparation in order to engage in conducting family therapy programs. Needed are a knowledge of family assessment, family therapy models and intervention skills to employ with families. Unfortunately, there has been a paucity of knowledge provided on family-centered approaches within most therapeutic recreation curricula. There is a real need for those preparing students for careers in therapeutic recreation to give more attention to the emerging area of family therapy.

All therapeutic recreation specialists should be aware of the danger in treating the individual in isolation, without giving consideration to other family members or including them in the treatment program. Secondly, therapeutic recreation specialists, through family therapy, are reminded of the advantages of programming in the nonthreatening atmosphere of activities where people can be themselves. Finally, family therapy approaches also remind therapeutic recreation specialists that therapeutic recreation programs often allow for the direct observation and learning of behaviors that may be used daily in interactions with family members and others.

Psychodrama

Psychodrama is a form of psychiatric treatment developed by Jacob L. Moreno. The goal of psychodrama is to help the client gain increased awareness of feelings and behaviors through personal insights and the perceptions of others resulting from dramatizing situations centering around past, current, or anticipated difficulties. The client discovers more about his or her difficulties and learns to cope with them by means of the cathartic expression of acting out problems. Corey (1995) has explained: "The techniques of psychodrama lend themselves very well to producing lively group interaction, exploring interpersonal problems, experimenting with novel ways of approaching significant others in one's life, and reducing one's feelings of isolation" (p.206-207).

Elements involved in psychodrama include the stage director, subject (client), alter ego, and auxiliary ego. The psychodrama takes place on a stage and is directed by the leader, who may interject comments when necessary and who interprets the drama. It is also the leader's job to convey a warm, caring, and supportive attitude conducive to encouraging spontaneity. The subject has the opportunity of playing the leading role, which may be himself or herself or someone else. This person, or any character in the drama, may have an alter ego (or double) who stands immediately behind the person and states aloud whatever that character is probably thinking (in contrast to what the person is actually saying). Thus the alter ego is an extension of the person's ego. The auxiliary ego is a person who portrays a significant other in the life of the subject (Matson, 1977; Cohen & Lipkin, 1979; Corey, 1995).

Implications for Therapeutic Recreation

Therapeutic recreation specialists should not be tempted to conduct psychodrama without extensive preparation. The psychodrama leader must obtain a high level of training under expert direction. Nevertheless, aspects of psychodrama such as role playing, role reversal and rehearsal for future situations may be used by therapeutic recreation specialists. Like the leader of psychodrama, the therapeutic recreation specialist should also attempt to create a warm, accepting atmosphere so clients feel free to express themselves.

Multimodal Therapy

The **multimodal therapy** of Arnold A. Lazarus is a systematic and comprehensive psychotherapeutic approach with the goal of reducing psychological suffering and promoting personal growth. Lazarus' principle of *technical eclecticism* encourages the employment of a diverse range of assessment and treatment methods drawn from different sources without adhering to the theories that spawned them. While operating within the framework of social learning theory, multimodal therapy transcends behavioral traditions to use an array of techniques ranging from behavioral (e.g., modeling, contracting, biofeedback, assertiveness training), to cognitive (e.g., Ellis' paradigm, thought-blocking, bibliotherapy), to Gestalt (e.g., empty chair), to sex therapy (e.g., tactile stimulation), to meditation. Flexibility is inherent in multimodal therapy since the therapist is constantly searching for new techniques or refining or eliminating old ones to determine what works best for each individual under particular circumstances (Lazarus, 1984; 1989).

The notion of multimodal therapy grew out of Lazarus' experiences as a student at the University of Witwatersrand in

Johannesburg, South Africa, where he discovered that behavioral interventions were usually superior to the purely verbal or cognitive approaches commonly practiced in the 1950s. Later, Lazarus found that behavioral techniques alone were not, however, sufficient. He came to advocate a "broad-spectrum" approach that transcended the behavioral approach. In the early 1970s, Lazarus accepted the term multimodal behavior therapy, which he ultimately changed to multimodal therapy to reflect the use of assessment and treatment strategies beyond those used by behavioral therapists (Lazarus, 1984).

While subscribing to the *principle of parity* (we are equal to one another), Lazarus views each of us as different and unique because he believes our personalities are produced out of an interplay among our genetic endowment, our physical environment, and our social learning history. From this belief, Lazarus developed the acronym BASIC I.D. (Behavior, Affect, Sensation, Imagery, Cognition, Interpersonal Relationships, and Drugs/biological factors) to represent the "human personality." In multimodal therapy, assessment and treatment are specifically and systematically divided into these seven discrete but interactive modalities (Lazarus, 1984; 1989). Meaningful improvement is expected only when concern is given to all of the modalities (Lazarus, 1992).

Because of this perspective, multimodal therapy is, by necessity, personalistic and individualistic. A fundamental premise of multimodal therapy is that clients are seen as usually being troubled by a number of specific problems that need to be treated using a multitude of techniques. Therefore, in multimodal therapy there is no typical treatment format. Instead, clients are assessed using the BASIC I.D. Chart or Modality Profile that is structured around the seven modalities. This assessment serves as a blueprint in that stipulating salient features of the client's BASIC I.D. enables the client and therapist to establish objectives, specify therapeutic techniques, and formulate a comprehensive evaluation plan (Lazarus, 1989).

Implications for Therapeutic Recreation

Multimodal therapists are drawn from a wide range of health service professionals including (but not limited to) psychologists, social workers, psychiatric nurses, and pastoral counselors. A multimodal therapy approach has been suggested for leisure counseling with elderly clients (Munson & Munson, 1986). Therefore, therapeutic recreation specialists with strong counseling backgrounds and who are well versed in multimodal methods, may utilize it in leisure counseling. More likely, however, would be the use by therapeutic recreation specialists of concepts shared between multimodal therapy and therapeutic recreation. The following represent such concepts.

- Multiple areas are covered in completing a comprehensive assessment.
- Following assessment information, treatment procedures are individually tailored to meet the unique needs of each client.
- A vast array of therapeutic approaches may be used with clients to meet a wide spectrum of concerns.
- An egalitarian approach is followed in the therapist-client relationship.
- Objectives are clearly stated and an evaluation plan is developed to measure results.

SUMMARY

Some approaches covered in this chapter, such as psychoanalytic psychotherapy and psychodrama, are beyond the normal bounds of therapeutic recreation and are utilized by other helping disciplines. Nevertheless, theoretical notions or actual techniques drawn from these approaches may have application in therapeutic recreation. Other approaches, such as behavior modification and transactional analysis, are more likely to be used in therapeutic recreation intervention and leisure counseling. The information from this chapter will hopefully act as a catalyst for the interested reader to develop expertise in several of these therapeutic approaches.

READING COMPREHENSION QUESTIONS

1. Provide an example from your own experience that shows how theory affects practice.

2. What is meant by the eclectic approach? Do you agree that therapeutic recreation is characterized by eclecticism?

3. Differentiate between the psychoanalytic and behavioristic approaches. Contrast these with the growth psychology approach.

4. What are the id, ego, and superego?

5. Think of possible conflicts you have personally experienced between your id and superego.

6. What is the narcissistic phase?

7. What is psychoanalysis? Transference? Counter-transference?

8. Do you accept the cathartic notion? Why or why not?

9. Describe play therapy.

10. How do behaviorists view "mental illness?"

11. Compare classical conditioning with operant conditioning.

12. Discuss what is meant by shaping, prompting, and fading.

13. What is modeling? Suggest ways to use it in therapeutic recreation.

14. What is time-out? Do you think it should be used by therapeutic recreators as a behavior modification technique?

15. What are token economies?

16. Should recreation be used as a privilege to be earned with tokens?

17. Explain the Premack principle. Do you think the response deprivation hypothesis is a better explanation of reinforcement patterns?

18. What is growth psychology? Who is associated with growth psychology?

19. What do you consider to be the major implications of Rogers' client-centered therapy for practice in therapeutic recreation?

20. Briefly describe Gestalt therapy. Do you see any way its techniques could be used in leisure counseling?

21. Which of the four major orientations do you personally favor (psychoanalytic, behavioristic, cognitive-behavioral, or growth psychology)? Why?

22. Do you agree that rational-emotive therapy can have useful application in leisure counseling?

23. Do you agree with Glasser's basic propositions regarding responsibility and reality? Would you place the same level of importance on involvements as Glasser does in his theory?

24. What are the four primary methods by which those using transaction analysis attempt to understand behavior?

25. What is an egogram?

26. What are the transaction analysis ego states?

27. Do you allow your Natural Child to come out in play and recreation?

28. What are positive strokes?

29. Should therapeutic recreation specialists be involved with family therapy?

30. Does psychodrama have implications for therapeutic recreation?

31. Do you concur with Lazarus' principle of technical eclecticism?

Chapter Three

FACILITATION TECHNIQUES

CHAPTER PURPOSE

In addition to the more developed and comprehensive helping theories and therapeutic approaches discussed in Chapter 2, there are a number of facilitation techniques that may be employed as interventions. This chapter will help the reader to gain an understanding of a variety of techniques that may be used by therapeutic recreation specialists.

KEY TERMS

- Values clarification
- Horticulture therapy
- Therapeutic touch
- Breathing techniques
- Autogenic training
- Benson's technique
- Self-massage
- Aromatherapy
- Debriefing
- Social skills training
- Cognitive Rehabilitation
- Attitude therapy
- Resocialization
- Reminiscence
- Bibliotherapy
- Therapeutic community
- Humor
- Progressive relaxation training
- Transcendental meditation
- Biofeedback
- Adventure/challenge therapy
- Aquatic Therapy
- Assertiveness training
- Animal-facilitated therapy
- Validation Therapy
- Reality orientation
- Remotivation
- Sensory training

OBJECTIVES

- Assess selected facilitation techniques to understand implications for practice in therapeutic recreation.
- Define basic terminology and concepts related to facilitation techniques.
- Evaluate facilitation techniques for possible use in therapeutic recreation.

The approaches discussed in this chapter are diverse. Some have been used primarily (but not exclusively) in psychiatric settings. Bibliotherapy, relaxation techniques, adventure/ challenge therapy and therapeutic community fall into this category. Others, such as reality orientation, remotivation, resocialization, sensory training and reminiscence, have been employed mostly with persons who are elderly. Still others, such as horticulture therapy, humor and values clarification, have been used in an array of settings with a variety of client groups. Because the approaches presented in this section do not fit together into neat packages, no attempt has been made to group or arrange them systematically (with the exception of those primarily employed with persons who are elderly, which are placed together). Therefore, the order in which a particular approach is presented has nothing to do with its importance or possible value to therapeutic recreation.

VALUES CLARIFICATION

According to Wilberding (1992), "The health care professions are increasingly recognizing client autonomy as a central feature of the client-provider relationship" (p.323). *Values Clarification* is a facilitation technique that can be used to help clients in making autonomous decisions consistent with their values. Health care professionals can assist clients to explore their values and to make decisions regarding their values (important beliefs and principles by which people live their lives).

Prominent among authorities associated with values clarification is Sidney B. Simon, who has presented an approach to valuing made up of seven steps. These seven steps fall under three major categories—choosing, cherishing, acting—each of which represents a plateau. The first category or plateau deals with choosing one's beliefs and behaviors. It has three subprocesses: option exploration or determining alternatives; appraising the consequences of a particular choice; and freely choosing a value after rational consideration. The second plateau deals with cherishing beliefs and behaviors. It contains the fourth step, which asks if you feel good or are happy with your choice and you are ready to let others know of your choice. The third plateau contains the final two steps. Step six is determining action or what you are willing to do about your value. Step seven is making the value a regular part of your life (Simon & Olds, 1977).

Simon has also presented a number of values clarification strategies. Included within these are many that directly concern leisure choices. Among exercises from the book by Simon, Howe and Kirschenbaum (1995) that I have used with groups are "The Pie of Life" (strategy 33) and "Twenty Things You Love to Do" (strategy 1).

Pie of Life

The purpose of this strategy is to take an inventory in terms of how time is spent during typical work or leisure days. Value/time inconsistencies may be discovered as participants find out if they are getting what they want out of life. The strategy also can produce thought-provoking issues about how individuals spend their lives.

The procedure involves the leader drawing a large circle on the board while indicating that the circle represents a typical 24-hour day. Participants are then asked to draw their own circles and divide them into quarters, representing 6-hour blocks, using broken lines. One circle can be used to represent a work day (or school day) and the other, a leisure day. Participants then use the following categories (additional categories may be included) to draw in slices of the pie to depict how they spend their time: sleep, school, work, with friends, alone, with family, on chores around the house, exercise or sports, eating or other miscellaneous pastimes.

After completing the pies, participants are asked to think about the following questions:

- Are you satisfied with the relative sizes of your slices?
- Ideally, how big would you want each slice to be? Draw your ideal pie.
- Realistically, is there anything you can do to begin to change the size of some of your slices?
- Is there a Self-Contract (see Strategy Number 59) you'd be willing to make and sign your name to?

Twenty Things You Love To Do

The question asked by this strategy is: "Am I really getting what I want out of life?" Rewarding living includes taking part in highly-prized activities. Until participants engage in this strategy, they may not know whether they are getting what they really want from life. In Appendix A at the end of this chapter (p. 118), you will find the directions for this activity. The activity encourages participants to evaluate how they really feel about things they do by insisting that they note various conditions about these activities.

Other exercises I have used from the 1995 Simon book are strategies 3, 4, 23, 27, 28, 57, and 71. With some of these the leader must choose parts or adapt them in a way that emphasizes leisure aspects. A very helpful strategy to use in conjunction with a number of exercises is strategy 15, "I Learned Statements." This exercise stimulates group discussion about the previous strategy by allowing participants to complete phrases such as "I learned that I....," "I realized that I....," and "I was surprised that I...."

It is important for those leading values clarification strategies to keep in mind that the goal of values clarification is not to impose a value or course of action on participants but to encourage them to look at alternatives and their consequences. Such clarification on leisure lifestyle can be meaningful to individuals who have not adequately worked through value issues related to leisure.

Implications for Therapeutic Recreation

Values clarification has direct implications for therapeutic recreation specialists who may employ values clarification strategies in leisure education and leisure counseling programs. Through these exercises individuals can discover leisure values and initiate plans to act on their values. Usually exercises are completed in a group, with the leader providing the instructions for each exercise. No particular equipment is necessary, although it is helpful to have a blackboard available. Participants may need paper and pencils to complete some exercises.

BIBLIOTHERAPY

Bibliotherapy employs reading materials such as novels, plays, short stories, booklets, and pamphlets to help clients become aware that others share problems similar to theirs and to help bring new insights into being. Bibliotherapy is usually used in psychiatric settings. Particular readings are selected for the client that contain characters with problems related to the client's problems. The client will then supposedly identify with the characters and project himself or herself into the story. This process results in an emotional reaction that can then be discussed with a helping professional (Eisenberg & Delaney, 1986; Carson, et al., 1996).

Implications for Therapeutic Recreation

Bibliotherapy has not become a popular technique among therapeutic recreation specialists, but it does reinforce the importance of structuring ways for clients to help themselves. Clients can engage in self-help activities without direct assistance from therapeutic recreation specialists if proper structures are provided.

HORTICULTURE THERAPY

Horticulture therapy uses the activity of working with plants to bring about therapeutic outcomes. A **horticulture therapy** program can be simple or complex. It can range from simply growing plants indoors under lights, or having plants on a window sill, to extensive outdoor gardens or a complete greenhouse.

Horticulture therapy takes place within a variety of treatment and rehabilitation settings in Europe, Canada, and the United States. Among settings applying this therapeutic approach have been: psychiatric hospitals, community mental health centers, schools with special education programs, corrections facilities, nursing homes and long-term care facilities, centers for physical rehabilitation, and alcohol and drug rehabilitation centers (Friedman, 1985; Rothert & Daubert, 1981).

Within such facilities, horticulture activities are used as means to develop therapeutic relationships, "for the dual purpose of helping with the problem of adjustment, and motivating a broader interest in the client's surroundings as a result of increased knowledge of the plant world," according to Rothert and Daubert (p.2). Horticulture therapy has been reported to provide the following benefits.

- Enhance life satisfaction, morale, and interaction with the environment.
- Increase socialization, peer support, and self-esteem.
- Establish commitment to a goal, a sense of responsibility, and feelings of control.
- Bring about physical therapy benefits during participation in personally meaningful activity.
- Stimulate contact with concrete reality and nature by working hands in soil.
- Develop appreciation for other living things, life cycles, growth, and development.
- Instill a sense of purpose and of being needed.
- Develop horticulture skills that may lead to employment.
- Develop a wholesome leisure activity that may be carried on following treatment and rehabilitation (Edinberg, 1985; Friedman, 1985; Rothert & Daubert, 1981).

It should be mentioned that horticulture therapy is gaining increasing use within programs that serve clients with physical disabilities. Because of this, more attention is being given to creating environments that are conducive to gardening for persons such as those who use wheelchairs, have had strokes, or have visual impairments. For example, elevated areas can be constructed to allow clients using wheelchairs to do gardening (Smith, Austin, & Kennedy, 1996). Long-handled tools reduce the need to bend or stretch for those who have had strokes (Growing Confidence, 1993). A variety of ideas to facilitate horticulture activities for persons with disabilities (including the use of cut and grab scissors, one-handed wheelbarrows and vertical planters) appear in a wonderfully illustrated booklet published by the Perkins School for the Blind (n.d.).

Implications for Therapeutic Recreation

Although scientific validity for horticulture therapy has not been established, clinical results hold promise that clients may receive therapeutic benefits through work with plants. Therapists must possess knowledge of plants and gardening, and be able to relate this knowledge to clients' problems or concerns in order to conduct horticulture therapy programs. The requirement of a high degree of facility with the medium employed in therapy or rehabilitation is, of course, a fundamental prerequisite to the application of any therapeutic approach, as is the ability to apply the medium to meet client needs. Some colleges and universities do offer a master's degree in horticulture therapy, although many horticulture therapy programs are conducted by therapists without such specialized preparation.

THERAPEUTIC COMMUNITY

Maxwell Jones originated the term **therapeutic community,** which has typically been employed to describe a way of operating a relatively small unit within a general hospital, a large psychiatric hospital, or other institution. Therapeutic communities have been used primarily on psychiatric services and with nursing home residents in the treatment of emotional and behavioral problems. Most recently, the concept has been applied in community-based transitional living facilities for homeless, chronically mentally ill persons (Murry & Baier, 1993).

Therapeutic communities are based on the concept that the entire social milieu may be used as an intervention because clients change and grow as a result of involvement in interpersonal relationships. It is reasoned that since client problems have resulted from faulty social learning, positive social learning can build the individual's ability to cope. The goal is for persons to help themselves by helping others, ultimately learning to be responsible for themselves. In the therapeutic community, staff and clients interact freely in work and recreation within an understanding atmosphere designed to utilize the total impact of group processes. The Director and Assistant Director of Nursing at Menninger Foundation have noted that one of the main areas where learning is needed is in regard to leisure activities and the use of unstructured time on the unit (Benfer & Schroder, 1985, p. 454). The concept of therapeutic community stands in contrast to the hierarchical, authoritarian organization often associated with hospitals and institutions. The student of therapeutic recreation may recognize that the therapeutic community has much in common with the moral therapy of the nineteenth century (Barnes, Sack & Shore, 1973).

Implications for Therapeutic Recreation

Even though there are problems related to the therapeutic community concept, including its abstractness and staff role blurring, the approach has implications for therapeutic recreation specialists. One is the importance of all staff in facilitating change, because all client experiences have therapeutic value and all transactions between clients and staff are seen as having therapeutic potential. Since therapeutic recreation specialists are regularly very involved with the daily activities of clients, their potential impact on the social milieu is obvious, calling for them to have extensively developed skills in interpersonal communications and group dynamics. Therapeutic recreation specialists should apply these skills with particular concern for clients who are learning to deal with unstructured time while in their "home away from home." The therapeutic community approach also shows that therapeutic recreation specialists must learn to function harmoniously in a team effort with staff and clients in order to create a positive social structure to enhance treatment.

HUMOR

Laughter results from **humor**, which develops out of incongruity. Things that appear funny are generally unexpected, ambiguous, inappropriate or illogical (Adler, 1989). Laughter and humor have been associated with both being healthy and becoming healthy. Healthy persons are generally perceived to have a sense of humor and are able to laugh with others and at themselves. The notion that laughter and humor have therapeutic value has long enjoyed popular support. All of us have no doubt used the phrase, "Laughter is the best medicine," on more than one occasion. Even so, the concept of using laughter and humor as therapeutic interventions remains controversial (Lumsden, 1986; Fry & Salameh, 1993); this may well be attributed to a previous lack of scientific evidence to support the use of humor in treatment.

Scientific Documentation

Interest in the therapeutic potential of humor has been largely triggered by Norman Cousins who widely wrote about his use of humor in recovering from Collagen disease (a crippling illness) and a myocardial infarction. The use of self-prescribed daily doses of humor in his recovery is well documented in Cousins' books, *Anatomy of an Illness*, published in 1979, and *The Healing Heart*, which appeared in 1983. Scientific evidence on the value of humor in therapy has, however, only recently begun to be published.

One study has been completed by Adams and McGuire (1986) in which these researchers tested the hypotheses:

(1) Individuals viewing humorous movies will experience more reduction in perceived pain than individuals viewing non-humorous movies;
(2) Individuals viewing humorous movies will experience more improvement in affect than individuals viewing non-humorous movies (pp.160,161).

Subjects in the study were persons residing in a long-term care facility who viewed movies for 30 minutes three times each week for six weeks. Both self-report and decreases in the use of pain medications confirmed the positive impact of the humorous movies on the subjects' pain. Support was also found for hypothesis 2. Affect Balance Scale scores indicated that the subjects who viewed the humorous movies had significantly higher affect scores than those who saw the non-humorous movies.

Other studies have likewise reported promising outcomes with the use of humor as an intervention. For instance, humor has been found to play a significant role in helping people to deal with stress (Simon, 1988). Deep laughter has been shown to increase heart rate and oxygenation to the lungs, stimulate the adrenal glands, and temporarily increase blood pressure, creating a state of relaxation (Hill & Smith, 1985). Laughter has been found to stimulate the endocrine system, causing the release of natural painkillers, and to lead to reductions in muscle tension (Lumsden, 1986). These and other findings lend growing support for the possible use of humor in treatment.

Implications for Therapeutic Recreation

According to the editors of *Advances in Humor and Psychotherapy* (Fry & Salameh, 1993), humor has begun to become an accepted element in mental health care. What Fry (1993) has termed the "amazing absurdity of the absolutist stricture against humor in therapy transactions" (p. xiii) is becoming a thing of the past. Humor is seen by many not only as no longer being a questionable treatment modality but as a "powerful tool" (Mosak & Maniacci, 1993) that can free us from shame and guilt (Fry, 1993), reduce stress (Kuhlman, 1993), liberate us from inhibitions (Yorukoglu, 1993), assist us in social bonding (Mosak & Maniacci, 1993) and produce feelings of mastery (Schimel, 1993).

Although it may be premature for therapeutic recreation specialists to open comedy clubs in their facilities, there is evidence to support the use of humor in treatment programs. Perhaps the first thing to gain from the recent interest in humor as therapy is that none of us should take ourselves too seriously. We all need to learn to laugh at ourselves and the situations we find ourselves in. Beyond modeling a sense of humor, we may wish to initiate humor in interactions with clients who display a sense of humor. We may also help clients to experience humor by showing humorous movies, as was done by Adams and McGuire (1986), or by helping them to select something humorous to read. Finally, Simon (1988) and Kuhlman (1993) have suggested that the use of humor may be taught within stress management programs as a coping skill that leads to relaxation and feelings of well-being.

THERAPEUTIC TOUCH

The use of touch as a therapeutic tool has a long history. Cave paintings in the Pyrenees some 15,000 years ago attest to the ancient use of the laying on of hands. Written history of healing by touch goes back 5,000 years. Both the old and new testaments of the *Bible* contain descriptions of its use. The terms "King's touch" and "Royal touch" came from early France and England where kings used touch to cure goiter and other diseases of the throat. Numerous accounts of healing by the laying on of hands appeared in church histories of the Middle Ages. While these events make it clear that the therapeutic use of hands had been employed widely throughout history, with the arrival of the scientific age such practices fell from favor. Only relatively recently has touch begun to be reexamined for its possible therapeutic value (Cohen, 1987; Krieger, 1979).

The term **therapeutic touch** was coined in the 1970s by Dolores Krieger, a nursing professor at New York University, who continues to be a leading advocate for the therapeutic use of human touch (Cohen, 1987). Krieger has conducted studies on therapeutic touch in which she has been able to show positive results, particularly in bringing about dramatic increases in subjects' hemoglobin counts (Krieger, 1979; Lawrence & Harrison, 1983). The theory underlying Krieger's therapeutic touch is that energy (termed *prana*) may be transferred from the healer to the patient. Healthy persons, according to her theory, have an excess of prana. Through therapeutic touch, the healthy healer transfers prana to the ill person who is suffering from a deficit in his or her level of energy. The transfer relieves pain and produces a relaxation response that creates a condition in which the patient's recuperative processes can take control. Krieger believes that humans have a latent potential to heal others through touch as long as they are healthy and have a strong desire to help meet the needs of others (Krieger, 1979).

Scientific Documentation

While scientific evidence supporting the general use of therapeutic touch as a medium is not abundant, some exists. McKechnie, Wilson, Watson, and Scott (1983) completed a study with subjects who had chronic muscle tension, aches and pains. Following a treatment of ten deep massage sessions these subjects displayed decreased muscle tension, slower heart rate, and lower arousal. They also were reported to be more verbal during psychotherapy. Aguilera (1967) reported increases in verbal interaction on the part of psychiatric patients who received touch from a nurse. Whitcher and Fisher (1979) found touch from a nurse prior to an operation lowered anxiety and blood pressure for female patients both before and following surgery. Touch for male patients, however, produced an opposite effect. It was speculated that touch for the men may have been interpreted as a sign of dependency that was a threatening reminder of their vulnerability. A study completed at the Harvard Medical School has been reported by Maxwell-Hudson (1988). Researchers there found that patients who received touch from an anesthetist, as part of a warm approach prior to surgery, required only about one-half the amount of drugs as the control group and, on an average, were dismissed three days earlier than the controls.

Social Barriers

Touch has been called the "most important" (Colton, 1983, p.14) and the "most fundamental" (Cohen, 1987, p.1) of all our senses. Infants have been found to need touch for normal development (Huss, 1977). Adults become depressed and irritable without it (Maxwell-Hudson, 1988). Psychologist Stephen Thayer (1988) has termed touch, "the most powerful of all communication channels" (p.31). Yet, while the beneficial and powerful effects of touch have been acknowledged in the scientific and professional literature, many people are hesitant about touching others. Perhaps this is due to our Puritan heritage that has frowned on touching and because of connections we have drawn between touch and sex (Colton, 1983; Huss, 1977; Maxwell-Hudson, 1988). Today there are signs, however, that touch is growing in acceptance. Indicators include books on therapeutic touch (e.g., Cohen, 1987; Ford, 1992; Macrae, 1993) and articles on therapeutic touch (e.g., Cassetta, 1993; Vortherms, 1991).

Implications for Therapeutic Recreation

Touch is a powerful form of communication. But as a nonverbal form of communication, it is open to misunderstanding. While touch may be meant to be warm and caring, it may be interpreted as invading personal space or as being demeaning or seductive. Caution needs to be exercised when using touch. It is important to consider the appropriateness of the use of touch. Factors that should be appraised include the following:

- The environment in which touch takes place;
- Whether others are present;
- The relationship with the person being touched;
- The gender of the person;
- The body part being touched (e.g., handshake, hand on shoulder, or hug);
- Whether the person is in a mood to be touched; and
- The history of the individual.

The history of the individual should be a particular concern. A person who is depressed or grieving may react to a touch as a gesture of concern. In contrast, a sexually promiscuous person may regard touch as a sexual advance. A child who has been abused may reject a touch meant to be comforting, while a person who is dying may feel a great deal of comfort from having his or her hand held (Shives, 1994).

Because touch can be misinterpreted, many therapists avoid it in order to protect themselves from legal or ethical charges from clients (Thayer, 1988). There are, however, times when words are not sufficient to express feelings. At these times clients may need caring touch (Huss, 1977). Additionally, many individuals are starving to be touched (Ornstein & Sobel, 1989).

Should therapeutic recreation specialists risk using touch with clients? Thayer (1988) has suggested that more therapists should consider the use of touch as a part of their therapeutic repertoire. This would seem to be good advice. Of course, each individual must engage in self-examination in order to determine if he or she will take the risks involved with touch. Huss (1977) has suggested that first becoming aware of one's feelings about touch is a good place to begin this self-examination and has recommended participation in Gestalt therapy awareness exercises such as those found in Stevens' (1988) *Awareness Exploring, Experimenting, Experiencing.*

RELAXATION TECHNIQUES

Stress, with ensuing tension, is a normal part of everyday life. Relaxation techniques are a means to deal with excess tension brought about by stress. In the section that follows, several methods for eliciting a state of relaxation are described. Covered are deep breathing, progressive relaxation training, autogenic training, imagery, meditation, Benson's technique, biofeedback, and massage. Step-by-step instructions for each of these techniques can be found in Appendix B: Relaxation Techniques (p. 119). Breathing and progressive relaxation training are given the most attention because these approaches are most commonly employed by therapeutic recreation specialists.

Deep Breathing

Mason (1985) has exclaimed that "Learning to breathe deeply...is the first step in learning to relax...." (p.13). Certainly learning **breathing techniques** is a skill crucial to most relaxation therapy techniques. This is not surprising when we consider how fundamental breathing is to our feeling of emotional states. Our breathing becomes shallow and irregular and our heart races when we become upset. When relaxed, our breathing becomes deeper and slower and our heart rate decreases. If we can develop the ability to control our breathing so we can breathe deeply, we can trigger the relaxation response (Mason, 1985).

Authorities (e.g., Lynch, 1989; Mason, 1985) offer the following suggestions toward helping individuals to learn deep breathing:

1. Breathe in through the nostrils.
2. Inhale very slowly and deeply.
3. When breathing in, remember to breathe from the diaphragm. The abdomen should rise as if it were a balloon expanding when breathing in, and fall as if it were a balloon deflating with the exhale.
4. Once the abdomen achieves full extension, the shoulders should draw back and the head should rise as the upper part of the lungs are filled.
5. The breath should be held for approximately 5 seconds.
6. Exhale slowly and fully through the nostrils or mouth. In doing so, draw in the abdomen and drop the shoulders slightly.
7. Once the exhaling has occurred, wait two seconds before drawing the next breath.
8. Avoid abrupt transitions.

Among specific breathing exercises that Mason (1985) has offered are "Three-part Breathing" and "Alternate-Nostril Breathing." Description of these techniques can be found in Appendix B: Relaxation Techniques (p. 119). When completing these or any deep breathing exercises, it is important that they are done in a quiet environment in order to remove distractions and that the individual be in a comfortable position. Many clients will wish to close their eyes while they perform the exercises.

A variation on the alternate-nostril breathing exercise may be attempted once the person is comfortable with the alternate-nostril breathing. The more advanced technique calls for the individual to close off each nostril through visualization, rather than actually placing the finger over the nostril (Mason, 1985).

Deep breathing can be a helpful relaxation technique for many clients. Once learned, deep breathing may be used at any time stress is felt or anticipated. For some others, deep breathing, in itself, may not be enough to bring about complete relaxation but it may be used in combination with other relaxation techniques such as progressive relaxation training.

Progressive Relaxation Training

Progressive relaxation training is a technique by which helping professionals train clients in achieving relaxation. Edmund Jacobson's name is usually associated with relaxation training. His progressive relaxation is based on becoming aware of the amount of tension in the body. By having people tense and release their muscles and attend to the resulting sensation of tension and relaxation, Jacobson discovered that a feeling of deep relaxation could be achieved. Joseph Wolpe, the noted behaviorist, later further refined Jacobson's original relaxation procedure. Today a number of variations of relaxation training exist.

Relaxation training is generally done with clients who are experiencing high levels of stress and tension. It takes place in a quiet room in which the windows and doors have been shut and the blinds or drapes drawn. This removes distracting stimuli. To create further a tranquil environment, lights in the room are kept dim. Clients assume a comfortable position in a chair or on a couch, or they may lie on their backs on blankets or mats on the floor. Comfortable, non-binding clothing is worn by clients. Glasses, jewelry, belts, shoes, and other such items are taken off, and clients are instructed to close their eyes during the actual relaxation exercises.

The helping professional's voice is also used to create the proper atmosphere in which to bring about relaxation. Voice volume and tone are instrumental in the process. An initial conversational level gives way to progressive reductions in volume as the session continues. Likewise, the pace of presentation is reduced, or slowed as the session goes on. Although the tone of voice is not hypnotic or seductive, it remains smooth and even.

The basic procedure is to move the client through the tensing and relaxing of a series of muscle groups. A similar five-step sequence is suggested by Bernstein and Carlson (1993) for relaxing each group of muscles. First, the client is told to focus attention on the muscle group. On signal, the muscle group is tensed. Tension is held for 5 to 7 seconds. Tension is then released on the cue of the helping professional. Finally, the client's attention is focused on the muscle group as it is relaxed.

Girdano, Everly, and Dusek (1993) suggest that as each gross movement relaxation exercise is completed, the client breathe in during muscle contraction and out during muscle relaxation. Appendix B: Relaxation Techniques (p. 119) provides other specific instructions that may be employed in the teaching of progressive relaxation training skills.

Learning relaxation skills is similar to learning any new behavior. In order to get better at it, practice is necessary. There really is nothing particularly magical or mysterious about it. And, as with any new skill, some will pick it up quicker than others.

Interested readers are referred to *Progressive Relaxation Training: A Manual for the Helping Professional* by Bernstein and Borkovec (1973), *Stress Power!* by Anderson (1978), *Relaxation* by Cautela and Groden (1978), *Teach Yourself Relaxation* by Hewitt (1985), *Guide to Stress Reduction* by Mason (1985), *Controlling Stress and Tension; A Holistic Approach* by Girdano, Everly, and Dusek (1993); and Bernstein and Carlson's (1993) chapter on progressive relaxation in Leher and Woolfolk's (1993) *Principles and Practice of Stress Management* for detailed information on relaxation training procedures. These seven publications were the major sources for this section and the specific directions for "Progressive Relaxation Training" found in Appendix B: Relaxation Techniques (p. 119).

Autogenic Training

Originated by Johannes H. Schultz in Europe, **autogenic training** (or autogenics) is similar to progressive relaxation training in that both deal with inducing a state of muscular relaxation. Like progressive relaxation training, it can be self-taught by reading books, although it is usually taught by a physician or psychiatrist. Unlike progressive relaxation training, autogenic training involves vasomotor and cognitive processes to teach an individual to exert control over physiological processes through a series of mental exercises involving sensations of heaviness and warmth (Hewitt, 1985; Marcer, 1986).

Autogenic training is a form of voluntary self-regulation in which the trainee concentrates on certain physiological functions normally regulated by the autonomic nervous system. The trainee maintains passive concentration while repeating a self-instruction (e.g., "my left arm is heavy") several times. He or she then observes the sensation that follows (such as heaviness) (Hewitt, 1985; Titlebaum, 1988). Linden (1993) has clearly described the overall process that involves a series of six "formulas" (phrases that are repeated in the mind of the trainee) that produce self-hypnosis. The first formula is an exercise for muscular relaxation (The Heaviness Experience) in which the trainee thinks "My right (or left) arm is very heavy" six times; then once thinks to himself or herself, "I am very quiet." Other exercises involve: "Arms and legs are very warm" six times and "quiet" once (Second Exercise: Experience of Warmth); "The Heart is beating quietly and strongly" six times and "quiet" once (Third Exercise: Regulation of the Heart); "It breathes me" six times and "quiet" once (Fourth Exercise: Regulation of Breathing); "Sun rays are streaming quiet and warm" six times and "quiet " once (Fifth Exercise: Regulation of Visceral Organs); and "The forehead is cool" six times and "quiet" once (Sixth Exercise: Regulation of the Head). Linden's chapter offers the interested reader a complete introduction to Autogenic Training.

Imagery

Imagery refers to the use of positive suggestions to create mental representations of things we know or can fantasize. While largely associated with visualization (mental "pictures"), imagery can involve mental representations of other senses as well. We have the capacity to hear a voice, taste a lemon, recall a pleasant smell, or feel ourselves lounging in a warm bath or swimming in a cool stream (Smith, 1992; Zahourek, 1988).

While the process is not fully understood, we know that our mental images can affect us physiologically and, thus, may be used to bring about relaxation. Zahourek (1988) has provided a specific application of how nurses use images to promote relaxation. I have included "Zahourek's Application of Imagery" in Appendix B: Relaxation Techniques (p. 119).

While information available on imagery is not as extensive as for some of the other relaxation techniques, imagery shows promise as a means to assist clients in achieving relaxation. An example of a relaxation exercise has been provided by Flynn (1980, p. 182). It is termed the "Lightness Relaxation Exercise" and is also in Appendix B (p.119).

Meditation

Because the **transcendental meditation** (TM) of Maharishi Mahesh Yogi received much media attention in the 1960s, and has continued to appear in the news since, many Americans have some knowledge of meditation (Marcer, 1986). Because TM is controlled by an organization that does not allow clinicians to practice it unless they are trained TM teachers, mental health professionals have developed their own modern meditation techniques. These techniques are Carrington's *clinically standardized meditation* (CSM) and Benson's *respiratory one method* (ROM). Such methods of meditation are easily learned and have produced excellent results (Carrington, 1993).

No matter the technique, meditation follows a relatively simple approach that involves sitting comfortably in a quiet place for 15-20 minutes one or two times each day, while passively dwelling on a single word or sound (Carrington, 1993; Marcer, 1996). The person meditating is told to concentrate only on the meditation object (sometimes termed mantra). Mantra are typically calming sounds that end in nasal consonants "m" or "n" and have no meanings. Examples are "Abnam" and "Shi-rim". When learning to meditate, the trainee first repeats the mantra, then whispers it and then finally, just silently thinks of it with his or her eyes closed. Any other thoughts, sensations or images that might be distracting are allowed to pass through the consciousness (Carrington, 1993). This is typical of all meditation as the individual narrows his or her focus to only one thing at a time in order to reach an altered state of awareness (Mason, 1995). Meditation stands in opposition to thinking about a topic. It transcends thought. As Hewitt (1985) states, "It aims at becoming detached from thoughts and images and opening up silent gaps between them" (p.117).

In his best selling book, *The Relaxation Response*, Herbert Benson (1975) has listed four elements basic to most meditation:

- A quiet place to meditate
- A comfortable or poised posture
- An object for attention-awareness to dwell upon
- A passive attitude

Research has found measurable effects for meditation in reducing physiological arousal and decreasing muscle tension to bring about deep relaxation (Benson, 1975; Titlebaum, 1988). Brain wave studies have displayed that the fullest relaxation occurs when there is an absence of thought or thoughts are few in number or of little importance (Hewitt, 1985). The meditator's conscious information-processing mechanisms seem to be temporarily shut off, providing a reprieve from stressful stimuli, resulting in a low level of arousal.

Benson's Technique

Benson's technique may be thought of as a type of meditation. He developed his technique after extensively studying the physiological effects of meditation and reported it in his book, *The Relaxation Response*. Benson's research led him to believe that there was no single, unique method to creating a relaxation response. Instead, he identified four common components of meditation whatever technique was used. These were: a calm quiet environment with few distractions; a mind shift to a mental device or constant stimulus (such as a word, sound, phrase, or fixed gazing at an object); a passive attitude in which people do not worry about how well they are performing the technique and let distracting thoughts pass through; and a comfortable position so there is no undue muscle tension (Benson, 1975).

Benson's technique involves all four of the elements. It is described by Benson (1975) in the six-step process that appears in Appendix B: Relaxation Techniques (p. 119). Benson views the relaxation response as the body's natural means to counteract the stress response (or fight or flight response), the body's involuntary response to threat. The body uses the relaxation response as a protection from stress. He believes that regularly eliciting the relaxation response can be a means to prevent or counteract diseases in which increased sympathetic nervous system activity is involved (Marcer, 1986; Titlebaum, 1988).

Biofeedback

Biofeedback is the use of devices to monitor physiological activities and provide a measurement of them. For instance, heart rate may be measured with the monitoring device producing a graph of the heart beat. Once the individual is given information about a process, such as heart rate, he or she can learn to consciously alter their functioning. In the case of heart rate, the person can affect it by controlling breathing. Mental states can also produce effects on physiological processes during biofeedback sessions. Just thinking about an anxiety-arousing happening can increase heart rate. Heart rate can be decreased when an individual imagines a restful scene (Mason, 1985).

The goal of biofeedback training is for the client to gain awareness of and control over physiological functions. This skill is then used in daily life to increase relaxation and manage stress (Gilkey, 1986; Titlebaum, 1988). Heart rate, skin temperature (blood flow), blood pressure, brain waves, sweat gland activity, and muscle tension may be monitored through biofeedback. Once the person knows what is occurring within the body, he or she can learn to regulate their biological responses since the mind can have a powerful influence over the body (Corbin & Mental-Corbin, 1983).

Biofeedback is usually employed in conjunction with other relaxation techniques such as breathing exercises, progressive relaxation training, imagery, and autogenic training. It has been used to treat a variety of health problems including tension and migraine headaches, anxiety, hypertension, insomnia, and teeth grinding (Titlebaum, 1988). It should be mentioned that biofeedback has the added advantage of helping clients to feel a sense of control and confidence in their abilities to cope with stressors (Stoyva & Budzynski, 1993).

Massage

Thousands of years ago, people of the Mediterranean nations realized the importance of massage not only as an approach to release tension in the muscles but as a means to pleasurable feelings of relaxation (Cohen, 1987). Today massage is enjoying renewed acceptance within the health care community (Cassetta, 1993; West, 1990).

Swedish Massage and Japanese Shiatsu

The Swedish massage is a smooth and flowing massage that leads to a feeling of total relaxation. The masseuse or masseur employs kneading movements in giving the massage. It is usually given in a warm, darkened room on a massage table, but may be given with the person lying on the floor (Cohen, 1987). Another popular method of massage is Japanese Shiatsu. Many massage therapists follow eclectic approaches, borrowing techniques from various sources (West, 1990). The problem with any type of full body massage is it takes an hour to an hour and one-half (Maxwell-Hudson, 1988), and, of course, it requires another person with training in order to give the massage. There is also a cost factor unless a spouse or friend knows massage techniques. **Self-massage** provides an alternative means to relaxation when time, money, or a masseuse or masseur are not available. As the name implies, in self-massage the individual learns to massage himself or herself.

Self-Massage

Experts generally agree (e.g., Dowing, 1972; Lidell, 1984; Maxwell-Hudson, 1988) that self-massage does not offer the potential for the same level of enjoyment and relaxation as traditional massage. Self-massage can nevertheless produce relief from tension. It can also offer an opportunity for clients who may not be aware of certain body parts, and related problems, to get in touch with their bodies (Lawrence & Harrison, 1983). Some self-massage exercises are ones many people do instinctively to reduce tension. For example, in the neck squeeze, the hand is placed over the back of the neck near the shoulders. The neck is squeezed moving from the shoulders to the area where the neck meets the head. In the shoulder tension release the shoulder is stroked with the opposite hand, molding the hand to grasp the top of the shoulder. The hand then squeezes the shoulder as far down on the back as can be reached. Most self-massage techniques are relatively easy to learn and many books on massage contain sections on self-massage. West's (1990) book offers a particularly extensive self-massage section.

Stretching

Some individuals prefer to combine stretching exercises with self-massage. Descriptions of various stretching exercises appear in Appendix B: Relaxation Techniques (p. 119).

Implications for Therapeutic Recreation

Traditionally, psychologists and psychiatrists have conducted relaxation therapy using many of the techniques covered in this section. However, other helping professionals, including therapeutic recreation specialists, may find these techniques helpful with tense clients. Brammer (1988) has stated that progressive relaxation training, in particular, is a simple skill to learn and possesses few hazards for clients. Progressive relaxation training and deep breathing have perhaps been the most utilized techniques by therapeutic recreation specialists. Other relaxation techniques, particularly self-massage, are beginning to be applied more widely in therapeutic recreation.

Another method to facilitate stress reduction is physical exercise. Physical activity as a means to stress reduction is discussed in the following section.

Stress Reduction and Physical Activity

Perhaps the most natural way to bring about the control of stress is through participation in physical activity. Physical exercise may be conceived to be nature's tranquilizer.

The overall value of exercise has been explained by Fillingim and Blumenthal (1993):

> Exercise has become an increasingly popular leisure-time activity in recent years, perhaps largely because of its potential health benefits, such as improved weight control and reduced risk of cardiovascular disease. In addition, there has been considerable interest in the potential psychological benefits of physical activity. Anecdotally, many individuals report "feeling better" following physical activity, and many health care professionals recommend exercise as a stress management technique (p. 443).

Conflicts, frustration, threats, and insults may bring about psychological stress. In reaction to stress the body activates itself for the occurrence of an anticipated "fight or flight" response. That is, the body becomes physiologically mobilized in anticipation of protective actions to deal with or remove danger. As a result, a widespread physical reaction is brought about. There is a general overall increase in arousal level to heighten alertness. The cardiovascular system shows increased activation, and respiration is increased. Adrenal cells secrete hormones into the blood, and the flow of blood is increased to the brain, heart and skeletal muscles (Sundeen et al., 1985, Dusek-Girdano, 1979). In short, the body becomes ready for a physical reaction to stress.

When the stress reaction occurs, Dusek-Girdano (1979) has proposed that physical activity can help handle stress by alleviating the stress state. She has written:

> This is not a time to sit and feel all of these sensations tearing away at the body's systems and eroding good health. This is the time to move, to use up the products, to relieve the body of the destructive forces of stress on a sedentary system. Appropriate activity in this case would be total body exercise such as swimming, running, dancing, biking, or an active individual, dual, or team sport that lasts at least an hour. . . .Such activities will use up the stress products that might otherwise be harmful and that are likely to play a part in a degenerative disease process such as cardiovascular disease or ulcers (p.222).

Research (e.g., Berger, 1987; Harper, 1984; Ismail & Trachtman, 1973; Muller & Armstrong, 1975; Palmer & Sadler, 1979; Smith, 1993) holds promise that running and jogging, in particular, may help many people by reducing stress and fostering positive psychological effects. (Treatment programs using these forms of exercise are sometimes referred to as "running therapy.") It might be speculated that the high level of interest in running in recent years may be correlated to people's need to cope with the stress of modern life. Some tips on "Running for Relaxation" and "Runners Stretches" have appeared in the literature. They are included in Appendix B: Relaxation Techniques (p. 119).

Some clients may wish to enter into a walking program because walking offers the benefits of running without a great amount of strain on tendons, muscles, and joints. Exercise (sustained brisk walking) is a natural form of exercise rs a particularly good option for older adults, those with limitations, and those who have been inactive.

_orbin and Mental-Corbin (1983) and Getchell (1988) have made a number of suggestions on "Walking for Relaxation" which are included in Appendix B: Relaxation Techniques (p. 119).

A third area for stress reduction through physical activity is that of engaging in a moderate to vigorous exercise program. Muscles that are exerted through exercise must respond with relaxation. Also, participation in a systematic exercise program requires concentration that focuses a person's thoughts away from stressful concerns. An exercise program may be a wise choice for old people who may not desire to run or walk, as well as for those individuals who have physical limitations that do not permit them to participate in a running or walking program. These individuals may particularly profit from water exercise, where the buoyancy of the water provides therapeutic value.

There are any number of resources that contain information on organizing and conducting exercise programs. Some have been designed to meet the special needs of persons who are elderly, while others are designed for individuals with physical disabilities. Getchell's (1988) *The Fitness Book* contains a well illustrated chapter on stretching, shaping and strengthening exercises. Most of the exercises could be easily adapted to the needs of elders or persons with disabilities. Specifically designed for elders is *Pep Up Your Life* (n.d.) published by the American Association of Retired Persons. This booklet provides a number of illustrated exercises for strength and flexibility. *A Handbook of Exercise and Dance Activities for Older Adults*, by Corbin and Mental-Corbin (1983), offers numerous examples of exercise programs including warm-up exercises and exercises done with bicycle innertubes. *Eldercise* (Penner, 1989) outlines a comprehensive exercise program for the frail elderly. Water exercise is discussed by Ekberg (1990) in an article in *Parks and Recreation* that details a senior adult water exercise class. *The New York Times* health section (Brody, 1990) has listed several videotapes for persons with disabilities, including: "Wheelchair Workout " (Janet Reed, 12275 Greenleaf Avenue, Potomac, MD 20854), "Fitness is for Everyone" (National Handicapped Sports, 1145 19th Street N.W., Suite 717, Washington, DC 20036), and

Richard Simmons' "Keep Fit While you Sit" (Stabo Productions, 1057 South Crescent Heights Blvd., Los Angeles, CA 90035).

Whenever an individual contemplates initiating a running, walking or exercise program it is always best for that person to check with his or her physician before beginning. Once the individual has received medical clearance, their program should start slowly and build from that point as greater fitness is developed (Whitmer, 1982).

Implications for Therapeutic Recreation

Physical activity has long been a popular program area in therapeutic recreation. The emergence of running on the American scene, along with the increasing amount of attention being given to "running therapy," has however, brought newfound recognition of the psychological benefits to be gained from physical activity. Running would seem to have particular promise for therapeutic recreation, since it is not a costly activity and can be done almost anywhere. Walking offers an alternative to running that is not costly and does not require any special facilities. In addition, walking offers a low risk of injury and it is a natural activity that can be done by most people. Perhaps some of the tension release properties of walking come from the enjoyment of being outdoors in a pleasant setting (since most walking is done outside) or in walking with others in a relaxed social atmosphere. Exercise programs offer still another approach to stress reduction through physical activity. Such programs offer an alternative to running and walking for older adults and persons with disabilities. Other physical activities such as swimming, boating, biking, and hiking seem to be particularly well suited to helping people handle stress because they are not normally approached on a competitive basis, which might lead to further threat, conflict, and frustration for participants. Heywood (1978) has found that stress reduction occurs to a greater extent when the activity engaged in is perceived to be a recreative experience.

AROMATHERAPY

Aromatherapy is the use of plant oils for health purposes. A holistic approach that seeks to help people to maintain a balance of mental, physical and spiritual health, aromatherapy attempts to go beyond the mere treatment of symptoms to deal with the cause of the disease. Although it has recently regained popularity, aromatherapy was practiced for medicinal purposes by the Egyptians 3,000 years before Christ. So too did the Greeks and Romans. The "Father of Medicine," Hippocrates, wrote of using a number of medicinal plants.

The use of essential oils in massage is perhaps the most common form of aromatherapy, although there is far more involved than simply a mechanical application of massage, as Davis (1995) has explained. Davis has written: "Massage with essential oils is the most important method of treatment, for it combines the effects of the oils themselves, with the important element of human contact between the aromatherapist and the person seeking help" (p. 7). Massage with essential oils may be of particular value by offering relief from stress and anxiety. Davis has exclaimed: "Essential oils exert a subtle influence on the mind and, combined with the loving care of a sensitive therapist, offer a truly holistic, gentle and natural alternative to psychotropic drugs" (p. 7).

The second most common aromatherapy application of essential oils is in aromatic baths where essential oils combine with the therapeutic properties of warm water. Other uses of essential oils are in hot or cold compresses (used with physical conditions) and skin preparations (mixed in cremes, lotions and water to treat skin diseases or to enhance the skin's complexion). Two of the aromatherapy treatment approaches may be applied in combination. For instance, aromatic baths may be taken between massage treatments. The use of essential oils used in these treatments may also be extended if the client particularly enjoys one. The client may apply small amounts as a perfume or may use it as a room spray.

Whatever the treatment approach, massage, baths, compresses, skin preparations or a combination of these, the essential oils are absorbed into the body through the skin and are inhaled through the nose. Massage has been termed by Davis (1995) as, "the most effective way of introducing essential oils to the body. The skin absorbs these oils very readily, and when the whole body is massaged, a useful amount of essential oil can be taken into the bloodstream in a fairly short time" (p.204). In regard to inhalation of essential oils, Davis has explained: "The aroma alone can have a subtle but real effect on the mind, and via the mind, on the body. Inhaling the oils also has a direct effect on the body, as some part of the oil will be absorbed via the lungs and will enter the bloodstream in that way" (p. 8).

What essential oils are used in aromatherapy? One example is the use of oil of Bergamot employed for its antidepressant properties. A second example is the use of Basil, Geranium, Nutmeg, Rosemary or Thyme (or a blending of two or more of these) to combat fatigue. A third example is Peppermint oil, used for its digestive properties in treating indigestion, diarrhea or stomach pain. It can be used to massage the stomach and abdomen. The drinking of Peppermint tea may be used as a further treatment. A final example is treating anxiety with sedative oils such as Benzoin, Jasmine, Melissa, Sandalwood or Ylang Ylang.

In closing this section, it should be noted that aromatherapy can often be employed in combination with other types of treatment. For instance, stress reduction techniques such as meditation, autogenics, and relaxation training may be used in combination with massage with oils with sedative properties (Davis, 1995).

Implications for Therapeutic Recreation

While not widely found in clinical settings today, aromatherpy is gaining acceptance in England, Canada, and the United States. It may be that some therapeutic recreation practitioners may wish to become skilled in using aromatherapy. Others may wish to simply borrow concepts from aromatherapy such as using a holistic approach to treatment that includes caring human contact. It would also appear that within therapeutic recreation programs that therapists could help clients to identify certain smells that they associate with past pleasant or relaxing times so that recalling this smell, or actually smelling the odor, may contribute to positive emotional reactions or to feelings of relaxation.

ADVENTURE/CHALLENGE THERAPY

One of the most rapidly growing areas of therapeutic recreation has been **adventure/challenge therapy**. Reflecting the swift acceptance of adventure/challenge therapy are a number of books published early in the decade of the 1990s. Among these have been: Gass' (1993) *Adventure Therapy*, Nadler and Luckner's (1992) *Processing the Adventure Experience* and Smith, Roland, Havens and Hoyt's (1992) *The Theory and Practice of Challenge Education.*

Many different terms have been used to describe **adventure/ challenge therapy**. Among these are: outdoor adventure activities (Voight, 1988), adventure-based programs (Voight, 1988), adventure recreation (Dattilo & Murphy, 1987), experiential challenge program (Roland, Summers, Friedman, Barton &McCarthy, 1987), adventure education (Sugarman, 1988), adventure programming (Witman, 1987), outdoor adventure recreation (Ewert, 1987), adventure/challenge programs (Richards & Myers, 1987), adventure therapy (Gass, 1993), and adventure/challenge therapy (Smith, 1987).

Likewise, many definitions have been set forth by authors in the area. Those by Ewert (1987) and Dattilo and Murphy (1987) seem to best capture the essence of this approach to therapy. Ewert, who employs the term outdoor adventure recreation, defines it as "a self-initiated, non-consumptive recreational activity engaged in a natural outdoor setting, that contains real or perceived elements of risk in which the outcome is uncertain but influenced by the participant and/or circumstance" (pp. 15, 16). Dattilo and Murphy use the term, adventure recreation, which they define as, "a subjective, challenging experience that occurs in the outdoors. It involves activities that are usually performed in the natural environment and contain elements of actual or perceived danger" (p.14). They go on to state, " Challenge is the essential feature of adventure recreation" (p.15).

· The most evident common component reflected in the definitions of the field is a perceived challenge on the part of participants, usually in an outdoor activity that contains the element of adventure (i.e., an unusual experience with apparent danger). Therefore, Smith's (1987) term of *adventure/challenge therapy* would seem to be the most descriptive when referring to this approach as a treatment modality.

Outward Bound

The origins of adventure/challenge therapy can be traced to the Outward Bound movement in England in the 1940s, which was begun to satisfy youths' desire for adventure (Richards & Myers, 1987). Winn (1982) has reported the original components of Outward Bound included: "an unfamiliar environment, physical activity, a controlled amount of stress, a collaborative small group context, and the use of newly acquired knowledge and skills" (p.163). Outward Bound programs emphasized the development of each participants' inner resources through meeting physical and mental challenges (Sugarman, 1988). Today, adventure/challenge therapy is employed with a variety of client groups including persons with a full range of disabilities and troubled youth. It is enjoying particularly wide use within psychiatric treatment programs (Richards & Myers, 1987; Roland et al., 1987; Witman, 1987).

Sugarman (1988) has listed the values of adventure/ challenge therapy programs. Included are:

- The activities tend to be non-competitive.
- Successful completion of a specifically designed sequence of activities results in a sense of accomplishment.
- The activities promote cooperation and trust among participants. The entire group must communicate and work together to achieve specific goals.
- The activities can be implemented at the level of participants, which enhances the opportunity for improvement of self-concept.
- The activities can be used as a metaphor for situations which occur in the participants' daily life.
- Participants have fun while improving flexibility, strength, coordination and endurance.
- Activities require cooperation with the elements of nature, which leads to a greater respect for an appreciation of the natural environment (pp.27, 28).

Program Benefits

A number of benefits resulting from adventure/challenge therapy programs have been identified by researchers. These include: enhanced self-confidence and self-esteem; increased feelings of empowerment; enhanced social skills and greater trust and cooperation; improved problem-solving skills; improved academic performance; increased muscular strength and cardiovascular efficiency; more realistic perception of self; reduced obsessive compulsive behavior; decreased anxiety and depression; less disorganized thinking; reduced recidivism among adjudicated adolescents; and reduced deviant behavior (Chakravorty, Trunnell & Ellis, 1995; Dattilo & Murphy, 1987; Ewert, 1987; Gillis & Simpson, 1993; Winn, 1982; Witman, 1987; Witman & Munson, 1992).

Debriefing

Roland, Keene, Dubois and Lentini (1988), Roland, Summers, Friedman, Barton and McCarthy (1987), Luckner and Nadler (1995), Nadler and Luckner (1992), Smith (1987) and Witman (1987) have all stressed the critical nature of **debriefing**, or group processing, in order for clients to achieve benefit from adventure/challenge therapy. Roland and his colleagues (1987) emphasized that activities serve as a bridge or address important client issues. Debriefing permits participants to express themselves about feelings, such as being supported or being pressured by the group. Being able to talk things out provides group members opportunities to express their perceptions and to raise and resolve conflicts.

The leader can and should participate in the debriefing, but the group members must take primary responsibility for the discussion. It is only when the group's discussion bogs down that the leader should step in. Even when it is appropriate to assert himself or herself into the discussion, it should be to stimulate the group members to come to understandings on their own. The leader does not resolve dilemmas for the group but raises questions or makes statements aimed at stimulating discussion within a group. As Rohnke (1989) has stated: "It is not that you (i.e., the leader) shouldn't share your knowledge. But you need. . . to get participants to do the thinking as much as possible, to dig into their feelings, to build up their own collection of observations, and provide an atmosphere to act on them" (p.23).

Roland and his colleagues (1987) reported using approximately a third of the time of the session on activities, with two-thirds devoted to debriefing, and warned that without this process there is the risk that the activities will become diversional. In Witman's (1987) program for adolescent psychiatric patients, the following three questions were used to stimulate discussion and insights: "How was the session for you?" "What did you most/least enjoy?" and "What were some of your feelings during the activities?" (p.25). Smith (1987) has suggested that leaders may wish to structure activities, such as candle ceremonies, to promote processing and bring closure to the session. It would seem that processing could be enhanced if activities were chosen that might lead to the discussion of issues with which the group as a whole or individual members were dealing. Bacon's (1983) book, *The Conscious Use of Metaphor in Outward Bound*, offers a helpful approach in the use of metaphor in processing that could prove valuable in adventure/challenge therapy.

The books, *Cowstails and Cobras II* (Rohnke, 1989) and *Islands of Healing: A Guide to Adventure Based Counseling* (Schoel, Prouty & Radcliffe, 1988), both emphasize the importance of sequencing in debriefing because group members need to warm up before they are ready to deal with difficult issues. Borrowing from earlier work by Terry Borton, authors of these books propose the use of the sequence: the "What," the "So What" and the "Now What."

In the initial "What" phase, group members are asked to review what happened during the group activity with the intent of raising issues about positive behaviors and those behaviors that participants may wish to change. Once the group has identified issues and is talking, it should be moved toward the "So What" phase.

At this point, participants express what they have learned from the experience. They move from the descriptive (i.e., "What") to the interpretive (i.e., "So What"). For example, they might be encouraged to describe their feelings about the activity and their participation in it. They might also be asked to reflect on goals on which they have been working.

Finally, the "Now What" phase provides opportunities to talk about what the group members will do with what they have learned as a result of their participation. It is the phase in which they generalize their learnings from the group to other parts of their lives.

Types of Adventure/Challenge Activities

What specific activities are found in adventure/challenge therapy programs? While many different activities may be used among the most popular have been: trust activities (e.g., trust walks and falls); cooperative activities (e.g., "lap sit"); group problem solving tasks (e.g., "human knot"); initiative games (e.g., "electric fence" and "wall"); low ropes courses (that involve maintaining balance while moving across a course made of rope, wire, and wooden beams that has been constructed a few feet off the ground); and high adventure activities (e.g., rappelling, caving, high ropes courses, zip lines, tree climbs, kayaking and wilderness camping) (Robb, 1980; Robb, Leslie & McGowan, n.d.; Roland, Summers, Friedman, Barton & McCarthy, 1987; Sugarman, 1988; Winn, 1982; Witman, 1987).

Havens' (1992) *Bridges to Accessibility* and Elmo and Graser's (1995) *Adapted Adventure Activities* provide suggested program adaptations for persons who are disabled. These books cover the analysis and modification of a wide variety of adventure activities.

Implications for Therapeutic Recreation

Some of the leading advocates for adventure/challenge therapy are in therapeutic recreation. Two of the best known therapeutic recreation specialists in the area are Gary Robb and Jeff Witman. Robb, the Director of Indiana University's Bradford Woods, and his staff have had extensive experience in using adventure/challenge activities as interventions and in training others on how to utilize the approach. Witman, when a practitioner in New Hampshire, conducted and researched adventure/ challenge therapy programs in a psychiatric facility.

Work by Robb, Witman and others has shown great promise in the use of adventure/challenge therapy, particularly for adolescents. The use of adventure/challenge therapy is still relatively new, however, and should be approached with caution by those without extensive training and experience in its application.   Therapeutic recreation specialists should seek consultation and training from those expert in the practice of adventure/challenge therapy before initiating programs.

Principles that guide adventure/challenge therapy can be applied with groups in other types of therapeutic activities. One is that the activity is focused on providing challenges that lead to the achievement of positive outcomes. Providing activities that offer a challenge but are still within reach of clients is a principle that can be applied throughout therapeutic recreation programming.

Another principle is that while the leader's role is critical, the emphasis remains on the participants who are seen as agents for their own change and who assume increasing levels of responsibility for their treatment as time goes on. The focus in therapeutic recreation always remains on the clients who are expected to be responsible for bringing about changes in themselves while taking greater responsibility for change throughout the treatment process.

A third principle from adventure/challenge therapy is that debriefing, sometimes referred to as group processing, is a critical part of the clients' total experience. Learning from experiences gained during therapeutic recreation programs can be enhanced by processing the activities following participation. Gains can be reinforced and feelings, behaviors and cognitions that need to be altered can be brought to the attention of clients as a result of group processing.

ASSERTIVENESS TRAINING

Assertiveness training is an offshoot of behavioral therapy that helps people to become more assertive in social relationships, sexual expression, work-related interactions, or other social situations. Assertiveness training assists persons to change habits or behaviors, allowing them to stand up for their legitimate rights and the rights of others. This new assertiveness, in turn, makes people feel better about themselves, thus increasing feelings of self-esteem.

Nonassertive behaviors are usually reflected by submissive actions, inability to communicate in social situations, difficulty in maintaining eye contact, and fear of rejection. Learning to respond in an assertive fashion begins with the client identifying situations in which he or she wishes to respond more assertively. The helper then assists the client to examine irrational beliefs behind timid behavior and to identify more rational beliefs. Once this is completed, the helper and client identify proper assertive responses that may be made. Role playing, rehearsal modeling, and reinforcement techniques are used to establish new assertive responses. When the client has demonstrated assertive responses repeatedly within assertiveness training sessions, he or she is encouraged to try out their behavior in real-life situations. Successful clients put aside their inhibitions about responding assertively in all types of circumstances as newly learned behavioral tendencies generalize to other situations (Hackney & Cormier, 1988; Eisenberg & Delaney, 1986; Matson, 1977).

Implications for Therapeutic Recreation

Assertiveness training provides a model for helping people reduce anxiety by developing responses that will enable them to say and do what they wish. Therapeutic recreation specialists can easily allow for opportunities for clients to practice healthy assertiveness and can reinforce this behavior. Therapeutic recreation specialists may also wish to gain skills to conduct assertiveness training. Assertiveness training has been suggested as a technique to be used in leisure counseling (Connolly, 1977).

SOCIAL SKILLS TRAINING

The use of **social skills training (SST)** is a relatively new development within rehabilitation. Perhaps it is the name of Michael Argyle, British social psychologist, that is most commonly associated with the beginnings of SST in the 1970s. The origins of SST came from the emergence of the behavioral approach, research on the connection between social competence and psychiatric problems, and social psychology research on verbal and nonverbal communication (Hollin & Trower, 1986).

Many people receiving therapeutic recreation services display deficits in social skills. Sneegas (1989) listed the following types of therapeutic recreation clients who often have social skills deficiencies: those who are chemically dependent; persons with mental retardation; residents in long-term care facilities; individuals experiencing problems in mental health (particularly depression or schizophrenia); and children with learning disabilities. Such clients may profit from social skills training. In addition, social skills training has been used with managers, teachers, social workers, medical doctors, and other professionals (Harré & Lamb, 1986), as well as with those experiencing developmental difficulties through the life span. Adolescents and young adults anxious about heterosexual relationships and elderly persons making adjustments to aging are examples of such populations (Hollin & Trower, 1986).

Definitions of Skills

What are social skills? A frequently quoted definition is that of Combs and Slaby (1977) who stated that social skills represent, "the ability to interact with others in a given social context in specific ways that are socially acceptable or valued and at the same time personally beneficial, mutually beneficial, or beneficial primarily to others" (p.162).

Cartledge and Milburn (1986) originally defined social skills as "socially acceptable learned behaviors that enable the person to interact with others in ways that elicit positive responses and assist in avoiding negative responses from them" (p.7). More recently, Cartledge and Milburn (1995) have defined social skills as "social behaviors that involve interaction between the child and his or her peers or adults where the primary intent is achievement of the child's or adult's goals through positive interchanges" (p.4). Whether for children or adults, social skills are then those competencies employed in relating effectively to others. Social skills are interpersonal or interactive skills.

Hewitt (1988) listed five characteristics of social skills. First, social skills behaviors are goal directed or are performed in order to achieve a specific purpose (e.g., smiling and moving closer are directed toward the goal of achieving friendship). Second, each social behavior relates to a goal and, therefore, should be interrelated and synchronized with other behaviors (e.g., the smile and moving closer together are seen to relate to the common goal of achieving friendship). Third, social skills, similar to motor skills, may be broken down into parts (e.g., the social skill of making friends is composed of smaller elements ranging from making eye contact to asking personal questions). Fourth, social skills are learned behaviors that are reinforced in ways that motivate the individual to choose the most appropriate social response (e.g., some behaviors are more appropriate in making friends with someone of the same sex than someone of the opposite sex). Fifth, social skills are under the control of the individual (e.g., the individual does not apply social skills to form friendships in situations where friendship would not be appropriate).

Hewitt (1988) has divided social skills into two categories, nonverbal and verbal communications. Under nonverbal communications she listed: bodily contact; proximity; orientation; posture; gestures and body movements; facial expressions; eye contact; appearance; and paralanguage. Hewitt listed verbal communications as: instructions and directions; questions; comments; suggestions and information; informal chat or gossip; performative utterances; social routines; expressive emotions and attitudes; and latent messages. Others, such as Cartledge and Milburn (1995), have perceived social skills more broadly. They present Stephens' (1992) wide range of classroom social skills listing 136 specific social skills within 4 major categories and 30 subcategories.

What are reasons for social skills deficits? Anxiety, depression, confusion and psychotic reactions may contribute to diminished social skills for clients who have undergone psychiatric difficulties. For some individuals, the skills may simply have never been learned (Birrell & Henderson, 1986). Still others have social skills, but negative experiences have convinced them that they lack these skills (Myers, 1996).

Skill Instruction

Social skills training is directed toward the correction of problems encountered in performing social skills with the aim of improvement both in social functioning and the way the person feels about himself or herself (Duck,1986). SST involves the teaching of skills of social interaction through a planned and systematic method that reflects social psychology, Bandura's (1986) social learning theory, and contemporary pedagogic procedures.

SST consists of using *modeling* or *demonstrations* by competent persons; *role playing* by group members acting out previously modeled behaviors; *feedback* from others or from videotapes; *instruction* in the form of comments to improve performance; *social reinforcement* to provide positive feedback for achieving established standards; and *homework* to practice new skills in real-life situations (Birrell & Henderson, 1986). Steps in the SST approach have been identified by Sneegas (1989) as:

1.   assessment of the problem area;
2.   task analysis of the behavioral components necessary to achieve the social skill;
3.   introduction to the social skill and a rationale for the learning of the social skill are given to the client;
4.   demonstration and modeling of specific social behaviors;
5.   practice and rehearsal of the new behavior;
6.   provision of feedback and reinforcement of the behavior; and
7.   generalization to a variety of situations.

Witman and Lee (1988) have provided a detailed description of a psychiatric hospital social skills group operated by an occupational therapy/therapeutic recreation department. Schleien and Wehman (1986) have discussed how social skills may be facilitated for children with severe disabilities through leisure skill programs.

Implications for Therapeutic Recreation

While the use of social skills training has not been widespread in therapeutic recreation, articles by Schleien and Wehman (1986), Sneegas (1989), and Witman and Lee (1988) display the promise that SST holds as a technique to help people receiving therapeutic recreation services. Therapeutic recreation shares much in common with social skills training. The development of social competence has long been seen as an important goal of therapeutic recreation specialists who have attempted to develop social skills in their clients through various means (although not formally utilizing the SST model). The development of social skills is viewed by both therapeutic recreation and SST as a means to enhance self-esteem as clients take pride in their abilities to gain new skills and receive social reinforcement during social interactions.

COGNITIVE REHABILITATION

Cognitive rehabilitation is a relatively new approach employed with head-injured clients to assist in their neuropsychological recovery. No single occupational group has the comprehensive training to conduct cognitive rehabilitation so it is provided as a team effort by a number of disciplines, including therapeutic recreation specialists. Sohlberg and Mateer (1989) have stated that cognitive rehabilitation "refers to the therapeutic process of increasing or improving an individual's capacity to process and use incoming information so as to allow increased functioning in everyday life" (p.3). They have gone on to say, "cognitive rehabilitation applies to therapy methods that actually retrain or alleviate problems caused by deficits in attention, visual processing, language, memory, reasoning/ problem solving, and executive functions" (p. 4).

Toglia and Golisz (1990) have emphasized that brain injury is particularly disruptive to interpersonal or social functioning. Individuals with head injuries often have a difficult time processing all the relatively subtle cues that are part of the social situation. Their book, *Cognitive Rehabilitation: Group Games and Activities*, contains many group games and activities that can be used with brain-injured individuals to help them to function socially. Of the use of games, they have written: "Games stimulate motivation and interest while providing a meaningful context in which behaviors can be tried out and practiced. Life situations and problems can be confronted in a nonthreatening environment" (p.17). They go on to stress that games and activities also allow clients to: gain insights regarding their strengths and weaknesses; overcome the self-centered behavior that sometimes accompanies brain injury; build ability to control behavior; and develop more flexible thinking. One particularly interesting portion of Toglin and Golisz's book for therapeutic recreation specialists is an eight-session leisure education module that contains several worksheets for client use.

Therapeutic recreation specialists doing cognitive rehabilitation typically employ a functional approach "to promote transfer of improved cognitive function to real-world activities. ..." (Sohlberg & Mateer, 1989, p.328). Sohlberg and Mateer (1989) have portrayed the role of TR specialists. They have stated:

> Within the rehabilitation team, the therapeutic recreation specialist's role is to increase the patient's leisure awareness, social interaction, and leisure participation. There has been a recent movement within this discipline away from serving a purely diversionary function toward taking a more active role in the rehabilitation process. For example, within most rehabilitation settings, the therapeutic recreation specialist is responsible for taking patients out into the community on recreational outings. Rather than viewing these events simply as field trips or one-time leisure experiences, the "state of the art" in therapeutic recreation is to encourage community outings as training opportunities in which therapy objectives targeted within the clinic can be transferred to naturalistic contents (p. 329).

Implications for Therapeutic Recreation

Still emerging is the relatively new area of cognitive rehabilitation. Therapeutic recreation specialists who work with clients with head injuries will apply cognitive rehabilitation methods with the aim of improving the functional abilities of those they serve. As members of the rehabilitation team, it is likely that therapeutic recreation specialists will take the lead in the application of games and activities to enhance clients' leisure awareness and social functioning and in conducting community reintegration programs. Like their colleagues in cognitive rehabilitation, most other therapeutic recreation specialists have concern for their clients' interpersonal or social functioning within a caring, nonthreatening environment. Developing client leisure awareness and building skills for leisure participation and community reintegration are also common goals for clients of therapeutic recreation specialists in many varied settings.

ANIMAL-FACILITATED THERAPY

The first documented therapeutic use of animals was at the York Retreat in England, a psychiatric hospital founded in 1792 by the Society of Friends. There patients gained self-control by feeding and caring for rabbits and chickens that totally depended on the patients for their care (Fogle, 1984). **Animal-facilitated therapy** today is being employed with clients of all ages in a variety of settings including hospitals, rehabilitation institutes, nursing facilities, group homes, special schools and day care programs for elders.

Because animal-facilitated therapy has been found to be effective in working with clients who have not been able to establish satisfying social relationships, it has been used extensively as a means to reach persons who are lonely, isolated or withdrawn (Jessee, 1982; Robb, Boyd & Pristash, 1980). The accepting, nonthreatening tendencies of pets are ideal to meet the needs of nonsocial clients.

Pets tend to seek attention, eagerly respond to attention, and are very accepting. McCandless, McCready and Knight (1985) have explained: "Animals naturally respond to their caretakers with a trusting innocence, unconditional love, affection and acceptance without judgment, criticism or unreasonable demands" (p.56). Perhaps animals with their nonjudgmental natures, represent the ultimate in Rogerian therapy!

Goals of animal-facilitated therapy include:

- increasing social interaction and communications;
- heightening emotional expression, particularly joy and pleasure;
- enhancing self-confidence and self-esteem;
- maintaining contact with reality;
- developing attitudes toward birth and death;
- reducing feelings of alienation;
- learning responsibility, cooperation, and social skills;
- experiencing self-expression and trust;
- maintaining responsibility and impulse control;
- providing sensory stimulation; and
- reducing stress.

(Center for Pet Therapy, n.d.; Damon & May, 1986; Gustafson & Dorneden, 1988; Jessee, 1982; McCandless et al, 1985).

While few controlled investigations have been conducted on animal-facilitated therapy (Damon & May 1986), some studies have been completed. A study of nursing home patients with dementia found pet therapy brought about improvement in levels of mood and alertness, along with higher levels of enjoyment, reality orientation and patient-staff interactions (Furstenburg, Rhodes, Powell, & Dunlop, 1984). In a Veterans Administration Medical Center study, Wadle, Augsburg, and Martin (1985) reported patients demonstrated less depression following an animal-facilitated intervention.

In a veterans home study, Kongable, Buckwater and Stolley (1989) found that the social behaviors of Alzheimer's residents increased due to the presence of a dog. Fick (1993) reported the presence of a dog increased verbal interactions of nursing home residents.

In a study of recently widowed women, investigators found that those who owned pets felt less anxious about their loss and less worried about their own deaths (Rucker, 1987). Other teams of researchers have reported significant decreases in mortality rates for heart patients with pets as compared to those without pets (Levitt, 1988).

There is much anecdotal evidence supporting the therapeutic benefits of pet-human interactions. The stroking and cuddling of pets may act as a substitute for intimacies in the lives of those who lack human companionship (Colton, 1983). Interacting with pets, such as puppies, may serve as a catalyst for social behavior for clients previously exhibiting isolating and withdrawn behaviors (Damon & May, 1986). Caring for animals may provide clients with pleasure and a purpose for life, thus enhancing self-worth (Jessee, 1982).

The attracting and viewing of wildlife may have a positive effect on the morale of clients (Cable & Udd, 1988). By playing with animals and caring for them with clients, therapists may build trust and rapport. Animals help create a safe and comfortable environment (McCandless et al., 1985). The bond with a loving pet may enable humans to feel safe and less anxious (Geis, 1986). Stress reduction may result from stroking a cat or dog for a few moments. Even birds have been known to create a calming effect on people (*Pet Update*, 1989).

The Center for Pet Therapy (n.d.) has advocated the use of consistency in animal-facilitated therapy programs. Center staff suggested that pet therapy sessions be held on the same day and at the same time each week. Further, they recommended the same staff be present and the same animals be used. An approach has been described by Damon and May (1986) whereby dogs were initially introduced by their owners to participants in an adult day care program. Later, a "wild" animal show, including a chicken, rabbit, opossum, and snake, visited the day care center. Clients reacted favorably to the assortment of animals.

McCandless and her colleagues (1985) have described an animal care program in a psychiatric hospital. The program featured the caring for sheep, rabbits, bees, doves and chickens by a group of five to eight patients who meet for 45 minutes five days a week. Field trips to a veterinarian's office and a university livestock department enriched the program. Finally, it has been suggested by Ferrini and Ferrini (1989) that interactions with pets may be used to reinforce behaviors. For example, residents in nursing facilities may be rewarded for positive behaviors by having ten minutes with a pet. Once a behavior has been established, the employment of pets as reinforcers is systematically reduced. It must be mentioned, however, that many professionals object to such a practice because they believe opportunities for positive experiences should not be withheld from individuals.

Implications for Therapeutic Recreation

Animal-facilitated therapy has direct implications for therapeutic recreation specialists who may employ it with a wide variety of clients. It is a relatively inexpensive program that has shown promise of bringing about therapeutic outcomes. As Damon and May (1986) have remarked with "tongue in cheek": "The use of pets for therapeutic purpose represents an interactional therapy that draws upon an abundant resource. Unwanted dogs and cats can be made available for more hours at a much lower cost and in greater numbers than psychiatrists, nurses, poets, and others. . . . (p.130).

AQUATIC THERAPY

Aquatic therapy uses the environment of water for treatment and rehabilitation. This relatively new therapy involves far more than just swimming. It is an intervention by which treatment and rehabilitation goals are reached through motor activities in pools. Benefits of aquatic therapy include both improved physical and psychosocial functioning. Physical benefits that may be derived are increased strength, endurance, flexibility, range of motion, balance and coordination (Beaudouin & Keller, 1994; Thomas, 1994; Yurcicin, 1995). Psychological benefits that have been identified are decreased depression, greater locus of control, enhanced self-concept and improved body image (Beaudouin & Keller, 1994; Thomas 1994). Additionally, Yurcicin (1995) has claimed that clients often have greater motivation to actively engage in their treatment programs when they begin to experience functional gains through participation in aquatic therapy. Aquatic therapy has been used to treat chronic pain arthritis, multiple sclerosis, heart disease, high blood pressure, obesity, diabetes, chronic fatigue and depression and in the rehabilitation of clients who have had strokes, amputations, spinal cord injuries, mastectomies and athletic injuries (Beaudouin & Keller, 1994; Thomas, 1994).

Elements that are often mentioned (e.g. Beaudouin & Keller, 1994; Yurcicin, 1995) as being particularly helpful to the success of aquatic therapy are the natural buoyancy and uniform resistance offered clients by the water in pools. The buoyancy of water reduces the force of gravity that clients encounter on land, allowing them to function in ways that they could not on land. The buoyancy of individuals in water permits them to take the weight and pressure off of their joints and other parts of their bodies, thus permitting them to stand, walk, jog and generally move with a maximum of independence and a minimum of pain or discomfort. Water also offers clients a "constant, uniform resistance, which stimulates the body to gain added strength and endurance by performing specific exercises" (Yurcicin, 1995, p. 50). Aquatic equipment, such as fins and paddles, may be used in these exercises (Thomas, 1994).

Aquatic therapy sessions may be one-on-one or in a group. A suggested format for aquatic therapy sessions has been presented by Beaudouin and Keller (1994):

> All treatment interventions begin and end with warm-up and cool-down periods (approximately five minutes each) consisting of simple stretching, toning, and flexibility exercises. Main workouts commonly start with range of motion exercises, followed by strength and/or endurance training (15-35 minutes). All activities focus on individuals' physical and psychosocial needs and goals (p. 197).

Aquatic therapy has become increasingly popular as a treatment and rehabilitative modality in recent years. It is still, however, in a relatively early stage of development. It is likely that this emerging form of intervention will continue to expand as more clients and professionals come to understand the treatment and rehabilitation benefits to be derived from it.

Implications for Therapeutic Recreation

As with any intervention that is growing in popularity, therapeutic recreation specialists should not initiate aquatic therapy programs simply because they are becoming more widely adopted. If it is determined that an agency's clients can benefit from the introduction of aquatic therapy, then it is important that staff acquire proper training in order to gain the skills necessary to deliver quality programs. Many professional organizations offer workshops and short courses in aquatic therapy.

Due to the current popularity of aquatic therapy, "turf battles" have loomed over which group of professionals should provide it. Professionals from physical therapy and occupational therapy, as well as therapeutic recreation, have laid claim to the right to use aquatic therapy as an intervention. It is likely that practitioners from all three professions will continue to provide aquatic therapy.

REALITY ORIENTATION

James Folsom is credited with designing **reality orientation** (RO) as a technique to meet the needs of elderly patients possessing moderate to severe degrees of disorientation and confusion. Reality orientation has been used primarily in homes for the aged, nursing homes, and geriatric units in psychiatric hospitals.

Reality orientation involves the technique of regular repetition of basic facts and constant orientation to time, place, names, events of the day, and things in the environment. Everyone who comes in contact with residents uses reality orientation 24 hours a day to combat confusion, depression, and apathy and generally to move the person toward reality.

All staff address residents by name, encourage them to use each others' names, and drill them on essential information such as place, time of day, date and day of week, the next meal, and object identification. Typical staff questions would be: "What is your name?" "What is the name of this facility?" "What city are we in?" "What is your hometown?" "How is the weather today?" Personnel may also engage in environmental engineering to provide stimulation by the use of bright colors, signs, clocks, and calendars.

Attitude Therapy

In conjunction with using reality orientation to influence the social milieu, an **attitude therapy** approach is employed whereby staff respond to clients with one of five attitudes. Carter, Van Andel and Robb (1995) have described the use of attitudes (kind firmness, no demand, active friendliness, passive friendliness, matter of fact) as follows:

> *Kind firmness* is used, for example, with depressed or insecure clients. For instance, a TRS might respond to a client with, "I'm not going to listen to talk like 'I'm no good.'" In contrast, a *no-demand* approach may be used with suspicious, frightened, or

out of control clients who might respond more effectively to: "I'm not going to harm you or interfere while you are upset." Encouraging clients with repeated verbal support, referred to as *active friendliness,* is the most appropriate attitude for apathetic, withdrawn persons who have had little success relating to others. Identifying these persons, spending extra time with them, and praising them for any accomplishments, no matter how small, is a key to positive outcomes. *Passive friendliness* is often used with clients who are suspicious, frightened, fearful of closeness, or distrustful of others. Staff make themselves available but do not, for example, insist that a client complete a task immediately. A *matter-of-fact* attitude is used with manipulative, irresponsible persons, or with those displaying expected behaviors. A therapist might respond to a late arrival with: "The program started at 10 a.m. Please read the instructor's materials and listen as directions are given, and see me after the session if you have any questions." (p.97).

From this quote, it may be seen that *kind firmness* requires a steadfast approach without being harsh or punitive. A *no-demand* attitude allows clients to vent anger without any requirement being placed on them. The attitude of *active friendliness* calls for the continual expression of attention, support, warmth and caring. *Passive friendliness* involves a more restrained form of friendliness so as not to overwhelm fearful and distrustful clients. The *matter-of-fact* attitude is direct and non-accusatory in an effort to help clients take responsibility for their actions (Edinberg, 1985).

In addition to the continuing informal RO, daily RO classes are conducted. Four or five residents generally meet for a 30-minute class at a routine time each day; again, the residents are provided with repetition and constant orientation. The course begins with simple name, date, and place recognition—usually using an RO board on which the name of the facility is posted along with the year, day of week and date, the weather for the day, the next holiday, and the upcoming meal. As time goes on, the staff person introduces the identification of various common objects such as utensils, food, and clothes. As the class progresses, residents may be asked to classify objects by shape and color, and, perhaps, abstract qualities (Folsom, 1968; Barnes, et. al., 1973).

Reality Orientation Procedures

Actual procedures for reality orientation have been provided by Edinberg (1985):

- Telling or reminding clients who they are, where they are, and what day, date, and time it is.
- Talking to the client directly and distinctly, using simple sentences.
- Correcting mistakes in orientation and rambling in a caring but direct manner.
- Giving simple instructions one step at a time.
- Asking for one answer at a time.
- Immediately praising oriented responses (this may require some shaping; that is, initially praising attention to a question, then praising closer approximations to an oriented response). If a client has difficulty remembering his or her name or where he or she is, prompting, giving the answers, and asking the client to repeat them are appropriate interactions.
- Allowing time for the client to respond.
- Reinforcing the attempt to respond.
- Being consistent in steps one through eight.
- Helping the client use props, a reality board, and other aids (p.178).

Use and Effectiveness

Research findings on reality orientation have been mixed. Verbal responses to questions explicitly covered in RO have shown improvement but other studies have questioned if there is any real generalization of RO training to client orientation and functional abilities (Edinberg, 1985; Hussian, 1981). Despite the lack of strong empirical research evidence, Folsom (1986) has defended the value of the RO approach by underscoring the point that RO makes a contribution in that its philosophical base directs staff to go beyond custodial care to focus on the needs and potential of each individual and emphasizes the team approach and the role of the provision of a therapeutic milieu.

Hussian (1981) has suggested that modifications are needed in the reality orientation approach. First, he called for employing more relevant environmental cues in RO training (such as the location of restrooms and dining rooms and the names of staff). Second, he suggested that RO should teach skills that can be generalized and not rote learned verbal responses. Third, he suggested expanding the level of the tasks taught in the RO classroom rather than "graduating" clients to other groups (e.g., remotivation or resocialization) while relying heavily on positive reinforcement to teach these higher level skills. Both Hussian and Edinberg (1985) have emphasized the need to not mechanistically apply RO but rather to carefully select those who might be expected to benefit from the approach since inappropriate applications can lead to anxiety and depression in clients.

The strength of reality orientation lies in its simplicity. It can be taught to staff relatively easily. Because of this, it has enjoyed widespread use, particularly in nursing homes. Research findings on reality orientation programs have been mixed, however, and the technique has been criticized in terms of approach and its indiscriminate application. Nevertheless, the central RO concept of regularly and consistently reinforcing oriented responses would appear to be a valid concept that can be useful in treating many confused clients (Edinberg, 1985).

Implications for Therapeutic Recreation

The technique of reality orientation suggests that the confusion experienced by some elderly persons may be due to factors other than an organic cause, such as social deprivation and lack of stimulation. Minimizing social deprivation and increasing stimulation for older people can promote improvement in persons who otherwise might be termed "senile" and simply be forgotten. The too common, stereotyped "bingo and birthday party" programming that prevails in some facilities becomes just another part of the monotonous institutional atmosphere. Such programming should not be tolerated. It must be replaced by creative programs that put variety into the residents' daily lives.

Additionally, Teague and MacNeil (1992) have suggested that therapeutic recreation specialists working with confused clients in nursing homes should incorporate RO techniques into their practice. They list the following:

- Briefly repeat who you are and what you do before starting each activity.

- Review programs/activities in which the residents participated in the recent past.
- Work information such as the time of year, current location, and weather conditions into program descriptions.
- Describe, when appropriate, the connection of a particular activity to a seasonal theme or holiday.
- Highlight programs and activities to be offered in your next meeting or the near future.
- Review monthly activity calendars with residents (p.246, 247).

VALIDATION THERAPY

Validation therapy is a popular intervention used in over 7,000 long-term care facilities in Australia, Canada, Europe and the United States. It was developed by Naomi Feil in the 1970s from her experience in working with very old persons with Alzheimer's-type dementia (Feil, 1993). In contrast to reality orientation (RO), validation therapy does not emphasize orientation to name, date, and time but, instead, uses a series of techniques in order to communicate effectively with disoriented "old-old" clients (those over 85) who need help in resolving their pasts. These are individuals who have not resolved key developmental tasks and must return to the past in order to resolve their unfinished life tasks. People who have met their developmental tasks at various life stages are able to achieve integrity and have no need for validation, according to Feil (1993).

The basic premise for validation therapy is that there is a sense of reality or logic that underlies the behavior of even the most disoriented individuals. These persons have certain unmet social and psychological needs: to express suppressed feelings; to regain equilibrium following physical losses; to restore formal social roles; to resolve past relationships that have not been satisfactory; and to resolve life tasks that remain unfinished. Validation therapy uses empathetic communication to assist clients to "regain dignity, reduce anxiety, and prevent withdrawal to vegetation" (Feil, 1993, p. 15). While other types of clients may benefit from validation therapy, it has been primarily directed toward very old people with Alzheimer's-type dementia (Robb,

Stegman & Wolanin, 1986). Validation therapy is not appropriate for old persons who are chronically mentally ill, mentally retarded or alcoholics (Feil, 1993).

Validation therapy can be used by anyone properly trained in its relatively simple techniques. The main qualities needed by a validation therapist are having the ability to accept people who are disoriented and to be empathetic toward them. Feil (1993) lists 14 techniques to be employed by therapists. Some of these are merely widely accepted counseling techniques, such as maintaining eye contact, employing rephrasing in responding, speaking with a caring tone of voice, using appropriate touch and avoiding "why" questions. Other techniques, such as mirroring motions and emotions and employing extreme examples of client complaints, are unique to validation therapy. All 14 techniques are covered by Feil (1993) in her book, *The Validation Breakthrough.*

In her book, Feil also has discussed conducting a validation group meeting. Validation meetings for groups of seven or eight members usually are conducted for 20 to 60 minutes at least weekly. There are four phases. *Phase One* is titled *Birth of the Group—Creating Energy,* which lasts 5 to 15 minutes. The therapist initially greets each group member in the circle. Care is given to greeting each person by his or her last name (e.g., Mr. Jones), while using touch and eye contact. At this time members are also reminded about their assigned roles in the group, such as the welcomer (who opens and closes the meeting), song leader, prayer leader or chair arranger. Members are encouraged to hold hands during the meeting. The therapist assists the welcomer to rise and open the meeting and then asks the song leader to begin a song and, finally, the poet or prayer leader to recite a poem or lead a prayer. *Phase Two* has the title *Life of the Group—Verbal Interactions.* During this phase lasting 5 to 10 minutes, the therapist introduces a topic (such as how to help overcome loneliness or what makes a happy person) and encourages each group member to respond at some level. The therapist then summarizes the discussion and gives praise to the group members for addressing the topic. *Phase Three* is termed *Movement and Rhythms.* This lasts 3 to 20 minutes. The therapist helps the group leader and other members of the group to engage in the movement activity, which might involve passing a ball, throwing a bean bag, completing arts and crafts projects, taking part in a rhythm band or dancing (e.g., "The Hokey Pokey"). The final phase is *Phase Four: Closing of the Group, with Anticipation for the Next Meeting*. This lasts 5 to 15 minutes. The therapist asks the song leader to lead the closing song. After this, the assigned host or hostess passes out the refreshments. Following refreshments, the group member who is the welcomer says goodbye to the members and reminds them of the next meeting. Then an upbeat song is led by the song leader with members holding hands. Finally, the therapist wishes each of the members goodbye while using touch and telling them he or she looks forward to the next meeting of the group.

According to Feil (1993), validation therapy: restores self-worth; reduces the need for chemical and physical restraints; minimizes the degree to which they withdraw from the outside world; promotes communication and interaction; reduces stress and anxiety; stimulates dormant potential; helps resolve unfinished life tasks; and facilitates independent living for as long as possible. Potential adopters of Feil's program should however be aware that research findings on validation therapy have not all found support for its use. For example, scientific investigations by Robb, Stegman and Wolanin (1986) and Scanland and Emershaw (1993) reported no significant effects of validation therapy on clients' mental status, morale or social behaviors.

Implications for Therapeutic Recreation

Validation therapy offers another approach for therapeutic recreation practitioners to use with "old-old" confused or disoriented clients, particularly those with Alzheimer's disease. Certified Therapeutic Recreation Specialists (CTRS's), through their professional preparation, should have a strong foundation for doing validation therapy. They should possess the counseling and interpersonal relations skills that are a central feature of validation therapy. CTRS's also typically have knowledge of activities and understandings of group leadership needed in validation therapy. Practitioners working with disoriented clients who do not wish to adopt validation therapy may well benefit from a review of Feil's (1993) techniques, as well as her suggested structures for groups.

It is apparent that there is a real need to conduct empirical investigations on validation therapy and other means of working with confused elderly persons since well-grounded interventions are increasingly needed as projections call for rapid growth in the numbers of persons having Alzheimer's disease. In the United States alone, it is projected that as many as 14.3 million persons will have the disease by 2050 (Scanland & Emershaw, 1993).

REMOTIVATION

Remotivation was originated by Dorothy Haskins Smith to be employed with moderately confused elderly residents. It is often used to augment other therapies with clients who have successfully completed an RO program. Clarke (1967) has reported the use of the remotivation technique with clients who are aging and mentally retarded.

The remotivation technique involves a group interaction process, usually conducted by a trained aide-level staff member called the remotivator. Groups usually meet weekly for 45 to 60 minutes and are composed of 8 to 15 residents. The purpose of this motivational technique is to promote discussions of topics that may bring participants closer in touch with the world outside of the institution. This is achieved by drawing participants out, remotivating old interests, and improving interpersonal relations with others with the intention of reducing feelings of isolation. It is the appropriate approach with clients who are semi-confused, clients who are regressed, those with substantial brain dysfunction, and older clients receiving psychiatric services who have been institutionalized in psychiatric hospitals for some time.

Remotivation participants are encouraged to take a renewed interest in their environment through a series of carefully planned conversations that stress simple, objective features of everyday life not related to the residents' emotional difficulties. The remotivator chooses a topic to discuss during each meeting of the group. Topics chosen may be wide ranging from baseball to gardening; the only restriction is that controversial subjects such as sex, politics, religion, or marital relations may not be discussed. The group meetings follow a five-phase process, with each phase lasting about 10 minutes—the first and fifth steps may be shorter (e.g., 5 minutes) while the second, third and fourth steps may be occasionally longer (e.g., 15 minutes). The five phases, or steps appear in Appendix C: The Five Phases of Remotivation (p. 129).

The interested reader may wish to refer to Leitner and Leitner's (1985) article titled, "Recreation Leadership Principles," that appeared in Volume 7 of *Activities, Adaptation, & Aging* in order to obtain examples of remotivation sessions. Two sample remotivation sessions appear in the article. In addition to Leitner and Leitner, other sources for this section on remotivation included: Barnes, Sack and Shore (1973), Carter, Van Andel and Robb (1995), Kraus, Carpenter and Bates (1981), Teague and MacNeil (1992) and Storandt (1983).

Implications for Therapeutic Recreation

The ideas expressed in the remotivation technique of establishing a warm, accepting atmosphere, dealing with the well parts of clients, and encouraging the rediscovery of interests have obvious merit in therapeutic recreation programming for older persons. Therapeutic recreation programs should help clients to feel wanted and comfortable in a group, assist in the development of positive attributes, and help encourage the reawakening of the interests that have brought gratification in the past.

As aging clients begin to take a renewed interest in themselves and their environment, it is critical that they are allowed to establish a sense of control over their leisure activities. Iso-Ahola (1980) has presented convincing evidence to support the contention that the sense of personal responsibility and control gained by clients over their behaviors and environment is the most important result of recreation participation for residents of nursing homes. According to this author, being able to pick and choose activities allows clients to experience responsibility for themselves. Through participation in self-selected activities, feelings of helplessness give way to feelings of mastery or control.

RESOCIALIZATION

Resocialization is a technique to increase the social functioning of residents in geriatric settings. Its goal is to increase awareness of self and others by helping clients to form relationships, establish friendships, and discover new interests. Through the group process, isolated individuals are encouraged to rediscover their surroundings, values, and potentials.

Resocialization groups are conducted by a staff member for groups of 5 to 17 residents, depending on the mental and physical abilities of the participants. Refreshments are served at group meetings, which take place three times a week. Sessions usually last 30 to 60 minutes. The leader serves as a role model by showing acceptance of participants, making nonjudgmental comments, displaying flexibility, and raising discussion questions. The focus of the group is on building relationships, discussing problems of living together in their social community, and reliving of happy experiences. The leader attempts to maintain a free and accepting group atmosphere where participants will feel at liberty to discuss interpersonal problems (Barnes et al., 1973).

Implications for Therapeutic Recreation

The restoration of social functioning through group processes is a common goal of therapeutic recreation specialists working with older clients who exhibit symptoms of withdrawal. Many recreation programs for older people follow structures and objectives similar to those of the resocialization technique. However, in recreation groups, the emphasis is not usually centered around discussions but around activities in which group members can find satisfaction. Programs attempt to provide opportunities for relatively isolated and lonely clients to establish involvements with staff and other clients. Through such social involvements clients hopefully develop the ability to interact effectively with their environments by acquiring skills and attitudes necessary to function successfully in social roles with others. Such programming requires a basic knowledge of group dynamics, interpersonal communications, and social learning on the part of the therapeutic recreation specialist.

SENSORY TRAINING

Originally developed to work with children with perceptual-motor problems, **sensory training** has been used extensively with regressed and disoriented older persons in psychiatric facilities and nursing homes. Sensory training attempts to maintain and improve the functioning of regressed patients through a program of stimulus bombardment directed toward all five senses. Its goal is to improve the individual's perception and alertness in responding to the environment.

Carter, Van Andel and Robb (1995) described the sensory training effects in the following way:

> The overall effect of sensory training is similar to the effects of physical exercise. When you exercise, you overload or stress certain muscle groups to strengthen and develop those muscles. So too, when a person participates in a systematic sensory stimulation program, his or her neurological function is effectively increased (p. 103).

In group sensory training, clients meet with a leader in groups of four to seven for sessions lasting 30 to 60 minutes. Each session begins with the group sitting in a circle. The leader introduces himself or herself and asks the participants to introduce themselves. The purposes of the session are explained, perhaps using a blackboard or bulletin board to note major points; then the leader conducts a series of activities requiring use of all the senses. At the conclusion of the session, the leader thanks each participant for taking part and reminds each individual when the following session will be held. Kraus, Carpenter and Bates (1981) suggest that the leader shake hands with each participant at the beginning and end of each session and that name tags be used. They state that after the introductions, the leader should orient participants to time, place, date, day of the week, and that they are at the treatment facility because they need specialized care and treatment. Finally, they stress the need for the leader to use a loud speaking voice and to speak slowly and clearly, repeating statements when required.

Actual activities include: kinesthetic awareness exercises (in which participants name and flex and extend part of their bodies from a sitting position); tactile stimulation activities (in which patients feel objects such as balls, sponges, or pieces of wood while being asked questions about the sensations received, preferences, and feelings); smelling activities (in which participants smell sharp or distinct-smelling substances and are questioned about feelings regarding them and uses the substances have); listening activities (providing a number of sounds through media such as records, simple instruments, clapping, and singing); tasting activities (using different foods such as candy and pickles to establish contrasts); and visual activities (employing mirrors and colorful objects) (Barnes et al., 1973; Kraus, Carpenter & Bates, 1981).

Sensory Stimulation

Not to be confused with sensory training is the technique **sensory stimulation.** Sensory stimulation has been used as a treatment for brain-injury patients who are in prolonged coma. Two types of sensory stimulation have been described in the literature, multimodal and unimodal stimulation. In multimodal stimulation, all of the senses are stimulated in every treatment session. Using this technique, each of the senses (visual, auditory, tactile, gustatory, olfactory) is stimulated to the highest degree a response can be achieved. For example, for the sense of smell, smelling salts are first tried, and if a reaction occurs then more pleasant strong odors (e.g., cooking spices) may be used. Unimodal stimulation follows a similar pattern but involves treating just one sense in any single session. Selecting the senses is done on a random basis (Wilson, Powell, Elliot & Thwaites, 1993). With either technique, therapists observe patient responses to stimulation to determine which are the most effective in producing consistent responses such as hand or head movement or an eye gaze. While limited, research (Doman, Wilkinson, Dimancescu & Pelligra, 1993; Wilson & McMillan, 1993) suggests that sensory stimulation can effect behavior in unconscious patients and can reduce the depth and duration of coma.

Implications for Therapeutic Recreation

Sensory training provides input to activate perception and increase alertness. It is important to recognize that older people can become more functional if they receive the proper stimuli to activate their senses. Therapeutic recreation specialists can conduct sensory training as well as recreation programs that emphasize the use of the senses. Through such programming, aging clients may be able to reactivate senses that have not received adequate stimulation from the dull, routine environments that exist in many long-term care facilities.

Therapeutic recreation specialists may be directly involved as members of the sensory stimulation treatment team. For example, therapeutic recreation specialists at the Drake Hospital in Cincinnati, Ohio, have been actively engaged in the provision of sensory stimulation programs.

REMINISCENCE

Reminiscing has been termed by Weiss (1989) as "the excursion into one's memory of the past" (p.7). While reminiscing, people recall objects, places, other people, and their own self-reflections. **Reminiscence** may be perceived to be a normal and healthy process that should be experienced by old people. Old people who engage in reminiscence are not indulging themselves in idle ramblings but, instead, are taking part in a positive process that should be encouraged (Weiss, 1989).

Teague and MacNeil (1992) have called reminiscence a "healthy adaptation mechanism" (p.249) that may be directly beneficial to individuals during the last portion of the life cycle when "life review" is taking place. The concept of life review was originated by Butler (1963). It has been explained by Ferrini and Ferrini (1989) who have written: "As an elder becomes conscious of the end of life, she or he will mull over past memories, goal fulfillment, and unresolved conflicts, and attempt to integrate and unify life's experiences" (p.209). Edinberg (1985) has also interpreted the benefit of reminiscing: "Verbal review of memories can be 'cathartic'; that is, the process of remembering and talking has a potential therapeutic value. By discussing old memories and achieving a 'new perspective' on them, a client can make substantial internal changes" (p.162). Thus reminiscing may be seen as helpful to the process of life review as the individual comes to terms with his or her life by resolving conflicts, regrets and disappointments from the past.

In addition to life review's therapeutic value; numerous benefits of reminiscence have been extolled in the literature. Reminiscing may:

- enhance self-esteem as people review their history of competence and productivity;
- reaffirm an individual's sense of identity;
- bring pleasure from relating the past to others;
- create joy in sharing with others who have lived through similar times;
- provide socialization, helping to overcome loneliness and separation;
- stimulate cognitive processes that might otherwise atrophy;
- increase orientation for time, person and space;

- provide feelings of cognitive competence as persons draw on their long-term memories;
- allow for the expression of feelings, producing a positive effect from fond memories or release of pent-up anger;
- reduce feelings of depression as individuals recall their lives as worthwhile;
- increase social interaction;
- increase individuals' respect by being able to express themselves clearly in front of others;
- comfort those who feel that their lives were in the past;
- provide opportunity for persons to "improve" their past lives by "redesigning" them to enhance self-images or public impressions.
- serve to enable persons to come to terms with old disappointments in order to gain a balanced perspective on their lives;
- allow persons to see that others have the same problems they do;
- encourage people to discover similarities with others, creating a common bond;
- reduce fear and anxiety as individuals learn to share experiences with others who are accepting;
- offer enjoyment by sharing old jokes and humorous events;
- provide opportunity for individuals to gain insights into themselves because listening to others' lives is a means to obtaining new personal perspectives into one's own life; and
- create self-awareness about leisure (Deig, 1989; Edinberg, 1985; Field, 1989; Gayle, 1989; Teague & MacNeil, 1992; Tabourne, 1995; Weiss, 1989; Weiss & Kronberg, 1986; Weiss & Thurn, 1987).

Scholars (Nugent 1995; Thornton & Brotchie, 1987) have warned, however, that formal research studies on reminiscence are sparse and those published have produced mixed results. It appears that many more empirical studies are needed to explore key variables represented in reminiscence. For example, varying social contexts (e.g., widowed men, widowed women, single women) may produce inconsistent findings (David, 1990), as may the lack of a standard model or approach to reminiscence (Soltys & Coats, 1995).

In contrast to approaches such as reality orientation and remotivation, reminiscence does not have a formalized set of structures or procedures. Nevertheless, several authors have provided guidelines and suggestions for conducting reminiscing groups. For instance, it has been suggested that group members should be approached individually about being in the group so that they may be given a choice regarding their participation and that they may know in advance who the other group members will be. They should also be briefed that the purpose of the group is simply not to talk about "the old days" but to review life experiences to learn to better appreciate themselves.

The size of the group should be kept under 10 to 12 members, with some groups as small as five or six, depending on the type of client. It is important to allow time for each individual to interact within the group session. Normally, groups meet at the same time and place once each week, with the flexibility to meet more often if desired. At times, however, sessions may be held in special locations in order to stimulate the reminiscing process. Sessions may be organized around a specific topic (e.g., most enjoyable vacation), a topical area (e.g., historical event, holidays, seasons), or developmental stage (e.g., childhood, adolescence). The group may be long or short term, depending on the purpose of the group and the length of stay within a facility (Deig, 1989; Edinberg, 1985; Field, 1989).

Weiss (1989) has suggested a one-on-one approach to reminiscing for those who do not have the capacity to interact successfully in a group setting. Staff, volunteers, and family members may be trained to facilitate reminiscing with individual clients during one-on-one contacts. Weiss' approach is described in detail in her article which appeared in the third quarter of 1989 in *Therapeutic Recreation Journal*.

Any number of approaches have proven effective as means to trigger memories of the past. Weiss and Kronberg (1986) used a "Lifeline" in order to facilitate reminiscence about leisure. Various formats, ranging from paper and pencil to verbal interactions, were used to consecutively (by dates) present major historical events (i.e., political, social, scientific events) of the past hundred years. Weiss, this time writing with Thurn (1987), has also described the use of mapping to stimulate reminiscence. Maps and mapping activities were successfully used with people residing in nursing homes who were mildly to moderately confused.

Other aids, or props, that have been employed to encourage reminiscing include visual aids (e.g., antiques, old photographs, scrap books, vintage clothing, art works), food (to stimulate recall of experiences related to taste or smell), scents (spices, flowers, perfumes), films and slides (of old news, political speeches, etc.), and music (to arouse memories and feelings) (Edinberg, 1985; Field, 1989; Karras, 1987). Whatever means are used to facilitate reminiscing about a chosen topic, it is important that the leader be an empathetic listener who displays acceptance and appreciation for each member of the group.

Implications for Therapeutic Recreation

Therapeutic recreation specialists need to understand that reminiscing is not simply an idle activity to fill time, but the process of reminiscing is a natural phenomenon that may provide valuable benefits for old people. Therapeutic recreation specialists who serve elders may conduct reminiscing groups or may wish to train other staff, volunteers, and relatives of clients to conduct one-on-one reminiscing sessions. Reminiscence may also be actively encouraged during various therapeutic recreation programs. Art and music programs, in particular, would seem to offer opportunities for facilitating reminiscence on the part of clients.

SUMMARY AND CONCLUSION

Therapeutic recreation is diverse in the types of populations it serves and the nature of the settings in which it is delivered. Diversity is, therefore, demanded in its methods. In this chapter a wide variety of facilitation techniques have been reviewed that have implications for, or direct application in, the practice of therapeutic recreation.

Several of the facilitation techniques covered in this chapter (e.g. meditation, therapeutic touch, biofeedback, imagery) could be referred to as *alternative therapies*. These are modalities not traditionally embraced by the medical community and, therefore, fall outside the mainstream of medical practice. Another term for such treatment approaches is *complementary therapies,* suggesting these therapies are to be employed in conjunction with conventional treatment approaches (Swackhamer, 1995).

Therapeutic recreation professionals have generally remained open-minded toward alternative therapies. Their holistic underpinnings provide a basis for practice that is accepting of modalities that treat the whole person in order to meet psychosocial, intellectual and spiritual needs, as well as physical needs. It is likely that alternative therapies will continue to be developed and will be used within therapeutic recreation. Examples of emerging alternative therapies are photo therapy (Fow, 1995) and tai chi (Yan, 1995).

No matter what methods or techniques are used, it is wise to keep in mind that therapeutic recreation is a very human enterprise. Any helping interaction must begin with the building of a person-to-person relationship based on mutual respect and a shared confidence in the abilities of both persons to meet the client's problems or needs. Good person-to-person relationships remain at the heart of therapeutic recreation, regardless of which particular approach is used.

READING COMPREHENSION QUESTIONS

1. Do you personally favor using values clarification exercises as a major part of leisure education or leisure counseling?
2. Can you suggest applications of horticulture therapy in therapeutic recreation?
3. Do you feel therapeutic recreation specialists should use bibliotherapy? Why or why not?
4. Do you see therapeutic recreation as playing a critical role in the therapeutic community? Please explain.
5. Have you ever observed the use of humor in therapy? Explain.
6. Do you believe it is "risky" to use touch in therapy? Explain.
7. Should progressive relaxation training be used by therapeutic recreation specialists?
8. What preparation do therapeutic recreation specialists need before leading adventure/challenge therapy?
9. What is social skills training?

10. Do you believe animal-facilitated therapy should be done by therapeutic recreation specialists? If so, with which client groups?
11. Compare and contrast reality orientation, remotivation, resocialization, sensory training, and reminiscence.
12. For what purposes might aquatic therapy be used?

APPENDIX A:
TWENTY-THINGS-YOU-LOVE-TO-DO ACTIVITY

Twenty Things You Love to Do

The procedure for Twenty Things involves each participant writing the numbers 1 to 20 down the middle of a sheet of paper. To the right of each number, participants are asked to "make a list of 20 things in life that you love to do." Sometimes the leader will encourage participants by telling them the things can be "big" or "little" and may give an example or two of things that bring him or her happiness or enjoyment. The leader also constructs a personal list and, when finished, he or she should tell the participants that it is fine if they have over or under 20 things listed.

Then the leader asks the participants to use the left side of their papers to review their list and code each behavior in the following way:

1. A dollar sign ($) is to be placed beside any item which costs more than $3 each time it is done. (The amount could vary, depending on the group.)
2. The letter A is to be placed beside those items the student (participant) really prefers to do alone: the letter P next to those activities he (or she) prefers to do with other people; and the letters A-P next to activities he (or she) enjoys doing equally alone or with other people.
3. The letters PL are to be placed beside those items that require planning.
4. The coding N5 is to be placed next to those items that would not have been listed five years ago.
5. The numbers one through five are to be placed beside the five most important items. The best-loved activity should be numbered 1; the second best, 2; and so on.
6. The participant is to indicate next to each activity when (day, date) it was last engaged in.

The list may be used in any number of ways. For instance, participants can discuss within a group what they learned from the exercise; they may describe to a partner how they like to do their number-1 rated activity; or, they may use the sheet to develop a plan to engage more frequently in enjoyable activities.

APPENDIX B: RELAXATION TECHNIQUES

Three-part Breathing

Take a deep, diaphragmatic breath. Imagine that your lungs are divided into three parts. Visualize the lowest part of your lungs filling with air. Use only your diaphragm; your chest should remain relatively still. Imagine the middle part of your lungs filling, and as you visualize the expansion, allow your rib cage to move slightly forward. Visualize the upper part filling with air and your lungs becoming completely full. Your shoulders will rise slightly and move backward. Exhale fully and completely. As you empty your upper lungs, drop your shoulders slightly. Visualize the air leaving the middle portion of your lungs, and feel your rib cage contract. Pull in your abdomen to force out the last bit of air from the bottom of your lungs. Repeat the exercise four times (Girdano and Everly, 1986, p.17).

Alternate-nostril Breathing

Place your right forefinger over your right nostril, pressing lightly to close off the nostril. Take a deep, full breath, inhaling with your left nostril. Visualize your lungs filling fully and expanding completely. Remove your finger from the right nostril and lightly close off the left nostril. Exhale slowly through the now open right nostril. Be certain to exhale fully and completely. Inhale through the right nostril. Close off the right nostril, and exhale fully and completely through the left nostril. Repeat slowly and rhythmically for three more breaths (Girdano and Everly, 1986, p.18).

Introduction to Progressive Relaxation Training

(Here is what might typically be provided as an introduction to progressive relaxation training. Naturally, the therapist should adjust the presentation for his or her own style.)

1. Start by making sure you are comfortable, whether you are sitting or lying down. You should remove any item that might constrain you. You may wish to take off your watch or glasses, or slip out of your shoes.
2. Please refrain from talking during the session. You can nod or give a hand signal to communicate. I will dim the lights

in the room to cut down on external stimuli (and, perhaps, turn on soft background music).

3.   We will tense each muscle, or muscle group, for five to seven seconds; then relax for 10 to 12 seconds. As we do this, remember to pay attention to the feelings of tension as you contract your muscles and the relaxation once you release the tension.

4.   Release the tension immediately upon my cue. Release it immediately, rather than gradually. Once you've relaxed a group of muscles, don't use them unnecessarily, except to move to make yourself more comfortable.

5.   Let's begin by closing your eyes gently, keeping them closed throughout the session. Get into a comfortable position. Take a deep breath from your diaphragm. Slowly and easily take deep breaths through your nose. Fill up your lungs as much as you can. Hold it briefly being aware of the contractions of the back and chest muscles. (pause) Now breathe more slowly. (pause) Keep this slow breathing going. Breathe deeply in (pause) and deeply out (pause) let the tension go from your body. (pause) As the air leaves your lungs, say to yourself, "relax" and notice how your muscles relax.

(In the section that follows, the actual relaxation training begins.)

Progressive Relaxation Exercises

By making a tight fist, tense the muscles in your dominant *hand*. Now (pause) concentrate your attention on the muscles of your hand and lower arm. Feel the tension in these muscles as they pull hard and tight (for 5-7 seconds). OK, relax. (pause) Notice how it feels to have those muscles limp and loose. (pause) Take a deep breath, feel the relaxation as the tension flows out as you exhale. Notice how the muscle group becomes more and more relaxed. (Some authors suggest repeating each exercise a second time. Do so, if you wish.)

Now tense your bicep in your dominant arm as much as possible by pushing down with your elbow. If you have trouble getting the amount of tension you want, pull your elbow inward toward the body as you press down. Hold it. (pause) Concentrate on the tension. (pause) Now, relax. Just let yourself relax. Note the difference between the tension you felt and the relaxation you feel now as you allow the bicep to become limp. (pause) Take a deep breath, then feel the relaxation as the air flows out of your body. Breathe deeply and fully as you allow the tension to flow away. (Once again, you may wish to repeat this exercise.)

Now let's repeat for the nondominant hand and lower arm. Ready, make a fist. (pause) Hold it. Feel the tension, (pause) notice the tension. (pause) OK, relax. (pause) Think of your hand going loose and limp. Be aware of the contrast between your feeling of relaxation and the prior tension. (pause) Breathe deeply and relax. (You may or may not wish to ask participants to do deep breathing with each exercise. Deep breathing is not included in each exercise in Appendix B but you may include it if you wish.)

Now your bicep for the nondominant arm. Push down with your elbow putting tension on your bicep as much as possible. Concentrate on the tension. (pause) Hold it. (pause) OK, now relax. (pause) Try to be aware of the feelings in your arm. It really doesn't matter how it feels, just learn to pay close attention to those feelings.

Just allow the muscles to go on relaxing while you shift attention to the next muscle group, the face and neck. We'll begin with the forehead. Use an exaggerated frown to do this—or lift the eyebrows as high as you can. Notice where your forehead feels particularly tense. (pause) OK, relax. Take a few seconds to notice your forehead as it relaxes; let it feel smooth and fully relaxed.

Let's do the central part of the face. Close your eyes very tightly and focus on your slow, calm breathing. (pause) Now with your eyes still tightly closed, wrinkle your nose. Hold the position. (pause) Now relax letting tension out. (pause) Feel the relaxation in and around your eyes and nose.

Next, tense the muscles in the lower part of your face. To do this, bring your upper and lower teeth together lightly and curl up your tongue hard against the roof of your mouth. (pause) Hold it. (pause) Relax, letting your tongue fall to the floor of your mouth. Notice how it feels to have those muscles loosen and relax.

Clench your teeth firmly. Bite your teeth together and pull the corners of your mouth back. Notice the tension. (pause) *LET GO* from the tension, so your jaw relaxes and your teeth and lips part slightly. Notice the difference in the way it feels. Notice the absence of tension in the jaw right up to your temples.

Pucker your lips. Keep up the pressure, noting where it feels tense. (pause) Now, let the lips go free and loose. (pause) Notice the difference in the way it feels.

OK, good, now let's go to the neck muscles. To tense the neck muscles, pull your chin down toward your chest, but keep it from touching. Do you feel just a bit of trembling? OK, relax. (pause) Notice how you feel with the neck muscles loosened.

Fine. Next we'll move to the chest and abdomen. Tense the chest by taking a deep breath, holding it, and at the same time pulling the shoulder blades together—try to get the shoulder blades to touch. Go ahead, deep breath, hold it with your shoulder blades pulled together. Do you feel tension in the chest, shoulders and upper back? OK, relax. (pause) Let your arms go loose. (pause) Notice the feeling as those muscles loosen.

Tighten your abdomen. Hold the tension by pulling it in and making it hard. Pull your muscles in even more. (pause) Hold it. (pause) Now, relax. (pause) Breathe calmly, releasing tension. As you exhale, let out even more tension.

Now we'll move to the legs and feet. Begin with the upper right leg. Try to make the large muscle on your upper leg get hard. Lift the leg slightly if you have difficulty hardening the muscle. Now, let your muscles go slack. (pause) Let go of the tension. Observe the relaxation.

Now let's do your lower right leg. Tense these muscles by pulling your toes toward your head or pointing your toes away from your head. Be aware of the tension. (pause) OK, relax. (pause) Let your leg go back to a relaxed position. Take note of the relaxation.

Now let's do your right foot. Turn your foot inward and at the same time curl your toes. Ready, begin. Not too hard, just enough to feel the tension. Feel the tension in the foot. (pause) OK, fine, relax. (pause) Notice the relaxation when the foot and toes are released to take their most restful position.

We'll now shift to the left leg, starting with the upper left leg. Make the large muscle on your upper left leg get hard now. (pause) Hold it. (pause) OK, good, relax.

Now for your lower left leg. Create tension by pulling your toes toward your head, now. Put tension on the calf of your leg. (pause) Hold it. (pause) OK, relax. (pause) The calf now feels loose and floppy. Be aware of that feeling in your calf.

Turn your left foot inward and, at the same time, curl your toes. Ready begin. (pause) Hold it for just a second. (pause) Now, relax. (pause) Notice the relaxation when the foot and toes are released to a restful position.

Try to be aware of the feelings in your legs. Do they feel relaxed? Whatever they feel like is fine, what's important is that you learn to pay close attention to these feelings.

Now slowly and easily, take a *deep breath*. Be sure to fill up the bottom part of your lungs as well as the top. Now exhale fully and completely, releasing even more tension with the exhalation. Feel your rib cage relax as you exhale. Keep this slow, deep breathing going.

With each in-breath, whisper a thin "re." With each out-breath, whisper or think "lax." No rush. (pause) Pause between breaths. Remember "re" as you breathe in and "lax" as you breathe out. (pause) Go ahead, try it now. (pause) Re-lax.

Don't force your breathing. Just let it flow, easy and slow. (pause) Re-lax. (pause) Try it now on your own for the next minute or so.

We've now relaxed the muscles of the whole body. Just allow them to continue relaxing. (pause) Let your whole body lie limp. Feel the relaxation spread throughout your body. (pause) If you feel any tension in any muscle group, let go of it. Let go of any tension anywhere. (pause) Relax, loose and easy. (pause) Just relax.

Enjoy your state of relaxation. (pause) Focus on the pleasant feelings of relaxation. (pause) Enjoy your relaxation.

Now before you get up, stretch yourself slowly and gently. Don't rush. (pause) Open your eyes slowly, feeling calm and relaxed, just as if you had a brief nap. (pause) Get up slowly, feeling relaxed and refreshed.

Zahourek's Application of Imagery

A person might be encouraged to experience a visit to a favorite vacation spot, the mountains, a fantasy place, or his or her most relaxing spot at home. Drawing on a past positive experience or reminding a patient that he or she has experienced previous relaxing times vivifies the scene. If a beach is visualized (a popular image for many people), instruct the patient to "see" the color of the water and the sky, to notice the "smell" of the salt air, and to "hear" the birds singing and the surf hitting the shore.

A sense of relaxation is encouraged and other bodily sensations are mentioned, such as, "feel the warm sun on your back and how the sand feels as it slips through your toes." Using words such as *relax, comfort, peace,* and *soft* all develop sensory responses to the images (Zahourek, 1988, p.76).

Lightness Relaxation Exercise
Get into a comfortable, relaxed position. . .
Allow your mind-body to relax. . .
As you gently allow your eyes to close
Take some relaxing breaths and notice your body
Relaxing even further. . .
And your mind becoming still and peaceful. . .
And your feelings calm. . .
As you remain in this peaceful state of relaxation
Concentrate your attention on your right arm
Just notice your right arm and a sensation of lightness
Your right arm is feeling lighter and lighter
It is so light as it begins to float higher and higher
You notice two helium balloons attached to your wrist
You notice the colors of the two light balloons pulling your arm up even higher.
Repeat to yourself. . .
My right arm is light. . .
I feel it floating. . .
The balloons are lifting my arm up even higher. . .
Just allow your arm to float without any effort. . .higher and higher
Fine. .
And now let your arm gently float down to its resting position and take the balloons from your wrist.
Let them float up to the ceiling or to the sky. . .
Take an energizing breath, open your eyes, stretch, and smile.
Notice how relaxed and refreshed you feel.
Go about the rest of your day calmly active
And actively calm (Flynn, 1980, p. 182).

Benson's Techniques
1.   Sit quietly in a comfortable position.
2.   Close your eyes.
3.   Deeply relax all your muscles, beginning at your feet and progressing up to your face. Keep them relaxed.

4. Breathe through your nose. Become aware of your breathing. As you breathe out, say the word "One," silently to yourself. For example, breathe IN. . .OUT, "ONE"; IN. . .OUT, "ONE"; etc. Breathe easily and naturally.
5. Continue for 10 to 20 minutes. You may open your eyes to check the time, but do not use an alarm. When you finish, sit quietly for several minutes, at first with your eyes closed and later with your eyes opened. Do not stand up for a few minutes.
6. Do not worry about whether you are successful in achieving a deep level of relaxation. Maintain a passive attitude and permit relaxation to occur at its own pace. When distracting thoughts occur, try to ignore them by not dwelling upon them and return to repeating "ONE." With practice, the response should come with little effort. Practice the technique once or twice daily, but not within two hours after any meal, since the digestive processes seem to interfere with the elicitation of the Relaxation Response (Benson, 1975, pp.162, 163; italics removed).

Running for Relaxation
- Loosen the face and drop the jaw, with the idea that if the face is relaxed the rest of the body will follow.
- Run upright, keeping the body perpendicular to the ground.
- Pull the shoulders back slightly and push the buttocks forward.
- Carry the arms low and slightly away from the body with the shoulders loose and relaxed, yet stable.
- Keep the hands softly closed and relaxed.
- Keep the stride at a comfortable length that allows for smooth striding, not too short and no overstriding.
- To move faster, keep the stride fluid, focusing on relaxation rather than power (Lynch, 1989).

Runners' Stretches
Each position is held for 10 to 15 seconds, unless otherwise noted. The *total body stretch* is a good one to use to begin and end stretching. The runner lies on his or her back with arms and legs fully extended. Fingers and toes are pointed and stretched as far as possible for five seconds, three to five times.

The *foot lift* involves standing on one foot while grasping the opposite ankle and slowly pulling the heel toward the buttocks where it is held during the stretch. Balance is maintained by supporting the other hand and arm against an object such as a wall or tree. The exercise is done for both legs.

The *toe touch* is done to prevent hamstring pulls, back pain, and pulled muscles. With the feet spread about shoulder width apart, the runner bends slowly from the waist until he or she can feel a pull in the back of the legs and then holds the position.

The *wall lean* is performed for the Achilles tendon, calf, and shin muscles. With the runner facing the wall and a couple of feet away from it, both hands are placed against the wall at about shoulder to eye level. Starting from the position of having the legs about shoulder width apart, one leg is placed forward of the other, bending the front leg and slightly bending the rear leg, while attempting to keep the heels flat on the ground. From this position, the person pushes his or her hips forward until the stretch is felt on the inside of the leg and in the Achilles. After holding the position for the usual 10 to 15 seconds, the legs are switched and the stretch is repeated for the other leg.

The *spinal twist* is completed while sitting with the right leg straight and the left leg bent so it crosses over the right leg with the foot resting to the outside of the right knee. The right elbow is bent slightly so it rests on the outside of the upper left thigh. The left hand and arm rest on the floor behind the person to provide support. From this position, the head is turned to look over the left shoulder while rotating the upper body toward the left hand and arm. After stretching, the same position is repeated for the other side of the body.

The final stretch is the *groin stretch*, which is used to relax the body and prevent groin pulls. Here the individual lies on his or her back with the soles of the feet together. The knees fall apart, and as this occurs, the hips are relaxed. The position is held for about 40 seconds (Coats, 1989).

Stretching Exercises
- neck stretch (drawing the head down toward the chest); neck turn (looking over the left and then right shoulder);
- shoulder shrug (drawing the shoulders up toward the ears);

- elbow waggle (with the hands behind the head, drawing the elbows backward);
- wraparound (extending the arms out to the sides from the shoulders parallel to the floor, then drawing the hands backward as though attempting to touch the back, and finally, bringing the arms across in front of the body to give yourself a hug);
- palms down (sitting on the floor with legs in front on the floor, bending forward from the waist in an attempt to touch the palms of the hands on the floor;
- shin clasp (sitting on the floor with legs in front, raising one knee while clasping the shin of the leg with both hands trying to pull the kneecap so the head rests on it. Repeat for other leg.) ;
- shoe stretch (sitting on the floor with legs in front, extending both legs while sliding both hands forward in an attempt to reach the shoe. Repeat for the other shoe.); and
- leg left (sitting in a chair with the back against the back of the chair, raising one leg so it is parallel to the floor, curling the toes toward the body as much as possible—then raise the leg upward. Repeat for the other leg.)

In presenting these stretches in *Unstress Your Life* (1987), the editors of *Prevention* magazine suggest that slow, deliberate movements should be used until a tug is felt and, at that time, the position should be held. At first, it should be held for 10 seconds; increasing to 30 seconds with practice. The editors recommend each exercise be done while seated and repeated two or three times.

Walking for Relaxation
1. Walk at a natural, comfortable pace that is brisk enough to increase heart rate and cause breathing to have greater depth than normal;
2. let the arms swing loosely and naturally with a rhythm in the walk;
3. walk upright with the head high, back straight, and abdomen flat;
4. lean forward slightly on hills or when walking rapidly;
5. land on the heel first and roll on to the ball of the foot;

6. swing the legs forward freely from the hips, taking long easy strides, but do not overstride;
7. take deeper breaths than normal while not becoming breathless;
8. pace and distance should increase as physical fitness improves;
9. the pace should always be brisk, challenging the cardiorespiratory system.

Walking requires a minimum of equipment, the choice of shoes and clothing needs to be given some thought. Shoes may range from running shoes to hiking boots (depending on walking style and terrain) with the main criteria for the selection of any shoe being comfort and good support. Clothing should be comfortable and suitable for weather conditions.

APPENDIX C:
THE FIVE PHASES OF REMOTIVATION

The Five-Phase Process

1. **Climate of acceptance.** The session begins with the remotivator warmly greeting each participant with a handshake while addressing the person by name and making some comment in regard to the resident's appearance. The purpose of this phase is to create a warm, supportive atmosphere.

2. **Bridge to reality.** The remotivator attempts to develop group discussion around a theme during this phase. The bridge to reality is built by the remotivator and, sometimes, some of the participants, by reading a poem, story, or article that relates to the theme. The purpose of the reading is to introduce the topic and stimulate imagery and thought about the topic. The remotivator then asks broad questions in order to encourage participants to recall and share related ideas and events concerning their relationship with the topic. For example, if the topic was desserts, the remotivator might ask: "Do you ever eat less of the main course in order to save room for dessert?"

3. **Sharing the world we live in.** This phase involves conversation about the particular topic of discussion for the day. Visual aids and questions are often used to encourage clients to share personal experiences related to the topic. For example, cookies or pictures of desserts might serve as visual aids when the topic is desserts. Questions related to personal experiences might be: "What is your favorite dessert?" or "What is the best dessert you can make?" During this phase, the leader may attempt to move the focus of the discussion on to the world as it is presently.

4. **Appreciation of the work of the world.** Purposes of this phase are to get participants to: think about pros and cons of the topic (e.g., "What are good (or bad) things about desserts?") relate the topic to other things in the world (e.g., "How do desserts affect your teeth?") (Leitner & Leitner, 1985), think about work world activities (e.g., "How many people do you think are employed by bakeries to make desserts?") (Carter, Van Andel & Robb, 1995), or think

about work in relation to himself or herself ("Do you still like to prepare desserts?") (Teague & MacNeil, 1992). Participants may be encouraged to rediscover past hobbies or occupations that they are reminded of as a result of the discussion. Projections into the future may also be encouraged.

5. **Climate of appreciation.** At the completion of each group session, the remotivator reviews what has been said, comments about the participation of each individual, and personally thanks them for attending, and then informs the group about plans for the next session.

Chapter Four

THE THERAPEUTIC RECREATION PROCESS

CHAPTER PURPOSE

It is critical that therapeutic recreation specialists become aware of basic philosophical beliefs that prevail in therapeutic recreation. Beliefs affect theoretical notions that, in turn, affect the principles on which professionals operate. It is equally important that a thorough understanding of the therapeutic recreation process be gained, since this process underlies the delivery of all therapeutic recreation services. This chapter will help the student to develop a more comprehensive and systematic perspective on these fundamental concerns that will ultimately pervade the delivery of services to clients.

KEY TERMS

- Humanistic perspective
- Holistic medicine
- Actualizing tendency
- Treatment
- Health protection/promotion
- Recreation
- Leisure
- Diagnosis
- Skilled observation
- Specific goal observation

- High-level wellness
- Stabilizing tendency
- Leisure education
- Special recreation
- Prescriptive activity
- Intrinsic motivation
- Assessment
- Casual observations
- Naturalistic observations
- Standardized observations

- Reliability
- Maslow's hierarchy
- Goals
- Strengths list
- Specific objectives
- Evaluation

- Validity
- General objectives
- Needs list
- Goals set
- Plan
- Activity analysis

OBJECTIVES

- Understand the humanistic perspective as it relates to therapeutic recreation.
- Recognize the relationship between therapeutic recreation and high-level wellness.
- Describe therapeutic recreation models.
- Appreciate the need to employ a systematic method of problem solving known as the therapeutic recreation process.
- Reduce the therapeutic recreation process to a series of logical steps, defining each in terms of its role in the total process.
- Explain methods of client assessment.
- Describe the setting of priorities to meet client needs.
- Relate guidelines for formulating client goals and objectives.
- Describe the elements of an individual (personalized) program plan.
- Know the importance of clearly defined implementation procedures.
- Recognize approaches to evaluation.
- State a rationale for involvement of clients in the entire therapeutic recreation process.

THE HUMANISTIC PERSPECTIVE

Therapeutic recreation may be perceived as a profession within the broad field of recreation and leisure service. During the 1970s the recreation and leisure service field began to assume a **humanistic perspective** that recognized that people have the ability to be self-directed, make wise choices, and develop themselves during leisure. This philosophical position has been reflected in the writings of Gray (1975) and Murphy (1973, 1975), among others.

The Approach Defined

From the humanistic position Murphy (1975) has stated:

> Recreation and leisure agencies which incorporate a humanistic approach to service seek to promote the capacity and ability of groups and individuals to make self-determined and responsible choices—in light of their needs to grow, to explore new possibilities, and to realize their full potential (p.2).

Murphy goes on to discuss the ramifications of the humanistic perspective for leisure service personnel. He states:

> . . . leisure service personnel need to have unconditionally positive regards for their clientele. They must relate person-to-person. The participants are respected for what they are, and accepted for that, with all their potentialities. Such unconditional relationships, which have often been fostered in therapeutic settings, are seen as fundamental to all areas of recreation and leisure service (p.3).

Among other concepts, those embracing the humanistic approach:

- take a holistic view of the person;
- believe both children and adults are capable of change;
- see people as being in dynamic interaction with the environment, not just reacting to the external world; and
- view people as healthy who strive for personal satisfaction, yet go beyond their own needs to understand and care about others (Chapman & Chapman, 1975; Borden & Stone, 1976; Sundeen et al., 1985).

The Approach Applied

Therapeutic recreation seems to epitomize the humanistic concepts brought forth in the writing of Gray (1975) and Murphy (1973, 1975) directed toward the general field of recreation and leisure service. As O'Morrow (1980) has stated: "Present-day therapeutic recreation specialists emphasize the concept that the 'whole person' is involved" (p.151). Therapeutic recreation specialists take a holistic approach with their clients. They see each client as an individual possessing a unique biological, psychological, and social background from which to react to the environment as a total person or whole being.

Also central to the humanistic orientation of therapeutic recreation are the beliefs that people have the freedom to change, make decisions, and assume responsibility for their own actions—particularly in regard to leisure. This "freedom to become" or ability to develop oneself more fully is in keeping with the provision of therapeutic recreation activities. Through activities clients express their natural motivation toward stimulus seeking in positive recreative experiences in contrast to waiting passively for the environment to act on them. Within the accepting atmosphere provided in therapeutic recreation, clients have the opportunity to reach unexplored potentials.

Finally, therapeutic recreation is interested in helping people feel good about themselves through personal satisfaction gained in recreation. The therapeutic recreation specialist assumes a caring, understanding attitude toward the client and attempts to create a free and open recreational environment where the client can experience positive interactions with others. Good person-to-person relationships are at the heart of therapeutic recreation, as are opportunities for self-expression and creative accomplishment. Through such experiences persons may enhance positive self-concepts and learn to grow beyond themselves to care about others.

The humanistic approach exemplified in the philosophy of therapeutic recreation provides an excellent theoretical framework from which to help clients grow and to assist them to prevent or relieve problems. In what better atmosphere than that achieved in recreation and leisure could growth be fostered and problems met?

HIGH-LEVEL WELLNESS

The humanistic perspective has also helped to bring about the concept of **high-level wellness** championed by Dunn (1961) and Ardell (1986). High-level wellness is defined by Dunn (1961) as ". . . an integrated method of functioning which is oriented toward maximizing the potential of which the individual is capable" (p.4). Dunn's approach, which centers around the wholeness of the individual, calls for not only an absence of physical illness but implies a psychological and environmental wellness. Thus the physical well-being of the total person is joined by mental and social well-being in forming the concept of health under the notion of high-level wellness.

Ridenour (1983), a mental health professional, has written:

> Wellness recognizes a balance between mental and physical functioning. The wellness philosophy encourages us to strive toward maximal health instead of merely overcoming or recovering from illness. By forming habits that promote maximal functioning, we can improve the quality of our everyday living and probably even increase the length of our lives (p.1).

People have generally become more aware of the need for health promotion as is reflected by the many individuals who belong to health and fitness clubs, jog, exercise at home, eat more nutritious food, and attend weight-reduction clinics. Hospitals, schools, industries, and health insurance companies have promoted wellness programs to encourage the development of the highest levels of health.

Lindberg, Hunter, and Kruszewski (1983) have stipulated that high-level wellness involves:

- A continuing improvement in the way we function;
- Continuing progress in our ability to respond to life's challenges; and
- Increasing oneness of our whole being—mind, body, and spirit—in the way we function (p.71).

High-level wellness is gained, according to Dunn (1961), when we exist in a "very favorable environment" and enjoy "peak wellness" (where illness and wellness are conceived along a continuum, with death on one end and peak wellness at the other). When limitations hinder the attainment of peak wellness, an optimal level of high-level wellness may be achieved by making the individual's environment as conducive to growth as possible. For example, intellectual potentials are difficult to alter, but we may enhance the opportunity for intellectual growth by providing a deprived child with a stimulating play environment.

Holistic Medicine

The **holistic medicine** proposed under the banner of high-level wellness treats the person, not the disease. Like therapeutic recreation, holistic medicine is concerned with the "whole person" and with allowing individuals to assume responsibility for their own health and well-being. According to Ardell (1986), the ultimate aim of "well medicine" (in contrast to the "traditional medicine" normally practiced by the medical community) is moving clients toward self-actualization and, therefore, the achievement of high-level wellness. While traditional medicine deals solely with illness according to Ardell, well medicine deals with wellness or health enhancement. This is not to criticize those who follow the traditional medical model where disease is eliminated by treatment without concern for the entire person. The medical model has been highly successful in developing specific treatments for diseases. The concept of wellness simply extends beyond traditional medical practices to encompass all aspects of the person—mind, body, spirit and environment—rather than dealing with isolated parts and symptoms.

Therapeutic Recreation and Wellness

The similarity between therapeutic recreation and the concepts expressed by Dunn (1961) and Ardell (1986) in their separate works entitled *High Level Wellness* is striking. Both have health enhancement and self-actualization as major goals, and both have seemingly been heavily influenced by the humanistic viewpoint.

Therapeutic recreation, like traditional medical practice, has long dealt with the problem of illness. Unlike traditional medicine, however, therapeutic medicine has not dealt exclusively with illness. Therapeutic recreation has historically promoted the goal of self-actualization, or the facilitation of the fullest possible growth and development of the client. Therefore therapeutic recreation may be conceived to be much like traditional, medically oriented, allied health professions in its concern for preventing and alleviating illness. At the same time, therapeutic recreation specialists join both other leisure service professionals and physicians practicing "well medicine" in their desire to bring about the self-actualization of their clients. Thus therapeutic recreation specialists may be perceived to have concern for the full range of the illness-wellness continuum (Figure 4-1).

FIGURE 4-1
ILLNESS-WELLNESS CONTINUUM

```
        | Illness                              Wellness |
Death   |------------------------------------------------| Peak health
        | (concern with disease)       (concern with growth) |
```

It may be seen by observing Figure 4-1 that the therapeutic recreation specialist may assume several different functions, depending on the needs and desires of the client. At one point, the function of the therapeutic recreation specialist may be to join with other clinical staff to help a client alleviate illness. For example, the therapeutic recreation specialist may function as a member of a treatment team in a psychiatric hospital. Moving along the continuum toward wellness, we may find the therapeutic recreation specialist conducting a leisure counseling program at a comprehensive mental health center for clients who reside in the community. Even further along the continuum, the therapeutic recreation specialist might be found working with a community-based recreator on a community recreation program aimed at bringing about stress reduction for health enhancement.

Similar examples may be provided in all areas of therapeutic recreation service. For instance, the therapeutic recreation specialist may initially assist the patient undergoing physical rehabilitation to prevent, curtail, or reverse secondary disabilities such as muscle atrophy or decubitus ulcers, which may be caused by inadequate care, neglect, or disuse (Avedon, 1974). This programming usually occurs within the hospital or rehabilitation center. Later, as the patient moves along the wellness continuum, the therapeutic recreation specialist may provide a resocialization program to begin to foster social and leisure skills necessary for community living. Still later, the patient may be introduced to organized, community-based recreation programs as a part of a leisure counseling program.

Finally, therapeutic recreation and high-level wellness are similar in that they both hold that each of us is responsible for our own health. We cannot simply entrust our health to medical staff, letting them "take care of us." We may use resources outside of ourselves to improve our health but the primary responsibility is ours. As Ridenour (1983) has stated, "No one else hurts when you are sick; no one else is left out when you can't keep up in the Sunday volleyball game. No one else dies when you do. Of course, others care, but the experience is yours alone" (p.1). Therapeutic recreation clients are active partners with therapeutic recreation specialists, rather than being passive recipients of treatment.

The therapeutic recreation specialist recognizes that helping clients strive toward health promotion is the main goal of therapeutic recreation. This belief rests on the right of all persons to achieve their highest state of well-being, or optimal health. It is based on a philosophy that encourages clients to endeavor to achieve maximum health, rather than just conquering illness. Therapeutic recreation is directed toward not only the provision of treatment but the dynamic process of health promotion.

Stabilizing and Actualizing Tendencies

Therapeutic recreation specialists then assist clients in both their quests for health protection (overcoming illness) and health promotion (the achievement of the highest level of wellness possible). Two central human motivational forces underlie health protection and health promotion: the **stabilizing tendency** and the **actualizing tendency** (Pender, 1987).

The stability tendency is directed toward maintaining the "steady state" of the organism. It is responsible for helping us adapt in order to keep stress in a manageable range and protect us from possible biophysical and psychosocial harm. It is the force behind health protection. The actualization tendency is the growth enhancement force brought to the forefront by humanistic psychologists. It is this tendency that is the motivational force behind the achievement of health promotion (Pender, 1987).

King (1971) and Pender (1987), among others, have offered definitions of health which emphasize the stability and actualization tendencies. King defined health as: "A dynamic state in the life cycle of an organism which implies continuous adaptation to stress in the internal and external environment through optimum use of one's resources to achieve maximum potential for daily living" (p.24). Pender defined health this way: "Health is the actualization of inherent and acquired human potential through satisfying relationships with others, goal directed behavior, and competent personal care while adjustments are being made as needed to maintain stability and structural integrity" (p.27).

Health is a complex concept that encompasses coping adaptively, as well as growing and becoming. Healthy persons are able to cope with life's stressors, as well as develop themselves to the fullest. The healthy individual is free of barriers to actualization so he or she may actively pursue personal growth and development. Therapeutic recreation specialists contribute to health by assisting clients to fulfill their needs for stability and actualization. Therapeutic recreation is a means to regain stability or equilibrium following a threat to health (health protection); and, it is a way to achieve high-level wellness (health promotion).

CONCEPTUAL MODELS

Each of us work from our own personal base of knowledge and beliefs. Our professional practice springs from certain philosophical notions, concepts, theories, and models. An individual's *philosophy* reflects his or her viewpoint. One's philosophy is made up of a set of learned beliefs and values that direct behavior and attitudes (Flynn & Heffron, 1988, p.62). Because our philosophies dictate what we do and how we feel about things, it is important that therapeutic recreation specialists engaged in self-examination reveal to themselves their personal philosophical perspectives.

Concepts are ideas or "vehicles of thought" used to describe objects, properties and events, and relationships among them. A concept brings together a number of items by focusing on attributes shared by the items. In a way, concepts are stereotypes that allow us to recognize similarities and differences and to make generalizations about a phenomenon. By so doing, we can tie together past experiences with the present in order to allow us to predict the future (Flynn & Heffron, 1988; Narrow & Buschle, 1987; Taylor, Lillis & LeMone, 1993). Concepts underlie all theories. They are "the building blocks of theories" (Flynn & Heffron, 1988, p.64).

A *theory* is a statement that relies on a set of interrelated concepts to form a systematic view of some phenomenon. Chinn and Kramer (1995) have defined theory as "a systematic abstraction of reality that serves some purpose" (p. 20). Theory organizes concepts and specifies relationships between concepts in an effort to present an understanding and explanation of a phenomenon. Examples are the psychoanalytic, behavioristic, cognitive-behavioral, and growth psychology theories of human behavior presented in Chapter 2. Professional practice disciplines, such as therapeutic recreation, may too have theories that form a basis for action. Such theories are derived from philosophical positions and from concepts drawn from personal experience and the scientific and clinical literature.

Models Defined

Closely related to theories are *models*. Models are representations of something. Chinn and Kramer (1995) have provided the following definition of the term model:

> A model is a symbolic representation of an empiric experience. The symbolic form of a model may be words, mathematic notations, or physical material, as in a model airplane. One key idea in understanding models is that they are not the real thing but are an attempt to objectify the concept they represent. A model of an object, property, or event replicates reality with various degrees of precision (p. 75).

Riehl and Roy (1980) illustrate the concept with the example of a toy model of a car. The model is not actually a car, of course, but it represents the actual car. In contrast to theories, which explain, models describe. Models provide an image or picture. In the case of a professional practice discipline, such as therapeutic recreation, models offer an image or picture of the components of the discipline and how its parts fit and work together.

Models Applied

But a model for a practice discipline, such as therapeutic recreation, must do more than allow the field to be visualized. Models must direct practitioners in the process of intervening in the lives of clients. Additionally, a sound model for practice must be based on something. This is where theory comes in. Theory provides the foundation for assumptions behind parts of the model and gives a theoretical basis for action. A sound model for therapeutic recreation should identify the essential components for therapeutic recreation practice (i.e., it should describe); and, it should offer a theoretical basis for each of the parts of the model (i.e., it should explain).

Therapeutic recreation, as an increasingly emerging profession, has begun to develop models for practice. It is critical that therapeutic recreation has well conceived models in order to interpret the profession to others and to provide a framework for practice in the field.

Therapeutic recreation specialists have had difficulty agreeing on what therapeutic recreation is, or should be. Some have endorsed an all encompassing approach that has portrayed the discipline to represent the provision of recreation to persons who are disabled. Others have taken a narrower perspective that emphasizes clinical interventions for treatment and rehabilitation. It may be argued that such differences are harmful to therapeutic recreation in that one single model of practice has not been endorsed by all members of the profession. Others hold that a multiple model approach is best in that diversity and conflict among theorists will bring about progress in the profession.

THE PETERSON/GUNN LEISURE ABILITY MODEL

The best known model of therapeutic recreation is the Leisure Ability Model developed by Peterson and Gunn and presented in their 1984 textbook, which served as the reference for this section. The Peterson/Gunn model holds that recreation and leisure are necessary experiences that all should enjoy, including those with "limitations" (their word, p.5). The purpose of therapeutic recreation is, "facilitating the development, maintenance, and expression of an appropriate leisure lifestyle" (p.15) for "individuals with physical, mental, social, or emotional limitations" (p.5), according to this model.

Leisure Ability Model Defined
Therapeutic recreation service is seen as existing along a continuum from client-oriented therapy at one end to special

recreation programs at the other. This continuum may be divided into these three components:

- Treatment
- Leisure education
- Special recreation

The **treatment** component is directed primarily toward therapy or rehabilitation. Therapeutic recreation specialists function chiefly as therapists who help clients gain the basic functional abilities that are necessary for leisure involvement and lifestyle. Recreation activities are means toward reaching specific behavioral changes or improvements in clients.

The **leisure education** component deals with the development of activity skills and social interaction skills as well as issues for leisure counseling. Therapeutic recreation specialists function primarily as teachers and counselors. In therapeutic recreation programs clients develop their leisure and social skills. Through leisure counseling clients gain leisure awareness and information on leisure resources.

Special recreation concerns the provision of recreation programs for members of special population groups. Therapeutic recreation specialists function as recreators who provide individuals with organized opportunities for recreation participation. The emphasis is on recreation participation, not behavioral or attitudinal change.

Leisure Ability Model Analyzed

I object to the suggestion that a *primary* role of the therapeutic recreation specialist is that of recreation leader or supervisor for the provision of recreation opportunities for members of special population groups. If the major function of inclusive or special recreation is the provision of opportunities for self-directed leisure, then those charged with the responsibility for the delivery of leisure services—community recreation personnel—should operate these programs. This criticism is shared by others (e.g., Smith, Austin & Kennedy, 1996), including Bullock (1987) who has written:

> Recreation and special populations, or special recreation, must be distinguished from therapeutic recreation. Therapeutic

recreation is the purposive use of recreation by qualified professionals to promote independent functioning and to enhance optimal health and well-being in persons with illnesses and/or disabling conditions.

Therapeutic recreation is not any and all recreation services for persons who are disabled. Merely being disabled does not qualify a person to receive "therapeutic" recreation services. . .To call recreation services "therapeutic" because they involve a person or group of persons with a disability is doing a disservice to the person who is being served (p.203).

The term "therapeutic recreation" should be reserved for the clinical application of recreation and leisure and not be used to describe the provision of recreation services for persons who require special accommodations because of unique needs they have due to some physical, cognitive, or psychological disability.

Contained in the statement by Bullock is a second point of criticism of the Leisure Ability Model. This criticism deals with the lack of attention given to health and to independent functioning (outside of leisure) as purposes for therapeutic recreation. The purpose of therapeutic recreation under the Leisure Ability Model is stated to solely be the achievement of independent leisure functioning. Because of this, the Leisure Ability Model goal of helping individuals assume an appropriate leisure lifestyle has a much better fit with leisure service agencies (which exist for the provision of leisure services) than it does with health care agencies.

Another criticism of the Leisure Ability Model is that it includes limited theoretical underpinnings. It offers a description of how its authors view the world of therapeutic recreation but remains on a descriptive level. It is what Stevens (1979) has termed a "descriptive theory" in that, "A descriptive theory is an existential statement, it asserts what is" (p.3). It is descriptive, not explanatory. To say that the Leisure Ability Model is descriptive in nature is not to detract from its importance. As Stevens has indicated, "Descriptive theory is not only the first level of theory development, but it is the most important level because it determines what entities will be perceived as the essence of the phenomenon under study" (p.3).

The Leisure Ability Model has been widely embraced by the therapeutic recreation profession. It served as the basis for the philosophical statement of the National Therapeutic Recreation Society. Recently, however, signs have emerged to indicate that professionals are more closely examining the model and finding it to be less than complete (Hamilton & Austin, 1992). Therefore, alternatives to the Leisure Ability Model are being sought. The Health Protection/Health Promotion Model is one such alternative.

THE HEALTH PROTECTION/
HEALTH PROMOTION MODEL

The **health protection/health promotion model** (Austin, 1996) regards the purpose of therapeutic recreation as enabling the client to recover following a threat to health (health protection) and to achieve optimal health (health promotion). The mission of therapeutic recreation is to use activity, recreation, and leisure to help people to deal with problems that serve as barriers to health and to assist them to grow toward their highest levels of health and wellness.

Therapeutic recreation specialists contribute to health by helping persons to fulfill their needs for stability and actualization until they are ready and able to assume responsibility for themselves. This is accomplished through client participation in prescriptive activity, recreation, and leisure.

Health Protection/Health Promotion Model Defined

As illustrated in the Health Protection/Health Promotion Model represented in Figure 4-2, prescriptive activities, recreation, and leisure fall along a continuum that ranges from poor health to optimal health. The continuum is modeled after continua presented by Ball (1970) and Frye and Peters (1972). Clients may enter the continuum at any point that is appropriate for their needs. As clients move toward optimal health they exercise increasing degrees of choice. While the clients' choices enlarge, the control of therapeutic recreation specialists continually decreases.

The first of the three broad areas along the continuum, that involves prescriptive activities, is where the stability tendency is paramount. At the extreme, clients experience poor health in an unfavorable environment. It is here that therapeutic recreation specialists help activate clients. Therapeutic recreation specialists provide direction and structure as means to interventions. The second area along the continuum, recreation, represents mutual participation on the parts of clients and therapeutic recreation specialists. At this point the actualization tendency starts to emerge as the stabilizing tendency begins its decline. In the third area, leisure, the actualizing tendency becomes paramount as the health of clients improves and they assume greater self-determination. Ultimately, clients assume primary responsibility for their own health.

Health Promotion Model Applied

As previously stated, clients may enter into therapeutic recreation anywhere along the continuum that ranges from poor health to peak health. For example, they may be in poor health where the stability tendency is primary. Such individuals typically lack energy and may experience feelings of depression. This is not to imply, however, that they never experience moments when they transcend their prevailing state of health. Even the most seriously ill persons have times when they "feel good." They may temporarily enter into recreation experiences, or even growth-producing leisure. Unfortunately, however, such occasions are not long lasting due to their existing health problems.

Potential for Change

The model is based on the humanistic assumption that human beings have an overriding drive for health and wellness. Combs (1989) has written: "From the moment of conception we begin an insatiable search for wholeness and health that never ceases until death has occurred in the last of our cells." He goes on to state: "The drive toward health is a built-in quality of every living cell including the millions which make up a complex human being" (p.19).

It is this drive for health that provides the motive for client participation in treatment and rehabilitation, including therapeutic recreation treatment and rehabilitation programs. Therapeutic recreation specialists, and other helping professionals, take on the role of fostering conditions that allow the drive for health and wellness to be fulfilled. Clients are perceived to possess almost a limitless potential for change (Combs, 1989).

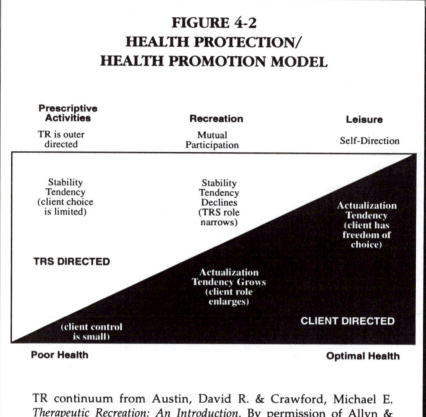

FIGURE 4-2
HEALTH PROTECTION/
HEALTH PROMOTION MODEL

TR continuum from Austin, David R. & Crawford, Michael E. *Therapeutic Recreation: An Introduction.* By permission of Allyn & Bacon, Needham Heights, MA 02194 ©1996.

Prescriptive Activity

When illness is initially encountered, people often become self-absorbed. They withdraw from their normal life activities and experience a loss of control over their lives (Flynn, 1980). Clients, at this time of threat to health, are not ready for recreation or leisure. For such individuals, activity becomes a necessary prerequisite to health restoration. In order to gain control over the situation and to overcome feelings of helplessness and depression, they must begin to actively engage in life. **Prescriptive activity** may be necessary in order to energize them so that they are not passive victims of their circumstances but begin to take action to restore their health.

At this point, therapeutic recreation specialists activate clients by providing direction and structure for activity. Client control is reduced only because of the temporary feeling of loss of control caused by the illness, injury or disorder that is interfering with the overriding drive for health. The role of the therapeutic recreation specialist is not to manipulate clients but to be supportive and to encourage new means for clients to move themselves toward health. Once engaged in activity, clients can begin to perceive of themselves as having the capacity for successful interaction with their environment, for making improvement, and for regaining a sense of control. As clients begin to become energized and gain confidence in themselves as a result of their successful participation, therapeutic recreation specialists gradually decrease the degree of client dependency with the intent of entering into a full partnership with clients during the recreation portion of the continuum.

Recreation

Recreation involves activity as one component but recreation is more than activity. Recreation is commonly linked with being restorative, offering refreshment or re-creation for participants (Kelly, 1982). It is this ability to restore or refresh the mind, body and spirit that has meaning to the therapeutic application of recreation in health restoration. Through recreation, clients may regain their equilibrium so they may once again resume their quest for actualization. It is in this sense that recreation is used in therapeutic recreation as a treatment modality. It is during this stage that the actualizing tendency begins to emerge as the stabilizing tendency declines due to gains made by clients.

Too often client interactions with health care professionals bring about feelings of helplessness in clients due to condescending behaviors, paternalistic approaches, and the mystification that accompanies many health care processes (Pender, 1987). Control is taken away from clients. Therapeutic recreation represents the antithesis of the controlling environment often encountered in health care facilities. In recreation, clients are allowed choice and control. They work in close partnership with therapeutic recreation specialists in choosing treatment programs that will meet their needs. There is mutual participation by clients and therapeutic recreation specialists. Through this relationship, clients learn to select recreation experiences that help them to achieve better health.

In recreation, clients are afforded opportunities to experience control over their environments within a supportive, nonthreatening atmosphere. Through participation in activities that allow mastery experiences and build a sense of accomplishment, clients learn they are able to be successful in their interactions with the world. They learn new skills, new ways of behaving, new means to approach interactions with others, new values and philosophies, and new ways to think about themselves. Positive changes in self-concepts occur as a result of clients proving to themselves that they are capable of achieving success and of learning new skills, behaviors and ways of thinking. Their personal evaluations of their abilities, or feelings of self-efficacy, are enhanced. Bolstered efficacy expectations allow clients to have confidence in themselves and to better face difficulties so that they can persevere even in the face of frustration (Bandura, 1986). Clients increase feelings of being able to control their lives and meet adversity as they become more and more healthy. When healthy (i.e., not having to engage in health protection), clients are in a position to confront potentially threatening situations and to react to these with a minimum of distress.

High-Level Wellness and Intrinsic Motivation

Once threat to health has been successfully met and good health is restored, clients are free to pursue high-level wellness or optimal health—or to move from health protection to health promotion. They can move from "not being ill" toward "becoming well." They can take charge of their lives with the help of therapeutic recreation specialists who serve to facilitate life changes. Old negative habits can be discarded to be replaced by positive ones. For example, smoking could be replaced by another means of stress reduction such as relaxation training. Or the habit of not exercising could be replaced by regular workouts several days a week. In order to promote wellness, a new lifestyle is built in order to replace old habits with positive ones. Leisure counseling and leisure education may be used as avenues for the achievement of such lifestyle changes.

Moving further along the continuum toward optimal health, the actualizing tendency enlarges as the health of clients improves.

Those who have achieved a degree of positive health and wellness are relatively free of barriers to actualization so that they may endeavor to achieve personal growth and development. The healthier individuals are, the better able they are to cope with stressors and to pursue actualizing experiences. It can be said that such individuals are intrinsically motivated because they are no longer ruled by external constraints or limitations.

Intrinsic motivation comes from our innate needs for competence and self-determination, needs that motivate us toward mastering tasks that challenge our abilities. When challenges are met and successes are encountered, feelings of competence and autonomy result together with the emotions of enjoyment and excitement (Deci & Ryan, 1985). Deci and Ryan have portrayed intrinsic motivation as the energizing force behind the actualization tendency that promotes change, growth, and maturation.

Leisure

Intrinsic motivation is also a central defining property of **leisure** (Austin, 1996). It is the intrinsically motivated, self-determined nature of participation, coupled with the match between abilities and challenges, that defines leisure and makes it so involving. Leisure allows people self-determined opportunities to stretch themselves by successfully applying their abilities in order to meet challenges. Such experiences are growth producing, leaving participants with feelings of accomplishment, confidence and pleasure. Leisure plays an important role in helping people to reach their potentials (Iso-Ahola, 1989).

Leisure experiences contain the elements of intrinsic motivation, self-determination, mastery, and competence, which, in turn, lead individuals toward feelings of self-efficacy, empowerment, excitement, and enjoyment. Leisure experiences provide opportunities for the expression of the actualizing tendency and enable individuals to develop themselves. Leisure can play a critical part in helping clients to actualize and to move toward optimal health.

Health and actualization are intimately intertwined. The attainment of high-level wellness permits actualization. Those who enjoy peak health are free of barriers to actualization so that they may actively pursue personal growth and development.

The achievement of a higher level of actualization is, in turn, a hallmark of high-level wellness that produces resources to further enhance the dynamic state of health and wellness.

Implications for Therapeutic Recreation

The basic goal of therapeutic recreation, under the Health Protection/Health Promotion Model, is for clients to achieve the highest possible level of health. Therapeutic recreation specialists nurture the drive in all humans for health and wellness through a partnership with their clients. Within this relationship, therapeutic recreation specialists provide a supportive atmosphere while helping clients move toward increasing levels of independence. Clients who are in poor health are most dependent on therapeutic recreation specialists. At this point the stabilizing tendency is protecting the client from biophysical and psychosocial harm brought about by an injury, illness, or disorder. Clients are assisted in their attempts to fight off the threat to health and stabilize themselves by therapeutic recreation specialists who engage clients in prescribed activities or recreation experiences in an effort to protect their health. Later, as the stabilizing tendency is reduced and the actualizing tendency comes to the forefront, clients are less and less dependent on therapeutic recreation specialists as they assume increasing responsibility for their own health and greater concern for health promotion. It is at this point that clients engage in leisure experiences, fostering health enhancement and allowing for the expression of the actualizing tendency. At this stage, clients assume primary responsibility for themselves with therapeutic recreation specialists taking minor roles. Clients hold the ultimate potential to assume complete responsibility for their own health, at which time they have no need for therapeutic recreation services.

The Health Protection/Health Promotion Model has been formulated as an alternative to the Leisure Ability Model and would appear to have a more complete theoretical basis than that presented by the Leisure Ability Model. Further, the Health Protection/Heath Promotion Model is more in keeping with the purpose of health care agencies—to restore, maintain, and promote health. Because the vast majority of therapeutic recreation specialists are employed by health care agencies, the goal of therapeutic recreation should coincide with the purpose of these agencies.

Students and practitioners need to adopt, adapt or construct their own therapeutic recreation practice models. All who are interested in the practice of therapeutic recreation are encouraged to explore the literature to learn as much as possible about models of practice. *Theory of Therapy* by Arthur W. Combs (1989) can be a great catalyst to stimulate thinking.

WHAT IS THE
THERAPEUTIC RECREATION PROCESS?

Because the therapeutic recreation specialists are foremost involved with purposeful intervention, the setting in which help is given is of little significance. Therapeutic recreation may be performed in virtually any setting. The concern of therapeutic recreation specialists should not be hospital therapeutic recreation, community therapeutic recreation, or any other type of therapeutic recreation—except people therapeutic recreation. No matter where therapeutic recreation specialists are based, their overriding mission is the provision of purposeful intervention designed to help clients grow and to assist them to prevent or relieve problems through activities, recreation and leisure. Purposeful intervention in therapeutic recreation is brought about through the employment of the therapeutic recreation process.

The therapeutic recreation process may be used with a client or group of clients at any point along the illness-wellness continuum. The needs of the client dictate where the process will be directed. No matter where along the continuum the client's needs lie, the therapeutic recreation process provides a systematic method of problem solving through a progression of phases. O'Morrow and Reynolds (1989) have listed four steps in the therapeutic recreation process:

1. Assessment
2. Planning
3. Implementation
4. Evaluation

Through the orderly phases of the therapeutic recreation process, the client's problems or concerns and strengths are determined (assessment), plans are made to meet the problems or concerns (planning), the plan is initiated (implementation), and an evaluation is conducted to determine how effective the intervention has been (evaluation). Each of the phases of the therapeutic recreation process is dependent on the other. No phase stands alone. It is a cyclical process (Figure 4-3) that can be repeated as often as necessary in order to meet client needs.

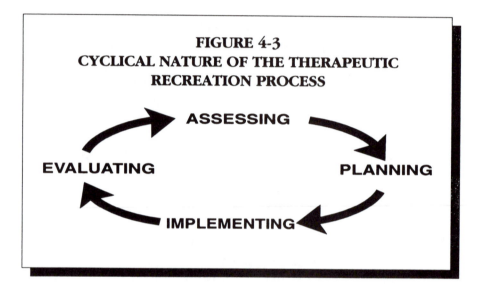

FIGURE 4-3
CYCLICAL NATURE OF THE THERAPEUTIC RECREATION PROCESS

Before discussing each of the four phases in detail, it is important to establish that the client and therapeutic recreation specialist should work together throughout the entire therapeutic recreation process to the greatest extent to which the client is capable. The importance of this cooperation is perhaps best illustrated when considering the planning phase. Inherent in a plan is a systematic effort to reach certain goals. If the client has not been included in the planning, the client's goals could differ from those developed by the therapeutic recreation specialist. Also, the likelihood is small that commitment and motivation will spring forth from the client to achieve aims he or she has not been involved in formulating.

CLIENT ASSESSMENT

The first step in the therapeutic recreation process, assessment, is concerned with data collection and analysis in order to determine the status of the client. Once baseline assessment information is available, the therapeutic recreation specialist can help identify and define the client's problems and strengths. Assessment provides a beginning point so the therapeutic recreation specialist can determine "where the client is," in order to determine a starting place in working with the client. Complete assessment is a *sin quo non* for meaningful therapeutic recreation intervention.

The critical importance of comprehensive assessment to therapeutic recreation has been documented in studies that have examined views of therapeutic recreation specialists. Beddall and Kennedy (1985) found practitioners in therapeutic recreation to positively value assessment. Winslow (1989) discovered the primary technique or method that practitioners wanted to know more about was client assessment.

Gathering Information

The purpose of therapeutic recreation assessment must remain clear. Therapeutic recreation assessment is not conducted in order to label or categorize the client. Instead, we assess to gain information that is useful in helping the client to profit from our services. Assessment should aid us to determine client strengths, interests, and expectations and to identify the nature and extent of problems or concerns. Determining client strengths and interests will allow us to construct a strengths list on which to base interventions during the planning phase. Identifying client expectations helps us to determine treatment or rehabilitation goals. Evolving from the exploration of client problems will come a needs list since a problem reflects an individual's inability to meet a need (O'Morrow & Reynolds, 1989).

Many of the different needs that may arise and become the focus for planning follow.

- Increasing confidence
- Feeling a sense of belonging
- Learning social or leisure skills
- Managing stress

- Reducing anxiety
- Developing a wholesome body image
- Improving fitness
- Becoming aware of values
- Developing a sense of humor
- Enhancing self-esteem
- Building positive expectations
- Establishing a sense of control
- Experiencing fun and enjoyment
- Increasing functional skills (e.g., ADL skills)

The primary source of information is usually the client. Secondary sources are, however, almost always used as well. Secondary sources include medical or educational records, results of testing (e.g., psychological testing), interviews with family or friends, the social history (usually taken by a social worker), case recordings or progress notes that staff have charted, and conferences and team meetings with other staff. Occasionally, therapeutic recreation specialists also assess the client's home and community to determine leisure patterns of the client, or to survey for recreation opportunities. Knowledge of the potential recreation environment found in the client's home and community are useful in understanding the client and in future planning with the client.

Diagnosis

A **diagnosis** is derived from the assessment by the therapeutic recreation specialist. This diagnosis is very different from a medical diagnosis that identifies a specific disease from the patient's symptoms and involves a classification system adopted by the medical profession. Therapeutic recreation diagnosis may relate to the medical diagnosis but pertains strictly to those problems that the therapeutic recreation specialist is able to diagnose and treat. O'Morrow and Reynolds (1989) have written:

> For a number of years diagnosis was a forbidden word in therapeutic recreation. A literal definition of the word, with no qualifier preceding it, suggests it is a good term to use when conveying the idea that we are seeking knowledge or information about what needs to be improved, what is causing the difficulty, or what is interfering with normal functioning. With this in mind, therapeutic recreators can use the word

"diagnosis" as effectively as the physician can or any person who is trying to discover where efforts must be applied to perform service for the benefit of the member (p.142).

Once data have been collected and analyzed, therapeutic recreation diagnosis can occur. Through assessment, the therapeutic recreation specialist attempts to obtain as complete a picture as possible of the client's life situation. In order to accomplish this, the client's history, present condition, and expectations for the future must be examined.

What are Methods of Assessing Clients?

Observing and interviewing are the two most used methods of client assessment. Both observations and interviews offer a number of perspectives from which to approach client assessment. Schulman (1982) has outlined several methods of observation. Among these are what he has termed casual observation, naturalistic observation, specific goal observation, skilled observation, standardized observation and time-interval observations.

Casual Observation

Casual observation is the type of nonsystematic observation in which we engage on a daily basis. It is responding to our environment in a somewhat random fashion and out of our personal bias and background. It is not "skilled observation" in that it is not directed or purposeful.

Skilled Observation

Skilled observations are carefully completed in an organized manner and are as free as possible from personal bias. Skilled observers learn to disregard irrelevant material in order to become selective in their observations. Knowing what to look for and what to expect in terms of normal behavior is important to doing clinical observation, as is the ability to describe observations in objective, factual terms (O'Morrow & Reynolds, 1989). Skilled observers also are unobtrusive so as to not alter or change client's behaviors (Wilkinson & Canter, 1982).

Naturalistic Observation

In **naturalistic observation** there is no attempt to manipulate or change the natural environment. This method calls for keeping an ongoing account of the client's behavior through written anecdotal notes, photographs, film, videotape, or a combination of these techniques. In therapeutic recreation, naturalistic observation might be accomplished while watching the hospitalized client interact during unstructured recreation on the ward or by observing children with disabilities on the playground in a free play situation.

Willson (1987) has suggested that naturalistic observations should be completed in a variety of settings while clients are engaged in a wide range of activities in order to gain as complete an assessment as possible. General areas for such observations as outlined by O'Morrow and Reynolds (1989) follow. *General appearance* to obtain signs of emotional and physical problems such as poor posture signaling depression. *Interpersonal interactions* to observe social interaction patterns and coping abilities. *Motor activity* to assess psychomotor abilities and levels of mobility. *Body language* to observe nonverbal communication from visual, vocal, spatial and temporal cues.

Areas of observation set forth by Willson (1987) include:

- Personal appearance (cleanliness, grooming, clothing);
- Posture and movement (sitting, walking, coordination);
- Manner (relaxed, tense, socially comfortable);
- Facial expression (eye contact, habitual expression);
- General level of activity (repetitive movements, lethargic, chain smoking);
- Intentional activity (spontaneous activity, things precipitating activity, initiative shown);
- Cognitive ability (follow instructions, recall, attention, sense of organization); and
- Communication (vocabulary, nonverbal communication, initiate conversation).

Specific Goal Observation

Specific goal observation requires precision in planning, since the observer sets definite goals for observation to meet a particular purpose or to assess a well-defined behavior. Here the therapeutic recreation specialist may observe how cooperative the client is in a co-recreational game situation or the client's response to frustration in an athletic contest.

With children, the therapeutic recreation specialist may confirm other information concerning the child while viewing the child at play. Takata (1974) has provided a list of questions to guide such observation.

- With what does the child play?
- How does the child play?
- What type of play is avoided or liked the least?
- With whom does the child play?
- How does the child play with others?
- What body posture does the child use during play?
- How long does the child play?
- Where does the child play?
- When does the child play?

Examples of goal observations calling for specific behaviors might include observing an adult playing a card game, such as bridge, or observing an adolescent square dancing. These activities make certain cognitive, psychomotor, or social demands on the client. The therapeutic recreation specialist observes to determine how the client meets these specific demands and to record this information.

A closely related assessment, that might be categorized as a specific goal observation, is *role playing*. The basis for role playing can be a standard social situation or a particular situation in which the client has experienced difficulty in the past. The client is told to act as though he or she normally would in the situation. Props (e.g., tables and chairs) may be used and the therapist may prompt those role playing either verbally or nonverbally. Wilkinson and Canter (1982) have suggested role playing as a means to assess client social skills.

Standardized Observation

Standardized observations take two major forms (Schulman 1982). One is the standardized or norm-referenced instrument. The other involves the use of time-interval observations. Norm-referenced tests provide a measure of how an individual performs in relation to others who are from the same classification of persons. In contrast, criterion-referenced assessments do not compare people. Criterion-referenced tests measure achievement toward some established standard (Hogg

& Raynes, 1987). An example of a standardized test that a therapeutic recreation specialist might apply is the Leisure Diagnostic Battery (LDB) developed by Witt and Ellis (1987). The LDB and several other standardized tests are covered in the next major section of this chapter. Although standardized tests have not been extensively employed by therapeutic recreation specialists, they are beginning to become more commonly used in therapeutic recreation assessment.

Determinations regarding the choice of standardized assessments are influenced by two major considerations, reliability and validity. **Reliability** deals with the question of whether an instrument yields reproducible results. A reliable instrument produces stable results over time. It reflects stability (Berger & Yule, 1987). A reliable assessment also demonstrates internal consistency within items contained in the instrument and equivalency between various forms of the instrument, if more than one form is available (Dunn, 1989).

Validity answers the question of whether the assessment measures what it is designed to measure. Or, can the results be interpreted as an accurate representation of the phenomenon being assessed? Or, does it test what it sets out to test? (Berger & Yule, 1987) A minimum requirement for any clinical assessment is that it has content validity, or that it makes intuitive sense. Another type of validity is criterion-related validity that is derived from a statistical comparison of the instrument against some previously established criterion. A third type, construct validity, deals with how well an instrument reflects the construct that underlies the assessment (Dunn, 1989). Information on reliability and validity should be provided in the manual that accompanies any assessment instrument.

Dunn (1989) has supplied a number of useful guidelines for the selection and application of standardized assessments in therapeutic recreation. These guidelines are listed in Table 4-1. The interested reader is referred to Dunn's original article in Volume 23, Number 2 of the *Therapeutic Recreation Journal* for further information.

TABLE 4-1
GUIDELINES FOR USING
STANDARDIZED ASSESSMENTS

Guidelines for Selection of Assessment Procedures
1. The assessment should provide evidence of validity.
   a. The assessment should be validated on a representative sample of sufficient size.
   b. The assessment should be valid for its intended use.
   c. There should be evidence of the relationship of subscores to total scores of those measures which produce subscores.
2. The assessment must provide evidence of reliability.
3. The manual and test materials should be complete and of appropriate quality.
4. A test user should demonstrate relevance for the assessment selection.
   a. The assessment should be relevant to the clients served by the agency.
   b. The assessment should be relevant to the decisions made based on assessment results.

Guidelines for Assessment Use
1. An assessment should be revalidated when any changes are made in procedures, or materials, or when it is used for a purpose or with a population group for which it has not been validated.
2. The assessment should be selected and used by qualified individuals.
3. The assessment should be used in the intended way.
4. Published assessments should be used in combination with other methods.

Guidelines for Administering, Scoring, and Reporting
1. The administration and scoring of an assessment should follow standardized procedures.
   a. During the administration of an assessment, care should be taken in providing a comfortable environment with minimal distractions.

TABLE 4-1 CONT.

b. During the administration of assessments, the administrator should be aware of the importance of, and effect of rapport with the client.

2. It is the responsibility of the test user to protect the security of materials.

Guidelines for Protecting the Rights of Clients

1. Test results should not be released without informed consent.

2. Data regarding a patient's assessment results should be kept in a designated patient file.

Source: Dunn. J. D. 1989. Guidelines for using published assessment procedures. *Therapeutic Recreation Journal.* 23(2), 59-69.

A type of assessment related to standardized instruments is the self-rating form that has not been normed. Self-ratings are, of course, completed by the client and then are later reviewed by the therapist. Most agencies have leisure interest instruments on which clients are asked to designate hobbies and other recreation interests by checking them on a checklist or by indicating a level of interest (e.g., high, moderate, none) or frequency of participation (e.g., often, rarely, never).

Some agencies have goal lists. Clients use these to check the goals on which they wish to work while in the program. Others have self-rating scales where clients may check problematic behaviors (e.g., to stop drinking too much, to feel at ease talking in a group, to stop swearing at other people). Cautela (1977) has compiled a book containing numerous self-rating forms that have clinical applications. Willson (1987) has offered these rules to guide those who might desire to design self-report questionnaires:

1. Be clear about what the information is to be obtained and why it is needed.
2. Choose a format that will be most easily understood.

3.   Construct the questions avoiding unnecessary words or ambiguities.
4.   Try it out on a sample of its intended respondents to see if it can be administered easily and if the results can be processed in a meaningful way (pp.119, 120).

Self-reports, of course, can only be employed with clients who are able to read and to complete the scale on their own. Additionally, the validity of the information drawn from self-reports is suspect because of mood variations and the fact that people wish to portray themselves in a positive light (Wilkinson & Canter, 1982). The problem of validity does, however, need to be weighed against the values of self-report instruments as Willson (1987) has indicated. Following a discussion of the problem of validity, she has written, "On the other hand, the way in which a patient rates himself (or herself) should be significant to the therapist and should also allow the patient to be more fully involved in the objectives and progression of his own treatment" (p.119).

Time-Interval Observation
Time-interval observations or observational probes are standardized observations in which clients are observed at predetermined times during the day. These observations may last for 15 minutes, 30 minutes, or any period of time. During the observation, the therapeutic recreation specialist looks for a specific behavior and records frequency counts when that behavior occurs. For instance, the number of verbal interactions with other clients, or the number of times a client behaves in an aggressive manner could be recorded.

Besides time-interval observations, Dattilo and Murphy (1987) and Levy (1982) have presented any number of behaviorally orientated types of observations. Included are frequency counting (or event recording), duration recording, interval recording, and time sampling. The interested reader is referred to either of these excellent resources for detailed information on these observational methods.

Assessment Instruments
Fine and Fine (1988), Howe (1984), Stumbo (1991) and Wehman and Schleien (1980) have provided extensive reviews of

various assessment instruments suitable for application in therapeutic recreation.

Fine and Fine

Fine and Fine's review in their 1988 book, *Therapeutic Recreation for Exceptional Children,* includes four categories of assessment instruments. Under the category of *developmental profiles and interviews* are listed: the Developmental Profile II, the Learning Accomplishment Profile—Diagnostic Edition (LAP-D), the Brigance Diagnostic Inventory of Development, and the Vulpe Assessment Battery.

Under *motor skill* and *psychomotor tests* are: the Purdue Perceptual Motor Survey, the Bruiniks-Oseretsky Test of Motor Proficiency, and the Ohio State University Scale of Intra Gross Motor Assessment (OSU-SIGMA). The *behavioral checklist* category contains: the Comprehensive Evaluation in Recreation Therapy Scale (CERT), the Haring and Phillips' Scale (Adapted Version), the Burke's Behavior Rating Scales (BBRS), and the Devereux Child Behavior Rating Scale (DCB). Under *leisure interest and skill instruments* are found: the Leisure Diagnostic Battery (LDB), the Leisure Activities Blank (LAB), and the Mirenda Leisure Interest Finder (MLIF).

Additional leisure interest finders are mentioned by Fine and Fine but are not analyzed. These include: the Leisure Interest Inventory, the Constructive Leisure Activity Survey, the Avocational Activities Inventory, and the Self-Leisure Interest Profile.

Howe

Howe (1984) has presented leisure assessment instruments under five clusters. Under *leisure attitudes,* she lists the Study of Leisure, the Leisure Ethics Scale, and the Leisure Attitudes Battery. In the *leisure states* category are the Walshe Temperament Survey and the Leisure Well-Being Inventory. The *leisure behavior* category contains Joswiak's Leisure Counseling Assessment Instruments and the Comprehensive Evaluation in Recreation Therapy Scale. Within the *leisure satisfaction* cluster are the Milwaukee Avocational Satisfaction Questionnaire, the Leisure Satisfaction Scale, and the Leisure Satisfaction Inventory. The largest grouping is that of *leisure interests* instruments. Here Howe lists the Leisure Interest Inventory, the Mirenda Leisure

Interest Finder, the Leisure Activity Blank, the Avocational Activities Inventory, the Constructive Leisure Activities Survey, and the State Technical Institute Leisure Activities Project.

Stumbo

Stumbo (1991) offers the most current, and perhaps most complete, review of assessment tools for application in therapeutic recreation. Stumbo reviews 45 assessment instruments, and in addition to providing a brief description of each of the instruments, she lists references related to each as well as information on how to locate and purchase it. The instruments are categorized under four headings: *leisure attitudes and barriers, functional abilities, leisure activity skills,* and *leisure interests and participation patterns.* Under the heading of *leisure attitudes and barriers* she covers tools such as the Leisure Diagnostic Battery (LDB), Leisure Satisfaction Scale (LSS), Leisure Attitude Scale (LAS) and Brief Leisure Rating Scale (BLRS). The *functional abilities* section has within it instruments such as the Functional Assessment of Characteristics for Therapeutic Recreation (FACTR), Ohio Leisure Skills Scales on Normal Functioning (OLSSON), Comprehensive Evaluation in Recreation Therapy—Physical Disabilities (CERT-Phys. Dis.), and the Comprehensive Evaluation in Recreation Therapy—Psychiatric/Behavioral (CERT-Psych.). Among instruments in the *leisure activity skills* category are Functional Hiking Technique and Downhill Skiing Assessment. The final category of *leisure interests and participation* contains 11 instruments including Joswiak's Leisure Counseling Assessment, the Recreation Participation Data Sheet (RPD) and the Family Leisure Assessment Checklist.

Wehman and Schleien

Wehman and Schleien (1980) have compiled a listing of assessment instruments appropriate for use in a leisure skill training program. Several of the instruments covered by Fine and Fine (1988) and Howe (1984) are contained in this listing. Others listed by Wehman and Schleien are: Bogan's Group Assessment, I Can, Davis' Recreational Directors' Observational Report, the Iowa Leisure Education Program Assessment Form, Know, Hurff & Takata Deaf-Blind Assessment, the Linear Model for Individual Treatment in Recreation (LMIT), the Leisure Skills Curriculum Assessment Inventory (LSCDD), the Minimum

Objective System, the Recreation Therapy Assessment, the Sonoma County Organization for the Retarded Assessment (SCOR), the State of Ohio Curriculum Guide for Moderately Mentally Retarded Learners, the Toward Competency: A Guide for Individualized Instruction, and the Vineland Social Maturity Scale.

The interested reader is referred to these four major reviews for additional information on the cited instruments. Still another good source is burlingame's and Blaschko's (1990) volume on assessment. In the remainder of this section a sampling of some of the most commonly applied and more readily available assessment instruments for therapeutic recreation are provided. Covered are the Leisure Diagnostic Battery, the Comprehensive Evaluation in Recreation Therapy Scale, and the Functional Assessment of Characteristics for Therapeutic Recreation Scale.

Witt and Ellis

The Leisure Diagnostic Battery (LDB) (Witt & Ellis, 1987) contains a group of instruments that have been designed to assess the leisure functioning of both disabled and nondisabled individuals. Long and short forms are available for most of the instruments in the LDB for both adults and adolescents.

The eight scales of the LDB have been categorized under two sections. Section One scales provide an indication of an individual's perception of freedom in leisure. They are: Scale A-Perceived Leisure Competence Scale, Scale B-Perceived Leisure Control Scale, Scale C-Leisure Needs Scale, Scale D-Depth of Involvement in Leisure Scale, Scale E-Playfulness Scale. Section Two scales deal with factors that may inhibit an individual's leisure functioning.

Under Section Two are: Scale F-Barriers to Leisure Involvement Scale, Scale G-Leisure Preferences Inventory, and Scale H- Knowledge or Leisure Opportunities Test.

Witt and Ellis (1987) have described the purposes of the LDB as:

- To enable users to assess their clients' leisure functioning;
- To enable users to determine areas in which improvement of current leisure functioning is needed;
- To enable users to determine the impact of offered services on leisure functioning;

- To facilitate research on the structure of leisure to enable a better understanding of the value, purpose, and outcomes of leisure experiences (p.7).

The *Users Manual* for the LDB is available through Venture Publishing, Inc. (1640 Oxford Circle, State College, PA 16803).

Parker and Colleagues

Comprehensive Evaluation in Recreation Therapy Scale (CERT) is one of the more established assessment instruments. It was developed by Parker and his colleagues (1975) for therapists to apply when assessing clients in psychiatric settings. The CERT contains three areas of assessment: general, individual performance, and group performance. Under the general section are five items covering attendance, appearance, attitudes toward recreational therapy, coordination, and posture. The individual performance area has ten items dealing with response to therapist's structure one-to-one, decision-making ability, judgment ability, ability to form individual relationships, expression of hostility, performance of organized activities, performance in free activities, attention span, frustration tolerance level and strength/endurance. The group performance section also has ten items. It addresses: memory for group activities, response to group structure, leadership ability in groups, group interaction, handles conflict in group when indirectly involved, handles conflict in group when directly involved, competition in group, and attitude toward group decisions.

The scoring system for the CERT is a five-point scale for each item ranging from zero to four. Zero is used to represent no problematic behavior while four is used to indicate the most problematic behavior. Therefore, the higher the score, the more problematic is the client's behavior.

A second CERT has been developed for use with clients who have physical disabilities. It has eight clusters of items. These include: (1) gross muscular function, (2) fine movement, (3) locomotion, (4) motor skills, (5) sensory, (6) cognition, (7) communication and (8) behavior.

Both forms of the CERT are available from Idyll Arbor, Inc. (25119 SE 262nd Street, Ravensdale, WA 98051-9763).

Functional Assessment of Characteristics for Therapeutic Recreation (FACTR)

The FACTR is designed to identify client needs related to basic functional skills and behaviors used in leisure participation. It covers functional skills in three domains. These are the physical, cognitive and social/emotional domains. Under each are 11 items for a total of 33 items.

Under the physical domain are items concerning areas such as sight/vision, ambulation, coordination, and strength. The cognitive domain possesses items concerning areas such as short- and long-term memory, literacy, and math concepts. Examples of areas covered by items under the social/emotional domain are social interest, cooperation, competition and decision making. Following each item is a list of descriptive statements. Staff check the one that best describes the client being assessed. Space is provided to indicate if the behavior can be improved through therapeutic recreation interventions and if the behavior warrants the application of an intervention. The FACTR is available through Idyll Arbor, Inc. (25119 SE 262nd Street, Ravensdale, WA 98051-9763).

Howe (1984) has discussed that the actual selection of assessment instruments is based on the therapist's philosophy, education, and past experience, as well as those factors outlined by Dunn (1989) regarding the selection of instruments to be completed by clients (See Table 4-1). A major practical influence on instrument selection is, of course, the availability of the instruments and background information to support their use.

THE INTERVIEW METHOD

The therapeutic recreation specialist will generally attempt to conduct at least one interview with every new client. The interview usually has three purposes. First, the interview provides an opportunity to gain information from the client and to observe the client. Second, the therapeutic recreation specialist wishes to begin to develop a relationship, or gain rapport, with the client. Third, orientation to the program or programs available to the client may be provided. Additional information on the process of conducting interviews is contained in Chapter 6.

A prime purpose of the interview is, of course, to gather information regarding the client and to provide the client with an opportunity to begin to identify his or her needs and how these may be met. This may be accomplished by talking with the client and observing the client's condition and behavior. (Table 4-2 lists areas of information that may be sought during assessment interviews.)

The client's leisure behaviors and interests are regularly the focus of discussion during the interview. The therapeutic recreation specialist will likely ask the client about past leisure patterns, including the amount of time given to leisure, the activities in which he or she has participated, and who has taken part in recreation with the client. Additionally, an attempt is usually made to help the client identify recreational interests for possible future participation.

TABLE 4-2
SUGGESTED AREAS FOR INFORMATION SEEKING
DURING ASSESSMENT INTERVIEWS

---

1. Readiness for treatment or participation in recreation activities or leisure counseling.
2. Degree of rationality (for psychiatric and other appropriate clients).
3. Strength and number of relationships with others.
4. Resources for support (financial, psychological, personal).
5. Leisure-related problems.
6. Leisure values held.
7. Awareness of resources available for leisure.
8. Basic skills needed to develop leisure skills.
9. Client's leisure history.
10. Personal appearance, hygiene and other habits.
11. Other problem areas.

Source: Items drawn from Ferguson, D.D. 1983. Assessment interviewing techniques: A useful tool in developing individual program plans. *Therapeutic Recreation Journal*. 17(2), 16-22.

Open-Ended Questions and Leisure Interest Instruments

Common techniques to facilitate the interview are using a list of open-ended questions related to leisure patterns and using formal leisure interest instruments. Typically, the open-ended questions appear on an interview form with a brief space following each one in which the client's response may be recorded. Leisure interest instruments are normally in a checklist format so that the client may complete them with the help of a therapeutic recreation specialist, or the therapeutic recreation specialist may read the items to the client and check the appropriate place on the forms. Examples of open-ended questions appear in Appendix A: Open-Ended Questions. Long, Higgins and Brady (1988, p.52) have suggested "Open-Ended Questions for Adults" and "Open-Ended Questions for Older Adults" that are also included in Appendix A: Open-Ended Questions, (see p.198).

It is important that these or similar questions be used only to form a guideline for interviewing and not be strictly adhered to. Instead the interviewer should feel free to deviate from any set of questions in order to follow up on a client's statement or probe more deeply into a particular area.

Most agencies or institutions offering therapeutic recreation service will adopt or develop some type of leisure interest instrument appropriate for use with their clients. Some instruments, such as the Mirenda Leisure Interest Finder (Mirenda, 1973), ask the client to indicate how much they like or dislike particular activities. In addition to Mirenda's instrument, other tools available for use in assessing client's interests include the Self-Leisure Interest Profile (SLIP) (McDowell, 1974), Leisure Activities Blank (LAB) (McKechnie, n.d.; 1974), and the Avocational Activities Inventory (AAI) (Overs, 1970).

Whatever the approach, clients should be given the opportunity to express themselves in regard to their perceptions of strengths, weaknesses, and problems. Knowing how each client views himself or herself, the environment, and his or her place in that environment is necessary to understand completely the client's behavior. An attempt should be made to acquire this knowledge when occasions arise throughout the interview process.

Children and the Questioning Process

For children, traditional interview methods may not be appropriate. When feasible, the therapeutic recreation specialist may begin assessment procedures with an interview with each child's parents. Stanley and Kasson (n.d.) have produced materials to be used by those faced with the task of interviewing parents of children with disabilities. These materials contain a series of questions that may be directed toward the parents regarding their child's play and social patterns. Questions based on those posed by Stanley and Kasson appear as "Open-Ended Questions for Parents" in Appendix A: Open-Ended Questions, (see p.198).

Stanley and Kasson also provide a list of suggested questions that might be used when interviewing the child. "Open-Ended Questions for Children" that have been adapted from that list appear in Appendix A (see p. 198).

When interviewing children, conduct the interview in an area conducive to creating a relaxed, friendly environment. A play area may help create this atmosphere and has the added feature of allowing for possible observation of the child at play. Stanley and Kasson have suggested that the interviewer should make sure that various age-appropriate playthings are available so the child may play in a variety of modes during the interview. They go on to state that if the interviewer invites the child to play, this should always be done in a friendly and sincere manner so that the child is not given the impression of being tested.

For the shy child or the child who has difficulty with verbal expression, Stanley and Kasson propose the use of pictures illustrating children taking part in various play or recreation activities. The child can be asked to choose those that he or she likes or would enjoy exploring. With all clients, nonverbal language is often the best indicator of the client's true feelings. Clues provided by bodily movement, gestures, and posture can prove to be more revealing than verbal expression. Most people would agree that the child's smile is a good indicator that he or she likes something.

Relationship Development

A second purpose of the interview is to develop a relationship with the client. Developing rapport is not usually a major hurdle for the therapeutic recreation specialist, who is customarily seen by clients as a nonthreatening person. In highly clinical settings clients may feel particularly alienated by the surroundings and too frightened to approach the doctor or nurse. In such situations the unique role of the therapeutic recreation specialist often comes to the forefront. With the therapeutic recreation specialist clients usually feel that they can relax, "drop their guards," and "be themselves." In the clinical atmosphere a therapeutic recreation specialist may become a "professional friend," since he or she is viewed as someone who enters into a mutual participation with clients instead of as someone who does something to clients.

Orientation to the Program

The interview is sometimes also used to acquaint the client with the program or services provided by the therapeutic recreation service. Even though this orientation is often limited and necessarily brief, the interview allows the opportunity to inform the client of basic program offerings. The therapeutic recreation specialist must exercise judgment in determining how extensive an orientation is appropriate for the individual client. This may range from a few general statements regarding the availability of selected programs to a review of the complete therapeutic recreation offerings provided by the agency or institution.

Secondary Sources of Information

There are many sources from which to obtain the different types of information that you will find useful when working with your clients. A discussion of a few such sources follows.

Medical records include the results of the physician's examination report, along with information on the client's medical history, physical assessment, and diagnostic studies. Also contained in the medical record is the medical diagnosis, a prognosis, a plan for medical treatment, physician's orders, progress reports, and other relevant medical information.

In educational settings, *educational records* may be a basis for client assessment. According to Stephens (1976), assessment information for children with learning or behavioral disorders should include an assessment of academic skills, a determination of which sensory modes are most effective in learning, an evaluation of the level of social skills, and an appraisal of the child's reinforcement system. Other information that might be found in educational records includes educational diagnoses and teacher and physician reports.

Testing provides objective data about the client. Results from tests administered by psychologists or staff from other allied disciplines can be useful to therapeutic recreation assessment.

Much can be learned about the client and his or her relationships with others by *interviewing family or friends* who may possess knowledge about the client's past leisure interests and behaviors. Information may also be gained in regard to future expectations and anticipated resources for the client's leisure participation.

The *social history* is normally completed by the social worker. It contains information on where the client was born, raised, and educated, the client's home and family, past occupations, family income, recreational pursuits, and religious affiliation.

Progress notes written by various staff contain objective comments regarding the client's behaviors as they deviate from normal. Charting is commonly accomplished daily in treatment and rehabilitation facilities by staff members, including nursing services and activity therapy personnel.

Where *treatment teams* exist, the therapeutic recreation specialist will likely be an integral part of the team. In this capacity he or she will confer regularly with other staff, both within and outside of formal team meetings. The formal and informal sharing of information with other staff will provide information that may be applied in therapeutic recreation assessment.

A great deal may be learned by *visiting the client's home and community*. What are the social and recreational opportunities accessible to the client? What specific recreational outlets are evident in the home? Are parks, community centers, libraries, or other recreational facilities available in the client's neighborhood or community? Some treatment facilities maintain an up-to-date inventory of recreational programs and facilities available in the communities they serve.

ASSESSMENT INFORMATION

Initial Information

General information that the therapeutic recreation specialist might wish to have on hand as soon as possible would include:

- Client's full name, address, and telephone number;
- Sex, age, and marital or family status;
- Date admitted;
- Education completed;
- Language(s) spoken;
- Occupation;
- Leisure interests briefly noted;
- Limitations or precautions (e.g., physical restrictions, suicidal);
- Medications; and
- Why the client is seeking service.

In a clinically oriented facility it would also be appropriate to note the names of the client's physician, social worker, and primary therapist when recording initial assessment information. In a community-based program it would be advantageous to list with whom the client is living and who should be contacted in case of emergency. This ensures that the information is readily available when required.

Factors Affecting the Assessment Process

Beyond general information, exactly what assessment data should be collected by the therapeutic recreation specialist? The answer to this question will vary depending on the setting in which therapeutic recreation services are being delivered and the personal preferences and theoretical perspectives of the therapist. In the section that follows, I discuss settings and personal preferences and theoretical perspectives as they affect assessment and then conclude with observations that reveal my biases toward assessment.

Setting

Variables within the *setting* that affect assessment include the type of client being served and the prevailing treatment or rehabilitation orientation of the agency. Data collected on psychiatric clients will differ from those needed in physical rehabilitation centers or centers for persons with developmental disabilities. The age of the client will obviously play a role. Different developmental information will be needed about children than adolescent or geriatric populations. The overall model adopted by the agency will likely affect assessment as well. For instance, does a medical model prevail where other health professionals serve under the direction of a physician? Or, does an educational model apply where the program is centered around children's educational needs? Goals, and, therefore, assessment procedures, will differ markedly according to the prevailing orientation of the agency. In sum, the therapeutic recreation specialist will have to adapt assessment procedures to take into account the setting in which his or her program is located as well as the prevailing orientation of the particular agency.

Therapists' Preferences and Perspectives

Therapists will likely collect data using assessment procedures with which they are most familiar. Therefore, past training and experiences will affect assessment practices. Students need to be particularly aware of the biases toward various assessment approaches present in their university instructors and clinical supervisors. Personal theoretical perspectives held by therapists also affect choices in the types of assessment data collected.

For instance, psychiatric therapeutic recreation specialists who favor the psychodynamic approach are apt to explore tensions underlying disorders whereas those who are behaviorally orientated are likely to examine directly observable behavior (Ellis, 1987). Similarly, therapeutic recreation specialists who adopt the Leisure Ability Model are likely to focus assessment on independent leisure functioning while those following the Health Protection/Health Promotion Model are apt to be more concerned with issues related to health and wellness.

Holistic Approach

I believe in taking a holistic approach to assessment. A person is a unified entity. One part of a person affects another. Clients' physical problems almost always have a psychological component and a social impact. Psychological difficulties inevitably involve a physical response, and so on (Yura & Walsh, 1988). Therefore, the total person needs to be assessed, taking into account all the parts that come together to make each of us a unique individual. Complete assessment will also encompass the client's developmental level, a sometimes neglected area of therapeutic recreation assessment. It is important that the therapeutic recreation specialist has knowledge of human development throughout the life span and developmental theories so that he or she may complete a thorough assessment in order to identify developmental problems with which the client may need help.

Data gathered by the therapeutic recreation specialist deals largely with psychosocial aspects of the person (i.e., emotional, behavioral, mental, environmental and interactional processes) in an effort to identify past and current levels of functioning. Therapeutic recreation assessment may also involve the physical domain, depending on the client population being assessed. Even when physical assessment is accomplished by another health professional (e.g., physician or nurse), information from that assessment is integrated into the overall therapeutic recreation assessment.

Areas for therapeutic recreation assessment include:

1. Clients' general perceptions about their present health status, how they are dealing with their health problems, and how their health problems may be impacting on regular recreation and leisure patterns.
2. Sensory or motor impairments, cognitive deficits, limitations in activities of daily living, and any precautions (e.g., heart problems) are noted.
3. Leisure values, interests and pursuits are explored along with client attitudes toward participation in therapeutic recreation programs.

4. The developmental level of the client is appraised to determine developmental tasks or issues with which the client may be dealing.
5. Problems are explored in order to reveal needs (e.g. need to belong, for self-esteem) in order to establish a needs list.
6. Strengths (e.g., abilities, support from family and friends) are identified in order to build a strengths list.
7. Client expectations and goals are identified.

The total therapeutic recreation assessment provides the therapeutic recreation specialist with data to determine where the client is along the illness-wellness continuum so an appropriate therapeutic recreation intervention can be designed. The overall purpose of therapeutic recreation assessment is to gain information that will be useful in the provision of therapeutic recreation interventions (assuming it is determined therapeutic recreation intervention is needed), although therapeutic recreation assessment data are likely to be helpful to other members of the treatment team as well.

Computerized Assessment Procedures
    Mention needs to be made of the development of computerized assessment procedures that have emerged in therapeutic recreation. Dattilo and Mirenda (1987) have demonstrated a computerized assessment system that allows children with severe disabilities to indicate leisure preferences. Olsson, Shearer, and Halberg (1988) have successfully used scales from the Leisure Diagnostic Battery with clients having spinal cord injuries. These clients both self-administered and self-scored the scales using computer programs.
    Software for the Leisure Diagnostic Battery (LDB) is available commercially. The LDB Computer Software can be used in administering and scoring the scales contained in the instrument. According to the publisher, the 1994 version permits the storing of test scores and calculation of local norms. This software is available through Venture Publishing Inc. (1999 Cato Avenue, State College, PA 16801-3238). It is likely that the use of computerized assessment procedures in therapeutic recreation will grow rapidly in coming years and that many more assessment instruments will appear on the market.

CONCLUDING STATEMENT
ON ASSESSMENT

Adequate assessment is a prerequisite to the provision of individual program planning. However, assessment is a continuing process that does not end after the initial work-up on the client. Clients, like all human beings, are in a dynamic state of change, necessitating that ongoing assessment be conducted with every client.

By assembling all available assessment data, the therapeutic recreation specialist will gain an overall picture of the client from which a statement of problems and needs may be made. Both objective data from various sources and subjective information gained directly from the client are usually required in order to formulate a clear definition of the client's needs.

Objective information includes data from medical records, educational records, results of standardized testing, interviews with family and friends, social history, case recordings or progress notes, information from staff conferences or team meetings, community survey information, systematic observations, and general client information, including demographic data.

Subjective assessment data are gathered directly from the client. Narrow and Buschle (1987) write: *"Subjective data* include information which can be provided only by the patient (the subject), such as his (or her) perception of what he (or she) is experiencing or his (or her) attitudes, desires, feelings, and needs" (p.253).

Client assessment employing objective and subjective data allows the therapeutic recreation specialist to explore both client strengths and weaknesses and then identify client needs. Once the initial assessment procedures have been completed, the therapeutic recreation specialist has formed the basis for individual program planning and can move to the second step in the therapeutic recreation process, the development or planning phase.

WHAT CONSTITUTES THE PLANNING PHASE?

After identifying the client's needs, they are examined to determine priorities, goals are formulated, and a plan of action is determined. As a result of this planning phase, the client's personalized therapeutic recreation program emerges.

A four-step procedure may be conceptualized for the planning phase: (1) setting priorities following examination of the client's needs; (2) formulating goals or general objectives; (3) determining strategies or actions to meet the goals; and (4) selecting methods to assess progress made toward the goals.

Setting Priorities

After the client's needs have been identified, the therapeutic recreation specialist should examine them carefully to determine if therapeutic recreation services can be helpful and to set priorities for dealing with the client's needs. Marriner (1983) suggests that for nursing plans it should be determined which needs the client can handle independently, which require professional help and what kind of help is indicated, and which needs are most urgent. She goes on to recommend that Maslow's needs hierarchy may serve as a guide to setting priorities. It would seem that Marriner's thoughts translate well to therapeutic recreation planning.

Maslow, the father of humanistic psychology, pictured humans as constantly striving toward self-actualization, or self-fulfillment, the highest level of need. Maslow's (1970) hierarchy contains five basic needs. At the lower levels are physiological needs (thirst, hunger, etc.) and safety needs (security, protection from threat of danger, freedom from fear). Next are social needs (belongingness and love needs) and self-esteem or ego needs (for self-respect, status, recognition). At the top of **Maslow's hierarchy** is the need for self-actualization (or the need to fulfill one's potentials). (See Chapter 5 for a more thorough explanation of Maslow's hierarchy.)

Once a need has been met it no longer evokes behavior. Satisfaction of lower-level physiological and safety needs provides a firm foundation from which the individual can move forward toward developing his or her potentials. Generally, there are fewer problems with these lower-levels needs than with the other needs, although physiological and safety needs certainly must be considered by the therapeutic recreation specialist. One area where this is particularly true is in dealing with the client's need for psychological safety. Psychological safety may be a problem if the client does not feel free from the fear of being labeled or discriminated against because of a disability or illness (Ringness, 1975). Neurotic anxieties also may threaten psychological safety (Maslow, 1970).

Recreation and leisure offer natural means by which the client's higher-level needs for belonging, self-esteem, and self-actualization may be met. Through gratifying recreation experiences, clients gain acceptance, validate their personal worth, and grow toward their potentials.

Employing Maslow's hierarchy, the therapeutic recreation specialist can analyze the client's needs and set priorities for the needs that require professional help. The client should be included in this planning if possible, although physical or mental conditions may prohibit the client's participation at times. Nevertheless, it is desirable to seek this involvement as soon as the client is ready to join the therapeutic recreation specialist in the planning process. Like all of us, clients are apt to become more committed to plans that they have helped to form. In recreation, where self-direction and independent decision making are hallmarks, client involvement becomes paramount.

Formulating General Objectives or Goals

Having **general objectives** or **goals** provides us with a sound basis for selecting activities or programs appropriate for client needs. General objectives or goals also are useful to evaluation, since they represent clear statements of sought outcomes. General objectives or goals give direction to the therapeutic recreation specialist and allow others to know what outcomes are intended.

It should be clear that general objectives or goals reflect sought outcomes that are directed toward satisfaction of our clients' needs. Therefore, goals are written in terms of the clients' behavior and not the activities or processes of the therapeutic recreation specialist.

The critical nature of clearly formed goals in therapeutic recreation planning is reflected in a statement by O'Morrow and Reynolds (1989). They have written: "Without goals or objectives, the plan has lost its therapeutic value" (p.144).

General Objectives and Goals Defined

Goals and general objectives describe proposed changes in the individual client or in the client's environment. When goals or general objectives are spelled out, the client knows just what is expected and will likely feel a real sense of accomplishment when goals are achieved.

Within this discussion, the terms goal and general objective are used to mean the same thing. They may be used interchangeably. Goals or general objectives may be contrasted with specific objectives, which deal with very specific behaviors.

Goals or general objectives are written at the level of specificity needed to direct action but not be overly restricting. Gronlund (1985) speaks of general objectives in terms of *educational outcomes* and likens specific objectives to the *training level*. General objectives provide direction toward a general type or class of behavior, while specific objectives deal with a narrow band of behavior. In fact, one way to conceptualize the difference between a general objective and a specific objective is to think in terms of having to realize several specific objectives in order to reach one general objective. Therefore, we may evaluate progress toward general objectives by sampling from a number of specific objectives that fall under the general objective.

We usually begin our therapeutic recreation planning by goal formulation, or stating general objectives. Then we stipulate specific objectives that will enable the client to achieve the long-range goal. The specific objectives of learning to breathe correctly in water and to float in water, for example, move the child toward the more general objective of swimming using particular strokes.

Characteristics of Useful Objectives

The chief characteristic of the useful objective is that it states what the client will *do* or, said another way, it identifies the kind of *behavior* expected. The lone exception to this would be the objectives having to do with changing the client's environment instead of seeking changes from within the client. Even with environmental goals, however, we should remain cognizant of the need to be explicit. But, in the main, the therapeutic recreation specialist will be working with behavioral changes; therefore, the discussion of objectives will stress behavioral objectives. Some rules for stating objectives, drawn primarily from Gronlund (1985) follow:

- *Begin with an action verb* instead of with a phrase such as, "The client will. . . " By placing the verb first, the focus of the reader is placed on the sought outcome from the beginning.
- *State the objective to reflect client behavior* instead of mixing client objectives with process objectives you may have for yourself in helping the client to reach goal satisfaction.
- *Only state one terminal behavior per objective* instead of placing several behaviors in the same objective. This allows you to tell more easily if the objective has been fully realized. Putting two or more behaviors in the same objective is confusing and creates problems in evaluation when one behavior has been achieved, but the other has not.
- *Aim the objective at the appropriate level of specificity* instead of being too broad or too narrow. This is a difficult rule to follow, since it involves a certain amount of "feeling" or "intuitiveness" to stipulate objectives at the proper level. General objectives should be definable by stating specific types of behaviors that fall under them. Specific objectives should be relevant to a more general objective.

Condition and Criteria Stipulation

Mager (1962) has suggested that specific objectives may also stipulate conditions under which the behavior is to be performed and criteria for performance. To use Mager's (1962) terms, a condition is a "given" or a "restriction." These further define terminal behaviors by stipulating exact conditions imposed on the individual who is striving for the objective. Criteria, on the other hand, state a standard, or "how well" the individual is to perform.

Some brief examples may help clarify the concepts of criteria and conditions. Say you have a specific objective reading:

- Locate the show times for films playing at local theaters.

You could begin by imposing a condition of the source information. So the specific objective might now read:

- *Given a copy of the* Herald-Telephone *daily newspaper,* locate the show times for films playing at local theaters.

In addition to this given you might add another condition to the objective. This could be a restriction such as:

- *Without the help of the therapeutic recreation specialist,* and given a copy of the *Herald-Telephone* daily newspaper, locate the show times for films playing at local theaters.

If you really want to become specific about your objective, you might add a criteria. The objective might then read like this:

- Without the help of the therapeutic recreation specialist, and given a copy of the *Herald-Telephone* daily newspaper, locate the show times for films playing at local theaters *within a 3-minute period of time.*

By now you may be thinking, "Come on, let's not overdo it." Perhaps the example is overstated, perhaps not. Just how detailed should you be in writing specific objectives? Mager (1962) answered the question when stating the following:

> You should be detailed enough to be sure the target behavior would be recognized by another competent person, and detailed enough so that other possible behaviors would not be mistaken for the desired behavior. You should be detailed enough, in other words, so that others understand your intent as you understand it (p.26).

Stating Objectives

Mager's (1962) *Preparing Instructional Objectives* is perhaps the best-known source for writing behavioral objectives. The book uses an easy-to-follow programmed learning format. It is an excellent basic reference to aid in the forming of specific objectives. Gronlund (1985) offers a well-written explanation of general and specific objectives. His chapter on a three-part taxonomy covering the cognitive, affective, and psychomotor domains clearly explains a useful classification system and offers examples of verbs that may be employed in writing objectives. For those with particular interest in the psychomotor domain, Harrow's (1972) book, *A Taxonomy of the Psychomotor Domain*, should prove helpful.

Determining Strategies and Actions

The individual program plan is a written document stating what the client and therapeutic recreation specialist intend to accomplish. The plan flows from the client's previously established goals set. This goals set must fit, of course, into any overall client plan and should coincide with the general objectives of the agency or institution. Furthermore, the goals should be realistic and attainable so that the client is not destined to failure. Goals may be classed as immediate or long range in order to direct the goal achievement process and more aptly assure feelings of success on the part of both the client and staff.

Many settings employ goal-directed planning, but the terms used to describe the individual program plan vary. In clinical facilities the individual program plan is usually referred to as a "treatment plan." The term "care plan" is often applied in long-range care facilities such as nursing homes and continued care centers. The term "Individualized Education Program" (IEP) has come to be commonly employed in educational settings such as public schools and residential schools for special populations.

The exact nature of individual program plans will necessarily differ from setting to setting. Common elements that are likely to transcend all plans regardless of setting are:

- An indication of the client's problems and needs, in order to formulate a **needs list** (Problems represent obstacles to meeting needs. Therefore, the identification of problems leads to needs).
- An identification of client strengths (e.g., abilities, family support) to formulate a **strengths list**.
- A prioritized **goals set** appropriate to guide the delivery of therapeutic recreation services.
- A listing of **specific objectives** for each goal.
- A **plan** of activities or programs indicated for participation by the client, approaches to be utilized by staff, and the proper environment in which to facilitate change.
- A brief description of procedures by which client progress will be periodically evaluated, or a plan for **evaluation**.

The *needs list* will lead directly to the development of the *goals set* because goals are derived out of client needs. The *strengths list* will be useful in the determination of the *plan* of activities or programs because therapeutic recreation interventions use client strengths to reach specific outcomes through the use of therapeutically designed programs. *Specific objectives* will flow directly out of the *goals* because specific behavioral objectives break down each goal into observable, measurable parts. The *evaluation* plan will provide information regarding the success of the planned interventions toward reaching treatment goals.

By constructing a plan containing these six elements, the client will have an individualized program plan based on sought behavioral changes, the needs and strengths of the client, and the anticipated impact of the client, environment and staff on behavioral change. The strategies formulated for the plan should meet the established goals and consider each client's unique background, psychological makeup, and personal needs and expectations. By doing so, each properly prepared plan will be distinctive and personalized. An example of a personalized program plan follows.

THE CASE OF MILLER L. BUSH

An example of an individual program plan appears in Figure 4-4. This is based loosely on a case study that appeared in Lamson (1986). The case involved a single male in his mid-twenties who became severely depressed after his girlfriend broke up with him. This psychologically threatening event was taken by the client as proof of his worthlessness and his inadequacy as a male. For those who might wonder, Lamson reported that the patient was able to overcome his depression, feel good about himself, and ultimately terminate treatment.

FIGURE 4-4
INDIVIDUAL PROGRAM PLAN

Data Line:
Who:

Miller L. Bush

Why admitted:

Complaints of severe depression

Subjective:

States he lacks motivation to participate in leisure activity or work. Feels tired. Wishes to have friends but does not know how. Says no one would want him for a friend. Claims he cannot sustain a conversation. Does not feel adequate in traditional male roles—"failure" in relationship with girlfriend, he says, confirms inadequacy. Likes sports, especially tennis and swimming. Wishes to continue them when he leaves the hospital.

Objective:

Extreme withdrawal from family and friends. Became depressed when he and his girlfriend broke up. Observed on the admitting ward to gain satisfaction from watching tennis on TV. Until recently, very active person. On college tennis and swim teams. Likes unit therapeutic recreation specialist.

Assessment:

Very reserved. Appears to want to talk with others but is not comfortable in doing so. Is not confident. Lacks positive self-esteem. Is bright as evidenced in several brief conversations with the therapeutic recreation specialist, but holds back information as if frightened to reveal too much of himself.

Strengths:
- Has athletic abilities, particularly in tennis and swimming.
- Likes therapeutic recreational specialist.

Needs:
1. To interact with others through verbal and nonverbal means.
2. To take part in some type of gratifying physical activity with others in order to begin working toward meeting esteem needs.

Goals:
1. Increases interaction with others.
2. Participates in physical activity.

Specific Objectives:
1.
   a. Greets the therapeutic recreation specialist.
   b. Answers questions posed by others.
   c. Uses nonverbal means of responding to others.
   d. Initiates conversations with others.
2.
   a. Takes walks around grounds in free time.
   b. Rallys tennis ball with therapeutic recreational specialist.
   c. Works out at gym with therapeutic recreation specialist.
   d. Swims at the hospital pool during ward swim.
   e. Plays co-rec volleyball on ward unit when encouraged by the therapeutic recreation specialist.

FIGURE 4-4 CONT.

Plans:
- Do not place on full activity schedule at this time.
- To participate in regular ward activities (swimming, volleyball) and in daily tennis or gym workout with the therapeutic recreation specialist.
- Don't demand the patient to interact with you but be pleasant; allow opportunities for interactions and encourage him when he does interact.
- Strive to gradually increase the length of interactions.
- Give approval for active participation in physical activity, praising his successes in an appropriate manner.

Evaluation:
- To discuss and reevaluate in team meeting at the end of the week.
- Keep daily progress notes of behavior on ward and in one-on-one activities.

October 16, 1997	David R. Austin, CTRS
(date)	(signature)

Obviously, the individualized program plan (IPP) for Mr. Bush is an initial IPP. The client has not been given a full activity schedule but will take part in activities involving his unit and will participate in daily one-on-one sessions with the therapeutic recreation specialist. These types of activities are appropriate for an individual at the client's place on the illness-wellness continuum. That is, these prescribed activities suit the needs of an individual who is clinically depressed and needs to be activated. Following evaluation of Mr. Bush's progress, another IPP will be constructed as he advances along the illness-wellness continuum.

A final comment on Mr. Bush's IPP needs to be made in regard to the second goal, "Participates in physical activity." At first, this statement may appear to be simply a means to an end, or a process completed in order to reach a goal, and, therefore, not qualify as a goal. It is likely that in later IPPs participation in specific physical activities may very well become a part of the planning section and not a goal. Initially, however, it is a meritorious goal to just get the client active with the anticipation that he will gain gratification from his participation and decrease his feelings of depression. To reduce confusion over the question of "means or end," an alternative could be to have the goal read, "Exhibits gratification from physical activity." Some, however, might argue that the client is not yet ready to exhibit gratification but simply needs to become activated. The point to this discussion is not to debate this particular example but to bring out the fact that goals (and the specific objectives that follow them) need to relate to sought ends or outcomes and not to the processes involved in achieving them (which should be represented in the planning section of the IPP).

Activity Analysis

Once goals and objectives have been specified in the individual program plan, the therapeutic recreation specialist must select activities to apply in the intervention process. The activities utilized in intervention must be thoroughly understood in order to help assure optimal therapeutic benefit for the client. The name given the procedure for systematically achieving a precise and complete understanding of activities is activity analysis. Peterson (1976) has defined **activity analysis** as follows.

> Activity analysis is a process which involves the systematic application of selected sets of constructs and variables to breakdown and examine a given activity to determine the behavioral requirements inherent for successful participation.

Activity analysis permits the practitioner to break down activities into their component parts. Thus a total comprehension of a given activity is acquired so that the activity may be properly utilized to meet the goals and objectives of the individual program plan.

Non-Adapted Activities

In some instances the activity will be employed "as is." That is, no alterations will be required in order for clients to gain maximum benefit from participation. For example, a dance for clients would be planned and conducted in much the same way as a dance for any group. At other times, the therapeutic recreation specialist may manipulate the activity to bring about therapeutic intents. In so doing opportunities are created for the activity to contribute directly toward sought behavioral objectives. For example, cooperation might be emphasized in a particular sports activity in order to reinforce cooperative behaviors on the part of a certain client or clients.

Adapted Activities

In still other cases, activities will need to be adapted or modified to accommodate clients with limitations. Adaptive equipment may be utilized, such as audible softballs for visually impaired clients or a handle grip bowling ball for those who have difficulty gripping. Games may be modified by reducing the dimensions of the playing area, simplifying rules, or through other similar means. Whatever the modification, it is important that the therapeutic recreation specialist has a detailed understanding of the activity so that artificial or unnecessary modifications are not made. As a general principle, the best modification is the least modification.

Behavioral Domains

Peterson and Gunn (1984) have suggested that activity analysis should include the three behavioral domains (i.e., psychomotor, cognitive, affective) as well as social or interactional skills. It is the task of the therapeutic recreation specialist to examine the demands placed on participants by the activity in regard to specificities. Each of the four components must be appraised to determine what behaviors and skills are required by those who take part in the activity. Examples of aspects for possible consideration follow under each of the four major components.

Psychomotor (physical) Domain:
- Is the full body involved or only part of the body?
- What types of manipulative movements are required (throwing, hitting, catching, kicking, bouncing, pulling, pushing, grasping, lifting)?

- What types of locomotor movements are required (crawling, walking, running, climbing, jumping, hopping, rolling, skipping)?
- What kinds of non-locomotor movements are required (twisting, turning, stretching, extending, bending, swinging, hanging, landing)?
- What level of exertion is required?
- What degree of fitness is necessary?
- Is a high level of skill development required (e.g., hand-eye coordination, balance)?
- Is rhythm required?
- How much endurance is necessary?
- How much repetitiveness in movement is required?
- What sensory demands are made?

Cognitive (intellectual) Domain:
- Is the level of complexity appropriate for the clients?
- Is there a high degree of repetitiveness in the activity?
- Are academic skills required (e.g., spelling, reading, or math)?
- How much recall (i.e., memory) is involved? For example, are there many rules to remember?
- What level of concentration is needed?
- What level of analysis (i.e., breaking down material) and synthesis (i.e., putting parts together) is required?
- What level of verbal skill is needed?
- Are participants called on to think quickly and make rapid decisions?
- Is abstract thinking called for?

Affective (psychological) Domain:
- Does the activity release tension (stress)?
- Does the activity allow the client to communicate feelings?
- Does the activity generally lead to fun?
- To what degree is it possible to display creativity?
- Does frustration commonly arise from participation?
- How much control (over the environment) can the client experience?
- Does the activity have potential for enhancement of self-esteem?

- Is teamwork emphasized? Sharing? Helping others?
- Is self-discipline necessary? Listening skills?
- Are democratic processes followed?
- Is the activity stimulating? Exciting?
- Are values apparent in the activity? If so, what values?

Social (interactional) Skills:
- Is cooperation emphasized? Competition?
- Do structures (rules) reinforce prosocial behavior?
- Is the activity individual? Small-group oriented?
- How many persons may participate?
- How much leadership must be provided?
- How structured is the activity?
- May all ages take part? All sizes?
- Are traditional sex roles emphasized?
- What types of interaction patterns occur?
- What amount of initiative is required?
- Is a high level of interaction called for?
- Is verbal communication necessary?
- Does the space dictate being close to others? Physically touching?

The therapeutic recreation specialist will also necessarily need to analyze activities for other aspects in addition to social skills and the psychomotor, cognitive, and affective domains. Elements for consideration, drawn primarily from the classic work of Fidler and Fidler (1954), and Lamport, Coffey, and Hersch's (1993) *Activity Analysis Handbook*, include the following aspects.

Several question for assessing an activity's *adaptability* and *variability* follow.

- How much time is required for participation?
- Does the activity have a sequence of steps to complete it? If so, what is the time required to complete each step?
- Is the activity adaptable to various chronological and mental age levels? To various educational levels?
- How much is speed emphasized in completing tasks within the activity and to what degree can this be controlled?

- How much variety is possible in selection of tasks, or projects within an activity (e.g., how many types and levels of leather-tooling projects would be available)?

Asking the following questions can help determine an activity's *usefulness.*

- Is cost of the activity within the means of clients?
- Will materials or supplies be available to clients?
- Does the activity have any carry-over value in terms of participating in it outside of the clinical setting?
- Do products made have any useful value to clients (i.e., to use themselves or give as gifts)?

Answers to these questions may help determine whether an activity is *practical.*

- What are the space and environmental requirements for the activity (e.g., size of room or outdoor space needed, requirements for light, equipment readily adjusted to the needs of clients)?
- Is the activity practical for bed patients when factors such as noise and equipment are considered?
- Is the activity too expensive for the agency in terms of equipment and supplies?
- How much staffing is required to conduct the activity?
- Are there precautions that need to be taken?
- When would the activity be contraindicated for particular types of clients?

A word of caution is in order here. The therapeutic recreation specialist must remember that for the individual client an activity is *not* an activity is *not* an activity. It is the individual's particular approach to the activity that defines his or her experience. *How* the client takes part in the activity has a primary impact on the experience. For example, those who are hard driven and competitive will approach an activity very differently from persons who have more relaxed dispositions.

Therefore, it is not entirely the activity itself but also the way someone approaches the activity that affects the experience. The therapeutic recreation specialist must be aware that although understanding behavioral requirements of the activity is important, employing activities with clients is a complex task that should not be started on a simplistic level in which prescribed outcomes are expected by having clients participate in a given activity.

Progress Assessment

It was previously mentioned that the last step in the planning process is to determine methods of assessing client progress. In the case of Mr. Bush, assessment took the form of progress notes and discussion of his progress after a week. Mr. Bush's program plan was an initial, preliminary effort to direct early stages of the helping process. In long-term care, there are likely to be three actual stages in planning:

1.   The initial plan to deal with essential interventions while full assessment is being completed.
2.   The total assessment plan based on a complete assessment utilizing the techniques mentioned earlier in this chapter and from which the major intervention strategies are evolved.
3.   The revised plan based on new data that leads to altered actions either to bring about revisions in unproductive change strategies or meet newly identified needs.

Therefore, each client may have several program plans developed as a result of the ongoing assessment process.

THE IMPLEMENTATION PHASE

Implementation is the actual provision of the program. In implementation the strategies developed in the planning phase are employed. Perhaps the most important item to be considered in the implementation of the individual program plan is consistency. A well-formed plan allows all involved to strive for similar goals following agreed-on approaches. Such planning also contributes to the continuity of care provided by establishing short-term, intermediate, and long-term goals.

Often an interdisciplinary team effort will be utilized in implementing the plan. In other instances the plan will be carried out by one or more therapeutic recreation specialists. The setting and needs of the client dictate the particular procedures to be pursued. In any case, it is necessary to determine who has the authority and responsibility for coordinating the client's activities. Without clear delineation as to who is in control of the plan, problems will likely arise, since much coordination is necessary in maintaining client plans.

Usually some type of written communication is sent to all appropriate staff members informing them of the individual program plan to be implemented. Additionally, in settings such as hospitals and residential centers where clients are in various types of activities throughout the day (therapeutic recreation, psychotherapy, physical therapy, etc.), an activity schedule is often provided for each client. This schedule usually lists the days of the week and the hours of each day so that the activities planned for the client may be recorded. Written communications, such as the individual program plan and activity schedule, provide sources of reference and serve as reminders of the client's program for all staff. By following a systematic routine and using written communication, misunderstandings are avoided and consistency is promoted in the carrying out of the program plan.

In some modern facilities, client information is placed on a computer so that a clerk can call up data desired by staff on a particular client. This technological innovation allows changes to be made easily in the client's day-to-day activity schedule. The problem of retrieving and reissuing typewritten copies of client schedules is eradicated, thus eliminating a major practical difficulty in making revisions in schedules. It is anticipated that the computer will continue to play a growing role in the implementation phase as time goes on.

Most departments administering therapeutic recreation programs have written descriptions that detail each treatment or rehabilitation program offered. Sometimes these are referred to as protocols. The therapeutic recreation specialist who is conducting a program should make sure he or she is familiar with the information detailing the program and that his or her actions are consistent with it. The therapeutic recreation specialist should likewise be certain his or her approach with the client is consistent with the approach directed by the IPP. Finally, the therapeutic recreation specialist implementing a client program needs to continually assess the results of the program on clients, as well as the reactions of clients to the program. This data provides information for the final phase of the therapeutic recreation process, evaluation.

THE EVALUATION PHASE

Evaluation is the final step in the therapeutic recreation process. Through evaluation, the effectiveness of the client's program is examined.

In therapeutic recreation we are concerned with individual client evaluation and program evaluation. Both are important, and each is difficult to separate from the other, since programs are the vehicles by which we in therapeutic recreation help individual clients to meet problems or needs. In individual client evaluation the client is central to our purpose. In program evaluation we target our concern on the program itself. In either case, distinctions may be conceived to be somewhat arbitrary and difficult to maintain.

For the purpose of this chapter, however, the focus will remain with the individual client. Therefore, discussion will center on completing client evaluation.

Individual client evaluation is closely tied to the planning process because part of the planning process is determining methods to assess client progress. The actual carrying out of these methods is client evaluation. In the case of Mr. Bush, progress notes and staff discussion served as means to evaluation.

The approach taken in Mr. Bush's case is very representative of the general approach taken to client evaluation. Although some readers may be concerned about the lack of "rigor" provided by this general approach, they should not be. Staff should not limit their analysis only to "measurable" items. Staff can and should utilize naturalistic observations, observations of behaviors related to specific objectives (i.e., specific goal observation), and subjective feelings. Nevertheless, the emerging therapeutic recreation specialist will be more apt to rely on more quantitative means, such as norm-referenced tests and time-interval observations, since it requires some experience to develop observational skills and to learn to place trust in feelings.

In addition to the observational methods that have been mentioned, other methods used in initial client assessment are appropriate for evaluation. For example, the interview method offers an opportunity for clients to respond retrospectively as to how they perceive themselves after participation in prescribed activities compared to their perceptions prior to beginning the program. Secondary sources of information offer another means for client evaluation. For instance, pretest and posttest scores on standardized tests given by a psychologist may be contrasted to measure gains on a variable such as self-esteem. Family and friends may be interviewed following a home visit by a hospitalized client. Information may be gained from other staff at a team meeting, or progress notes may be reviewed.

If several different sources of information agree on the progress of the client, it can be said that congruence exists among them. Generally, the therapeutic recreation specialist should attempt to structure evaluation procedures to retrieve data from several independent sources to see if the data stand up to the test of congruence (i.e., the information is consistent).

Of course, all methods of client evaluation exist to determine if the hypothesized results transpired as a consequence of whatever therapeutic recreation intervention was applied. In other words, evaluation answers the question, "Were sought outcomes achieved as a result of the program?" If evaluation is not completed, the therapeutic recreation specialist has no basis on which to judge the effectiveness of the program in bringing about the objectives stated in the client's individual program plan.

It is essential to involve clients in the process of evaluation. Just as clients should be involved in the prior phases of the therapeutic recreation process, they should be involved to the fullest extent of their capabilities in evaluation. By engaging in evaluation, clients can help staff to judge the effectiveness of the program in reaching sought outcomes.

SUMMARY

The therapeutic recreation process has commonly been associated with highly clinical programs; however, its application goes far beyond the bounds of the clinical setting. The therapeutic recreation process of assessment, planning, implementation, and evaluation can be applied in any setting in which goal-directed programs are desired. Thus the therapeutic recreation process is not restricted to hospitals or rehabilitation or treatment centers. The systematic process outlined in this chapter can guide therapeutic recreation specialists who practice professionally in community-based programs, corrections facilities, nursing homes, and all other facilities where recreation is used with therapeutic intent. Conversely, if this process is not followed, therapeutic recreation service is not being provided, no matter what group is being served. The simple provision of recreation service for individuals from special population groups does not constitute in itself the delivery of therapeutic recreation service. Recreation programs for special populations that do not utilize the therapeutic recreation process should make no claims on the term "therapeutic recreation." They are better called special recreation programs.

READING COMPREHENSION QUESTIONS

1.   What is the humanistic perspective? Is it reflected in therapeutic recreation?
2.   Describe the concept of high-level wellness.
3.   Construct and interpret a continuum of service for therapeutic recreation.
4.   Outline and describe briefly the phases in the therapeutic recreation process.
5.   What is the purpose of therapeutic recreation assessment?
6.   List methods the therapeutic recreation specialist might use in completing client assessment.
7.   Would you approach an interview with a child in the same way as with an adult? If not, how might these interviews differ?
8.   What secondary sources are used in assessment?
9.   What basic general information might the therapeutic recreation specialist wish to gain on the client as soon as possible?
10.   What is objective assessment data? Subjective data?
11.   What are four steps in the planning phase?

12. How may Maslow's needs hierarchy be used to assist in setting priorities?
13. How do goals, or general objectives, differ from specific objectives?
14. Why formulate goals? Specific objectives?
15. Outline rules useful in stating objectives.
16. Clarify what Mager means by conditions and criteria as applied to specific objectives.
17. What common elements are likely to be found in individual (personalized) program plans?
18. Why is it important that each client's individual program plan is personalized?
19. Do you agree with the personalized program plan developed for Mr. Bush? Why or why not?
20. Can you apply activity analysis to a recreation activity of your choosing?
21. What are the three stages of planning described by Burgess?
22. Outline considerations for the implementation phase.
23. With what types of evaluation are we concerned in therapeutic recreation?
24. Should the client be involved in decision making during the therapeutic recreation process? Why or why not?
25. Do you agree with the distinction made between "therapeutic recreation" and "special recreation?"

APPENDIX A: OPEN-ENDED QUESTIONS

Open-Ended Questions for Adults

- Do you think leisure is important?
- How much leisure time do you have?
- Do you like the balance between your work and recreation?
- What kinds of things do you do for fun in your spare time?
- What are some of your hobbies?
- What would you like to do?
- Do you own any recreational equipment such as golf clubs, a tennis racket, or canoe?
- Do you watch television, and, if so, what programs do you watch?
- What things do you do with your family (spouse, children)?
- With whom do you take part in recreation?
- When do you usually participate in recreation?
- Would you rather do things with others or alone?
- Of the things you do in your free time, which do you like best?
- Do you like outdoor activities such as fishing or camping?
- Do you take vacations and, if so, what do you usually do on vacation?
- What would be your ideal vacation?
- Do you experience any problems with the expense involved in your recreation participation?
- Are there any other reasons for not participating in leisure activities?

Open-Ended Questions for Older Adults

- Are you retired? (Consider adjustment, future plans, time spent in leisure/pleasurable activities.)
- Do you feel safe going out during the day, evening? Why or why not?
- Is there someone to go with?
- Do you have your own transportation; if not, what means do you have?
- Do you belong to retirement or senior groups? (Consider political activity, veterans' organizations, volunteer work.)

- Do you use a community or senior citizen center?
- How do you relax and unwind?
- Have your leisure activities changed?

Open-Ended Questions for Parents

- What kinds of things does (child's name) do after school? On the weekends?
- Who does (child's name) play with? Other children? Parents? By himself or herself?
- If (child's name) does play with other children in the neighborhood, do they invite him or her to play?
- Does (child's name) indicate a preference for certain activities, such as sports, art, or music?
- What recreation equipment does (child's name) have?
- What sorts of recreation equipment or toys does (child's name) like to buy?
- Does (child's name) get excited easily or is he or she calm and easygoing?
- Does (child's name) like to try new things?
- Does (child's name) stick to projects or give up easily?
- Does (child's name) tend to be a self-starter or does he or she rely on others to get things started?
- Is (child's name) outgoing or shy? Can you give examples of this behavior?
- Does (child's name) enjoy helping around the house?
- Does (child's name) like to make decisions?

Open-Ended Questions for Children

- What sorts of things does your family do together for fun?
- What sort of hobby would you like to learn?
- Tell me the best birthday or Christmas present you ever got. What made it so good?
- What things do you do after school? On the weekend? With whom do you play?
- Did you like your summer vacation? What was good about it?
- What are your three favorite things to do?
- If you get an allowance, what do you spend it on?

Chapter Five

HELPING OTHERS

CHAPTER PURPOSE

Professional helping relationships have much in common with social relationships. Nonetheless, there are distinctions between helping as a professional and helping as a friend. To be an effective helping professional requires certain characteristics. One of these is possessing self-awareness. This chapter will clarify the role of the professional helper and will discuss characteristics of professional helpers with particular attention to the development of self-awareness. The chapter also contains information on professional ethics and concludes with a discussion of burnout as a problem for professional helpers.

KEY TERMS

- Self-awareness
- Physiological needs
- Love and belonging needs
- Self-actualization
- Value-free professional
- Client autonomy
- Privacy
- Professional competence
- Multiculturalism
- Self-concept
- Safety needs
- Self-esteem need
- Metaneed
- Professional ethics
- Confidentiality
- Socio-sexual relation
- Burnout

OBJECTIVES

- Comprehend the nature of a professional helping relationship.
- Appreciate the qualities or characteristics necessary for those who desire to be effective professional helpers.
- Recognize characteristics that should be possessed by therapeutic recreational specialists in order to practice as helping professionals.
- Appreciate the necessity for therapeutic recreation specialists to increase and refine their level of self-awareness.
- Analyze self-conceptualizations.
- Analyze fundamental personal needs.
- Recognize how values help to define behaviors.
- Recognize some of your own values.
- Evaluate basic philosophical beliefs for practice as a therapeutic recreation specialist.
- Know issues related to professional ethics in therapeutic recreation.
- Understand burnout as a problem for helping professionals.

PROFESSIONAL HELPING

One of the most widely read books within the clinical psychology and psychiatric communities has been Schofield's (1964) *Psychotherapy: The Purchase of Friendship*. In this book, the author likened the role of some clinical psychologists, psychiatrists, and psychiatric social workers to that of a "professional friend." Schofield stated that the long-term relationships often provided to clients by these professionals were simply substitute friendships for those in need of someone to talk to about problems and concerns.

Helping relationships do share similarities with friendships; despite these similarities, however, they do differ. With friends we are regularly giving of ourselves, and we, in turn, are helped by our friends. There is mutuality in the relationship. There is a norm of reciprocity at work. If we find ourselves constantly giving and never receiving, in all likelihood we will end the relationship; and, in such cases, we may even claim we have been taken advantage of.

Professional helping relationships differ from social relationships in that the primary focus is always on one person: the client. The client has come for professional help with no intent of reciprocating. The mutuality existing in friendships is not present in the professional helping relationship because those involved have different roles. One role is to give help (the helper), and the other is to receive help (the client). The fundamental reality that the relationship exists to meet the needs of the client, not the helper, is basic to maintaining a healthy helping relationship (Brill, 1995).

This, of course, is not to say professional helpers, including therapeutic recreation specialists, are not human. Helping others certainly does meet very real human needs. Through helping we gain satisfaction in seeing others succeed and we feel needed. Perhaps helping professionals need clients as much as clients need them; however, help is given by the helping professional without the expectation of personal gain. Mayeroff (1971) has presented the concept of helping in an insightful work titled *On Caring*, in which Mayeroff states: "To care for another person, in the most significant sense, is to help him grow and actualize himself. . . . Caring is the antithesis of simply using the other person to satisfy one's own needs" (p. 1). Through helping others we help ourselves. We fulfill, or actualize, ourselves through caring for others.

THE AIM OF HELPING RELATIONSHIPS

The helping relationship is, as stated previously, directed toward maximizing the client's growth potential and preventing or relieving problems. Helping is *not* resolving problems or handling crises *for* the client. Instead, in a helping relationship we *assist* the client to meet pressing needs and then further, in preparation for the future. Therefore, the ultimate goal of the helping relationship is to facilitate growth leading to independence and self-sufficiency.

NEEDED PROFESSIONAL CHARACTERISTICS

What characteristics should the effective helper possess? Many answers have been given to this question. Eubanks (1976, pp. 187-189) has listed the following as core elements in the helping relationship.

- *Awareness.* Helpers should understand their own strengths, limitations, and needs as well as those of their clients.
- *Honesty.* There should be no front or facade put up by the helper.
- *Acceptance.* Helpers should show willing acceptance of the client by expressing trust and a caring attitude.
- *Freedom.* The helper must be able to allow the client to grow.

Carl Rogers has had a significant impact on the helping professionals who have followed him. In fact, the triad of elements originally stipulated by Rogers (1961, pp. 61-62) are reflected in all subsequent lists. His three elements are:

- *Congruence (Genuineness).* Helpers are themselves. They do not put up a false front or facade.
- *Unconditional Positive Regard.* A warm, positive, accepting attitude is displayed by the helper. The helper prizes the client as a person.
- *Empathetic Understanding.* Helpers experience an accurate understanding of the client's private world.

Okun (1992, pp. 34-40) has provided a practical list of helping characteristics. Her list includes the following qualities.

- *Self-awareness.* Helpers who possess self-awareness have a basis for helping others in the development of self-awareness.
- *Honesty.* A crucial quality for helpers is to express themselves honestly and to develop trust.
- *Congruence.* Helpers who have congruence between their values and beliefs and their style of communication are seen as more credible and as more potent models.
- *Communication Skills.* Helpers' behaviors involve the ability to communicate observations, feelings, and beliefs.

- *Knowledge.* Helpers know and interpret theories on which effective helping is based.
- *Ethical Integrity.* Helpers' behaviors are responsible, moral and ethical.

Characteristics of effective helpers have been portrayed by Cormier and Cormier (1991, pp. 11-15) to be:

- *Intellectual Competence.* Helpers need intelligence to learn the skill required of helping professionals and, once in the field, to search for data in order to make informed decisions about client treatment and progress.
- *Energy.* Helpers have the energy to meet both emotional and physical demands made on them.
- *Flexibility.* Helpers are flexible so they can adapt methods and technologies to meet the needs of individual clients.
- *Support.* Helpers are supportive of clients.
- *Good Will.* Helpers have positive motives for helping clients and behave in ethical and responsible ways with clients.
- *Self-Awareness.* Helpers are aware of personal feelings and attitudes as well as strengths and limitations.
- *Competence.* Helpers need to possess feelings of personal competence and adequacy.
- *Power.* Helpers must be comfortable with issues of power and control.
- *Intimacy.* Helpers need to have resolved their intimacy needs so they do not fear rejection or feel threatened by closeness.

THERAPEUTIC RECREATION HELPING

It can be seen from the lists of characteristics that the helper's self-awareness and ability to communicate are overriding themes. Effective helpers also need to possess more than good intentions. Again, Okun (1992) and Eisenberg and Patterson (1977) state that a knowledge base is a prime quality for a helping professional. Therapeutic recreation specialists additionally need to project a strong belief in recreation and leisure experiences and the values inherent in these experiences. The following are proposed as characteristics of the effective therapeutic recreation specialist:

- *Self-Awareness.* Therapeutic recreation specialists must know themselves; they must have a developed sense of self.
- *Ability to Communicate.* The ability to communicate effectively is basic to the helping process.
- *Knowledge Base.* Therapeutic recreation specialists must possess special knowledge in therapeutic recreation to be effective.
- *Strong Belief in Recreation and Leisure Experiences.* Therapeutic recreation specialists prize the positive consequences to be gained through meaningful recreation and leisure experiences.

These characteristics are a working list and so are not intended to be complete. However, these elements are, I believe, the *sin qua non* of the therapeutic recreation helping relationship.

SELF-AWARENESS

Therapeutic recreation specialists should pursue **self-awareness** from a personal viewpoint and from a professional one. Therapeutic recreation specialists must know themselves and feel reasonably satisfied with themselves as persons before entering into fully effective helping relationships.

Concern About Self

In a curriculum study completed at Indiana University (Austin & Binkley, 1977), practitioners were asked to rate competencies needed for practice as a master's degree-prepared therapeutic recreation specialist. "To increase and refine self-knowledge" was one of the highest-rated competencies. It is logical that practitioners would rate this competency high because we must know ourselves in order to help others. If we are overly concerned about ourselves and our personal needs, we are apt to have a difficult time helping others. Chapman and Chapman (1975) have reported that beginning helping professionals are often concerned first about themselves and second about the client. Such preoccupation with the self is a part of the natural evolution in becoming an effective helping professional.

Knowing ourselves helps us to understand the client more quickly. Having a personal experience with any problem enables us to identify and relate more readily to similar problems in clients. This, in part, is the logic behind having those who have had drinking problems work with individuals diagnosed with alcoholism. By being aware of our personal value system, we can also monitor ourselves to make a conscious attempt not to force our values on our clients. Finally, professionals are also people and, like clients, have strengths and weaknesses. Knowing ourselves helps us to realize when we reach the limits of our helping abilities (Chapman & Chapman, 1975).

Introspection and Interpersonal Communication

Within the therapeutic recreation literature little mention has been made of the need to know ourselves or how to go about the critical task of gaining self-awareness. There are various ways to achieve self-knowledge. Brill (1995) has suggested we can get to know ourselves in two general ways: introspection (looking within ourselves) and interpersonal communication (interacting with others). In the remainder of the chapter, specific techniques employing these two methods will be discussed.

A word of warning should accompany this section. That is, it is often an anxious experience to learn or relearn things about ourselves. It may even be a painful experience when we discover things that we dislike. Although learning about ourselves is not an easy process, it should be kept in mind that none of us is perfect. Even the best helpers possess limitations in addition to strengths.

Some questions to be pondered by the reader as a means to self-learning follow. They were inspired by a similar list constructed by Brill (1995).

- What is my sense of self?
- How do I deal with my personal needs?
- What are my values?
- What is my basic philosophy?

What is My Sense of Self?

Perhaps no other question is as central to knowing ourselves as this one: "What is my sense of self?" Our concept of self is composed of all of the information, perceptions, beliefs, and attitudes we have about ourselves. Our self-conception is viewed by many social scientists (e.g., Coopersmith, 1967; Gordon & Gergen, 1968; Gergen, 1971; Samuels, 1977) as a vital factor in determining what we do and what we become. For example, Eisenberg and Patterson (1977) propose that persons who feel inadequate and insecure see outside forces as controlling their lives. In contrast, secure individuals perceive themselves as maintaining their own control of their lives.

We do not have to be social scientists to understand that the images we have of ourselves can have considerable impact on our thinking and behavior. Can you remember days in which you have felt really good about yourself and imagined that you could tackle the whole world? You could do anything. On the other hand, have you ever felt, as my daughter would say, lower than a snake? When we do not feel good about ourselves, we avoid setting high goals and may literally stay in bed instead of facing what we perceive to be a dismal world.

We can see that our self-concept is perhaps more accurately referred to as our self-concepts. Our self-concepts are relatively stable, but we do hold differing opinions of ourselves at different times and in various situations. Likewise, self-concepts are not carved in stone. It is possible to change them.

Different authors hold varying views on exactly what core elements compose our self-concepts. Samuels (1977) states that the critical dimensions of **self-concept** are body image (feelings about your body), social self (your racial, ethnic, cultural, and religious self), your cognitive self (your perceptions about self), and self-esteem (your evaluation of self-worth). Eisenberg and Patterson (1977) propose the central elements of self-concept to be personal adequacy and worth ("I'm O.K."), appraisal of one's abilities or competencies ("I can't do anything with my hands"), and interests and activities ("I like the solitude of walking in the woods"), along with self-attributions or explanations people provide for their own behavior ("I work hard to achieve, because success means a lot to me").

How do you see yourself? Are you obese, slim, weak, strong, young, old, handsome, pretty, or sexy? Are you able to reach personal goals? Do you meet personal standards or ideals you have set for yourself? What are your preferences for specific interests or activities? Do you like yourself? Do you feel worthy of being loved? A few of the suggested exercises found in Appendix A: Self-Concept Exercises deal with sense of self and personal needs, values, and basic philosophy, including the "Who Am I ?"exercise (p.229).

How Do I Deal with My Personal Needs?

One of the first steps to success as a helping professional is to gain an understanding of one's needs. The helper who is aware of his or her own personal needs can then examine the ways in which he or she meets them. By doing so, the helping professional can:

- gain personally from this knowledge,
- better understand similar needs and expressions in clients, and
- avoid using helping relationships to meet personal needs rather than needs of clients.

Like most things, saying we should become aware of our personal needs is easier than doing it. A scheme useful in client assessment may prove helpful to self-assessment as well. Maslow's (1970) hierarchy of needs can serve as a means to self-understanding.

According to Maslow (1970), all people possess an innate tendency to become self-actualized, or to become what they have the potential to become. This need is the fifth, and highest, of the needs found on the hierarchy. Four other needs exist below that of self-actualization: (1) physiological needs, (2) safety needs, (3) belonging or love needs, and (4) self-esteem needs. Once a need has been met, it no longer evokes behavior; therefore, we know that a need has been at least partially satisfied before a higher need appears.

Let us review briefly the five needs in the hierarchy. We will begin with the lowest, physiological needs, and proceed to the highest need, self-actualization.

Physiological needs are basic for survival. Included are physical needs for food, water, air, and sleep for self-preservation, and sex for reproduction. Few helping professionals have to be concerned about the satisfaction of survival needs.

The second set of needs is **safety needs**. Safety needs are concerned with psychological safety and security. Stability is needed in all of our lives, but so is some amount of risk-taking. In meeting our safety needs we keep tension resulting from uncertainty in a range that is comfortable for us as individuals.

The third level of need is **love and belonging**. This social need has to do with feeling wanted and accepted by others and with the giving and receiving of friendship and love. This need may be met through belonging to clubs or organizations, family relations, friendships, and intimate relationships. If we feel lonely or isolated from others we may resort to unproductive or attention-getting behaviors ranging from pouting and disruptive acts to severe depression and aggression. Scarf (1980) has suggested recently that promiscuous sexual behavior may result from depression brought on by feeling unloved and uncared for. Empirical evidence presented by Henderson (1980) strongly suggests that experiencing deficiencies in social relationships causes neurosis.

The fourth level of need is **self-esteem**. High self-esteem means having self-confidence, self-assurance, and a general feeling of adequacy and worth as a person. It means feeling good about ourselves. To achieve a genuine sense of self-esteem we must be able to conduct valid self-evaluation. We have to know our own strengths and weaknesses. One of the paramount outcomes of our work as helping professionals is to assist our clients to develop positive self-esteem. A lack in our esteem or our clients' might be reflected by *having to* drive the latest model car or live in the "right neighborhood" to prove to others that we are persons of worth.

The highest-level need is **self-actualization**. This represents the growth drive that moves us toward meeting our highest potentials. In self-actualization we have continued self-development leading us to a rich, full, and meaningful life.

Schultz (1977) has provided an excellent interpretation of Maslow's theory. He discusses the concept that those who have reached the level of satisfaction of self-actualization are no longer in a state of becoming but, instead, are in a state of being. They are no longer attempting to remove deficiencies (the lower-level needs). Instead, these extremely healthy persons experience metamotivation (otherwise known as growth motivation, or being, or B-motivation). **Metaneeds** (also known as B-values) represent a state of growth for self-actualizers. Among the metaneeds are concepts such as truth, beauty, unity, aliveness, uniqueness, justice, order, simplicity, meaningfulness, and playfulness. For most of us, metaneeds remain in the realm of ideals for which we strive.

In a moment you will be asked to think about yourself. First, read the remainder of this paragraph, which will invite you to engage in specific types of self-reflection. Close your eyes and reflect on yourself for a few minutes, thinking about your personal needs. Which have been past concerns? Which are most pressing now? How are these expressed in your actions and thoughts? Stop at this point in your reading and, for the next few minutes, engage in self-reflection.

Now that you have thought about yourself for a few minutes, what did you discover or rediscover? Are your adjustments to meeting your needs satisfactory to you? Are you engaging in any attention-getting or self-defeating behaviors? What things made you feel good about yourself?

If, through your self-analysis, you find that you are not perfect, welcome to the club! Schultz (1977) states that Maslow found that even his self-actualizers could occasionally be irritating, temperamental, vain, stubborn, and thoughtless. Nor were they totally free from anxiety, guilt, and worry. Also, if you are young, it would be anticipated that you would be still evolving as a person and would not yet be expected to be self-actualizing.

A general characteristic of self-actualizers reported by Schultz (1977), was that they were middle-aged or older. According to Schultz, Maslow assumed that younger persons had not yet had the necessary life experiences to enable them to develop a powerful sense of identity and independence. It follows that you, if you are a young person, are in a natural state of becoming and should be optimistic about your ability for future growth. In fact, we all should remain optimistic about our abilities to change because all of us possess the potential to grow and expand throughout our lives.

To stimulate further self-examination, I have constructed a list of questions. These "Self-Examination Questions" appear in this chapter's Appendix A (p. 229). It is not to be taken as an inclusive list, but the questions will reveal areas for exploration for you as an emerging, or even established, therapeutic recreation specialist.

On Becoming a Helping Professional

One serious question that all therapeutic recreation specialists must address at some point is if they truly desire to become helping professionals. When students actually begin to gain field experience, they sometimes find that the helping relationship does not meet their personal needs. For example, they may learn that while they like being with other people, they do not enjoy participating in actual helping relationships. It is critical that students gain experiences in the real world of the helping professional in order to confirm or challenge their suppositions. It is also important that students gain exposure to several different client groups. Some people work well with children who are mentally retarded. Others find enjoyment in serving adults with problems in mental health, individuals undergoing physical rehabilitation, old people, or members of some other group. Professional exploration is essential for the helping professional. There is nothing wrong with students making alternative career choices. In fact, it reflects the development of self-awareness on their part.

What are My Values?

When I began my professional career in therapeutic recreation, two myths existed. One was that professionals were value-free. That is, their personal values were not allowed to enter into their professional lives. The second was that even the beginning helping professionals held the highest of professional values. Young professionals presumably gained these through some unknown means because, to my knowledge, no college instructors ever helped us to develop them as students.

The myth of the **value-free professional** has passed. Professionals today are allowed personal values (i.e., values we hold as individuals). We have also come to understand that there is a place in professional preparation programs for examination of both personal and professional values (i.e., values accepted by our profession).

Values Defined

Before proceeding further, it may be wise to make explicit exactly what is meant by values. To value something is to attribute worth to it. Beliefs that we prize form our value system and are one basis for determining our behavior. Reilly (1978) has defined a value as "an operational belief which an individual accepts as his or her own and serves as a determinant of behavior" (p. 37). Values are critically important to us. They are the principles by which we live our lives (Simon & Olds, 1977).

Values Knowledge

Simon and Olds (1977) have discussed the ways by which we learn values. Included are "The Three Misleading M's." These are moralizing, manipulating, and modeling. These authors recommend none of the three methods. Few readers need convincing regarding the problems with moralizing. Manipulation limits choices and does not teach us how to think through conflicts. And, although modeling can be a potent force, learning by example does not afford the opportunity to make personal choices or wrestle with issues. Instead, Simon and Olds recommend the values clarification process developed by Raths. Through analysis of our choosing, accepting, and acting on values, the values clarification process helps us to determine our values for ourselves.

Values Clarification Strategies

Perhaps the most noted book on values clarification and values clarification strategies is *Values Clarification: A Handbook of Practical Strategies for Teachers and Students* (Simon et al., 1995). Because Simon and his colleagues have prepared this book and several others, values clarification will not be discussed in detail in this section. Instead, the reader is encouraged to seek out works on values clarification. The exercises, or strategies, found in these books offer enjoyment and insights to those who complete them. They are highly recommended. Among the topics covered are work, sex, friendship, family, ethics, authority, material possession, self, culture, and leisure. (See Chapter 2 for a listing of specific values clarification exercises on leisure.)

Other ways of clarifying our values have been proposed by Reilly (1978). Among them are reading and discussing values found in good literature, such as Shakespeare's sonnets. A second method is listening to popular music and analyzing it to determine the values it reflects. Role playing value-laden situations is a third method. Another is taking field trips to unfamiliar environments in order to broaden understandings of values represented in other life-styles, cultures, and socioeconomic strata.

Through the process of examining your own values, you will learn to aid clients in clarifying their value systems, because exercises and experiences useful to you may be equally valuable to clients. A note of caution should, however, be sounded if you do deal with client values. Clients have the right not to have your values imposed on them. Avoid placing on them your personal values toward achievement, sexual behavior, conformity, work, leisure, and other issues (Brill, 1995).

What is My Basic Philosophy?

It is important that we become aware of our basic philosophical beliefs, because these influence our theoretical notions which, in turn, affect the principles by which we operate. Or, as Frye and Peters (1972) said, "philosophy is the rudder that gives guidance and direction" (p. 32).

Brill (1995, p. 33) has listed the following seven beliefs that form her overall philosophical base for human service:

- The individual is a social animal.
- The individual exists in interrelationship with other people and with all other life forms. This relationship may be defined as one of mutual rights and responsibilities.
- The welfare of the individual and of the group cannot be considered apart from each other.
- Each person, and all living things, possess intrinsic worth.
- Each person, and all living things, are characterized by a need to grow and develop toward the realization of a unique potential.
- The individual and the society can be understood by use of the scientific method.
- The individual and the society possess the capacity for change as a part of their intrinsic natures.

Do you subscribe to Brill's philosophical beliefs? If not, with which ones do you disagree? It might be anticipated that beliefs such as the necessity for play in the developmental process, the importance of recreation and leisure as means to attainment of basic human needs, and the fundamental right of all people to engage in the pursuit of happiness might be added by therapeutic recreation specialists. Do you agree with these? Can you add others?

Obviously, philosophical beliefs are required to direct our practice. For some time, we in therapeutic recreation struggled with the development of a philosophical statement to represent our field. It is important for the evolution of therapeutic recreation that such a process occurred, but it is more critical that budding therapeutic recreation specialists develop personal philosophies. The emergence of newer, creative philosophies will cause us to examine continually past beliefs and will ultimately strengthen the profession.

Resources For Self-Examination

There are many resources from which to draw in order to facilitate development of self-awareness. Some have been mentioned previously. Others are listed here.

- *Tape Recordings.* You may listen to tape recordings of interactions you have had with friends or actual clients. My students complete an interview tape with a person with whom they are not in a close relationship. Then they critique it with a classmate, discussing needs, values, and behaviors that reveal themselves. The information on communications in Chapter 6 may be helpful in such an evaluation.
- *Videotapes.* You may videotape the role playing of various situations typical of practice in therapeutic recreation and then review them. Students in my classes have videotaped role-playing situations of interviews and recreational groups and then reviewed and discussed them to gain insights.
- *Diaries.* Keeping a diary in which you express feelings about your self-concepts, values, and beliefs may be helpful. Students completing internships may find this technique particularly valuable to gaining self-awareness.
- *Small Group Discussions.* Self-disclosure in small groups offers the opportunity to share information and insights. It is important to foster an open atmosphere conducive to such dialogue. Of course, confidentiality should be maintained.

Other Characteristics

Other helping characteristics previously listed for therapeutic recreation specialists included the ability to communicate, possession of a knowledge base, and a strong belief in recreation and leisure experiences. So important are communications that a separate chapter (Chapter 6) has been devoted to this topic. Hopefully, a knowledge base for practice will be built from many sources. Throughout this book specific information on theoretical approaches and practical techniques utilized in therapeutic recreation will be found. The therapeutic recreation specialist, in developing a personal and professional philosophy, will arrive at a belief in the values to be found in recreation and leisure.

ETHICAL ISSUES

Professional ethics comprise a system of principles or standards of behavior that govern conduct in terms of right and wrong in the performance of professional responsibilities. The term ethics comes from the Greek word *ethos,* which translates to our word "custom." Custom, in this sense, has to do with established duties and obligations instituted by common consent to insure uniform practice in a profession in order to protect human rights (Potter & Perry, 1987). **Client autonomy, confidentiality, social-sexual relations,** and **professional competence and training** are ethical issues covered in this chapter on helping others.

Client Autonomy

As professionals who have strongly cherished the ideal of freedom of choice in recreation and leisure, the issue of client autonomy is one to which therapeutic recreation specialists can easily relate. "The autonomous person," stated Sylvester (1985), "is one who is self-governing, being morally free to make the choices that direct the course of his or her life" (p. 13). Shank (1985) said that autonomy deals with "the person's freedom to form and act upon their judgments. Individuals are free to determine their own destiny" (p. 33).

Autonomy deals with the client expressing his or her freedom to make choices. A part of client autonomy concerns *informed consent.* Clients need to know what the therapist plans to do and why. As Sylvester (1985) has stipulated, "Informed consent provides that the client has the right to know, in adequate detail and comprehensible terms, what is likely to occur during and as a result of professional intervention" (p. 15). But what happens when after you have explained the program, there is a conflict between what you believe in your best professional opinion to be good for the client, and what the client wishes?

Should clients be allowed to refuse to take part in therapy programs that are part of their treatment plan? This type of ethical dilemma related to client autonomy is one with which the therapeutic recreation specialist must learn to deal.

As is the case with all ethical problems, it is not easily solved. It is, however, within the therapist's prerogative to ask reluctant clients to participate if such participation is clearly seen to be in their best interests. As Shank (1985) has explained, "the use of recreation as a therapeutic modality, especially in a health care setting, may necessitate action which restricts or reduces the autonomy of the patient" (p. 33). What about clients who express values that stand in opposition to yours? What if you know their values are "wrong"?

Sylvester (1985) has raised some interesting questions regarding leisure values. He asks:

> Is astrology an appropriate form of leisure, even when clients use it to make major life decisions? What about witchcraft or satanic worship? How should professionals deal with clients who neglect their families by devoting all their discretionary time to religious activity? What about clients who claim to receive "meaning and enjoyment" from child pornography, or who use their free time to support white supremacist causes? (p. 14).

Thank goodness we do not regularly encounter clients who hold the values reflected in Sylvester's questions! Nevertheless, we do encounter clients with values that may differ from those we hold. What should we do when this occurs? Should we ignore the obvious conflict out of respect for the client's right to autonomy? Should we tell them how wrong they are and how they need to change their values?

Most authorities probably agree with Corey's (1985) and Corey and Corey's (1987) thoughts regarding handling value conflicts. First, the Coreys stated it is unreasonable to believe that we can divorce our values from our professional practice: "Your values are a fundamental part of the person you are. Thus, they cannot help but influence how you lead a therapeutic group" (p. 63).

They go on to say that every therapist must first address possible values conflict by knowing himself or herself. If you are to be an effective leader you must become aware of your own values and direct and indirect ways in which you may try to influence your clients. It is suggested that once this is done you may choose to resolve conflicts between your values and those of a client's by *expressing* your views so the client may have the advantage of a new way of thinking about something. But you need to let the client discover what is right for her or him and *not impose* your values. To use Corey and Corey's terms, you need to *expose* but not *impose*.

Confidentiality

According to Shank (1985), "The rules of confidentiality and privacy are associated with the right to govern one's own affairs and is therefore considered a derivative of the principle of autonomy" (p. 35). Shank explains that the concern of **privacy** deals with a person's right to control personal information, while confidentiality has to do with an individual's right to control access to *information* that others have gained about them.

Confidentiality may present a problem for young professionals who are naturally extremely interested in their work and may be anxious to share their excitement for what they are doing by relating details of their on-the-job experiences with family, friends, or even fellow staff members. The impulse to tell a good story must be held in check if client confidentiality is to have meaning.

Are there times when confidentiality may be broken? Yes, there are occasions when confidentiality may be broken when harm may befall either the client or others. If a client indicates she is planning to commit suicide, for example, this information should be reported. Or if a client informs you that he is going to harm another individual, this intent needs to be made known. Authorities (Corey, 1985; Corey & Corey, 1987; Okun, 1992) agree that therapists need to inform clients of these instances when confidentiality will not be honored as a part of initial informed consent procedures.

Confidentiality within group leadership situations presents complexities not encountered with individuals. Corey and Corey (1987) have explained:

One of the central ethical issues in group work is confidentiality. It is especially important because the group leader must not only keep the confidences of members but also get the members to keep one another's confidences (p. 55).

It is important for group leaders to initially raise the issue of confidentiality with the group and then to remind clients from time to time of the necessity of maintaining confidentiality. While there is no way to insure confidentiality when working with groups, some suggestions to the groups may prove helpful. Besides raising the need to avoid malicious gossip, the therapist can provide pointers for the group members regarding talking about their experiences with significant others outside the group. These should include that it is permissible to talk about *what* therapeutic gains they have made as a result of their group participation but not discuss specifics about interacting with other group members (Corey & Corey, 1987).

It is critical that therapeutic recreation specialists are clear about their positions with regard to confidentiality. Therapeutic recreation specialists will interact with clients in recreational settings marked by informality and an accepting atmosphere. Additionally, many clients perceive therapeutic recreation specialists to be less threatening than other staff and some will view them as friends. For these reasons, clients have a tendency to share much personal information with therapeutic recreation specialists.

Social-Sexual Relations

It is generally accepted that sexual relationships between helping professionals and their clients are unethical. Nevertheless, sexual relations between therapists and clients do occasionally occur (Sylvester, 1985), although the prevalence of such practices in therapeutic recreation is unknown due to a lack of research on sexual behaviors of therapeutic recreation specialists.

Therapeutic recreation specialists encounter many occasions when warm, accepting gestures may be taken as sexual overtures by clients. Examples are hugs to demonstrate pleasure with a client's performance or embraces following success within an activity.

It is therefore important that therapists monitor their own behaviors in order to (1) minimize misunderstandings with clients, and (2) become aware of any romantic feelings that they might possess toward a client (Sylvester, 1985).

Social relationships with clients should not be encouraged by therapeutic recreation specialists. The bounds of the role of "professional friend" should not be exceeded by the therapeutic recreation specialist while the client is in the dependent position that is a natural part of the helping relationship. Professionals need to enter into close self-examination before pursuing a social relationship with a client even after the professional relationship has ended (Sylvester, 1985). Some agencies have personnel policies prohibiting social relationships with former clients. It is important that professionals become aware of any such ethical policies that may govern their behaviors.

Professional Competence

It is critical that therapeutic recreation specialists know their levels of professional competence and that they do not exceed them. Corey and Corey (1987) have suggested the following to leaders of therapy groups. Their sentiments have application to therapeutic recreation specialists. They have written:

> Group leaders must provide only services and use techniques for which they are qualified by training and experience. Leaders have the responsibility of accurately representing their competence to the participants in their groups (p. 42).

Okun (1992) has stated that helping professionals tread on unsafe ethical grounds when they administer or interpret tests without sufficient training and supervision. Similarly, those without extensive training and experience in conducting programs that may involve potential psychological or physical risks to clients (which would include most therapeutic recreation programs) should not assume responsibility to lead those programs. For example, those leading adventure-challenge therapy need to have had sound training and adequate clinical supervision before leading this clinical program. The need for therapeutic recreation specialists to upgrade their clinical skills becomes apparent whenever they contemplate initiating a new technique or program area. Equally evident should be the need for therapeutic recreation specialists to continually update themselves in order to remain current in the program areas that they regularly apply as clinical modalities.

A second area related to competency deals with guarding against impaired performance on the part of the helping professional. Professionals need to seek help when they themselves encounter personal problems that may interfere with professional performance. For example, a professional who is under an exceptional amount of personal stress may need to seek counseling, or a professional who is abusing substances may need to enter a drug rehabilitation program.

A final and growing concern facing all helping professionals is that of learning to offer quality care to clients of ever increasing cultural diversity. It is important for professionals to avoid thinking and acting according to their own monocultural orientation in a society that is becoming more and more multicultural. In fact, it has been suggested within the counseling literature (Ivey, Ivey & Simek-Morgan, 1993) that it is unethical for helping professionals to not be competent in the provision of services to clients from culturally diverse populations. Multicultural aspects enter into any helping relationship where the helper and client(s) have different perceptions of their social worlds. Professionals employing a multicultural orientation are sensitive to how issues such as race, ethnicity, age, gender, disability, affectional orientation, class, and religion may affect the provision of professional services to persons with culturally diverse backgrounds (Corey, 1995). They understand that their clients often possess views, attitudes and values that differ from those they hold. They do not assume their ways of thinking and behaving are the only "right" ones and that any others are "wrong." All of us learn our perceptions of the world and it is only logical that individuals coming from different cultural backgrounds will have different perceptions of the world. Those embracing multiculturalism recognize and value diversity.

It is vitally important that therapeutic recreation specialists educate themselves so that they are competent to serve clients with different ethnic and cultural backgrounds. To do so requires maintaining freedom from bias, becoming aware of and welcoming diversity, learning about various cultures, having contacts with clients from a variety of cultural backgrounds and completing clinical affiliation with clients from minority groups (Bernard & Goodyear, 1992). It is reasonable to assume that each of us will wish to gain cultural understandings of those specific client groups that we will be most likely to encounter in our practice. At the same time we need to acknowledge that there are ties that bind all of us, regardless of cultural differences. We will always wish to maintain the understanding that our clients are individuals, as well as members of a specific cultural group (Corey, 1995).

BURNOUT

The importance of the topic of **burnout** is reflected in a quote by Shinn, Rosario, Morch, and Chestnut (1984). These psychologists have written: "Staff burnout is a critical problem for the human service professions: It is debilitating to workers, costly to agencies, and detrimental to clients" (p. 864). Individuals who burnout face negative impacts on their physical, emotional, and mental health. Organizations have to deal with problems caused by staff who have burned out or have to replace those who resign. Clients suffer due to reductions in the quality of services performed by staff who are burned out (Szymanski, 1989).

Freudenberger (1975) originated the term "burnout" to describe the emotional and physical exhaustion experienced by professionals working in health care agencies. Cherniss (1980) has termed burnout "a process in which the professional's attitudes and behavior change in negative ways in response to job strain" (p. 5). Edelwich and Brodsky (1980) have defined burnout as a "progressive loss of idealism, energy, purpose, and concern as a result of conditions of work" (p. 14).

Maslach (1982) has used the framework of a three-phase process to describe the burnout syndrome. The initial phase of the process starts when a person experiences emotional exhaustion. A burned out individual lacks the energy to face another day. During the second phase, an individual begins to reduce client contact and treats clients in a depersonalized fashion. In the final phase, an individual feels a reduced sense of personal accomplishment resulting from his or her work.

Who are candidates for burnout? Patrick (1981, p. 12) has listed the following job characteristics that fuel burnout. They are:

- *Repetitive contact with people.* Nature of the job demands ongoing contact with recipients of services.
- *Intense interpersonal contacts.* Contact with people may occur to an extreme degree, and thus a finely tuned interpersonal communication style is required.
- *Long-term involvement.* Intensity of contact and interaction may be unremitting and chronic.
- *The "giving" role.* Health workers generally are defined as "givers"—a requirement that may not always result in a sense of reward or satisfaction.
- *Job monotony.* Job responsibilities or duties may be monotonous, which fosters a feeling of boredom and stasis (p. 12).

Do therapeutic recreation specialists encounter any of these job characteristics in their roles as health care professionals? Of course, they do. Especially common are the first four of the foregoing characteristics. Unfortunately, some people may also encounter job monotony in positions where they are not allowed to enlarge or enrich their responsibilities.

If therapeutic recreation specialists are at risk for burnout, for what signs or symptoms should they be alert? Patrick (1981, pp. 18-22) has listed the following objective and subjective signs of manifestations of burnout. Objective signs include:

- Overtime work increases as it becomes more difficult to get work accomplished during normal hours;
- Rest breaks and lunch are skipped to get work done;
- Vacations are delayed or cancelled;
- People lose their sense of humor, often being overly serious and, perhaps, affectively flat;
- Physical fatigue occurs;
- People become more irritable;
- Susceptibility to illness increases;
- Physical complaints of muscle tension, headaches, low back pain, and gastrointestinal irritability increase;
- Social withdrawal occurs in the form of pulling away from co-workers, peers and family or taking part in life activities but without true participation;

- Job performance declines as reflected in absenteeism, tardiness, use of sick days, accidents, and decreased efficiency and productivity; and
- Self-medication begins or increases.

Subjective signs of burnout include the following, according to Patrick (1981, pp. 23-29):

- Emotional exhaustion occurs as people experience emotional emptiness and drained inner resources;
- Self-esteem declines;
- People feel trapped in their jobs;
- Emotional withdrawal occurs ;
- Depression commonly appears;
- People experience increasing difficulty receiving support from others;
- Boredom and apathy occur;
- Helpers shift from understanding clients to blaming clients for their dysfunctions;
- Feelings of frustration increase;
- Feelings of anger appear; and
- Feelings of aloneness and isolation occur.

Austin and Szymanski (1985) conducted a research study with counselors in a residential camp serving campers with disabilities. Staff experiencing burnout reported:

- A lack of control over their environment;
- Little support from fellow staff members;
- A lack of recognition from camp administrators;
- Focusing on finishing tasks rather than long-term goals;
- Viewing the schedule as being without flexibility; and
- Experiencing a lack of self-fulfillment from their roles as camp staff.

Such findings are, no doubt, very representative of those that might be reported by helping professionals who encounter burnout in other settings.

There are any number of contributing factors to burnout. Chief among them are inadequate social support, lack of autonomy and clarity, work pressure, and a work environment that is not conducive. Those who burn out repeatedly report that they do not receive adequate social support from fellow workers or supervisors or reinforcement from clients. They often experience difficulty with role ambiguity and a lack of encouragement to be self-sufficient, along with problems related to not knowing what to expect in their daily routines, and rules and policies not being explicitly communicated. Work pressure results when people are overloaded with excessive responsibility or have inadequate preparation to do the job. Finally, staff often have to work in environments that are less than attractive and comfortable (Austin & Voelkl, 1986; Constable & Russell, 1986; Patrick, 1981; Rosenthal, Teague, Retish, West & Vessell, 1983).

Now that we have reviewed what burnout is, its signs and its causes, the obvious question is, "Can burnout be prevented or is it a malady that helping professionals cannot escape?" The answer is happily, yes, burnout can be prevented. McBride (1983, pp. 228,229) has offered an extensive list of actions that individuals can use to reduce stress and prevent burnout.

- *Development of a support system.* It is very important to have people who care about you and what you do. A close relationship with at least one other person is vitally important.
- *Take responsibility for what you do with your own body.* Exercise regularly, eat properly, limit the use of tobacco, alcohol, and drugs.
- *Learn how to manage time effectively.* Prioritize what needs to be done—do high-priority items first.
- *Know and respect your own limits, skills, energy, and level of commitment.* Do those things that are your responsibility—learn to say no.
- *Spend time out of your usual role.* Develop a hobby. Don't compete—just enjoy yourself.
- *Look upon life as a challenge.* Take risks.
- *Take time off*—"mental health" days, vacations, planning periods during the day. Use relaxation techniques, self-hypnosis, or other ways to "escape" daily pressures for a few minutes every day.
- *Seek professional help*-Career or personal counseling may be appropriate.

- *Learn to cry "Uncle" when you need to.* Realizing that stress is affecting you adversely is the first step in dealing with it.
- *Enjoy "strokes" when they occur.* Get thanks, recognition, and validation from all available sources.
- *Stack the deck in your favor.* Take on assignments, when possible, at which you will be successful.
- *Learn to laugh at yourself and the absurdities of life.* Learn to live life with a sense of humor. Angels can fly because they take themselves lightly.

Of course, the relaxation techniques mentioned previously in Chapter 3 can be applied as "self-help" methods in order to reduce feelings of tension. These techniques can prove to be very helpful to emerging professionals who are subject to burnout. Emerging professionals, who are the most susceptible to burnout (Bedini, Williams, & Thompson, 1995), should also have concern for gaining the highest degree of professional competence they can achieve through their higher education preparation. While certainly not assuring the prevention of burnout, having the necessary competencies to meet job expectations can reduce the probability of burnout occurring. Once in the field, the importance of keeping up with recent developments through continuing education opportunities needs to be underscored. Finally, it should be emphasized that therapeutic recreation specialists need to "practice what they preach" in terms of restoring themselves through recreation pursuits and expanding themselves through leisure experiences (Horner, 1993; McGuire, Boyd & Tedrick, 1995).

SUMMARY

Helping others is a very human enterprise aimed toward the development of independence and self-reliance on the part of our clients. Certain characteristics are required of therapeutic recreation specialists in order to function as effective helping professionals. The characteristic receiving primary attention in this chapter was self-awareness. It is clear that we, as helping professionals, have a responsibility to know ourselves so we know what we bring to the helping relationship and what we have to offer clients. We must also be responsible for understanding issues in professional ethics. Finally, it is clear that we must learn to recognize burnout and how to prevent it.

READING COMPREHENSION QUESTIONS

1. How do professional helping relationships differ from social relationships?
2. Explain how helping others is a very human enterprise that meets the helper's needs.
3. What is the ultimate goal of the helping relationship?
4. Analyze the lists of characteristics of effective helpers. With which do you most fully agree?
5. Do you concur with the list of primary helping characteristics for the therapeutic recreation specialist? If not, how would your list differ?
6. Explain why we need to know ourselves in order to serve effectively as helping professionals.
7. Do you agree that gaining self-awareness may be a painful experience?
8. Review the list of questions posed for self-examination. Are there others that you might add? If so, think about yourself in regard to these questions.
9. Does self-concept influence our behavior and expectations? How?
10. Do you agree with Eisenberg and Patterson that those with high self-esteem are more likely to feel they have control over their lives?
11. Did you participate in the "Who Are You?" Activity? Did it help you to examine yourself? How do you see yourself?
12. Why might it be important to become aware of your needs?
13. Can you outline Maslow's hierarchy? Do you recognize any of these needs in yourself?
14. Why might it be assumed that the majority of students are in a state of becoming?
15. Have you had firsthand experiences in helping relationships in therapeutic recreation? Were they what you thought they would be?
16. Why are values important? Can you recognize some of the values you hold in regard to work? Leisure? Other areas?

17.   Do you agree with Brill's list of philosophical beliefs? Would you add or subtract any beliefs to form your own list of beliefs as a philosophical base for practice in therapeutic recreation?
18.   Have you tried any of the resources suggested for self-examination?
19.   Name issues related to professional ethics.
20.   Have you observed health professionals experiencing burnout? What behaviors did they exhibit?
21.   Have you experienced burnout as a student? What steps have you taken to deal with it?
22.   What are actions individuals can take to prevent burnout? Are there things agencies can do to help prevent burnout from occurring?

APPENDIX A
SELF-CONCEPT EXERCISES

Who Am I?

Eisenberg and Patterson (1977) suggest that most of us are not fully aware of our beliefs about self. They submit that the "Who Am I?" exercise, often used to bring about self-learning, causes difficulty for all but a few people. This activity requires two people. One simply repeats the question, "Who are you?" To each inquiry the other person must respond by providing a new description of self. Eisenberg and Patterson claim most people do not go beyond their roles (e.g., wife, husband) and cannot respond to more than 10 inquiries.

Collage

A self-awareness exercise that many students enjoy is completing a two-sided collage. [This exercise was adapted from Borden & Stone (1976)]. On one side of a piece of poster paper, a collage is prepared to represent how you think people see you. On the reverse side, a collage is constructed representing the way you see yourself (the "real you"). The collages can be made out of pictures, advertisements, cartoons, or words from headlines from old newspapers and magazines. These can be cut out and pasted or taped to the paper. Or, you may draw or write things that represent you. The poster paper should be covered with collages on both sides in about an hour's time. Once completed, you may get together with another person to describe your artwork and have the other person describe theirs to you. After this, you may wish to display your collage for all to see. If done as a part of a class, you may desire to share information about your collages with your classmates and instructor.

Self-Examination Questions

On Physical Contact
- Do you enjoy being touched?
- Do you feel comfortable in touching others?
- Do you feel touching has sexual connotations?

On Giving and Receiving Compliments
- Can you receive compliments without discounting them?
- Are you comfortable with issuing compliments?

On Self-Esteem
- Do you have a feeling of being esteemed by others?
- Do you continually seek support or reassurance from others?
- Do you have a need to boast about exploits?

On Being Assertive
- Are you able to reveal what you think or feel within a group?
- Do you attempt to make things happen instead of waiting for someone else to do it?

On Social Relationships
- Are you free to let friends expand themselves or are you possessive or jealous when close friends make new acquaintances?
- Can you enter into intimate, honest relationships with others?

On Leadership Style
- Are you people oriented?
- Are you task oriented?

On Play
- Are you playful?
- Are you competitive, placing a priority on winning?

On Sharing Yourself
- Are you willing to transcend your own needs in order to facilitate growth in others?

Chapter Six

COMMUNICATION SKILLS

CHAPTER PURPOSE

Therapeutic recreation is action oriented, not talk oriented. Even though therapeutic recreation specialists do regularly interview clients and may engage in leisure counseling, the thrust of therapeutic recreation is toward active participation instead of purely the discussion of client problems and concerns. Nevertheless, the ability to maintain effective interpersonal communication is important and is a basic competency needed by the therapeutic recreation specialist in order to perform as a viable helping professional. If the therapeutic recreation specialist cannot communicate with his or her clients, the therapeutic recreation process is almost certainly doomed to failure. This chapter will help you to develop a fundamental understanding of communication processes and refine specific **communication skills**.

KEY TERMS

- Communication skills
- Nonverbal communication
- Medium
- Feedback
- Paraphrasing
- Checking out
- Effective listening
- Message
- Receiver
- Mental set
- Minimal verbal responses
- Clarifying

- Probing
- Interpreting
- Informing
- Attribution theory

- Reflecting
- Confronting
- Summarizing
- Self-disclosing

OBJECTIVES

- Comprehend the pragmatic approach (i.e., practical approach) to communication taken in this chapter.
- Know determinants of successful verbal communication.
- Translate theoretical knowledge of effective listening into practice.
- Demonstrate knowledge of verbal responses that may be used to facilitate client self-understanding.
- Use feedback principles appropriate in learning and performance situations.
- Appreciate the importance of studying nonverbal communication.
- Analyze specific cues in nonverbal communication.
- Recognize the importance of a proper setting for interviews.
- Apply basic interview skills.

One day a student of mine excitedly exclaimed as she entered the classroom, "I used some of those verbal responses we've been practicing in class with my friends and they really worked!"

Students are often surprised when they initially find that the interpersonal communication skills taught in their therapeutic recreation classes are useful in their everyday lives. Such skills have application because the things we do to be effective in our everyday encounters with others are the same skills we need to be capable helping professionals.

EFFECTIVE INTERPERSONAL COMMUNICATION

It is important to recognize that there is nothing particularly esoteric about the interpersonal communication skills employed in our relationships with clients. They are the skills used practically every day of our lives and are not the exclusive domain of therapeutic recreation specialists or any other group of helping professionals. As difficult as it may be to admit, therapeutic recreation specialists possess no magical means by which to relate to clients.

All of this is not to detract from the communication process, but it does underscore the fact that the business of helping is a very human enterprise that employs communication skills used in our day-to-day lives. It follows that the higher our level of personal communication skills, the higher our potentials will be to perform successfully as helping professionals. This chapter emphasizes the communication skills necessary for effective listening, interviewing, counseling, and activity leadership.

WHAT IS COMMUNICATION?

There are several frames of reference from which to view communication, including syntactics (information theory), semantics (dealing with meanings), and pragmatics (behavior) (Waltzlawick, 1967). In this chapter we will deal with all three, but our primary concern will be with the pragmatics, or the behavioral effects of interpersonal communication. This practical approach will concentrate on basic communication processes in interacting with clients.

Because there are several perspectives from which to approach communication, there is no one single definition of communication that is appropriate to all. For the purpose of our pragmatic approach, communication may be defined as the verbal and nonverbal transmission of ideas, feelings, beliefs, and attitudes that permits a common understanding between the sender of the **message** and the **receiver**.

Thus communication implies the exchange of information and ideas between at least two people, resulting in a common understanding. The word communication is derived from a Latin word meaning common, or shared by all alike, (Gibson et al., 1988; Killen, 1977). If, through verbal and nonverbal symbols, people are able to achieve a common or shared understanding, communication has taken place.

The communication process has five elements:

- **communicator**—who
- **message**—says what
- **medium**—in what way
- **receiver**—to whom
- **feedback**—with what effect (Gibson et al., 1988).

Therefore, communication is clearly a two-way sharing of meaning in which a message is both sent and received. Feedback provides assurance that the intended message has been received. Through feedback the receiver either verifies that the message was understood, or discovers that the message was misunderstood. Since feedback may be subtle, it is important that the sender be alert and sensitive to those with whom he or she is communicating. Okun (1992) has stipulated that effective helpers utilize verbal messages (containing cognitive and affective content) and nonverbal messages (including affective and behavioral content) and respond verbally and nonverbally to feedback.

To say that communication skills are important is an understatement. Satir (1972) has stated in regard to the human being that "communication is the largest single factor determining what kinds of relationships he or she makes with others and what happens to him or her in the world about him or her" (p.4, italics removed).

Therapeutic recreation presents an environment conducive to the development of positive interpersonal communication. In the open, nonthreatening atmosphere of the recreation situation clients often feel free to communicate with the therapeutic recreation specialist. This openness is, however, only one element in client-therapist interpersonal communications. Also critical is the appropriateness of the therapeutic recreation specialist's responses. Unless the therapeutic recreation specialist is prepared to respond appropriately, communications may break down. It follows that the therapeutic recreation specialist must learn to develop effective communication skills.

COMMUNICATION IMPROVEMENT GUIDELINES

Four factors influencing successful verbal communication:

- How material is presented;
- The speaker's attitude or feeling toward the client;
- The voice tone and volume; and
- The speaker's and receiver's abilities to listen (Purtilo, 1984).

The information that follows is based largely on Purtilo's discussion of these four influences.

Presentation of Material

Presentation of material has to do with the vocabulary used, the clarity of the speaker's voice, and the manner in which the message is organized.

Vocabulary

Failure to choose the right words will produce an unclear message. Acquiring an adequate professional vocabulary will allow the therapeutic recreation specialist to avoid using inappropriate words, or giving rambling descriptions to clients or other staff. This does not mean you should use large, technical words in conversations with clients. Although a certain amount of professional jargon is necessary in staff communication, problems arise when highly technical terms are used when speaking with clients.

Once a colleague of mine jokingly remarked, "I never use a two-syllable word when an eight-syllable one will do as well." This man was noted across campus for his eloquent utterances. In the academic community, where a command of language is valued, my colleague succeeded as a communicator because he knew how to gear his message to that particular audience. He knew that presenting material that was too simple would fail, and throwing in a few eight-syllable words here and there might earn him some amount of credibility! But being a good communicator, he also knew that presenting a message that was too complex would be equally bad. As all effective communicators know, failure to assess properly the receiver's ability to comprehend will severely hinder communication.

A good rule to follow is to state your ideas in simple terms in as few words as possible (Chartier, 1976). Although my colleague was an apparent exception to this rule, most of us are better off using everyday words, even when communicating with highly intelligent and well-schooled persons. In short, each of us should "be ourselves" and use our regular vocabulary.

Voice Clarity

Articulation is important in getting a message across. A clearly spoken sentence is not spoken too softly, nor is it rushed. Professionals who are regularly asked by clients to repeat instructions are probably speaking too softly or too fast. The rate of speaking must always keep pace with the listener's ability to comprehend. Therefore, we should monitor ourselves to make certain that we are communicating with our clients. For example, we may find we are speaking too softly to be understood by older people who may have difficulty hearing, or we may be speaking too rapidly to effectively get our message across to children.

Organization

Chartier (1976) has presented several communication guidelines, some of which may be used to help avoid rambling communications.

- Good organization begins by having a clear picture of what the sender wants the other person to understand. It is particularly imperative that the communicator hold a clear conception of what he or she wishes to say when dealing with complex or ambiguous topics.
- Define terms before discussing them and explain concepts before amplifying on them. New terms and concepts cause problems for those not acquainted with them, and thus require explanation before they are utilized.
- Organize messages into a series of sequential stages so that only one idea is developed at a time and it leads to the next idea.
- Redundancy leads to clarity. Repetition is a good form of learning, and is helpful in communication. Summarizing at the end of the message is an example of a common form of repetition. As Chartier (1976) says, "Repetition is important. Very important" (p.153).

- Relate new concepts and ideas to old ones. Here the rationale is that an individual can better understand a new idea if he or she has been able to relate it to a previously held one.
- Determine which ideas in the message need special emphasis. Underscored ideas have increased impact. For example, Chartier (1976) has stated, *"this last principle is an important one-remember it and use it"* (p.153, italics added).

Attitudes

The second of Purtilo's (1984) determinants of successful verbal communication deals with the communicator's attitudes or feelings toward the client. When the sender and receiver have high regard for one another, the effectiveness of communication is aided. Displaying genuine concern for the client through a warm, caring attitude enhances the prospect for successful communication.

On the other hand, the therapeutic recreation specialist who is not honest with clients will run into difficulties with interpersonal transactions. Confronting a client about his or her behavior may be difficult. However, displaying an accepting attitude toward what is seen to be inappropriate behavior is not an honest or helpful response; in the long run, the nonconfronting professional is running the risk of destroying the helping relationship. Neither is it wise not to admit anger on the rare occasions when the professional is obviously feeling anger toward a client. Providing the client with an understanding of why the anger arose displays an open, honest attitude.

Voice Tone and Volume

Have you ever had persons remark to you, "You didn't say it like you meant it?" They were probably indicating that they detected a lack of commitment in the tone of your voice. Voice inflection can be more important in projecting understandings than the actual choice of words. For instance, uncertainty reflected in the voice may communicate "yes," even though the speaker says "no."

The tone of voice can express a variety of attitudes and emotions, ranging from pleasure and exuberance to dejection and depression. When clinical psychologists refer to the client as having a "flat affect," they are no doubt basing this observation at least partly on the client's tone of voice. Occasionally, a speaker will not realize the emotion accompanying his or her speech until another person makes an observation regarding it. When leading activities, the therapeutic recreation specialist needs to monitor his or her voice to make certain that it is projecting excitement, enthusiasm, or whatever the appropriate feeling.

Closely related to voice inflection is volume. Volume can be used to control others. Speaking loudly will keep people at a distance, while a whisper may be used to draw others closer. In therapeutic recreation leadership, the attention of a group is usually better gained by speaking at a relatively moderate volume instead of using a loud voice. By doing so, the group must become quiet in order to understand you. This technique also has an added advantage in that clients feel irritated if you shout at them. As with tone of voice, it behooves the therapeutic recreation specialist to be constantly aware of implications of the volume of the voice. *How* you say things does make a difference.

Effective Listening

To improve communication, therapeutic recreation specialists must seek not only to be understood but also to understand. The final, and perhaps most critical, of Purtilo's (1984) determinants of successful verbal communication is the ability to understand, or the ability to be an effective listener.

All of us who have ever had fun playing the gossip game know that listening can be difficult. This is a game in which everyone sits in a circle. The leader whispers a tidbit of information to the next person in the circle, who in turn passes on the gossip. The gossip continues to be passed from person to person until it gets back to the leader. Rarely, if ever, are the original and final versions of the gossip even slightly related.

One author has stated that distortion may occur with the sender, the message itself, or with the receiver (Simmons, 1976). Primary factors influencing the sender are the physical ability to produce sound and motivation. Disease processes affecting the client's teeth, mouth, nose, or throat may impair speech, as may conditions such as aphasia. Motives such as fear or embarrassment may also cause the sender to distort or conceal information. For example, negative information may be forgotten for fear it may be upsetting to someone, or information may be slightly altered to give a more positive picture of an event.

The message itself may also become distorted. Words or phrases may be interpreted in several ways, causing semantic difficulties. For example, the phrase "Go jump in the lake," may be taken as either a helpful suggestion to beat the heat on a hot day, or as a derogatory remark.

Finally, communication may break down with the receiver. As with the sender, physical problems may be a factor in message distortion. A hearing problem can drastically alter the message's meaning. Additionally, there are several other ways in which the listener may distort what he or she hears. Chief among these are the listener's mental set, perceptual defenses, problems with directiveness, and sensory overloading.

Mental Set

The listener's **mental set**, or frame of reference resulting from previous experience, often brings about unintentional distortions of communication. One author has listed stereotypes, fixed beliefs, negative attitude, lack of interest, and lack of facts as pitfalls that may lead to distorted messages (Killen, 1977).

- *Stereotypes* are widely held generalizations about people or things. Although stereotypes may contain a grain of trust, they rarely hold when applied to a particular person or thing. It is a pitfall to engage in close-minded, stereotyped-based thinking instead of being open to new perceptions.
- *Fixed beliefs* are barriers to listening somewhat akin to stereotypes. The accurate listener does not filter out or automatically dismiss information just because it is not congruent with his or her own beliefs.
- A *negative attitude* toward the sender may interfere with listening. If the sender is not liked or trusted, the result will be a lack of credibility that will negatively affect how the receiver perceives the message.
- A *lack of interest* in the communication will cause the receiver to tune out the sender. The attention of others is aroused when people see how the message relates to them.
- A *lack of facts* causes people to complete information gaps with their own ideas, because people do not like incomplete information. Thus the listener must be aware of information

gaps and seek to obtain all necessary facts rather than fill them in as he or she wishes them to be.

Perceptual Defenses

Another barrier to communication is to ignore aspects of a message or to distort material so it is congruent with the self-conceptions of the receiver. It may be expected that the client whose self-concept is threatened by an illness or disorder will experience difficulty in accepting information that might further threaten self-image.

Problems with Directives

Directives are phrases that instruct people to do certain things. For example, instructions given to clients or other staff are directives. A problem with directives is that sometimes clients can take them more literally than they are intended.

I can recall an experience during my first summer of working in therapeutic recreation at a state hospital in Indiana. At the time I conducted an afternoon program for a group of older male patients at a park on the hospital grounds. Each day I would scurry around beginning one activity and then another in an effort to get as many of the men active as possible. I began one afternoon program by tossing a playground ball with two of the men. As soon as I was sure they were thoroughly engaged in tossing and catching the ball, I withdrew to try to interest others in activities. When I returned a full half-hour later, much to my dismay I found the two men (who were now obviously tired and totally bored) still dutifully tossing the ball to one another! Of course, I did not wish for them to keep up the activity to the point of exhaustion. I had no idea that they would interpret my communications to mean that they should continue until I instructed them to stop.

Professionals in clinical settings must be particularly alert to problems with interpretation of directives: clients may place a great deal of credence in instructions given by staff, perhaps feelings that they will become well if they do exactly what they are told. In such settings miscommunication can lead to false expectations, disappointment, and loss of trust.

Sensory Overloading

Sometimes people cannot absorb or adequately respond to all of the information directed toward them. At such times they are experiencing sensory overload. Limitations in the receiver's capacity to hear and comprehend all incoming stimuli cause barriers to communication. It was mentioned previously that talking too fast may cause problems for the receiver. The presentation of too many ideas or too much complexity may also cause difficulties. To prevent sensory overloading, the therapeutic recreation specialist must attempt to speak at a rate that the client can understand.

LISTENING SKILLS DEVELOPMENT

Effective listening transcends structured interviews or leisure counseling sessions. Effective listening can be employed in any interpersonal transaction in which the therapeutic recreation specialist engages. It is an active process involving four major skills. These are attending, paraphrasing, clarifying, and perception checking (Brammer, 1979). Brammer's discussion of effective listening is the base from which the following materials spring.

Attending

Attending behaviors let the client know you are interested in him or her and are paying attention to what he or she has to say. In my years of going to the inevitable receptions found at conferences and meetings, I have had the opportunity to view a number of humans behaving. One type of behavior I have regularly observed at these events is that of the person who I initially think wishes to speak with me, but who turns out to be more interested in looking past me to see if he or she can spot anyone they would rather be talking with. They do not attend to me or my conversation because they are much too preoccupied with their own hunting expedition. I usually feel as though I am being used as nothing more than a prop, and start looking around myself for a more stimulating, or, at least, more attentive person with whom to share a conversation.

Having others pay attention to us is something most of us appreciate. Clients are no different. If anything, attending behaviors have even greater impact with clients, particularly those who are insecure and easily experience feelings of rejection. Attending skills are basic to our interpersonal transactions if we hope to develop and maintain positive helping relationships.

Attending is accomplished through four primary means:

- Eye contact
- Posture
- Gestures
- Verbal behavior

Eye Contact

All of us have heard the expression "He (or she) gave her (or him) the eye," meaning that one person was indicating a particularly high level of interest in another person. Our eyes offer an expressive mode of communication. Frequent eye contact is one way by which we indicate we are attending to clients.

Eye contact with clients should occur on a regular basis when communicating. This, of course, does not mean staring at the client. You do not continually fix your eyes on friends during social interactions. Clients also dislike being stared at, but they find frequent eye contact reinforcing.

Posture

As with eye contact, extremes should be avoided in posture. Neither appearing too tense nor too relaxed is good. You should not sit or stand in a rigid or stiff position with arms crossed, nor should you present yourself in a slouching fashion. Instead, sitting or standing in a relaxed and open body position, in which you lean forward slightly, should help the client feel comfortable while indicating that you are interested in what he or she is saying.

Gestures

When speaking with friends you may occasionally nod your head as if to say nonverbally, "Yes, I see." This is a type of body movement that indicates interest in what the other person is saying. Other bodily movements, such as hand gesturing, can also be used to suggest that attention is being extended to the client.

Verbal Behavior

The fourth attending channel is verbal behavior. What you say as well as what you do indicates how attentive you are. Refraining from interruptions, questions, and topic jumping displays that you are interested in listening to what the client has to say. Hackney and Cormier (1988) have suggested that minimum verbal responses such as "ah," "I see," "mm-hmm," and "mm-mm" can be effective in indicating you are listening while not interfering with the client's verbal expressions. These authors also have stated that using animation in facial expression, such as an occasional smile, can create the feeling that you are attending to the client's communication.

Paraphrasing

A second listening skill discussed by Brammer (1979) is **paraphrasing**. In paraphrasing, the client's basic communication is restated in similar, but ordinarily fewer, words. This tells the client that you are listening. It also gives feedback to confirm your understanding of the client's central message.

A three-step process for paraphrasing is outlined by Brammer (1979): (1) listen for the basic idea or ideas expressed: (2) restate these in a brief way, summarizing what the client said; and (3) note the client's response to your restatement to determine the accuracy and helpfulness of your paraphrasing.

An example of paraphrasing follows.

Client: I really think it's neat to go out to the beach; it's so nice with the sand and all. It's fun. I could spend days there.
Helper: You really do enjoy going to the beach.
Client: Yes, I like it a whole lot.

Clarifying

The clarifying response is admitting to the client that you are confused about what was said and wish to clarify its meaning. When you are confused by an ambiguous or cryptic message, you can simply request the client to rephrase what was said, or you can ask the client to respond to your interpretation of what he or she said.

In the first instance you might say, "I'm confused. Would you go over that again for me?," or "I'm afraid I don't follow you.

Could you describe your feeling in another way?" When using the second clarifying technique, you are actually using a form of paraphrasing. This response might begin, "I think I got lost there. Let me try to restate what I thought you said."

Perception Checking

Perception checking, sometimes referred to as checking out, is very similar to clarifying. Here you are checking on the accuracy of your perceptions of what the client said. You are validating your understanding of the client's communication. You might say, "You seem to be happy—is that right?" Another example would be, "You really seem to care about attending the dance. Did I understand you correctly?"

A three-step process for perception checking has been provided by Brammer (1979):

- Paraphrasing what you think you heard;
- Asking for the client to confirm or disconfirm your understanding; and
- Permitting the client to correct inaccurate misperceptions.

Exercises in Appendix A: Listening Exercises provide an opportunity to try out the four major listening skills: "Attending," "Paraphrasing," "Clarifying," and "Perception Checking" (p. 267).

Additional Verbal Responses

Major verbal responses for helping professionals to employ in promoting the understanding of self and others have been reviewed in the literature (e.g., Corey, 1995; Evans, et al. 1993; Okun, 1992; Sundeem, et al.,1994). Included are:

- Minimal verbal responses
- Paraphrasing
- Checking out
- Clarifying
- Probing
- Reflecting
- Interpreting
- Confronting
- Informing

• Summarizing
• Self-Disclosing

A review of the list of verbal responses may bring to mind visions of formal interviews or counseling sessions in which a therapeutic recreation specialist helps a client to gain self-understanding. Therapeutic recreation specialists do conduct interviews and engage in leisure counseling, but these structures account for only one segment of the total delivery of therapeutic recreation services. As with listening skills, it is more likely that these verbal responses will be a part of day-to-day contacts with clients. Thus, while particularly helpful in facilitating client self-understanding during interviews and leisure counseling, the effective use of these verbal responses has much wider application.

Neither is the list as mysterious and foreboding as it might initially seem. As a matter of fact, four of the ten responses have already been reviewed in the last section on listening skills. Thus the reader is referred back to the listening skills material for information on minimal verbal responses, paraphrasing, checking out (perception checking), and clarifying.

TABLE 6-1
VERBAL RESPONSES

Minimal Verbal Responses are verbal cues such as "mm-mm," "yes," "I see," and "uh-huh." Their purpose is to indicate interest without disrupting the client's communication.

Paraphrasing involves rephrasing the content of the client's message in slightly different words. It is used to assist the helper understand the client's statements and to provide support and clarification.

Checking Out provides the helper with a chance to confirm or correct perceptions or understandings. It is used to clear up confusion about perceptions of the client's behavior or to try out a hunch.

Clarifying facilitates understanding the basic nature of the client's statement. Its purpose is to help the client sort out conflicting and confused thoughts and feelings and to assist the helper to understand what is being communicated.

TABLE 6-1 CONT.

Probing involves searching for additional information with such statements as "Tell me more," or "Let's talk about that." It is used to obtain more information.

Reflecting is rephrasing the affective part of the client's message. Its purpose is to help the client to understand his or her feelings.

Interpreting involves offering possible explanation for certain behaviors, thoughts or feelings. Its purpose is to add new perspectives to the client's understanding of his or her behaviors, thoughts, or feelings.

Confronting challenges clients to examine discrepancies between their words and actions. Its purpose is to encourage honest self-examination.

Informing transpires when objective and factual information is shared with the client. Its purpose is to convey information and not to advise the client.

Summarizing pulls together and condenses the important elements of the session. It is used to avoid fragmentation and give direction. Often, it is employed as a means to draw a session to a close.

Self-disclosing is sharing personal information with the client about the helper's experiences, attitudes or feelings. Such information is disclosed when it appears it will help the client.

Two final comments are necessary before reviewing specific verbal responses. First, another response that can be made is no response, or the use of silence. Brief periods of silence provide clients with a chance to consider what they just said and to prepare to speak again. For clients who are not verbal, silence may also provoke anxiety on their part and cause them to become more verbal. When silence is used, the helper must be aware of his other nonverbal communication in order to indicate interest in what the client has to say. The other comment is that the verbal responses presented do not by any means constitute the universe of verbal responses that the therapeutic recreation specialist can employ. These particular responses are designed to facilitate self-knowledge in contrast to developing client skills and attitudes.

Probing

A probe is a question that is directed toward yielding information in order to gain empathetic understanding. Probes are open-ended questions requiring more than a yes or no reply. Okun (1987) suggests probes such as, "Tell me more," "Let's talk about that," and "I'm wondering about. . ." (p.76). A brief example of a probe in a client-helper interaction follows.

Client: There are lots of things I like about hiking.
Helper: Tell me some of them.

Reflecting

The reflection response is a statement to reflect feelings received from the client through verbal or nonverbal means. Its aim is to mirror the feelings or emotions of the client. An example is: "It sounds as if you were really pleased to learn the outcome." An example of a client-helper exchange follows.

Client: I was mad as hell that they didn't ask me to join the team.
Helper: It seems you were feeling very angry about not being chosen.

Interpreting

Through interpretation something is added to the statement of the client. Here the helper is trying to help the client understand his or her underlying feelings. These responses are based on direct observation of what the client does and says, not on deep psychology. After the interpretation has been given, immediate feedback is sought from the client to see if your interpretation is correct. For example:

Client: I just can't seem to get my act together to join the club. I tend to put it off even though I really want to do it.
Helper: You seem to be frightened to take the first step in joining.

Confronting

The purpose of the confronting response is to assist the client to achieve congruency in what he or she says and does, or to help him or her be fully aware and honest in gaining self-understanding. Confrontation involves "telling it like it is," without being accusatory or judgmental. If the client does not seem to be genuine in his or her communications, this is pointed out. Okun (1992) has given these examples: "I feel you really don't want to talk about this," "It seems to me that you're playing games with her," and "I'm wondering why you feel you always have to take the blame. What do you get out of it?" (p.71). In raising discrepancies the helper expresses what seem to be contradictions in the client's comments or behavior. The following are examples of pointing out discrepancies. "You say you're angry, yet you're smiling," or "On the one hand, you seem to be hurt by not getting that job, but on the other hand you seem sort of relieved, too" (Okun, 1992, p.71).

It has been suggested that confrontation should not be used until rapport has been fully established and a positive helping relationship has developed (Egan, 1994). Another author has mentioned that the wise helper will limit confrontations to strengths instead of picking on the client's imperfections (Schulman, 1982).

An example of a confronting verbal response follows.

Client: I don't want to be around any girls.
Helper: You say you don't want to associate with girls, yet I saw you dancing with both Nancy and Joyce last night and you seemed to be having a very good time.

Informing

Informing transpires when objective and factual information is shared with the client. Informing is providing factual information to the client. Its purpose is to convey information only, and not to advise the client. In therapeutic recreation this might be describing types of programs available to the client. Informing is *not* telling the client what to do. For example:

Client: I don't know what to get into.
Helper: Let me describe the choices you have here at the center.

Summarizing

Summarizing pulls together and condenses the important elements of the session. It is used to avoid fragmentation and give direction. Often, it is employed as a means to draw a session to a close. Summarizing brings together the client's central ideas, feelings, or both. The summary synthesizes what has been communicated so the client can see significant patterns. It is normally applied at the conclusion of a counseling session or after several sessions. An example of a summarizing response follows.

Client: A lot of time I'd rather stay home and watch a game on TV, or read the paper or something like that. My wife always wants to go out and I don't think I should have to go just because she wants to.

Helper: You would prefer to stay home, while your wife wishes for you to go out with her.

Self-disclosing

Self-disclosing allows personal disclosures on the part of the helper with the intent of providing the client with an opportunity to perceive the helper as another human being who has encountered situations, thoughts or feelings similar to those faced by the client. Revealed may be personal experiences, thoughts, attitudes or feelings. In so doing, the helper not only reveals his or her reactions but may create trust and presents a model of how to reveal oneself to others (Corey, 1995). The use of limited self-disclosure has been suggested to be particularly effective during the beginning phase of the therapeutic relationship at which time the client may seek information about the helper such as hometown, marital status, and years in his or her profession (Sundeen, et al., 1994). An example of self-disclosure follows.

Client: This is my cat, Plato. I don't know what I would do without him. He is like a friend.

Helper: I love my cat, Sam, too. He greets me every evening when I get home and sleeps on the bottom of my bed at night. I guess he is like a friend to me also.

In closing this section it should be mentioned that the verbal responses presented here may seem at first to be very similar in nature. They are actually distinctive types of responses that the emerging helping professional should learn to discriminate among. Once familiar with them, their use will become more natural. Just as word processors differentiate among the keys on a keyboard without having to think about striking a particular letter, helping professionals learn to use the verbal responses without consciously defining the type of response before employing it.

It should also be reiterated that the verbal responses outlined bring about an expanded understanding of self and others. Although these responses are generally employed in formal interviewing and counseling sessions, they may also be appropriately applied in less structured interpersonal communications that typify therapeutic recreation. With the knowledge of these responses also comes the responsibility to resist any temptation to become a pseudo-psychotherapist. In Appendix B: Verbal Response Identification Exercise, you will find a verbal response exercise (see p. 269).

COMMUNICATION IN
SUCCESS-FAILURE SITUATIONS

Therapeutic recreation specialists spend a great deal of time interacting with clients while the clients take part in recreation activities. It is important, therefore, to explore communications between leaders and clients so that an understanding of effective feedback patterns can be gained. In the following section, feedback patterns and their effects are discussed.

Feedback
Research strongly suggests that therapeutic recreation specialists need to develop both an awareness of the messages given their clients during recreation participation and a working knowledge of the types of effective **feedback** that may be applied in leader-client communication. In a study completed at a camp for children with disabilities, researchers (Bullock, Austin, & Lewko, 1980) examined the nature of feedback counselors provided to campers. Prior findings (Panada & Lynch, 1972) had

indicated the importance of proper feedback, but Bullock and his colleagues found that no feedback at all was supplied in more than 20 percent of the interactions where campers experienced success on a task. As pointed out by these researchers, lack of feedback may be interpreted by the child as an indication of failure.

Furthermore, these researchers commented that for feedback to be most useful in failure situations, it should be specifically related to the task at hand (i.e., contingent), should give the participant information to make corrections in performance (i.e., informational), and should give some amount of encouragement (i.e., motivational). In situations where the campers did not succeed, the researchers found that less than 50 percent were furnished this type of feedback. In approximately 16 percent of the failure situations, no feedback at all was provided.

Attribution Theory

The Bullock team also considered the attributional nature of counselor feedback. The theoretical basis for this portion of the study was Weiner's (1974) **attribution theory**, which theorizes that people formulate explanations for their own and others' successes and failures. Basically, these explanations involve two dimensions, stability (stable, unstable) and locus of control (internal, external), and four determinants of success or failure, ability (a stable internal factor), effort (an unstable internal factor), task difficulty (a stable external factor), and luck (an unstable external factor).

Therefore, the camp counselor might judge that a camper was successful because he or she had a high level of ability (a stable-internal attribution); because he or she tried hard (an unstable-internal attribution); because it was an easy task (a stable-external attribution); or because of chance (an unstable-external attribution). On the other hand, the counselor could stereotype the child with a disability and, therefore, reason that any failure was due to a low ability ascribed to the disability. This would result in the expectation that the child could not succeed unless the task was made easier. If, instead, the failure was judged to be because of an unstable factor (low effort or bad luck), a more optimistic expectation would follow.

Feedback Awareness and the Attribution Theory

The possible effects of voicing these judgments in feedback statements seem obvious. Naturally, the child might develop certain concepts of his or her abilities (or lack of abilities) through communication from significant others. Thus, in addition to possibly establishing a "self-fulfilling prophecy," a child's self-concept could be seriously affected as a result of feedback. Much to the distress of Bullock and the other researchers, observations of counselor-camper interactions revealed relatively few explicit attributional statements by counselors that either attributed unsuccessful performance to unstable determinants (effort or luck) or offered praise directly tied to the camper's ability.

All in all, the study by Bullock and his colleagues revealed that staff generally seemed unaware of their feedback patterns, or of the possible effects their feedback might have on the children. The results have obvious implications for leader-client feedback patterns in all therapeutic recreation settings.

Guidelines for Feedback

Bullock and his colleagues (1980, pp.147-148) presented several explicit guidelines for providing feedback in therapeutic recreation leadership situations:

- Feedback should be given in nearly all if not all performance situations.
- In successful outcomes, the feedback should be contingent, informational, and positive and/or motivational.
- Attributional statements should be made more frequently.
- Attributional information must be explicitly stated in order for a clear understanding to (be given) the client.
- Reinforce success with internal stable attributional statements such as "Nice shot, I knew you could do it!"
- Encourage the child with unstable attributional statements following unsuccessful attempts. For example, "You'll have to try harder."

An exercise on feedback can be found in Appendix C: Feedback Exercise of this chapter (see p. 272).

NONVERBAL COMMUNICATION

Although we usually think of communication as involving verbal behavior, words represent only a small part of our total interpersonal communication patterns. The vast majority of our communicating is done on a nonverbal level (Sundeen et al., 1976). One author has stated that in face-to-face communication, only one-third of our communicating takes place on a verbal level, while two-thirds is nonverbal (Brill, 1995). Additionally, **nonverbal communication** is important in therapeutic recreation, because it can be particularly effective as an outlet for expressing feelings and attitudes that clients cannot express or do not wish to express verbally. Expressive recreation pursuits such as music, physical movement, and creative writing allow for the manifestation of feelings and attitudes through nonverbal means.

Nonverbal communications are, of course, the messages passing between a sender and receiver that do not rely on the spoken word. It has been specified that nonverbal communication is expressed continuously in human interactions. With or without accompanying verbal behavior, nonverbal communication is continuous in the presence of others, since all nonverbal behavior has potential message value (Brill, 1995). From this perspective ". . .it follows that no matter how one may try, one *must* communicate. Activity or inactivity, words or silence all have message value: they influence others and these others, in turn, cannot *not* respond to these communications and are thus themselves communicating" (Waltzlawick et al., 1967, p.49). For example, even silence or inactivity in the company of others may carry a message that a person is sad, bored, or perhaps depressed. Nonverbal communication is going on all the time, making it impossible not to communicate.

Nonverbal communication is obviously of great importance in interpersonal transactions. Therapeutic recreation specialists must become aware of nonverbal communication in order to pick up nonverbal cues from clients and staff, and be aware of possible effects of their own nonverbal communication on others.

Specific Examples of Nonverbal Behaviors

Tubbs and Moss (1981) have classified nonverbal behaviors into three categories: visual cues, vocal cues, and spatial and temporal cues. The information about these cues that follows has been drawn primarily from the work of Tubbs and Moss.

Visual Cues

Some visual cues to nonverbal communication have been mentioned as a part of the discussion on listening skills. Nevertheless, information on eye contact, body movement, and gestures is important and is repeated in the visual cues that follow.

Facial Expression

Our faces express numerous feelings and emotions. A friendly smile invites further interaction. A frown may indicate sadness. Grimaces may be a sign of anger. Blushing often indicates embarrassment. An animated face may show excitement and vigor, while a "poker face" may project the image of a bland person.

Eye Contact

It is reinforcing to receive eye contact. When someone does not look us in the eye, we may feel they are shifty or that they are hiding something. Of course, we must be aware that there are cultural differences in the use of eye contact and remain sensitive to these.

Body Movements

Our bodies are used to signal others in various ways. Biting our nails may indicate nervousness. Physical touch may be used to demonstrate caring and support. Fidgeting may distract from other messages.

Hand Gestures

The peace sign and the hitchhiker's raised thumb are two gestures we all recognize. Most people would also recognize the drumming of fingers on a table as a sign of impatience. Hand gestures may substitute substantially for verbal behavior, as in the case of sign language for those who are hearing impaired.

Physical Appearance and the Use of Objects

Rightly or wrongly, as documented by the classic social psychology study of Kelley (1950), first impressions have a potent effect. Therefore, it becomes important to realize that we may project a negative impression through extremes in clothing or jewelry. Equally important is that therapeutic recreation specialists guard against the pitfall of stereotyping that may result from generalizations made about clients after only brief contact.

The term *object language* is used by authors to denote the message value in physical objects. How people dress, decorate their homes and offices, their choices of magazines, the car they drive, and many other physical objects communicate nonverbal messages about them. Bumper stickers and t-shirts are popular means today for passing along nonverbal messages about ourselves. When we see a bumper sticker stating "I'm a Leisure Lover" or a t-shirt reading "Let's park and recreate," these bring certain connotations to mind.

Vocal Cues

Earlier in this chapter, vocal cues such as tone of voice and volume and rate of speech were discussed. These, and voice pitch and quality, constitute vocal phenomena that accompany speech and are sometimes termed paralinguistics. Various vocal cues are briefly reviewed here.

Volume

Speaking too loudly is likely to offend others. Speaking too softly also can be irritating. However, what is an appropriate level of volume to one group of people may not be for another group coming from a different cultural background. Therefore, it is best to test which volume works best in each situation.

Rate and Fluency

Our rate of speech may be taken by others as evidence of our mood. We often speak rapidly when we are excited and exhibit slower speech when depressed. Speaking too rapidly or too slowly may cause tension to be revealed in the listener. Fluency has to do with the continuity of speech. Pausing frequently and inserting "ah" or "er" distracts from the central message.

Pitch

The unvarying use of one level of voice pitch can be monotonous. An expressive person will vary voice pitch to reflect attitude or mood naturally.

Quality

Voice quality deals with how pleasant we perceive a voice to be. For example, a harsh, piercing voice may be distracting.

Spatial and Temporal Cues

To be effective in our interpersonal communications, we should be aware of the factors of time and space and the possible effects they may each have on communications.

Time

The concept of time varies from culture to culture. Americans generally seem to be very aware of time and may react when normal customs regarding time are violated. For instance, arriving late for a social invitation or a business appointment may offend those who are expecting you. This behavior may say to them that you do not hold them in high regard.

Space

Human communication may be affected significantly by the way people position themselves in relation to others. We might stand or sit very close to someone with whom we are in an intimate relationship. On the other hand, we normally attempt to maintain some social distance with clients so as not to infringe on their sense of personal space. As Sommer's (1969) work has shown, interaction patterns can be affected by something as simple as how furniture is placed. Certain seating arrangements foster interpersonal transactions, while others have the opposite effect. Unfortunately, many times this variable has not been considered by those in helping relationships.

To summarize this section, it seems clear that nonverbal communication processes are extensive. In face-to-face communication with clients we must take advantage of all the cues available to use. Therefore, the development of skills in interpreting nonverbal communication is essential. Several excellent exercises related to perceiving and giving nonverbal cues are available. The exercises in Appendix D: Nonverbal Cue

Exercises (p. 273) are drawn and adapted from Hackney and Cormier (1988), Okun (1992), and Stevens (1988).

COMMUNICATION WITH CLIENTS WITH SPECIAL NEEDS

Therapeutic recreation specialists may need to communicate with individuals with special needs. The guidelines that appear in Table 6-2 can prove helpful when communicating with clients who have visual or hearing impairments, use wheelchairs, or speak a foreign language.

TABLE 6-2
COMMUNICATION WITH CLIENTS
WITH SPECIAL NEEDS

Clients Who are Visually Impaired

- Speak to the person in a normal volume. Having a visual impairment does not imply hearing loss.
- Do not worry about using words such as "see." Persons with visual impairments desire that you speak to them as you would to anyone.
- Acknowledge your presence in a room and tell the client who else is present if anyone else is with you. Identify yourself by name.
- When you first meet someone who has a visual impairment, feel free to shake hands. If the other person has not extended his or her hand, say "How do you do, let me shake your hand." Of course, the process of aligning and making contact is up to you.
- Describe the environment, people, and events in the area to increase the client's understanding.
- Orient the client to the arrangement of the room or area and its furnishings.

TABLE 6-2 CONT.

- Provide orientation to the area by helping the person to use all senses to become oriented. If the individual tends to rely on one sense more than others, the dominant sense should be emphasized.
- Consistency in language and terminology is important when orienting a client as is the reference system. Compass directions can be used or boundaries (of the room, playground, etc.) can be identified by permanent landmarks.
- When orienting, provide a general familiarization by describing the area and encouraging the client to walk around the area to become comfortable with it.
- Tactile maps and signs can be used to help persons to orient themselves to new surroundings.
- Indicate to the client when the conversation has ended and when you are leaving the room.
- When offering assistance, do so directly, asking; "May I be of help?"
- All directions should be clear, concise, and consistent. Use directional words such as "left" and "right" and cite landmarks (e.g., "Walk through the exit. Then immediately turn to the right.").
- Use tactile, hands-on demonstrations along with verbal instructions.
- The client should be near enough to see or touch when demonstrations are provided.
- Use verbal instructions to create mental images for person with adventitious visual impairments.
- Never leave the client without a way to secure help by means of a signal of some kind.
- Never leave the client in an open area. Lead the client to the side of a room, to a chair or some landmark.
- Never grab the client's arm to guide him or her. Allow the client to take your arm.
- To assist a client to a chair, simply place his or her hand on the back or arm of the chair.

TABLE 6-2 CONT.

Clients Who are Hearing Impaired

- Do not let any object (e.g., hand, cigarette) cover your mouth. Men cause difficulty for the client if they wear big mustaches that obscure the lips.
- Speak distinctly but naturally. Speak moderately loudly but do not shout. Do not exaggerate your speech patterns or speak extremely slowly. On the other hand, do not speak too rapidly.
- When coming to the end of a sentence, do not drop your voice because the last two or three words can be important to understanding. Pause slightly at the end of a sentence to allow for the client to comprehend the message.
- When conveying a lengthy message, get some intermediate feedback along the way to make sure you are communicating.
- Alert the client to your presence before starting a conversation. This may be done by gently touching the client on the arm or shoulder or by moving so you can be seen.
- If someone is having difficulty understanding you, do not simply repeat what you have said but substitute synonyms.
- If the person has an unaffected ear, stand or sit on that side of the individual when you speak. (In referring to disabilities, learn to use the terms *affected* and *unaffected* to distinguish conditions. The use of these terms does not open you or your client to the possibility of thinking in negative terms regarding his or her abilities. They are also used by other helping professionals who deal with people with disabilities.)
- If you are having a difficult time communicating, write key words on a pad of paper. Of course, you do not have to restrict yourself to words. A map, picture, or diagram may be a better idea.

TABLE 6-2 CONT.

- An interpreter with sign language or fingerspelling skills should be made available for group presentations.

Clients Who Use Wheelchairs

- When having a conversation with a person who uses a wheelchair, make an effort to position yourself so that it will not be uncomfortable for him or her to look at you. It is usually best to seat yourself at eye level with the individual. For a very short conversation, do whatever seems easiest.
- Ask whether help is wanted before beginning to assist the person. This includes pushing the person in the chair.

Clients Who Speak a Foreign Language

- Use an interpreter if one is available.
- Use a dictionary that translates foreign words so you can speak a few words in the client's language.
- Use a normal tone of voice (do not speak loudly).
- Demonstrate or pantomime ideas you wish to convey, as appropriate.
- Be aware of nonverbal communication. Many nonverbal cues are universal.

Sources: Kelley, J. (ed.). (1981). *Recreation Programming for Visually Impaired Children and Youth.* New York: American Foundation for the Blind; Maloff, C. & Wood, S.M. (1988). *Business and Social Etiquette with Disabled People.* Springfield, IL: Charles C. Thomas Publisher. Murry, R.B. & Huelskoetter, M.M.W. (1991). *Psychiatric/Mental Health Nursing.* (3rd ed.). Norwalk, CT: Appleton & Lange; Smith, R.W., Austin, D.R. & Kennedy, D.W. (1996). Inclusive and Special Recreation: Opportunities for Persons with Disabilities (3rd ed.). Madison, WI: Brown & Benchmark Publishers; Taylor, C., Lillis, C. & LeMone, P. (1993). *Fundamentals of Nursing* (2nd ed.). Philadelphia: J.B. Lippincott Company.

INTERVIEWING: A FORM OF COMMUNICATION

The interview is a structured, face-to-face method of communication directed toward a particular end. Intents for interviews in therapeutic recreation will vary, but probably the most common type is the initial assessment interview discussed in Chapter 4. Therapeutic recreation specialists may additionally conduct interviews with clients' families and friends, during new client orientation programs, during leisure counseling, and for other purposes.

The Setting

Ideally, the interview setting should offer a quiet, relaxed atmosphere where privacy is assured. Too often, it seems, therapeutic recreation specialists are expected to conduct interviews on busy admissions wards or in active recreation areas. Do not trap yourself, or the client, into approaching the interview too casually because it concerns "only recreation." There is a great deal of difference between being relaxed and being careless in your approach.

Interviews can be structured to be formal or informal. Formal interviews are often conducted in an office or in a special room designed for interviewing. An informally structured interview might be conducted in a recreation area. In fact, some clients (and interviewers) feel most comfortable in an informal recreation setting. If this is the case, interviews might be conducted while shooting baskets in a gym, playing a table game, or having a soft drink in a quiet area of a snack bar. Psychological privacy, or feeling that you have a place to yourselves, is perhaps as important as the actual physical setting that is chosen.

Whatever the area selected to conduct the interview, it should be free from interruptions. There is nothing more distracting than to have clients called away in order to take medication, see the social worker, or participate in some seemingly "more important" activity. Protect yourself by scheduling your interviews at times when competition for the client's time is minimum and clearly inform other personnel of the need for an uninterrupted interview.

Phases

Most authorities agree that interviews have three phases, the beginning phase, the working phase, and the termination phase.

Beginning Phase

In any interview the first step is to help the client feel as comfortable as possible (Bernstein & Bernstein, 1985). The therapeutic recreation specialist should strive to create an atmosphere displaying openness, warmth, and respect for the client.

Just how the client should be greeted varies from interview to interview and person to person. It would be inappropriate to approach a small child with a strong handshake, or to provide a depressed individual with a vigorous welcome (Schulman, 1982). It has been suggested that a good beginning may be simply welcoming the client with a smile, introducing yourself, and inviting the person to sit down. Early in the initial interview you may indicate the length of time available for the session, your role, and the purpose of the interview. You may wish to inform the interviewee how you prefer to be addressed and also inquire as to how he or she would like to be addressed. Finally, you may want to talk with new clients about the confidentiality of the situation. Will you share the information with anyone? If you are taking notes or tape-recording, who will have access to these? Depending on your agency and situation, particular questions on confidentiality may or may not be important. You will have to determine which specific confidentiality issues are seen as important at your agency or institution (Hackney & Cormier, 1988).

Working Phase

During this stage, both you and the client have settled into comfortable positions and are ready to begin work. At this time, you direct the interview toward the primary goal for the session. This might involve any number of general objectives, such as gaining information regarding a client's leisure interests or allowing the client to express how he or she would expect to profit from therapeutic recreation programming.

Termination Phase

Toward the conclusion of the session, the therapeutic recreation specialist should indicate that it is almost time to stop. This may be done with a short, clear statement ("It seems our time is almost up for today"), summarization, or mutual feedback. By briefly summarizing the information and/or feelings expressed, the therapeutic recreation specialist and the client leave the interview with similar ideas about what has been communicated. Mutual feedback involves both the client and helper. This termination strategy is recommended if a plan has been formed, or specific decisions made. Both participants can clarify and verify what has been decided and what future steps are to be taken (Hackney & Cormier, 1988). Of course, it is appropriate to use the last few seconds of the session to make arrangements for the time and place of the next session if additional interviews are necessary.

TABLE 6-3
TECHNIQUES FOR THE
PRODUCTIVE INTERVIEW

- *Establish rapport.* Create a warm, accepting climate.
- *Control the external environment.* Minimize external distractions in a comfortable environment that offers privacy.
- *Wear clothing that conveys the image of a professional and is appropriate for the situation.* In some cases, clients will respond more readily to casual dress. With other clients, professional dress may inspire feelings of confidentiality.
- *Begin by stating and validating with the client the purpose of the interview.* You may begin with social conversation but should move relatively quickly into the purpose of the interview.
- *Use a vocabulary on the level of awareness or understanding of the person.* Avoid jargon and abstract words.
- *Avoid preconceived ideas, prejudices, or biases.* Do not impose your values on clients.

TABLE 6-3 CONT.

- *Be precise in what you say, so the meaning is understood. Say as little as possible to keep the interview moving.* Careful timing of your communications and allowing time for the client to understand and respond are important.
- *Avoid asking questions in ways that get only socially acceptable answers.* Otherwise, clients may tell you what they think you want to hear.
- *Be gentle and tactful when asking questions about home life or personal matters.* Things you may consider common information may be seen as being very private by some clients. You may inquire tactfully by asking indirect and peripheral questions.
- *Be an attentive listener.* Show interest by using attending behaviors such as eye contact, posture, gestures, and minimal verbal response.
- *Carefully observe nonverbal messages for signs of anxiety, frustration, anger, loneliness, or guilt.* Encourage the free expression of feelings and look for feelings of pressure hidden under attempts to be calm. Allow ventilation of feelings.
- *Encourage spontaneity.* Provide movement in the interview by picking up verbal leads, cues, bits of seemingly unrelated information, and nonverbal signals from the client.
- *Ask questions beginning with "What. . .?" "Where. . .?" "Who. . .?" and "When. . .?" to gain factual information.* Words connoting moral judgments should be avoided because they are not conducive to feelings of acceptance and freedom of expression.
- *Keep data obtained in the interview confidential and share this information only with the appropriate and necessary health team members.* The client should be told what information will be shared and with whom.
- *Evaluate the interview.* Was the purpose accomplished?

Source: Murry, R.B. & Huelskoetter, M.M.W. 1987. *Psychiatric/Mental Health Nursing* (2nd edition). Norwalk, CT: Appleton & Lange; pp.139-145.

In Appendix E at the end of this chapter, you will find an interview exercise.

SUMMARY

Success in helping relationships depends to a large degree on the ability of the therapeutic recreation specialist to communicate effectively with clients. The interpersonal communication skills employed in client transactions are basically the same skills used in everyday encounters. In social relationships, however, they may be casually employed. In contrast, in professional helping relationships where our primary focus is always on the client, our communications are consciously directed toward client needs in order to facilitate growth leading to independence and self-sufficiency.

READING COMPREHENSION QUESTIONS

1. Define the term communication in your own words.
2. Why are communication skills important to therapeutic recreation specialists?
3. Is professional jargon appropriate in client communications?
4. What are some guidelines to help avoid rambling communication?
5. How may attitudes enter into interpersonal communication?
6. How may voice tone and volume affect communication?
7. What things may cause the receiver to distort a message?
8. Explain why listening may be termed an active process.
9. What behaviors let the client know you are attending to what he or she is saying?
10. Explain the four major listening skills discussed in the chapter.
11. Briefly explain each of the verbal responses outlined in the chapter.
12. Do you understand the rationale behind each of the guidelines for feedback?
13. How much of our face-to-face communication is transmitted through nonverbal means?

14. What is the importance of studying nonverbal communication?
15. Why might it be said that one cannot not communicate?
16. Give some specific examples of nonverbal cues.
17. What does an "I'm a Leisure Lover" bumper sticker have to do with nonverbal communication?
18. Can you make any suggestions as to the setting for interviews?
19. What may be stipulated as the initial step in any interview?
20. Outline the phases of an interview.

APPENDIX A:
LISTENING EXERCISES

Attending Exercises

Eye contact, posture, gestures, and verbal behavior can have a powerful reinforcing effect on clients' communication. Although attending seems like a simple process to grasp and an easy thing to do, lack of attending in interpersonal relations is very common (Egan, 1994).

One simple attending exercise you might try is nonresponse. Get a partner and decide who will be A and who will be B. For two or three minutes, A should talk about any topic of his or her choosing. B should not attend to A (e.g., avoid eye contact, look around the room). Discuss how this felt. Did A feel frustrated? What sort of attending behaviors would A have appreciated receiving? Did B wish he or she could have responded? How? When?

Now switch roles. A should assume the B role and vice versa. At first, B should not attend to A as this person talks about something he or she likes very much. But after two minutes, B should try out his or her best attending skills. For the next two or three minutes B should use eye contact, gestures, posture, and verbal responses to encourage A to talk. Stop after a total of four or five minutes and discuss the differences between minimal and appropriate attending behaviors.

Egan (1994) has suggested an exercise that involves four persons. In this group of four, decide who is A,B,C, and D. A and B should spend five or six minutes discussing what they like or do not like about their styles of interpersonal communication. C and D should act as observers, with particular attention paid to nonverbal behavior, voice tone, pitch, volume, pacing, and so on (sometimes referred to as paralinguistic behavior). C and D should give feedback to A and B regarding their observations. Then roles should be exchanged and the exercise repeated.

Paraphrasing Exercises

Following this paragraph are some client statements. Practice restating these by writing your restatement either in the space that follows each or on a separate piece of paper.

Client: I really have an awful time with trying to remember everyone's names.

Response:

Client: Probably the worst thing I have to do is see Dr. Smith.

Response:

Then, with a partner, practice using paraphrasing while a third person observes. After you have used this technique for three or four minutes, the observer should report his or her observations, and these should be discussed among the three of you. Following this discussion, you may wish to change roles and repeat the exercise.

In completing the exercise, keep in mind that trite phrases prefacing your remarks such as, "I hear you saying. . . ." should generally be avoided (Brammer, 1979). It has also been warned that the overuse of paraphrasing can lead to a "parrotlike" effect (Hackney & Cormier, 1988), so attempt to interfuse other types of responses with the paraphrase. You may, for instance, try out some of the attending techniques.

Clarifying Exercise

College students have been exposed many times to clarifying in their classes as other students have attempted to clarify what instructors were saying. Within a small group of students, discuss occasions when you or other students have sought clarification in class. Do you remember any particularly well-stated clarification responses? Have any sounded like criticisms of the instructor instead of requests for clarification? For example, a student seeking clarification may, instead, sound critical by saying, "I haven't understood one word you've said all day. What in the world are you talking about?"

Listening Exercise

To listen effectively, the four major types of responses must become a natural part of your behavior repertoire. Again, with a partner, try out perception checking, clarifying, paraphrasing, and attending listening skills. Discuss the importance of developing effective listening skills (or any other topic of your choosing) while being observed by a third person. After 5 minutes, this person should present feedback to you and your partner on the use of listening skills. The observer may wish to jot down behaviors to aid the discussion.

APPENDIX B
VERBAL RESPONSE IDENTIFICATION EXERCISE

Verbal Response Exercise

Okun (1992) has presented an exercise on identification and recognition of the ten major verbal responses. This exercise is adapted from that of Okun. Each of the helper statements uses one of the ten responses. Read the helper's response, then identify it as one of the following: minimal verbal response, paraphrasing, checking out, clarifying, probing, reflecting, interpreting, confronting, informing, or summarizing. Record the responses you identify on a piece of paper. Then check them with the answers provided.

(1)
Client: I really felt good about being at the dance last night.
Helper: You were glad to be there.

(2)
Client: I don't even want to think about the swim team, let alone join it.
Helper: I saw you at the pool yesterday and you are an excellent swimmer, yet you always back off when the swim team is mentioned.

(3)
Client: I used to be really involved but during the last term I haven't done anything for recreation. I guess I've been too busy...but that's not it either....I just don't know exactly why I've gotten into this rut.
Helper: You have been active in recreation in the past but you have been inactive for the last few months, and you are unsure as to the cause for this.

(4)
Client: I can't really get with it.
Helper: I see.

(5)
Client: I really like being in a group.
Helper: Let's talk about that.

(6)
Client: Which program is the best for me?
Helper: I would advise you to look at three of the programs offered here at the center. Let me tell you about them.

(7)
Client: As I've said before, I just don't like it.
Helper: I want to check out with you what I'm hearing. You said that you really didn't enjoy it.

(8)
Client: At any rate, I just can't do it because it's too far away and in addition they aren't interested in helping me anyway.
Helper: I'm not sure I follow you. Could you tell me some more about it?

(9)
Client: I just don't know what to do. One time he tells me do this. The next time he says just the opposite.
Helper: He seems to confuse you.

(10)
Client: All they care about is themselves and not what happens to me.
Helper: It is tough when you don't feel people care about you.

Answers
(1)   Reflecting
(2)   Confronting
(3)   Summarizing
(4)   Minimum verbal response
(5)   Probing
(6)   Informing
(7)   Checking out
(8)   Clarifying
(9)   Paraphrasing
(10)   Interpreting

Now you may wish to get together with others who have independently completed the exercise so you can discuss the responses. Did all of you agree with the above answers? Did members of the group feel any of the helper's responses were inappropriate or poorly phrased? If you have time, half of the group should rewrite the helper's statements 1 to 5; the other half should rewrite 6 to 10. Share your statements and discuss which were most difficult to write.

APPENDIX C
FEEDBACK EXERCISE

Feedback Exercise

This exercise involves three people. A should take the role of the leader and B the role of the client. The third person should serve as an observer. A and B should complete a three to five minute role play in which the client is learning or performing a task. This might be making a leather belt or taking part in archery. As B takes part in the activity, A should attempt to offer helpful feedback. The observer should review the guidelines for feedback stated in the chapter. He or she should then take notes regarding the feedback of A. At the conclusion of the role play, these observations should be discussed by all three members of the group. If time is available, change roles and repeat the exercise.

APPENDIX D
NONVERBAL CUE EXERCISES

Portraying Feelings
(Hackney & Cormier, 1988)

This exercise is done with a partner. A is the speaker and B assumes the role of the respondent. The idea of the exercise is to portray feelings exclusively through nonverbal means. A selects a feeling from the following list without identifying it to B. A then portrays it, and B should attempt to identify the feeling. After a feeling has been identified, choose another feeling and repeat the process. Then reverse roles so B may portray the feelings. Choose feelings from the following.

- Contented
- Puzzled and confused
- Angry
- Discouraged

Magazine Pictures (Okun, 1992)

From magazines, cut out pictures of people but leave out any captions. First, ask a partner what he or she believes to be the message in each picture. Then ask for the responses in a group of four to six people. After you have looked at several pictures, see if your group can identify any common patterns for the group members' identification of feelings expressed in the pictures. The exercise is designed to examine different responses to the same nonverbal stimuli. Was there agreement on rationale behind the identifications? Was there disagreement? If so, what was the basis for it? Can you explain the diversity in perceptions?

Identifying Feelings (Okun, 1992)

This is similar to the portraying feelings exercise but involves three or more people. In this exercise A identifies a specific feeling or emotion and informs an observer of what it is. A then attempts to communicate the feeling or emotion nonverbally to a partner or to members of a small group. When it has been identified, another person should take the place of A, and the exercise should continue until all in the group who wish to participate have had an opportunity. When you have finished, process your experience to determine reasons for agreements and disagreements in identifications.

Self-Analysis (Okun, 1992)

Self-awareness is the purpose of this exercise, which asks you to list nonverbal behaviors used with each of the four major emotions: anger, fear, happiness, and sadness. For example, list what nonverbal behaviors you engage in when angry (such as frowning or clenching your fist). After recording these behaviors for each emotion, share your list in a small group, noting similarities and differences. As an alternative, you may share your list with a close friend. See if the friend agrees with how you express yourself in the ways you have listed. If your friend disagrees, what is the basis for this?

Nonverbal Canceling (Stevens, 1988)

The object of this exercise is to become aware of possible nonverbal messages you or others provide. A should purposefully cancel out everything stated to B with an accompanying nonverbal cue. Whatever the spoken message, cancel it out with an opposite gesture, facial expression, body movement, eye contact, or any other nonverbal means of communication. A and B should switch the sender-receiver roles back and forth for five minutes. At the end of this time, each should sit quietly and reflect on the exercise before processing on it. Begin the processing by telling each other what you experienced during the exercise. How did you feel when canceling verbal messages? Did you recognize any of the canceling behaviors from previous personal experience? As an alternative, you might complete this exercise in a small group, allowing all members to take both the sender and receiver roles.

Shoulder Massage (Stevens, 1988)

This is a group exercise in which a circle is formed by standing behind someone to whom you would like to give something. Once you are in a circle, you should face clockwise, sit down, and silently begin to massage or rub the shoulders, neck, and back of the person in front of you. Everyone should close their eyes and refrain from speaking. The only communication is with your hands. After several minutes, you may make noises (but do not use formal language) to let the person giving the massage know how it feels. Your noises should tell the person behind you what kind of things you like best. After five minutes, silently turn around in the other direction and give the massage to the person who has been massaging you. Again, communicate with noises to inform the person what feels good to you. Do this for three to five minutes more. Before you begin, tell those in the group that the exercise may make them slightly uncomfortable and, if this happens, not to laugh and talk but to follow the directions. After you have finished, share your ideas on the experience with the person in front of you and the person behind you. How did you communicate? Was this nonverbal expression natural? Did you feel uncomfortable in touching others of the opposite sex or others of the same sex?

APPENDIX E
INTERVIEW EXERCISE

Hackney and Cormier (1988) have outlined an exercise that involves videotaping two persons in an interview situation. The exercise that follows has been based on that of Hackney and Cormier.

In this exercise A is the interviewer and B is the client. Their communications are videotaped for four or five minutes. During this time, A should try to accomplish the following:

1. Welcome B appropriately;
2. Set B at ease (less bodily tension, voice not tense);
3. Project being at ease (relaxed, open posture);
4. Use reinforcing attending behaviors (e.g., eye contact, gestures);
5. Get B to start talking about anything; and
6. Get B to identify a current concern or problem in regard to his or her leisure.

After this, A and B should reverse roles and repeat the exercise. Again, this segment should be videotaped. Once all parts have been videotaped, the tapes should be replayed and critiqued for strengths and weaknesses displayed in the interviewers' skills.

Chapter Seven

BEING A LEADER

CHAPTER PURPOSE

Leadership is vital to therapeutic recreation. Even so, leadership has remained a relatively neglected area in therapeutic recreation literature. Few researchers have carefully examined the dynamics of leadership processes in therapeutic recreation. Neither have professionals in the field taken on the cause of writing extensively of their leadership experiences.

Nevertheless, all would probably agree that there is no substitute for effective leadership. In fact, many therapeutic recreation specialists would propose that the effectiveness of the leader is the single most important factor affecting therapeutic outcomes with clients. This chapter will help you to develop a general understanding of leadership and to gain exposure to specific information applicable to leadership in therapeutic recreation.

KEY TERMS

- Administrative leadership
- Team leadership
- Expert power
- Legitimate power
- Coercive power
- Democratic leadership
- Overjustification effect
- Director

- Supervisory leadership
- Direct program leadership
- Referent power
- Reward power
- Autocratic leadership
- Laissez-faire leadership
- Controller
- Instigator

- Stimulator
- Advisor
- Enabler
- Socio-emotive functions

- Educator
- Observer
- Task functions
- Nonfunctional behavior

OBJECTIVES

- Understand leadership, its levels, and its basis.
- Comprehend major leadership styles.
- Recognize factors influencing choice of leadership style.
- Identify possible leadership roles.
- Know ways to deal with dependency.
- Evaluate principles listed for the therapeutic recreation leader.
- Explain the function of the group leader.
- Distinguish between various structures for therapeutic recreation.
- Recognize types of therapeutic and growth groups.
- Know categories of games, exercises, and activities used with groups.
- Show awareness of what constitutes a sense of "groupness."
- Interpret stages of group development.
- Recognize leader concerns in group development.
- Distinguish between functional and nonfunctional behaviors in groups.
- Interpret principles for group leadership.

BASIC LEADERSHIP COMPONENTS

Authors of early books in recreation (e.g., Stone & Stone, 1952) often wrote of the personal characteristics of the recreation leader. Now we realize that leadership involves much more than the personality traits of the leader. The myth of the "born leader" has been dispelled.

Good leadership in therapeutic recreation involves the ability to influence the activities of clients toward accomplishing sought outcomes. Therefore, at a specific level, a leader's effectiveness may be primarily measured by how well clients do in achieving prescribed objectives. More generally, the therapeutic recreation specialist's success as a leader may be evaluated by his or her ability to facilitate the movement of clients toward an optimal level of independence and healthful living.

Levels of Leadership

Kraus, Carpenter and Bates (1981) have listed four levels of recreation leadership:

- Administrative leadership
- Supervisory leadership
- Team leadership
- Direct program leadership

Administrative Leadership

Administrative leadership is one task of the administrator who must also plan, organize, coordinate, evaluate, and generally control the operations of the agency. In heading the agency, the administrator provides overall direction and leadership for all subordinates within the organization.

Supervisory Leadership

Supervisory leadership involves providing supervision for other staff. On this level, the therapeutic recreation supervisor may supervise therapeutic recreation specialists and/or other agency staff, depending on the organizational structures of the agency.

Team Leadership

Team leadership may involve teamwork with other therapeutic recreation specialists or teamwork with an interdisciplinary team. In either case, the therapeutic recreation specialist may be called on to exert leadership within a peer situation.

Direct Program Leadership

Direct program leadership deals with the actual delivery of therapeutic recreation programming to clients. Here the leader is directly involved in face-to-face leadership with individuals in recreation or leisure-related activities. It is with this last level of leadership that this chapter is concerned, although much of the information presented may have application at the other leadership levels as well.

Basis for Leadership Influence

It is useful for the therapeutic recreation specialist to understand the basis for the leader's influence and power. Five types of power have been proposed from classic studies by French and Raven (1959). These are **expert power** (gained by being viewed as having knowledge or expertise), **referent power** (gained by the identification or closeness others feel for the leader), **legitimate power** (gained by being designated by those in control who bestow the right of the leader to be influential), **reward power** (gained by being viewed as having the ability to give rewards), and **coercive power** (gained by being perceived as being able to levy punishment).

The therapeutic recreation specialist is likely to have legitimate power, because he or she is designated for leadership by those in authority. Clients are also apt to bestow reward and coercive power on the therapeutic recreation specialist. Depending on the particular situation, the therapeutic recreation specialist may also be attributed expert power, since he or she may have a high degree of skill or knowledge in a certain activity. The leader who develops rapport with clients obtains referent power.

Research has shown that the development of referent power is particularly important for therapists. Nicholi (1988) has concluded from the results of several studies:

> . . . the therapist's ability to convey an intrinsic interest in the patient has been found to be more important than his (or her) position, appearance, reputation, clinical experience, training, and technical or theoretical knowledge. . . . Close, detailed attention must therefore be given to how, within the confines of a professional relationship and without patronizing or condescending, the therapist conveys genuine interest in the patient (p.8).

Schmuck and Schmuck (1988) have suggested it is important for teachers to attempt to gain expert and referent power to accompany the legitimate, reward, and coercive bases of power usually granted them so that they may be able to maintain control over the classroom. In doing so, teachers are able to meet occasions of conflict with high-power students, who usually gain their influence through being good at things (expert power) or who possess highly valued personal characteristics (referent power).

In order to understand the atmosphere within a therapeutic recreation group, it is important that those in leadership positions be able to analyze the power structures that are present. The leaders should know who has power and how it is being employed.

Schmuck and Schmuck have further stated that a positive group atmosphere generally exists when members see themselves as having some amount of power. Most persons want to feel they have influence in relation to important others (such as the leader) and, when they have some degree of influence, they feel more secure.

Therefore, it is the wise therapeutic recreation specialist who understands the issues of power within groups, and uses his or her leadership position to create a positive social climate by encouraging feelings of influence among group members.

LEADERSHIP STYLES

Most discussions of leadership center around three leadership styles: autocratic, democratic, and laissez-faire (Posthuma, 1989). These styles are outlined next.

Autocratic leadership is a directive style of leadership. The autocratic leader has superior knowledge and expertise. He or she makes all decisions and expects obedience from others. All authority and all responsibility remain with the leader. Autocratic leaders allow minimal group participation. There is never any question as to who is in charge.

Democratic leadership involves others in decision making. The leader draws on group members for ideas, thus creating a feeling of participation and teamwork. Under democratic leadership, people sense that their participation is important.

Laissez-faire leadership is an open and permissive approach. The leader does not exercise authority. Instead, minimum control is used so that participants may take on responsibility for decision making. Laissez-faire leadership is participative and client centered.

There really is no one best leadership style in therapeutic recreation. A number of factors influence the best style for any given situation. These factors include:

- The ability and personality of the leader;
- The characteristics and needs of clients; and
- The environment in which the leadership occurs (e.g., pediatrics unit, adult psychiatric unit, nursing-home).

Leader Abilities and Personality

As discussed in Chapter 5, it is very important that each therapeutic recreation specialist gains self-knowledge. This includes becoming aware of which leadership style best suits the abilities and personality of the individual. Good leaders choose a style with which they feel comfortable most of the time, but remain flexible enough to deviate from it when clients or situations dictate another style.

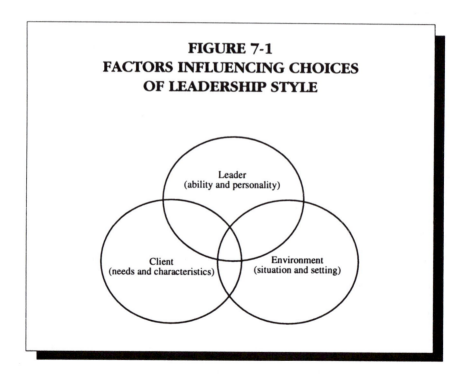

FIGURE 7-1
FACTORS INFLUENCING CHOICES
OF LEADERSHIP STYLE

Client Needs and Characteristics

The second factor to consider in selecting a leadership style under the interactional model of leadership is the type of client being served. No one style can be said to be the best overall style for therapeutic recreation because the leader must match his or her style to fit the characteristics of the group members. Information in this section on matching leadership style with client needs has been drawn primarily from Higginbotham, West and Forsyth's (1988) excellent presentation on the leader/ therapist.

An autocratic approach may be the logical choice when working with a group of clients with severe psychological problems. Clients who are pathological, aggressive, or resistant will likely not respond to influences within groups but, instead, need structure imposed by the leader. Directive leadership might likewise be called for when working in a behavior modification program for clients with mental retardation who have clearly defined tasks or behaviors to learn. Still another example where an autocratic style could be appropriate would be with confused nursing-home residents who, like the psychiatric clients, require a structured environment. With any population, an autocratic leadership style works best when group members respect the leader, and are willing to accept the leader's recommendations. With directive leadership, the more status the leader has with the clients, the more influence he or she will exert over the group.

Directive leaders must maintain their status within the group to be effective. When French and Raven's (1959) bases of power are considered, it would appear that the reward power and coercive power would lead to influence on the part of the directive leader. The problem with these approaches is that they do not result in internal acceptance of behaviors and values that have been imposed through a system of reward and punishments. Anger and hostility can result when clients feel coercive power is being used by directive leaders to influence them. Reward power must be used with caution because rewards can undermine intrinsic motivation for behavioral change.

An **overjustification effect** may occur that changes the person's motivational system from being internally motivated to one of external motivation. If extrinsic rewards are repeatedly given for a desired behavior, the individual may become personally less favorably disposed toward performing that behavior as the motivation becomes more and more extrinsically driven (Iso-Ahola, 1980). Consequently, leaders using an autocratic or directive approach need to attempt to base their influence on legitimate, expert, and referent power.

Democratic or laissez-faire leadership is best suited to groups in which members will accept social influence from others within the group, have group goals, and do not need or desire autocratic direction. Unlike clients in autocratic groups, clients operating under group-centered approaches can make decisions and can accept responsibility.

Leaders of therapeutic recreation groups ideally strive to employ a group-centered style of leadership that allows as much control on the part of clients as they are willing and able to assume. While doing so, leaders of therapeutic recreation groups have to keep in mind that no one leadership approach is always effective in promoting client change.

Leadership Situation or Environment

The final factor to be considered under the interactional model of leadership is the situation or the environment in which leadership transpires. The situation will sometimes dictate the type of leadership style that will be effective. For example, when working with very large groups, a more directive, autocratic leadership style will apt to be required. Small, intimate groups will likely need a group-centered approach.

Generally, the environment is closely tied to client needs and characteristics, because policies and practices of organizations are based largely on the type of clients being served. For example, confused psychiatric patients may be placed on a locked unit for their own safety and protection. The types of activities provided in such an environment might likely be highly structured, allowing for a minimum of control by the clients.

The type of clients discussed in the prior example (confused psychiatric patients), coupled with the environment (a locked ward with a highly structured program), might well dictate an autocratic style of leadership. If a therapeutic recreation specialist is not comfortable with this style, he or she may be better suited to another client population or setting. It is important for emerging therapeutic recreation specialists to realize that various types of leadership styles are needed because of the diversity of clients and variety of settings in therapeutic recreation. There is no one best leadership style. A wide variety of persons with varying abilities and personalities may become successful therapeutic recreation practitioners, each fitting into the type of leadership position for which he or she is most ideally suited.

Continuum of Leadership Styles

The three major leadership styles—autocratic, democratic, and laissez-faire—may be conceptualized to exist along a continuum, with autocratic leadership on one end and laissez-faire leadership at the other extreme. This continuum is represented in Figure 7-2.

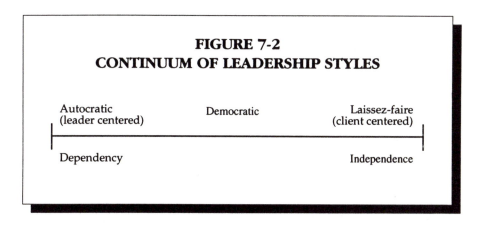

FIGURE 7-2
CONTINUUM OF LEADERSHIP STYLES

Autocratic (leader centered)	Democratic	Laissez-faire (client centered)
Dependency		Independence

Even when therapeutic recreation specialists must initially be autocratic in leadership, it is important to remember that the ultimate goal is to help each client move away from dependency on the leader and thus gain greater self-dependence. Progressive movement along the continuum of leadership style from a controlling, autocratic style toward the client-centered, participative leadership style is the goal of all leadership in therapeutic recreation. The therapeutic recreation specialist sincerely believes that all clients are first-class citizens who deserve the right to move toward the greatest possible level of independence.

The process of allowing clients to move past planned activities to choosing their own leisure pursuits requires a supportive atmosphere that provides for—and fosters—the growth of the individual. The leader moves toward ultimately reaching the role of an enabler who promotes the greatest possible level of independence and self-determination on the part of clients.

LEADERSHIP ROLES

Avedon (1974) has listed eight diverse roles that the therapeutic recreation specialist may assume as clients move from dependence to independence: controller, director, instigator, stimulator, educator, advisor, observer, and enabler.

The **controller** exercises a high level of control over clients, making all decisions regarding the activities of the group. The **director** still holds most of the power and leads the activities of the group, but does allow clients some latitude in decision making. The **instigator** incites action on the part of the group and then withdraws, leaving the group members in control. The **stimulator** begins activities by generating interest on the part of clients and then helps maintain this interest by encouraging participation. The **educator** instructs clients in activities and social skills. The **advisor** provides counseling and guidance to clients. The **observer** provides leadership by his or her presence and evaluates and reacts to clients' responses. The **enabler** role fits well into the laissez-faire style, where the leaders simply provide opportunities for participation in activities determined by clients.

The leadership styles and roles discussed in this section exist only as means by which to help clients move toward their optimal level of independence and healthful living. During this process of moving away from dependency, the therapeutic recreation specialist will necessarily have to help clients with problems and feelings related to dependency.

Leadership and Dependency

Dependent clients rely on staff for psychological and social support. They accept a subordinate status in which they depend on others instead of acting independently.

Dealing with dependency is a concern in almost every therapeutic recreation setting. In fact, Kutner (1971) has suggested that a certain amount of dependency is a natural part of successful rehabilitation because clients must give their consent to be influenced by those directing the treatment or rehabilitation program. However, some individuals may use their role as client as a means to gain excessive attention and/or escape personal responsibilities. If reinforced, such behavior can produce clients who learn to be "helpless," relying on others instead of on their own initiative (Schmuck & Schmuck, 1988).

Haber and her colleagues (1992) have suggested various ways to deal with dependency on which the guidelines that follow are based.

- Be conscious of demands for advice and answers to problems by clients who lack the confidence to make decisions for themselves.
- Show acceptance of clients, but do not give in to their demands if demands are excessive or irrational.
- Help clients become aware of their feelings of dependency and develop new ways to seek gratification of their needs through more independent means.
- Build the self-esteem of clients by making ability statements in which they are assured they have the ability to succeed.
- Provide opportunities for clients to make decisions and accept responsibility.

The Function of Group Leaders

Much of the therapeutic recreation specialist's time is apt to be spent in working with groups of various types. Knickerbocker (1969), Schul (1975), and Gordon (1977) have stated that human beings participate in groups because they believe that their needs will be satisfied as a result. People accept the influence and direction of leaders in order to meet their individual needs.

Gordon (1977) has provided a model as an explanation of group leadership. The model rests on the assumption that people are continually in the process of *satisfying needs* or *relieving tension*. In order to satisfy their need,s some means is necessary. Most needs in our society are satisfied through *relationships with other individuals* or *groups*. Persons take part in groups because they anticipate that this participation will result in meeting their individual needs. Individuals accept direction from a leader because this behavior is considered to be a means to needs satisfaction. The relationship with the leader is seen as an avenue through which they will get their needs met.

Our clients join therapeutic recreation groups in order to satisfy needs. Consequently, it is the function of the therapeutic recreation specialist to organize the activities of client groups so that individuals may reach needs satisfaction.

PROGRAM GROUPS AND STRUCTURES

Austin (1987) has extended Avedon's (1974) original outline of structures for group participation in therapeutic recreation to include the following:

Informal Lounge Programs

An informal lounge program is a casual program of low organization in which a multipurpose area is made open to clients on a drop-in basis. Activities vary from agency to agency but usually include pool or billiards, table shuffleboard, electronic games, card games, and table games. The choice of activity is left to each participant. Staff may provide some informal instruction and guidance, but their main roles are as observers and enablers.

Clubs

Clubs are made up of clients who meet regularly to pursue a common interest. They generally have officers who are elected by the club members. Examples are current-events clubs, art clubs, and teen clubs. Clubs may be completely client-run or may rely heavily on staff for leadership. Most would probably fall somewhere between these extremes.

Special Interest Groups

Special interest groups, like clubs, are scheduled on a regular basis. They are for clients who share a common interest in a particular recreation or leisure activity. For instance, a group of clients might get together regularly to pursue an interest in photography. In all likelihood, leadership would be shared, depending on the specific activity being engaged in at the time.

Classes

Classes are scheduled opportunities for instruction. They generally have a regular membership of clients who have sought the class or have been placed in the class as a part of their individual program plan. Classes range from instruction in bowling or swimming to sewing and flower arranging. Usually the instructor is the therapeutic recreation specialist, although volunteers with expertise in an area may be utilized as instructors.

Leisure Counseling Groups

Leisure counseling groups are typically led by a single therapeutic recreation specialist or two therapeutic recreation specialists serving as co-leaders. They provide small group counseling to help clients develop appropriate leisure attitudes and behaviors.

Adventure/Challenge Therapy Groups

Adventure/challenge therapy groups involve activities containing elements of perceived risk or danger that are engaged in by client groups in natural outdoor settings. Examples range from trust and cooperative activities to high adventure activities such as wilderness camping and high ropes courses. While participants may take part in such programs as a part of a club or special interest group, it is more likely that adventure challenge experiences will be organized and conducted as specific entities unto themselves.

Leagues, Tournaments, and Contests

Competitive structures are leagues, tournaments, and contests. These are organized by therapeutic recreation personnel. Examples would be bowling leagues and card tournaments. In some settings staff and clients participate together in team sports in public leagues and tournaments.

Special Events

Special events typically are large-scale affairs held by institutions at holiday times. Events such as Christmas dinner-dances and Independence Day carnivals were annual occurrences at most state psychiatric hospitals, state residential schools, and Veterans Administration hospitals. Similar activities are found at hospitals and other institutions today, but the concept of special events has been broadened to include many different types of occasions such as dining in restaurants, theater parties, and special tours.

Mass Activities

Mass activities are for large numbers of clients and perhaps their families and friends. Movies, concerts, and dances are examples. Staff organize and conduct these events.

Other Types of Groups

What other types of therapeutic groups are found within clinical settings other than those conducted by therapeutic recreation specialists or other action-oriented therapy disciplines such as occupational therapy, art therapy, or music therapy? A number of therapeutic groups may be conducted by agencies including counseling groups, psychotherapy groups, encounter groups, marathon groups, sensitivity groups, T-groups, systematic human-relations training, structured groups, stress-debriefing groups, self-help groups, and actualization groups. These are briefly reviewed here to provide emerging therapeutic recreation specialists with an acquaintanceship with the various types of groups. Therapeutic recreation specialists with specialized training occasionally may lead some of these groups. It is more likely, however, that therapeutic recreation specialists will simply encounter such groups being conducted by other members of the health care team.

Counseling Groups

Counseling groups usually have a particular focus, which can be educational, vocational, social, or personal. Members are well-functioning individuals who do not have extensive personality problems but whose problems relate to developmental tasks during the life cycle. A growth orientation is evident in these groups that emphasize the discovery of inner resources that will help clients to deal with barriers to optimal development (Corey, 1985; Corey & Corey, 1987).

Psychotherapy Groups

Psychotherapy groups focus on remediation, treatment, and personality reconstruction. Because psychotherapy groups deal with "deep" psychological problems; they tend to be of relatively long duration. Therapists are typically psychiatrists, clinical psychologists, psychiatric social workers, or psychiatric nurses (Corey, 1985).

Encounter Groups

Encounter groups (sometimes referred to as personal-growth groups) are intense experiences for persons who are functioning well but desire to develop more positive attitudes and improved interpersonal skills. Their emphasis is on the "here and now," rather than the past, as they focus on group interaction and communication skills. Most members of encounter groups join in order to increase intimacy with others and to explore blocks within themselves that prohibit them from achieving their full potentials. Encounter groups often meet for several days in a residential setting removed from the distractions of everyday living so participants may have the time and environment that help foster increasing awareness of feelings and greater risk-taking to discover or rediscover things about themselves (Brammer, Abrego & Shostrom,1993; Corey, 1985; Corey & Corey, 1987).

Marathon Groups

Marathon groups extend encounter groups to represent a blend of personal growth and therapy groups. Sessions are highly intensive and may go on nonstop for 24 hours or more with time out only for vital functions. This format, which allows continuous contact and produces fatigue, is meant to break down inhibitions and defenses in order to promote total honesty and the free expression of feelings. Participants are encouraged to discover genuine aspects of themselves and to give up pretenses they use in their everyday lives (Brammer, Abrego & Shostrom, 1993; Corey, 1985).

Sensitivity Groups

Sensitivity training is one of the first terms used to describe a type of awareness group. It originally referred to a small group training conducted by the National Training Laboratories. Sensitivity training is an educational method that involves experiential learning dealing with some aspect of human interaction. The term, sensitivity training, however has become so broadly employed that many feel it has little meaning (Gazda, 1982).

T-groups

T-groups were developed out of social psychology, rather than clinical psychology. Group members learn through direct experience with the social psychological forces that work within groups. T-groups are learning laboratories in which participants are taught how to observe their own processes as attention is directed on the analysis of interactions among members in order to improve individuals' sensitivity to themselves and others. Objectives include increasing awareness of individual's own feelings, learning how others see them and how they impact on others, and becoming aware of how people interrelate and how groups work. T-groups are commonly conducted in educational and business settings (Corey & Corey, 1987; Harré & Lamb, 1986).

Systematic Human-Relations Training

Systematic human-relations training is an adaptation and extension of the T-group laboratory approach. Carkhuff (1969a, 1969b) originally developed this group approach to train counselors. Later, Egan (1976) applied Carkhuff's model with persons who desired training in the skills of interpersonal living. Egan's training involves participants cooperating to achieve group goals, actively listening to others, responding in a concrete way to others, revealing personal information, giving others feedback and receiving feedback from others, and dealing with feelings that arise out of group participation (Corey, 1985).

Structured Groups

Structured groups, sometimes referred to as skill groups, focus on one theme or topic area. In contrast to relatively unstructured and intense person-growth groups, these groups are structured to provide participants with increased understanding of a specific life problem and means to better cope with it. Such groups are often offered by university counseling centers and cover such topics as stress management, women in transition, and overcoming perfectionism (Brammer et al., 1993; Corey, 1985; Corey & Corey, 1987).

Stress-Debriefing Groups

Stress-debriefing groups offer help for police, firefighters, rescue workers and others who are vulnerable to Post-Traumatic Stress Disorder (PTSD). This group process provides for debriefing workers as soon as possible in a site removed from the trauma scene (Brammer et al, 1993).

Self-Help Groups

Self-help groups are led by people who are not professionals but who struggle with the same issues as others in groups such as Alcoholics Anonymous, Adult Children of Alcoholics, Weight Watchers, and other similar organizations. In recent years there has been a tremendous growth in the number of self-help groups (Brammer et al, 1989; Corey & Corey, 1987).

Actualization Groups

Actualization groups are intensive group experiences that share similarities with structured groups, encounter groups, and psychotherapy groups. They combine the didactic and experiential group exercises of structured groups with the feeling emphasis of encounter groups and are similar to therapy groups in their depth and breadth. Actualization groups focus on specific outcomes and evaluate progress through the use of formal instruments such as the Actualizing Assessment Battery (Brammer et al, 1993).

GAME, EXERCISE, AND ACTIVITY CATEGORIES

Whitaker's Categories

Whitaker (1985, p. 126, 127), in her book titled *Using Groups to Help People*, proposed seven categories of games, exercises, and activities that can be used with therapeutic groups. Each category has its own character, purposes, and likely consequences. Whitaker's categories follow:

Pleasure Providing

A game, activity, or exercise is sometimes done for its own sake or for the intrinsic value it holds for participants. The purpose is pleasure and enjoyment.

Interaction Generating

Games, activities and exercises can be used to stimulate interactions between participants that can be used for therapeutic benefit. For instance, competitive games become the basis for a discussion of feelings dealing with winning or losing or about occurrences that transpired during an event.

Protective Rehearsing

A game, activity, or exercise offers an opportunity for rehearsal, in a protected environment, of behaviors clients desire to use once they leave the group. Skill development groups often use activities that provide chances to try out behaviors that are being learned.

Analogous Activities

A game, activity or exercise, may be chosen because it is analogous to, or representative of, something. For example, the situation of a game may be analogous to decision making in actual life situations. Through the experience, members learn how decisions are made in groups and how they themselves participate in the decision-making process.

Thought Stimulation

A game, exercise, or activity may be employed as an alternative route to raise an issue that otherwise might occur in open discussion. For example, a card-sorting exercise could be used in which members examine cards that contain descriptive words or phrases and then place the cards that best describe various members of the group face down in front of them. Once the cards are distributed, each person can read the cards in front of him or her to learn how he or she is perceived by others.

Planned- or Expected-Action Facilitating

The chosen activity, game or exercise can simply speed up the process to make some naturally occurring event in the life of the group occur faster. Examples are ice breakers to facilitate members getting acquainted, trust-building exercises, and self-disclosure games.

Empathy Building

An exercise or game can be used to help members to empathize with others whose points of view they would not normally take into account. An example would be a member taking on the part of his or her own mother or father in a role playing situation.

Other authors, such as Nickerson and O'Laughlin (1982) in their book *Helping Through Action: Action-Oriented Therapies* and Schaefer and Reid (1986) in their work *Game Play: Therapeutic Use of Childhood Games,* have also categorized games, activities and exercises. It is interesting to note that while some categories overlap with those of Whitaker (1986), there exist a surprising number of unique categories.

Nickerson and O'Laughlin's Categories

The six categories offered by Nickerson and O'Laughlin (pp.118, 119) have been taken from an article by Crocker and Wrobleski (1975) in which they suggested recreational games that could be applied in counseling. They are summarized as follows:

Assessing Clients

Commercial games such as "Risk" and "Kinetic Psychotherapy" may be used to surface behavioral patterns for their interpersonal significance.

Confronting and Dealing with Issues

An example of confronting and dealing with issues via games is the use of "Monopoly" to enable group members to deal with anxiety raised by feelings of poverty and helplessness generated during their participation.

Learning Rule Conforming

Players learn to operate within the rules of the game in a way analogous to accepting the rules of society.

Play and Fantasy Facilitating

Games allow players to feel free to be playful and engage in fantasy, thus freeing up more creative potentials for living and problem solving.

Security Enhancing

The use of games tends to create the feeling of a safe and permissive environment in which members can try out new behaviors.

Developing Coping Mechanisms

Participation allows opportunities to develop new and more adequate means of coping. For example, a competitive game can assist the person to learn coping skills to deal with aggressiveness, being defeated, defeating others, and being criticized or rejected.

Schaefer and Reid's Categories

In their book on the therapeutic use of children's games, Schaefer and Reid (1986, pp.11-13) discuss games in terms of the following therapeutic facets or categories:

- *Diagnosis.* Observing how children play games offers an opportunity for projective assessment.
- *Pleasure.* Pleasure and enjoyment may serve to prevent and alleviate psychological disturbance.
- *Therapeutic alliance.* Games offer means to help children become more comfortable so they may engage in the therapeutic process.
- *Self-expression.* Restraints can be loosened and defenses relaxed because "it's just a game."
- *Ego-enhancement.* Games provide opportunities for children to confront, work through, and gain mastery over feelings that are uncomfortable.
- *Cognitive.* Games can be used to develop cognitive skills such as concentration, memory, and creative problem solving.
- *Socialization.* The nonthreatening nature of games, positive peer pressure, and acceptance of authority provide an atmosphere for social learning.

Additional Thoughts on Categories

Other categories for the use of games, activities, and exercises could, of course, be added to those enumerated. Among these are: providing opportunities for clients to exercise control over their environment; exposing clients to new experiences that provide challenges so they may learn what they are capable and incapable of doing; offering feedback on clients' thinking, emotions, and behaviors; becoming aware of attitudes and values;

providing for a sense of purpose and commitment to a team or group; and enhancing self-esteem through successes enjoyed during activities, games, and exercises. You may be able to add other categories. In the end, it must be concluded that there are a vast array of ways that games, activities, and exercises may be applied therapeutically with groups.

Selecting Games, Activities or Exercises

Several areas for group leaders to consider in selecting games, activities, or exercises have been listed by Whitaker (1985, pp.128, 129). These areas for consideration follow:

- Experiences likely to be generated for those participating in the game, exercise, or activity.
- All consequences of utilizing the device, including both intended and unintended likely consequences.
- Likely consequences for the various specific members of the group.
- Likely damaging consequences for the members in general or for specific persons. If any of the consequences are likely to be damaging, modifications should be made in the device to prevent any damaging effects from occurring.
- The use of a device that allows for choice on the part of the participants.
- Preparation or follow-up required in order for potential benefits to be achieved and potential damages to be averted.
- Ways the device could go wrong and if it does, what the leader should do.

Finally, Whitaker (1985) has warned that the selection of games, activities, and exercises for therapeutic purpose must be done in a careful and reasoned manner. Games, activities, and exercises should always be chosen with the needs of the clients in mind, rather than the needs of the leader. Some leaders, for instance, may be worried about filling the time the group is scheduled for with activities and may select an activity as a time-filler only on the basis that they are familiar with it. This is a risky action because activities, games, and exercises can be powerful devices and, therefore, their choices need to be based on specific therapeutic needs of the group members with an awareness of the range of potential consequences that may ensue.

GROUP ELEMENTS

Do the clients involved in the types of therapeutic recreation program structures outlined earlier in the chapter really constitute groups? Think for a moment of the groups of which you are a member. What makes each of them a group? Is there a difference between a collection of individuals and a group?

Most of us have a feeling about what constitutes a sense of "groupness." First, we want to be a part of the group. There is a conscious *identification* with the group, or a sense of belonging. We also have some sort of *interaction* with others in the group. We communicate with and react to others in our group. Finally, there is a sense of *shared purpose*, or group goals or ideals that are held by members (Knowles & Knowles, 1959; Posthuma, 1989; Whitaker, 1985).

Are therapeutic recreation "groups" really groups? It is perhaps best to not answer this question in absolute terms but to recognize that most therapeutic recreation groups can be described as ranging somewhere along the previously identified dimensions of identification, interaction, and shared purpose by which groups may be defined. In some therapeutic recreation situations a sense of groupness exists; in others a complete sense of group does not form because the members have not developed along one or more of the dimensions. This may occur in situations in which there is continual change in the composition of the membership, in instances where the program itself is structured in a way that discourages client interaction (such as an art class in which clients engage in separate projects), or in cases where members are not yet ready to interact with others. Therapeutic recreation groups that do remain intact, enjoy structures conducive to group formation, and are constituted of members who feel comfortable interacting, go through several stages of group development.

STAGES OF GROUP DEVELOPMENT

Different phases of group development have been proposed by various authors (e.g., Hansen et al., 1980; Longo & Williams, 1986, Tubbs & Moss, 1981). Usually authors talk of four stages that groups encounter. They are the orientation or forming stage, the conflict stage, the group cohesion stage, and the performance or production stage. Some authors add a fifth stage, the termination stage, in which members may revert to old behaviors typical of the conflict stage.

During the *orientation stage* or *forming stage*, the natural insecurity and apprehension about being in a new group is paramount. There is a great deal of reliance on the leader because group members still feel dependent on the leader for direction. Here we are likely to observe group members all looking at the person speaking and then shifting their focus to the leader for his or her reaction. At this time, the leader must help the group break the ice so that members get to know each other and become comfortable in the group.

In the second phase a period of *conflict* is likely to occur. As people reveal more of themselves, their personalities, beliefs, or values may begin to clash. They may become hostile toward each other and toward the leader. This may be overt or covert. Generally, groups work through this phase.

As they do, they resolve conflicts, develop sensitivity to one another, and begin to enter a stage of *group cohesion*. During this stage, individuals begin to identify with the leader and other group members. Longo and Williams (1986), who refer to this as the "we stage," suggest members may find such pleasure in the cohesiveness of the group that they may even set aside their tasks just to enjoy being part of the group.

In the fourth stage, *performance or productivity*, members become functional and devote themselves to achieving individual and group goals.

Although it is true that groups go through somewhat predictable stages, each individual group will be different from other groups. As various writers have discussed (Hansen et al., 1980; Longo & Williams, 1986), groups vary in the amount of time spent in any stage and may move through several stages in the space of one meeting of the group. Groups also may not move precisely from one stage to the next in a sequential fashion. Instead, they may bypass a stage or may move backward to a previous phase. Nevertheless, it is important for the leader to develop an understanding of the developmental stages so that he or she may better help members in their individual and group development.

LEADER CONCERNS AND STRATEGIES

The following material discusses some of the special challenges that confront group leaders.

Anxiety as a New Leader

Most of us have some amount of anxiety when we try something new. Emerging therapeutic specialists are no exceptions. They may wonder about their abilities to lead a therapy group and commonly experience accompanying anxiety. It is important for beginning leaders to recognize and acknowledge that self-doubts and anxiety are common among practitioners at their stage of professional development. In fact, a moderate amount of anxiety can be good in that it can move the new leader toward self-appraisal. Of course, when anxiety becomes overwhelming, it may interfere with functioning. It is therefore important for students completing clinical experiences, and for those with limited experience, to discuss their feelings with other students or staff and with their clinical supervisors. Once the new leader admits feelings of anxiety, he or she will likely learn that other emerging leaders are experiencing similar anxiety or that more seasoned staff experienced it when they were emerging professionals. Unwarranted anxiety can be dissipated through such exchanges (Corey, 1995) and emerging leaders can learn strategies to help them to deal with being a new leader.

New Clients

Many clients want to be a part of a therapeutic recreation group but, like most of us, they are likely to find new situations threatening. They will have a natural concern about how they will be accepted by the leader and other clients and whether or not they will be able to perform to the expectations of the group. With such uncertainty, it is not surprising that the defense mechanisms of new clients may cause blocks to group participation. Persons may approach new situations by simply repeating old behaviors (Hansen et al., 1980), even though these behaviors may not be functional.

Fears of rejection or incompetence must be understood by the therapeutic recreation specialist. He or she must not ridicule the client who attempts to adjust to a new experience by employing some nonfunctional defense mechanism.   Understanding potential client problems will allow the leader to assist clients to overcome fears that interfere with their adjustments. Instead of becoming angry at clients for their inappropriate behaviors, the therapeutic recreation specialist must learn to ask the important question "Why?"

Thus the first task of the therapeutic recreation group leader is to reduce threat to new members by helping them to become comfortable. This involves expressing a warm, accepting attitude toward new clients, interacting with them in an open, nonjudgmental way, and helping them become acquainted with other members of the group. In doing so the leader creates a positive atmosphere for new members and functions as a model for the total membership of the group.

Modeling

One way for people to learn new behaviors or strengthen existing behaviors is to observe others who exhibit the desired behavior. Many of us can recall how our coaches and physical education teachers would model motor skills for us to imitate and then reinforce us for following their example. Or, we can remember how we learned a new dance step or some social behavior by watching older brothers and sisters and their friends. Our clients also learn from imitation. Therefore, it behooves the therapeutic recreation group leader to consider the potentially potent effect of modeling.

Because modeling can play a large role in shaping clients' behaviors, the emerging therapeutic recreation specialist particularly should engage in self-examination to become aware of the picture he or she is presenting to group members. This requires that he or she first think in advance about which social-recreational behaviors are desired and, therefore, should be demonstrated and, second, monitor his or her own behavior to assure that appropriate behaviors are displayed. Of course, once appropriate social-recreational behaviors are imitated, the therapeutic recreation specialist should reinforce clients for performing them.

Self-Disclosure

The question of *how much* self-disclosure is appropriate is a concern for both new and experienced group leaders, although more experienced leaders may have more comfort in the use of self-disclosure due to past experiences. Appropriate self-disclosure is a vital part of group leadership. Corey, (1995), taking his lead from Yalom (1985), has suggested that the leader should keep in mind that self-disclosure should only be used in order to benefit members of the group. Self-disclosure should provide group members with feelings of encouragement, acceptance and support while helping them to reach their goals. Corey believes the most productive use of self-disclosure relates to the dynamics of the group. For example, if group members are not actively participating and taking responsibility for the group, the leader may wish to disclose how he or she is affected by this lack of participation. Corey (1995) has learned that thought needs to be given before self-disclosure is employed. He has written:

> It is a mistake to assume that "the more disclosure, the better." It is also inappropriate to "let it all hang out" without evaluating the reasons for your disclosure, the readiness of the members, the impact that your sharing of intimate details is likely to have on them, and the degree to which you disclosures are relevant to the here-and-now process of the group (p. 59).

Conflict

Perhaps as critical as any understanding of group leadership is the realization that the leader is occasionally apt to encounter direct conflict and confrontation with group members. This may occur initially because the leader may not fit the preconceived stereotype of a leader formed in the mind of the client. As discussed by several authors (Knickerbocker, 1969; Hansen et al., 1980), people possess previously developed concepts of what a leader should be like based on prior experiences with significant others such as parents and teachers. If the leader refuses to fit this stereotype, conflict can arise and hostility may result. Another possible occasion for conflict is when the relationship between the group leader and members begins to change as a result of group members becoming less dependent on the leader. Conflict can develop if the members see the leader as being unwilling to play a reduced role in order for them to assume more leadership. If, in either case, conflict occurs the leader must handle any resulting personal attacks in a mature manner without retaliating against the attacking client or clients so that a positive example of dealing with aggression is provided for the group.

Difficult Group Members

Group members may meet the leader with resistance. For example, they may remain silent, try to monopolize the group, be overly dependent, or display hostility and aggression. When members of our groups behave this way, we have a tendency to label them as being "difficult." Corey (1995) has suggested that therapeutic group leaders need to understand that all of us are subject to using avoidance or resistive strategies when we are attempting to change and, therefore, as leaders we must accept that such behaviors will occur within our groups. Instead of labeling individuals as "problems" or "difficult," leaders should consider that there is a reason for the member's behavior and try to understand the individual and behaviors exhibited. Further, Corey has explained that leaders need not take resistance personally. We are not bad leaders because our group members engage in resistance. Finally, if we are honest with ourselves, it may be that client "problem behaviors" that disturb us the most are those that "hit too close to home." In other words, they are ones that we see in ourselves but would like to deny. We must be alert that we do not overreact to clients' behaviors because they may remind us of ourselves.

Working Within a System

Whether within a community-based agency or an institution, the group leader must learn to cope within the system. For example, in an "institutional environment" the administrators may be more concerned with maintaining the status quo than with providing meaningful treatment or rehabilitation programs. Such administrators may also employ top-down, bureaucratic administrative styles that do not encourage or reward innovations by group leaders. Still another challenge within a system may be overworked staff who lack continuing education opportunities and, thus, have to use their own time and pay their own expenses to attend professional workshops and conferences. Even when faced with such challenges, group leaders need to find means to offer quality programs despite the systems in which they work. Professionals must not let the system "win" but must continue their efforts to remain competent and to offer therapeutic groups (Corey, 1995).

Group Development

A primary dimension that affects the growth and development of a group is the climate that is created by both *environmental* and *emotional factors*. Other dimensions that can influence the growth and development of a group are the interaction, involvement, cohesion and productivity of its members (Posthuma, 1989).

Factors Affecting Group Climate

"The importance of the effects of the environment on the process and functioning of a group cannot be overemphasized," according to Posthuma (p.54). The leader first needs to become familiar with *environmental factors* that may affect the group. Then the leader needs to take steps to reduce group members' fears and anxieties by structuring elements in a way that will make the group setting as conducive as possible to achieving the outcomes sought by its members. Is the room an appropriate size? It should not be so small that members feel closed in or so large that members feel insecure in an undefined space. Is the room a comfortable temperature? Any group will suffer if the room is too hot or too cold, or if there is poor ventilation. Does the seating arrangement facilitate the sought outcomes of the group? For instance, if the leader wishes to downplay his or her role in order to encourage participant involvement, he or she needs to take a seat other than at the end of the table. With groups where verbal interaction is primary, it is important to place seats in a circle so participants can easily see each other. With task-related groups, a round table is a good selection because it provides work space while still allowing ease in interaction patterns among group members. In placing members in a rectangular configuration, or any seating arrangement other than a circle, the leader is in danger that the total group will not interact because the seating arrangement will encourage interactions only among subgroups.

Emotional Factors

Emotional factors can likewise affect the climate of a group. Posthuma (1989) has stated: "It is important to realize that the leader-therapist, by virtue of her (or his) status, has the power to influence the emotional climate of the group. If you are enthusiastic, open and caring, you have a better chance of eliciting these behaviors from the group members" (p.48). The group leader needs to ask himself or herself, "Am I aware of my own behavior and how it is affecting the group?" and "What is the mood of the group today?" The leader can alter his or her behavior to facilitate the group process. If members are not enthusiastic, he or she can encourage the members to discuss the mood of the group (Posthuma, 1989).

Interaction
"The more group members interact among themselves the more likely is the group to grow and develop," stated Posthuma (p.50). Of course, the activity in which participants take part will dictate interaction patterns. Some activities require a great deal of social interaction, others do not. The leader needs to be aware of the demands of potential activities and select those that will meet the needs of the group.

Based on Hall's (1966) early work in proxemics (the study of human spatial behavior), most authorities categorize space into four zones. With someone we know and like, we interact in the *intimate* zone, which is up to 18 inches apart. For casual friends or acquaintances, the *personal* zone runs from 18 inches to 4 feet. For other interpersonal encounters, the *social* zone is from 4 feet up to 12 feet. For public speaking, the *public* zone represents the 12 feet or more that the speaker stands away from the rest of the group (Duck, 1986). It is important for the leader to recognize these zones so members have enough personal space and do not feel as though it has been invaded.

Involvement
Posthuma (1989, p.52) has stipulated, "The more members that are involved in a group the greater the probability of the group growing and developing." People are attracted to a group because they like: the leader, others in the group, or the group's activities; believe the group can help them; or observe others gaining enjoyment and benefits from their participation. Once in the group, members' involvement can be encouraged by allowing them to make decisions about the group to build feelings of group "ownership" (Posthuma, 1989).

Cohesion and Productivity
Finally, positive outcomes may be expected from groups in which members feel a sense of group cohesion and believe the

group is accomplishing its purposes. Group cohesion is experienced when a climate of openness and trust has been established. Feelings of productivity grow when members are able to integrate their individual goals into the group goals and gain a sense of accomplishment. The leader needs to continually monitor the group to maintain a positive climate and ensure therapeutic outcomes (Posthuma, 1989).

Obviously, there are many other concerns and strategies with which the therapeutic recreation group leader must deal. However, the eight areas covered in this section (anxiety, self-disclosure, new clients, modeling, dealing with conflict, difficult group members, working within the system, and controlling factors affecting group development) merit particular attention on the part of emerging therapeutic recreation specialists.

GROUP FUNCTIONS

The activities of members of groups can be analyzed in terms of the function performed by the members. Two major functions are generally discussed in group dynamics literature. These are **task functions** (or content functions) and **social-emotive functions** (or maintenance functions). Task functions promote the work or task of the group. They are activities that help group members to achieve their goals. Social-emotive functions have to do with group building or promoting group development. They include activities that produce a positive group atmosphere in which members can find satisfaction through their group participation. Longo and Williams (1986) have used the term **nonfunctional behavior** to describe a third class of activities in which group members may engage. These activities interfere with the processes of the group.

In the section that follows, guidelines are offered to assist the group leader to analyze functional and nonfunctional behaviors in groups. These guidelines have been drawn from several sources (Beal, Bohlen & Raudabaugh, 1976; Jones & Pfeiffer, 1972; Knowles & Knowles, 1959; Longo & Williams, 1986; Posthuma, 1989).

Participation
- What percent of the members actively take part?
- Which members are high participators?
- Low participators?
- Do participation patterns shift? Why?
- Do those who participate too much realize this?
- How are quiet group members treated?
- Do certain members regularly withdraw?
- Who speaks to one another? Why does this interaction take place?
- Are members included in goal setting and major decisions, or does the leader set goals and make decisions without involving group members?
- Does the leader consciously try to involve members in the activities of the group?
- Are activities analyzed to bring about the type of participation desired?

Influence and Control
- Which members have a high amount of influence?
- Which members have a low level of influence?
- Is there rivalry or competition for leadership in the group? If so, between whom? How does this affect the group?
- Do any members seek recognition by drawing attention to themselves by presenting extreme ideas, boasting, or other behaviors?
- Are rewards or incentives used to influence others? How?
- Are formal and informal controls used to maintain group standards?
- Are members ever involved in deciding the means to enforce group standards?
- Are standards enforced relatively uniformly?
- Is the group self-directed?
- Is responsibility and leadership shared within the group?
- What is the relationship between the group and leader? What type of rapport exists?
- What is the role of the leader within the group?

Standards or Norms
- Are members overly nice or polite? Do they agree too quickly? Do they express only positive feelings?

- Are norms of behavior made explicit to all?
- Are certain areas avoided (e.g., sex, feelings)?
- Does the leader reinforce avoidance of certain areas?
- Does the formal leader serve as a model by living up to group standards? What about informal leaders?
- How much variety is there in the types of activities that are done with the group? Little? Some? Considerable?
- Are members consulted regarding group standards?
- Are standards realistic and reviewed periodically?

Atmosphere
- Is the physical setting conducive to the group atmosphere (e.g., size of meeting room, furniture arrangement, lighting, ventilation)?
- Are new members helped to feel a part of the group?
- Do members seem involved and interested? Do they seem to gain satisfaction?
- Is there much disruptive behavior such as clowning around or making fun of others?
- Which members seem to prefer and encourage a friendly atmosphere?
- Which prefer conflict and disagreement?
- Do members share and cooperate?
- Does the leader set a good example by projecting a warm, accepting attitude?
- Are basic needs for security, belonging, recognition, approval, and achievement met through the group?

Membership
- Do any subgroups exist? Do some people almost always agree and others consistently oppose one another?
- Are some members "outsiders" in the group? How are they treated?
- Does the body language of some members (i.e., leaning forward or backward) indicate moving in or out of the group?
- Is the size of the group about right for group involvement and participation?
- What is the degree of group unity, cohesion, or "we-ness"?

Feelings
- What signs of feelings of group members are observed (e.g., anger, frustration, warmth, boredom, defensiveness)?
- Do members attempt to block the expression of feelings?
- Do they stop discussion by blaming or insulting others?

Social-Emotive Functions
- Which members help others get involved? Which ones are friendly and encouraging?
- Which members cut off or interrupt others?
- Do members feel free to be themselves?
- How are disagreements resolved within the group?
- Do members attempt to mediate conflict by bringing about compromise or reconciling divergent ideas?
- Do members encourage others to express ideas and feelings?
- How are ideas rejected?
- Are members supportive of others by recognizing others' ideas and actions?
- Do members relieve tension through a healthy sense of humor?
- Do members assume follower positions by going along with the group and listening to others during discussions?
- How good are members about accepting new members?
- Do members really identify with the group?
- Is there really two-way communication with the leader?

Task Functions
- Do members initiate ideas and suggestions?
- Do members ask others for ideas and suggestions?
- Are there attempts to gain feedback and clarification?
- Are there attempts to elaborate on the thoughts of others?
- Does anyone attempt to summarize what has happened?
- Do members check out or evaluate the opinions of others in regard to making group decisions? Do they test for consensus?
- Who keeps the group on target?
- Does the leader underestimate or overestimate how much members really know and understand?

PRINCIPLES FOR GROUP LEADERSHIP

Hansen, Warner, and Smith (1980, pp.435-442) have developed principles to guide the practice of leaders in groups. Although they were developed specifically for group counselors, many of their principles apply in therapeutic recreation group leadership. Selected principles of Hansen and his colleagues have been stated here, followed by implications for therapeutic recreation practice.

> Group leaders have a responsibility to develop a theoretical rationale for group practice that will enable them to identify goals of their activity.

Therapeutic recreation group leaders need to recognize that their practice must rest on a philosophical base. They must know the "why" underlying the goals for their groups as well as the "how" of conducting the group. If the purpose of the therapeutic recreation group is not clearly articulated by the leader, it will be extremely difficult to set directions for the group's activities.

> Group leaders have a responsibility to limit their group practice to developed levels of competence and skills and to reveal these limits to clients.

The principle holds in any type of therapeutic recreation programming, but has particular application in leisure counseling and adventure/challenge therapy groups. Leaders of leisure counseling groups must have the competencies called for to conduct the type of counseling in which they are engaged. Once that level has been determined, its limits should not be exceeded. Because adventure/challenge therapy involves psychological and physical risks, only therapeutic recreation specialists with proper training and supervised leadership experiences should lead adventure/challenge therapy groups.

> Group leaders should be relatively congruent and stable individuals free from gross pathology and with developed insight into their own unique characteristics and needs.

Leaders of therapeutic recreation groups must know themselves and feel reasonably satisfied with themselves as persons before they can help others. If overly concerned about his or her own ego, the leader will have a difficult time helping others because it takes ego strength to deal with the stresses of group leadership.

> Every effort should be made to ensure the maximum privacy of participants in the group process by appropriate discussion of the principles, needs, and implications of the concept of confidentiality. Leaders should frankly confront the fact that they are able to guarantee only their own commitment to the privacy of discussions.

Professional ethics dictate that therapeutic recreation specialists maintain confidentiality in helping relationships. In one-to-one situations this simply means that the therapeutic recreation specialist must maintain discretion in the use of client information. Group leaders face a different situation because others are involved. Particularly when dealing with the discussion of potentially sensitive topics—as might be discussed in some types of leisure counseling—the issue of confidentiality should be discussed with group members.

> Individuals and institutions that offer and support group activities have the obligation to evaluate those activities periodically. Furthermore, those professionals and institutions have an obligation to participate in research activities designed to reform and refine practice and to determine the effectiveness of variations in practice.

Ongoing evaluation is necessary for the improvement of services offered in therapeutic recreation groups. Additionally, therapeutic recreation specialists should feel an obligation to conduct research efforts themselves and/or cooperate with university faculty and others in carrying out research investigations.

READING COMPREHENSION QUESTIONS

1.   Define leadership in your own words.
2.   What are four levels of leadership?

3. What are the major types of power? In what ways may power be possessed by therapeutic recreation specialists?
4. How will the wise leader deal with power?
5. Explain autocratic, democratic, and laissez-faire leadership.
6. Is there one best leadership style for therapeutic recreation? Why or why not?
7. Describe the continuum of leadership styles outlined in this chapter.
8. Do you understand the eight leadership roles of Avedon?
9. What is dependency? Have you felt dependent? How can dependency be dealt with positively?
10. What is the overjustification effect?
11. What types of power should directive leaders employ? Why?
12. What is the function of the group leader?
13. Can you name and describe structures for group participation in therapeutic recreation?
14. What types of therapeutic groups can you identify?
15. Do you agree with the categories of games, exercises, and activities that appear within the chapter?
16. What makes a collection of people into a group?
17. What are stages of group development? Can you describe each?
18. What are some things you might do as a leader to ease the entry of a new member into a therapeutic recreation group?
19. Why is the leader's example important to the group?
20. Do therapeutic recreation specialists ever have to face conflicts with clients? If so, how should they be handled?
21. What are dimensions that can influence the growth and development of the group that the leader must consider?
22. Can you identify major types of functions performed by group members?
23. Can you successfully employ the guidelines for group leader observations ?
24. Do you agree with Hansen's principles to guide the practice of group leaders? Which do you feel have particular application to therapeutic recreation groups?

Chapter Eight

SPECIFIC LEADERSHIP TASKS AND CONCERNS

CHAPTER PURPOSE

Critical to the success of therapeutic recreation specialists is their development in terms of gaining understanding of several leadership tasks and concerns. This chapter offers information on a number of these tasks and concerns including: (1) individual client documentation; (2) the therapeutic recreation specialist as teacher; (3) leisure counseling; and (4) understanding transactions. Areas covered within the section on understanding transactions are self-concept, learned helplessness, the self-fulfilling prophecy, labeling, loneliness, self-efficacy, and attributional processes.

KEY TERMS

- Source-oriented records
- Problem lists
- Progress note
- Problem-oriented-record (POR)
- Affective skills
- Self-concept
- Playing a role
- Self-esteem
- Self-reported handicap
- Reactance
- Data base
- Initial plan
- SOAP
- Cognitive skills
- Psychomotor skills
- Social comparisons
- Social distinctiveness
- Self-handicapping
- Learned helplessness
- Self-fulfilling prophecy

- Response-outcome expectancy
- Self-efficacy
- Attributional processes
- Internal attributions
- External attributions
- Self-serving bias
- Fundamental attributional error

OBJECTIVES

- Justify charting.
- Analyze a progress note.
- Know categories of behavior for progress note writing.
- Understand major principles in the teaching/learning process.
- Define the term counseling.
- Recognize the state of the art of leisure counseling.
- Appreciate topics of concern in understanding leader transactions: self-concept, learned helplessness, the self-fulfilling prophecy, labeling, loneliness, self-efficacy, and attributional processes.

THE CLIENT DOCUMENTATION TASK

An important function for therapeutic recreation specialists is the documenting of the therapeutic recreation process through charting. "Charting is the concise, accurate, factual, written documentation and communication of occurrences and situations pertaining to a particular client," as defined by Hoozer, Ruther and Craft (1982, p. 13) in their book titled *Introduction to Charting*.

All members of the health care team depend on the information communicated in client charts. The quality of the client's care may be jeopardized if information is not successfully communicated because a critical occurrence is not recorded or a note is poorly written. The chart is also a legal document that can be subpoenaed for use in a court of law. Legal action can be taken against an individual who falsifies or helps to falsify a client's chart. Because of possible legal ramifications, "charting is one of the most significant responsibilities that the health care professional assumes," according to Hoozer, Ruther and Craft (1982, p. 14). Therefore, the therapeutic recreation specialist needs to be sensitive to how the client is responding to clinical interventions and to record both subtle and dramatic changes in clear writing and charting.

Record Purposes

The client's record is used for several purposes. Two have already been mentioned; they are its use in communication and as a legal document. These and other purposes are discussed in the following section.

Communication

All members of the health care team are able to record in the client's chart and all have access to the documentation found in the chart. Communication is thus enhanced by use of the chart by health care professionals from various disciplines who interact with the client at different times.

Legal Document

Because the chart is a legal document admissible as evidence during malpractice or negligence suits, or other court proceedings, entries must be signed and dated by the health care professional making the entry.

Evaluation

First, the client's chart is an invaluable source to discover what changes have occurred in a client's condition since you last saw him or her. Secondly, chart information provides a basis for assessing the client's current status against his past or usual condition. Written records are certainly far more reliable than memory in drawing such comparisons. Third, information recorded by other health care professionals supplements your own assessments. Finally, reading documentation by yourself or others can prove helpful in explaining, confirming, or refuting current observations. It allows you to seek an explanation for behavior as well as to observe and report it (Narrow & Buschle, 1987). Of course, chart recordings allow the health care team to assess how the client is responding to the individual program plan and to provide a basis for what should be done next.

Education

The client record offers health care students and professionals a means to learn as they read about the clinical manifestations of particular problems and analyze the thinking process and judgments of others. Charts also provide examples of progress notes that may be helpful to emerging professionals who are developing their note writing abilities.

Research

The chart may be studied by researchers to identify researchable problems or to identify similar cases in order to determine how best to diagnose and treat particular health problems.

Audit

Charts may be systematically reviewed and evaluated as a part of a quality assurance program. Visiting teams from outside accrediting organizations, such as JCAHO (Joint Commission for the Accreditation of Healthcare Organizations), customarily complete chart audits as a part of their evaluations.

Types of Records

Each setting will adopt a standard method of charting and will supply forms for the client's chart that reflect the particular type of system that is used by the agency. Two systems are commonly found in agencies. These are the traditional *source-oriented record*, sometimes termed the *narrative record*, and the *problem-oriented record* that has gained popularity since coming on the scene during the 1960s.

Source-oriented Records

The traditional means of recording has been the **source-oriented** or narrative record. In contrast to the problem-oriented record that groups information from all health care disciplines according to the client's specific problems, the source-oriented record separates recordings according to source or discipline. Sections of the chart are designated for medical notes, nursing notes, therapeutic recreation or activity therapy notes, and so on. The obvious advantage of a source-oriented record is that each discipline's entries can be easily located. Those favoring the source-oriented record state that it is easier for each discipline to record all their data in one section of the chart. Those opposing the approach claim that it places data in too many locations making it fragmented and cumbersome to retrieve information (Peterson & Gunn, 1984).

Because recordings from the various disciplines are kept in separate sections of the chart, staff may neglect to read what others have written with the result that they are not aware of problems or successes experienced outside of their area. The use of the source-oriented system does not, of course, negate the possibility of a true interdisciplinary team effort. It may, however, make it more difficult unless team members make a concerted effort to employ a holistic approach by reviewing the notes of other disciplines and engaging in teamwork during team conferences and staff meetings (Narrow & Buschle, 1987).

Notations are made in chronological order with the most recent being nearest the front of the section. There is no strict format for each entry as the professional charts a narrative description of the client's participation in the program, or observations are made of the client on other occasions. The lack of formal structure can be a disadvantage in that inexperienced note writers may not focus their observations on specific client problems or goals. Because of this, some agencies have turned to the use of problem-oriented records that offer a set structure for charting.

Problem-oriented Records

The problem-oriented record (POR), or problem-oriented medical record (POMR), was originated by Dr. Lawrence Weed in 1958 as a means to improve the documentation of client care (Peterson & Gunn, 1984). Today it is frequently used for documenting client care with many agencies adapting the system to meet their particular needs. In some settings the approach is referred to as a problem-oriented health record (POHR) to reflect a broadened concern beyond medical care.

The objectives of the POR have been outlined by Lindberg, Hunter, and Kruszewski (1983, p. 243) to be:

- To individualize care by focusing on the client and his (or her) needs;
- To encourage health professionals to look for relationships among problems;
- To promote communication among health-care members involved in direct care of the client; and
- To organize the health-care record so that all information from all health disciplines is recorded in the same way.

The problem-oriented record is organized around the client's problems, rather than around the sources of information. It contains four basic parts. Those components are a defined data base, a problem list, care plans, and progress notes.

All members of the interdisciplinary team contribute to the data base. In the **data base** is contained information collected during the assessment phase of the therapeutic recreation process. Analysis of the data base leads to the establishment of a comprehensive **problem list**. Problems are numbered in chronological order based on the date each was stipulated. The list of numbered problems appears in the front of the chart with the date each was identified and is used as a table of contents to be referred to when recordings are made. The **initial plan** outlines an approach to be used to meet each of the identified problems. **Progress notes** record the results of interventions and the client's progress. Entries follow the acronym **SOAP**.

S stands for *subjective data*. Subjective data are those gathered from the client. **O** stands for *objective data*, which is collected through observation, measurement, and sources such as documentation by other health care professionals. **A** represents *assessment*. Assessment answers the question, "What do the subjective and objective data mean?" The professional records his or her conclusions following a review of the subjective and objective data. **P** is for *plan*. Under this part of the progress note, the professional formulates a plan or approach that he or she believes will resolve the problem. This may mean following the initial plans, revising them, or developing plans.

"Soaping," as therapeutic recreation specialists sometimes refer to completing progress notes using the SOAP format, has been widely accepted by numerous agencies in its original or an adapted form. Some staff, however, complain that the technique is too restrictive and too narrowly focuses on identified problems. They favor a return to the traditional narrative format (Taylor, Lillis & LeMone, 1989).

The following progress note, which employs the SOAP format, is based on an example provided by Shannon, Wahl, Rhea & Dyehouse (1988, p. 159).

Date	Number	Title
3-8-90	2	Anxiety

S Stated feeling less anxiety: "I'm not feeling so nervous as I had been."

O Engaged in a table game for 45 minutes on the unit with two other clients and the therapeutic recreation specialist without notable restlessness. Concentration and attention span were adequate to meet the demands of the game.

A Anxiety level is slowly decreasing. Still inability to express other emotional states.

P Continue care as outlined in initial plans.

Effective Progress Note Writing

A number of useful guidelines for writing progress notes have appeared in the literature. Those that follow have been drawn from a variety of sources, including Hoozer, Ruther, and Craft (1982), Narrow and Buschle (1987), O'Morrow and Reynolds (1989), Peterson and Gunn (1984), Potter and Perry (1987), and Taylor, Lillis, and LeMone (1993).

1. *Use simple descriptive terms.* Avoid the use of jargon as much as possible. The use of "big words" does not make a person into an expert. For instance, in working with clients who have problems in mental health, avoid such terms as "psychotic," "schizophrenic," and "bizarre" to describe behavior. Instead, describe the specific event or activity that was seen or heard. If a particular professional term is used, define it or tell what you mean by it.

2. *Be informative.* Ask yourself, "Does the note contain the information I intended it to?"

3. *Be accurate.* Information must always be correct. Never falsify a client's chart. Discriminate in a clear fashion whether subjective or objective data are being presented. Normally record only observations of behavior; when interpretations are made, differentiate these from behavioral observations.

4. *Be brief.* Eliminate unnecessary words. The term "client" or "patient" is not usually required and may be omitted from progress notes. Incomplete sentences may be used, along with appropriate symbols and abbreviations. (See Table 8-1 for a selected list of abbreviations and symbols.)

5. *Be precise.* Attempt to be as precise as possible. For example, state "six times in one hour," not "often." Avoid such words as "bad", "good," "average," "normal," and "better", that may mean different things to different readers. Do not use vague phrases such as "seems to be" or "appears to." Avoid generalizations such as "seems uncomfortable today."

6. *Avoid stereotypes.* Avoid the use of stereotypes or derogatory terms when charting.

7. *Use present tense* and correct grammar and spelling.

8. *Write legibly.* While some notes are entered directly on computers, most are still handwritten or printed. Use clear handwriting or printing and always write in ink. If others cannot read the note it will not serve its intended purpose.

9. *Employ a format.* Use a systematic format or logical order. For example, when recording observations about physical conditions, start with the head and go down the body. When presenting a series of behaviors, record them in the order in which they occurred.

10. *Use original source if possible.* Attempt to obtain firsthand information from the client. Write only what you know is correct, always verifying secondhand information. If you must report unsubstantiated information, label it as such and identify the source of the information.

11. *Document incidents.* Accidents or unusual occurrences need to be documented in the progress notes as well as on special incident forms. Record when and where the incident occurred, findings at the scene (facts; visual and material information), care of client before and after the incident, client's comments, who was notified, and what preventive steps were taken.

12. *Consider confidentiality.* Always preserve the dignity and privacy of every client. Progress notes should be used only as a means to improve client care and treatment.

13. *Correct errors.* No erasures should appear in progress notes (because others would not know if you or someone else

erased the information). Likewise, correction fluids should not be used. Errors should be corrected by drawing a line through the error and writing the word "error" over or next to the mistake.

14. *Never leave blank space.* Do not leave blank space in a note because another person can add information to the blank space that is incorrect. Draw a single line through blank spaces so no one may write in the space.

15. *Do not use ditto marks.* Ditto marks are not allowed in progress note writing.

16. *Chart entries chronologically* on consecutive lines. Do not skip lines.

17. *Be familiar with agency policies.* Agencies have specified forms that should be used to make progress note entries. Agencies also have policies as to who may place information in the client's record, or they may require different staff (e.g., nurses, social workers, therapeutic recreation specialists) to use a particular color of ink when writing notes.

18. *Determine frequency of recordings.* Determine precisely how often entries are to be made (e.g., daily, weekly). This schedule should be strictly followed. As a rule, it is best to record after each session with the client. Delaying charting is a dangerous practice because during a busy day it is easy to forget important details.

19. *Date and sign entry.* Be certain to date and sign each progress note you write. You should normally sign with your first initial and last name, along with your title (e.g., CTRS). Check your agency policy to be certain you sign the note as is required by your agency.

Examples of what *not* to do and what to do in writing progress notes follow.

How NOT to Write a Progress Note

The client often becomes angry when he plays basketball and when he is not playing he is always pacing the sidelines. He is uncooperative and more psychotic than before.

Obviously, the writer did not have access to the information provided previously in this section. Some apparent criticisms appear next. You may add others.

1.   The phrase, "The client," is not necessary. It would have been fine to use an incomplete sentence.
2.   The use of the word "often" is not precise. Does this mean every day, three times a week, or once every hour?
3.   What is meant by the word "angry?" What behavior is the writer describing? Did the client hit, kick, get red in the face?
4.   In what kind of basketball activity was the client engaged? Was this a scheduled game, a team practice, or an informal pickup game?
5.   The word "always" is not precise. Does this mean the client never stops?
6.   The terms "pacing" and "uncooperative" are not defined. What exactly was the client doing?
7.   The expression "more psychotic than before" employs jargon (i.e., psychotic) and lacks precision (i.e., more than before).
8.   Finally, the writer failed to date and sign the entry.

How to Write a Progress Note

Below is another progress note. Look it over. Is it superior to the previous example? If so, in what ways?

> *Unable to sit for 5 minutes while teams were being organized for basketball game during informal recreation for the unit in the gym. Instead, rapidly walked back and forth in front of bleachers where others were sitting. Said he did not wish to play, but decided to participate when told he would have to sit and watch others, or return to the unit if he chose not to take part. Displayed anger 2 times during 15 minute game. Once kicked ball when teammate missed a pass and once shoved opposing player when client felt he was fouled. Appeared to experience verbal hallucinations throughout 10 minute group processing following the game. Kept mumbling about, "Going to Heaven or Hell." 10-16-97 D. Austin, CTRS.*

Progress Note Content

The problem-oriented records format, of course, stipulates that each entry should be related to a problem and outlines the information that needs to appear. Some agencies, however, adapt or modify the POR system. Others use narrative note. Even those using the POR system may find some guidelines helpful in preparing progress notes.

Problems

Just what sort of information should be contained in progress notes? A good beginning place is to consider the problems on which the client is working. How is the client responding to the treatment or rehabilitation program? Are interventions accomplishing the stated specific behavioral objectives in the IPP? Is he or she changing? What does the client report in terms of his or her reaction to the program? Does he or she indicate feeling improvement?

TABLE 8-1
SELECTED ABBREVIATIONS AND SYMBOLS

aa	of each
ADL	Activities of daily living
adm	admission
a.m.	morning
amb.	ambulatory, walking
approx.	approximately (about)
c	with
c/o	complains about
dept	department
et,+, &	and
exam	examination
h	hour
med.	medical or medication
OD	right eye
OS	left eye
p	after
p.m.	afternoon
pt	patient or pint
q	every
qd	every day
s	without
via	by way of
>	greater than
<	less than

Symptoms

What about symptoms? Have there been episodes you have observed? What was the severity? What was the frequency? Duration? When was the onset? What precipitating factors were involved? What aggravating factors were noted? Relieving factors? Associated symptoms?

Confusion or Aggression

Were client behaviors such as confusion or aggression observed? When did this occur? Under what circumstances? What precipitating factors were involved? What specific behaviors were observed? What did you do? How did the client respond to your actions? (Potter &Perry, 1987)

General Progress

O'Morrow (1980) has suggested that routine progress notes might properly include general progress (or lack thereof), specific symptoms or problems interfering with progress, alterations or modifications made in client plans, client proficiency in the use of any device or adaptive equipment employed, and various evaluations made by staff. Quattlebaum (1969) has proposed that progress notes in psychiatric hospitals should include information on response deficits and excesses, deviant and inappropriate responses, and the people and situations causing these responses.

Miller (1989, pp. 16, 17) has relied on guidelines developed by the Pennsylvania Department of Health in suggesting that documentation in long-term care facilities should consider: *progress* (or lack thereof), *activities* (with frequency of participation), *resistance* (i.e., instances when the resident resists or refuses participation and strategies for seeking the resident's involvement), *participation* (level or extent), *relating and interacting* (social interaction with others), *group behavior* (acceptable and appropriate), and *size of events* (most appropriate size for resident such as one-on-one, small group, large group).

Peterson and Gunn (1984, p. 244) have offered the following list of guidelines for the relevance of content for progress notes:

- Progress toward attainment of client goal
- Regression from attainment of client goal
- New patterns of behavior
- Consistency of behavior

- Verbal information provided by the client
- Successful or unsuccessful attempts at a task
- Appropriate or inappropriate interactions with staff, peers, visitors
- Client responses to questions, instructions, requests
- Initiative with actions, ideas, problem-solving, decision making
- Follow-through or lack of follow-through with commitments

Behaviors

Different categories of behavior are utilized in various types of settings for the reference of those writing progress notes. Through my personal observation of materials prepared by agencies, it seems that there are several broad categories of behavior that therapeutic recreation specialists employ as guides to writing progress notes. Frequently used categories seem to be participation, performance, interpersonal relationships, personal habits, and state of consciousness and/or mental activity. These major categories follow along with items that relate to them.

Participation
- Interest in activities
- Extent and nature of involvement
- Attention shown (attention span)
- Appropriateness of energy output
- Initiative in choosing activities
- Attitude expressed toward own participation
- Attitude toward rules, winning, competition

Performance
- Level of performance
- Quality of performance
- Hindering factors
- Ability to make decisions
- Quality of judgment
- Ability to express self adequately
- Ability to express self appropriately
- Physical movement (e.g., slow, rigid)
- Use of any device or adaptive equipment
- Attitude expressed toward own performance

- Ability to follow rules and directions
- Special incidents
- Summary of change and performance

Interpersonal Relationships
- Relationships with therapeutic recreation specialist and others (e.g., dependency, hostility)
- Acceptance of limits
- Manipulative
- Passive, aloof, or withdrawn
- Reserved, insecure, timid, or shy
- Outgoing, confident, or extrovert
- Ability to make friends
- Acceptance by others
- Agreeable, cooperative, or helpful
- Resistive or stubborn
- Verbalizes appropriately

Personal Habits and Appearances
- Appropriateness of dress
- Grooming
- Cleanliness and neatness
- Concern with appearance
- Walk or gait
- Tics, rituals, habitual movements

State of Consciousness and/or Mental Activity
- Orientation to time
- Orientation to place
- Orientation to persons or objects
- Preoccupied (responsiveness)
- Slow in answering or thinking
- Distracted by others or events
- Ability to remember (retention)
- Hallucinations or delusions
- Intellectual functioning
- Stability of mood

PRINCIPLES IN THE TEACHING/ LEARNING PROCESS

Many situations require the therapeutic recreation specialist to help clients to learn. In fact, much of what is done in therapeutic recreation can be thought of as educational as clients learn to acquire and apply knowledge and analyze and evaluate information (**cognitive skills**), develop self-awareness in terms of values, attitudes, and opinions (**affective skills**), and gain and refine abilities that require the integration of mental and muscular activities (**psychomotor skills**).

Basic Teaching/Learning Principles

There is not a set formula for learning, but there are basic principles that can be used to guide the teaching/learning process. The principles that follow have been drawn from Blattner (1982), Dainow and Bailey (1988), Kibler, Barker and Miles (1970), Kraus, Carpenter and Bates (1981), Marriner (1983), Mosey (1973), Potter and Perry (1987), and Taylor, Lillis and LeMone (1993).

1. *Start at the level of the client and move at a rate that is comfortable.* It is important to assess the client's ability so the leader will not place too much or too little demand on the client. The rate of learning will vary, so the therapeutic recreation specialist must be prepared to adjust instruction accordingly.

2. *Individual differences must be given consideration.* Each client is an individual and will learn in a unique way. Individuals differ in their abilities, backgrounds, interests, ages, and readiness for learning. Intellectual capacities, physical health, and energy levels are ability factors demanding consideration. Educational and cultural background also influence learning, as does the level of client interest in the particular activity. Additionally, the individual must perceive the activity being learned to be age appropriate or it will likely be rejected. Finally, readiness plays a large part in learning. If the client does not have the physical and cognitive development to cope with the learning situation, he or she will probably fail.

3. *Active participation is essential for learning.* Active participation in planning for and engaging in learning means the client has a thorough involvement in the total learning process. It may be said that the best teaching is the

least teaching. People do learn by doing, so it is generally better to engage them actively in learning to the fullest possible degree. After all, it is what the learner does—not the instructor—that determines learning.

4.   *Reinforcement strengthens learning.* People tend to repeat the things that they enjoy or find rewarding. Teaching new behaviors then depends on clients finding the behaviors rewarding. Therefore, the therapeutic recreation specialist should strive to provide social reinforcement when clients perform appropriately. Usually social reinforcers take the form of attention, encouragement, and approval. Another reinforcer comes in the form of the client feeling mastery or a sense of accomplishment. Extrinsic rewards, such as money or food, may also be used to reinforce behaviors. The timing in delivering all types of reinforcers is critical to their success. Rewards have the most effect when administered immediately after the behavior. When new behaviors are initially being learned, a continuous schedule of reinforcement should be used. Once the behavior has been established, it does not need to be rewarded each time it is performed. It is possible to reward the client infrequently. (More detailed information on reinforcement as a technique is found in Chapter 2.)

5.   *Opportunities for trial and error can enhance learning.* Trial-and-error learning allows the learner to use a variety of approaches until he or she finds one that works. Of course, trial-and-error learning works best in an atmosphere that allows the time and freedom for people to work things out for themselves. Errors are perceived as a natural part of the learning process, and clients are not told what they should do. The therapeutic recreation specialist must remain flexible when using the trial-and-error approach in order to encourage inventive problem solving.

6.   *Imitation and modeling can enhance learning.* When making projects, clients should be shown models or examples of what they are to produce at the end of the learning experience. For example, a completed arts-and-craft project might be displayed so that clients have an idea of what the finished product will be like. In teaching sports activities the leader can demonstrate proper form, or audiovisuals (films, film strips) can be used to show clients correct

methods. Social behaviors for adults and play behaviors can be gained more quickly if the learner can see a model demonstrate the desired behavior. As discussed in Chapter 2, modeling can also be combined with reinforcement to make it an even more potent means to learning.

7.   *Practice facilitates learning.* The actual amount of practice needed to master a new skill or behavior will vary with the level of complexity of that skill or behavior. Therapeutic recreation specialists must remember that clients are sometimes taught new skills, but are not given enough time to practice them. Therefore, therapeutic recreation programs should offer many informal opportunities for clients to try new recreational and social skills. It may be that the therapeutic recreation specialist will help the client to arrange for post-discharge opportunities to practice while undergoing treatment.

8.   *Feedback facilitates learning.* Leaders should provide learners with feedback as they learn and practice new skills. This feedback can take the form of positive reinforcement for doing well, encouragement for trying hard, or corrective instruction that will allow the client to improve. The general thought of many clients is that "no news is bad news." Therefore, it is critical to provide regular feedback to clients who are acquiring and practicing new skills.

9.   *Clients should know what is to be learned and why they are learning it.* Our clients, as all learners, need to have prelearning preparation. They must be prepared for what is coming and the reasons for learning. Little learning will occur if clients do not understand what it is they are supposed to learn and why they are being taught something new.

10.   *Move from simple to the complex.* A general rule of learning is to move the learner from the simple toward the complex, or from the familiar to the unfamiliar. However, Mosey (1973) stresses that the teacher should not fall into the trap of teaching meaningless parts that learners are somehow supposed to connect to a whole on their own. She gives the example of teaching clients how to use public transportation as a natural detail of a pleasurable outing instead of taking the client on a meaningless trip for the sake of learning how to ride the city bus.

11. *Perception affects learning.* A client's perceptions come about as a result of the brain's processing of stimuli received through the sense organs. Maturation and learning both impact on the client's perceptions of the environment. A child may miss subtle cues, or an older adult may perceive things much differently than a relatively young helping professional. Also, a person with sensory problems may experience difficulty in receiving stimuli. Therefore, the therapeutic recreation specialist must become aware of possible client problems in receiving sensory impulses (e.g., sight, hearing) as well as differing perceptions on the part of individual clients.

12. *Anxiety affects learning.* Some anxiety, in the form of general arousal and interest, positively affects learning, but too much anxiety can interfere with the learning process. The therapeutic recreation specialist must attempt to identify the optimal level of anxiety for each client and gear the learning situation accordingly. Many clients require an accepting, nonjudgmental atmosphere in which to learn and try out new skills and behaviors. They learn best with individual instruction or in a small group where support and cooperation are emphasized. Once the skill is acquired, they may be ready to practice or perform gradually the skill in larger and larger groups. It is the role of the therapeutic recreation specialist to judge, with the client, what pace is appropriate for each individual.

13. *Relate new learning to existing knowledge.* There needs to be a link between what the client is learning and his or her present knowledge so new skills may be logically connected with what is already known. The therapeutic recreation specialist needs to build on the client's existing knowledge. This calls for the therapeutic recreation specialist to conduct an assessment in order to determine existing knowledge.

14. *Sensory stimulation can aid learning.* The use of a combination of sensory experiences (sight, sound, touch, smell, taste) together with varied teaching strategies (e.g., role playing, audiovisual aids) may promote learning. We learn better when more than one of our senses is activated.

15. *Timing affects learning.* Teaching needs to be timed to coincide with the client's readiness to learn. The best learning will occur when the client is attentive, receptive, and alert.

At times, side-effects of drugs can interfere with the client's readiness to learn so it becomes important for the therapeutic recreation specialist to be aware of possible side-effects of medication.

16. *Enthusiasm is contagious.* Clients will be more apt to remain interested in learning if the therapeutic recreation specialist is enthusiastic about the area of learning. The therapeutic recreation specialist should not remain stationary behind a lectern or desk, but should be an active teacher/therapist who makes eye contact with clients, uses gestures, and varies his or her voice tone and intensity. Teaching and learning are fun and should be approached with enthusiasm.

17. *Match teaching strategies to clients' needs.* Psychomotor skills are perhaps best taught through demonstration and practiced under supervision. Group discussion may prove effective when adult clients are exploring leisure values. Information on leisure resources might be provided to adolescents by means of an interactive computer program or a question and answer session. Play skills may be better taught to children with mental retardation through imitation and modeling rather than explanation. With whatever group you are working, choose a teaching strategy that fits them and the skill or knowledge being taught.

Summary of Teaching/ Learning Principles

The basic principles of teaching/learning have been presented to help therapeutic recreation specialists facilitate client learning. Remember, however, that every principle presented will take on a different level of emphasis or importance with each individual client and each new learning situation. Learning is obviously far more complex than is reflected by the traditional teacher-learner paradigm where the teacher's role is that of dispenser of information for eagerly waiting learners. Certainly the role of the therapeutic recreation specialist as a leader is far greater than this as he or she helps clients to find ways to learn.

It has been reported by Dainow and Bailey (1988), "that people generally remember 10 percent of what they read, 20 percent of what they hear, 30 percent of what they see, 50 percent of what they hear and see, 70 percent of what they say and write, and 80 percent of what they say as they do something" (p. 4). If this is true people need a variety of means to learn. There are any number of strategies available to assist clients to learn. These include modeling behaviors for clients, demonstrating techniques, lectures, group discussions, panel discussions, role playing, programmed instructional materials, computer-instructional programs, printed material, games and other experiential education approaches (e.g., adventure-challenge activities). When carrying out these strategies, "active participation" and "learning by doing" are key phrases for the therapeutic recreation specialist who strives to actively engage the client in educational experiences that have recreation properties. Learning and enjoyment should go hand in hand.

LEADERSHIP IN LEISURE COUNSELING

Leisure counseling is an area of interest to many therapeutic recreation specialists. In this section counseling is defined, factors distinguishing leisure counseling are presented, general orientations to leisure counseling are detailed, and conclusions are made regarding leisure counseling.

Most therapeutic recreation specialists would probably agree that counseling is an interpersonal process involving communication between a skilled helper and a client, or clients seeking help in attempting to discover and/or change feelings, thoughts, or behaviors. Counseling usually is entered into voluntarily with assurances that the counseling relationship is private and confidential, thus providing a condition in which clients freely express themselves (Blackham, 1977; Hackney & Cormier, 1988). The broad goal of counseling is to help clients enhance personal development.

Factors Distinguishing Leisure Counseling

Two primary factors distinguish leisure counseling from other types of counseling. First, the main intent of leisure counseling is to help the client in regard to his or her leisure well-being. Many variables impact on an individual, but they are of concern only to the extent that they affect leisure. The prime focus always remains on the client's leisure. Second, because of the nature of leisure counseling, the counselor must be conversant with the dynamics of leisure participation and with concrete information related to leisure opportunities. This assures that the counselor will be knowledgeable of the leisure experience and with problems related to leisure participation. It is also assured that the counselor will be well versed on particular leisure programs or situations that may be valuable to clients.

McDowell (1980) has provided what perhaps has become the most accepted formulation of major orientations to leisure counseling. These deal with:

- leisure-related behavior concerns,
- leisure lifestyle awareness concerns,
- leisure resource guidance concerns, and
- leisure-related skills development concerns.

Leisure-Related Behavior Orientation

The goal of the leisure-related behavior orientation is to help clients resolve behavioral concerns. These concerns may exhibit themselves in the form of feelings such as obligation, anxiety, guilt or boredom, or through escape behaviors such as chronic television viewing or excessive drinking. During leisure counseling, the counselor attempts to assist clients to express themselves so that their concerns may be clarified, understood, and resolved. Therefore, the focus of facilitation is with clarifying and understanding leisure-related behaviors so that clients may make reasoned decisions regarding their leisure patterns. This orientation is the most complex one and perhaps most closely resembles traditional counseling. Because of the complexity of the orientation, well-developed listening and facilitation skills are demanded of the counselor.

Leisure Lifestyle Awareness Orientation

Leisure lifestyle awareness counseling is directed toward helping improve clients' self-knowledge and understandings pertaining to leisure values, beliefs, and attitudes. This orientation also encompasses counseling regarding personal leisure and lifestyle needs, particularly as they relate to felt difficulties surrounding life events such as retirement, career change, marriage, or divorce. Here the counselor's role is active in initiating awareness on the part of the clients through the employment of experiential exercises and self-help leisure learning exercises. Often leisure lifestyle awareness concerns are met through group counseling.

Leisure Resource Guidance Orientation

The leisure resource guidance orientation deals with matching clients' interests with community resources. The leisure counselor helps clients to identify past, present, and potential leisure interests, perhaps using one of the leisure inventories. Interests are then matched with opportunities available to clients. Thus, this model of leisure counseling essentially is a referral service. The basic assumption underlying this approach is that clients can function adequately in the community and require concrete information in regard to their interests and resources available to meet those interests.

Leisure-Related Skills-Development Orientation

Underlying the skills-development orientation is the assumption that clients lack certain leisure-related skills or abilities. Under this model, personal, social, and recreational skills are appraised and remedial counseling is begun to help clients attain these skills. This counseling may be provided in coordination with client participation in therapeutic recreation programs that provide opportunities for mastery of skill deficiencies. The facilitating focus of the counselor is initially with identifying concerns of each client in regard to skills, prioritizing these concerns, and stipulating criteria for goal attainment. Once this has been accomplished, the counselor plays an active role in helping the client to establish means to move toward alleviation of the concerns. Evaluation of client progress is completed by the counselor while maintaining a supportive/confrontive role.

As McDowell (1980) has indicated, the four orientations discussed in this section are not mutually independent. Although each has a particular focus, in actual practice it is likely that the orientations will overlap.

TABLE 8-3
MCDOWELL'S LEVELS OF COUNSELING

Leisure-Related Behavioral Problems

To help clients resolve behavioral concerns. Clients develop effective coping skills and problem-solving abilities to deal with chronic or excessively expressed leisure-related behavioral concerns (e.g., boredom, TV watching, etc.).

Leisure Lifestyle Awareness Orientation

To help clients improve self-knowledge and understanding pertaining to leisure values, beliefs, and attitudes. Clients develop understanding regarding leisure and issues such as personal lifestyle, family relations, and transitions (e.g., aging, retirement, relocation, divorce).

Leisure Resource Guidance Orientation

To help clients match leisure interests with community resources. Clients need to identify leisure interests, or what to do in their free time, and information regarding opportunities needs to be provided to them.

Leisure-Related Skills-Development Orientation

To help clients develop the leisure-related skills and abilities that they lack. Clients develop skills in areas such as assertiveness, social skills, grooming, motor abilities, effective use of transportation, and recreation activities.

Source: McDowell, C.F. 1984. Leisure: Consciousness, well-being, and counseling. In E.T. Dowd (ed.). *Leisure Counseling: Concepts and Applications*. Springfield, IL: Charles C. Thomas.

Leisure Counseling Conclusions

I wrote in the first edition of this book that while leisure counseling had been a much discussed topic since the 1960s, it was still in the infancy of its development during the early 1980s. This observation was based on my own experience as a therapeutic recreation practitioner and educator, as well as several extensive reviews of the leisure counseling literature that had appeared around the time (Compton, Witt & Sanchez, 1980; Fikes, 1979; Shank & Kennedy, 1976). I must report my personal experiences and the literature (e.g., Hultsman, Black, Seehafer & Hovell, 1987; Munson & Munson, 1986) still indicate that leisure counseling has not outgrown the infancy stage in its development. Granted, there has been some growth, but the problems that have kept the field from thriving have only recently begun to be addressed. Persistent confusion regarding an agreed on set of goals or outcomes for leisure counseling and the related problem of the lack of a clear definition of leisure counseling have continued to create a high level of ambiguity. However, over the past 10 to 15 years, those concerned with leisure counseling have begun to define the service more precisely in an effort to promote the growth and acceptance of the field.

Authorities (Tinsley & Tinsley, 1981; Munson & Munson, 1986) agree that, although ill defined, what went on in leisure counseling in the early years was largely information giving. Staff assisted clients to identify leisure interests and then gave them the information needed to locate opportunities to pursue those interests. This type of service would fall under McDowell's leisure resource guidance orientation described earlier. Such efforts were performed without any theoretical basis. Even more recent and advanced approaches (that would come within McDowell's leisure lifestyle awareness orientation) have generally not been based on theoretical formulations (Hultsman et al, 1987; Tinsley & Tinsley, 1981). Also, many conducting leisure counseling have not been adequately prepared in the dynamics of counseling and, therefore, have lacked a conceptualization of the counseling process and knowledge of counselor skills (Tinsley & Tinsley, 1981).

Happily, out of experiences gained over the years, understandings have come that hold promise for the future of leisure counseling. There is a growing sophistication reflected by leisure counseling programs that extend beyond mere information giving. For instance, Wolfe and Riddick (1984) have reported on a program for adult psychiatric outpatients directed toward bringing about changes in leisure attitudes and self-esteem. Li (1981) has discussed the use of leisure counseling in stress reduction for a psychiatric population. Caldwell, Adolph, and Gilbert (1989) have reported research findings regarding the long-term effects of leisure counseling on leisure participation and satisfaction. The need for establishing theoretical underpinnings for practice also seems to be better understood. Iso-Ahola (1984) has formulated social psychological foundations for leisure and has provided implications of these for leisure counseling. Tinsley and Tinsley (1981) have identified leisure counseling models that have theoretical bases, including those by Remple, Gunn and Peterson, and Tinsley and Lindrud. Both Munson and Munson (1986) and Hultsman and his colleagues (1987) have offered specific theory-based models for leisure counseling.

As leisure counseling has begun to grow beyond the guidance-orientated, information-giving approach toward more advanced models built on theoretical foundations, the need for leisure counselors to possess counseling skills and knowledge has become increasingly apparent. Fortunately, therapeutic recreation specialists should have a solid foundation for doing leisure counseling, if they possess the basic helping characteristics for therapeutic recreation specialists (outlined in Chapter 5) that include the ability to communicate.

While it is too soon to predict a bright future ahead for the use of leisure counseling in therapeutic recreation, the future seems brighter than ever before. The goals and outcomes of leisure counseling are perhaps better understood today than at any time since its inception. The development of models (such as McDowell's, 1980; 1984) and the appearance of thoughtful writings (e.g., Iso-Ahola, 1984; Tinsley & Tinsley, 1981) have allowed us to realize that leisure counseling can extend beyond the narrow bounds of information giving into defined areas such as lifestyle awareness and leisure-related behavior problems, which more closely resemble traditional counseling. Other lessons that have been learned have been the necessity to adopt models and theory to support practice and the need for those conducting leisure counseling to possess counseling skills. These understandings have provided the opportunity for those doing leisure counseling to better define their efforts and to bring sharper focus to their work. Professionals now appear poised to move leisure counseling out of its infancy stage into its early childhood.

LEADERSHIP AND
UNDERSTANDING TRANSACTIONS

Self-concept, learned helplessness, the self-fulfilling prophecy, labeling, loneliness, self-efficacy, and attributional processes are topics of concern in understanding leader transactions with clients.

Self-Concept

One's concept of self plays a large role in influencing behavior. For instance, one's **self-concept** affects whether a particular situation is viewed as routine, challenging, or threatening. If we perceive ourselves to be highly competent we are apt to enter into new experiences and challenges. Conversely, perceiving oneself as inadequate can be debilitating (Borden & Stone, 1976; Iso-Ahola, 1980).

Origins

Our self-concept is the result of our life experiences, including the feedback received from those around us. Research reviewed in a major work on self-concept in early childhood by Samuels (1977) has substantiated that successful experiences can enhance self-concept. Furthermore, in Samuel's review she found that if significant others enhance self-concept through realistic evaluation of a person during the performance of a task, intrinsic satisfaction may eventually develop from the performance itself. Accordingly, less and less external feedback will be needed as time goes on and feelings of competency and control are instilled.

Influences

Self-concept development may certainly be affected by successful performances that are reacted to positively by significant others. Of course, poor performances met with negative evaluations by others can adversely affect self-concept as well. This "looking glass self" as Herbert Mead (1934) originally termed it, is one of four processes that affect self-concept according to Gergen and Gergen (1986).

In addition to coming to know ourselves by seeing how others react to our behavior, we also develop or change our self-concepts through social comparisons, from performing social roles, and by focusing on distinctive aspects of ourselves. Through

social comparisons, people compare themselves to others to see how they measure up. Individuals in social situations make observations as to how they compare with others and then draw conclusions about themselves. Have you ever compared yourself with someone you felt was clearly superior to you and, as a result, felt badly about yourself? My guess is that every one of us has done this at some point so we can all understand how our clients may form opinions about themselves through such comparisons.

Another means to altering self-concept is by **playing a role.** The idea here is that people who are forced into playing certain roles over time begin to take on that role and start to believe that the role represents the way they are. In short, their self-feelings follow actions.

The final means to developing or changing self-concept is through **social distinctiveness.** People tend to focus their attention on those aspects that make them different from others. When individuals observe something that sets them apart, that uniqueness comes into consciousness as a characteristic that is seen as a reflection of a personal identification. For example, Gergen and Gergen point out that we would not first think of ourselves or identify ourselves as a person with two legs because most others have two legs. However, were we to be missing our legs, we might well reflect this trait in our self-concept.

Ramifications for Therapy

Are there ramifications for therapeutic recreation practice of these means by which people define their self-concepts? Of course, there are. One important means to self-concept is receiving positive evaluations following performance. The therapeutic recreation specialist must keep in mind that he or she can have a great impact on client self-concepts and regularly strive to provide feedback that is both positive and realistic.

We also need to bear in mind that our clients will be making social comparisons that feed into their self-concepts. Placing a client in situations where everyone else is clearly superior in some way can negatively impact one's self-concept. Therefore, the therapeutic recreation specialist must analyze situations carefully before assigning a client into a group where he or she will likely pale in comparison to others.

Playing social roles may be used as a means to positively affect self-concept. It may be very therapeutic for the therapeutic recreation specialist to help a client to enter into a social role with which he or she does not feel comfortable, if in the judgment of the therapist the client will achieve success. For example, if a client is reluctant to join in a group because he or she is shy, encouraging participation by the client may lead to feelings of new found confidence when the client is able to achieve success within the group.

Because people identify themselves with those things that they perceive as being special or distinctive about themselves, the therapeutic recreation specialist can use this human trait to positively influence self-concept. For example, the therapeutic recreation specialist can help clients to realize positive characteristics about themselves that have not been a part of their consciousness. If a client is a particularly good checker player or a sharp dresser, the therapeutic recreation specialist can emphasize these positive characteristics that set the client apart. Clients who have collections as hobbies may be encouraged to make others aware of their interests because their collections represent symbols of their distinctive selves in which they can take pride.

Self-Concept and Self-Esteem

A question that often arises when discussing self-concept is how it differs from **self-esteem**. Most authorities concur that self-esteem is the affective part of self-concept. It represents how people regard themselves or value themselves. Self-esteem describes how favorable persons feel about themselves (LeUnes & Nation, 1989). Positive feelings result when our self-esteem is bolstered. Negative feelings occur when our self-esteem is deflated. When we feel good about ourselves, we perceive ourselves as having the ability to take on and meet the challenges we encounter in life. Negative thoughts about ourselves, however, can lead to feelings of loneliness, guilt, anxiety, and depression.

We human beings are unique in our ability to think consciously about ourselves. Further, we not only have the ability to reflect about ourselves, we possess a tendency to evaluate ourselves and, in doing so, we attempt to protect and enhance our self-esteem. Healthy striving can lead to maintained or improved self-esteem as persons take on tasks and experience success. Unfortunately, unhealthy behaviors can also arise as individuals attempt to protect self-esteem through the mechanism of self-handicapping. The information in the following section on self-handicapping is taken from an outstanding presentation of the subject by Leary and Miller (1986).

Self-Handicapping

Self-handicapping is the term that has been used to describe the action in which people actually arrange impediments that they can later blame for their poor performance. Strangely, people do not always want to admit the truth about themselves so they self-handicap by providing plausible excuses for their behavior. Self-handicapping allows them to avoid receiving negative information about themselves. The phenomenon may occur when the threat of failure is such that it would greatly shake confidence. For example, an individual may "pull an all-nighter" before an important examination to set up the opportunity to blame failure on lack of sleep. Another student may not study for an examination to insure that any possible failure will be attributed to a lack of study, rather than a lack of personal competence. Clients may self-handicap themselves by not putting effort into socializing with others so they can maintain they would be successful in their social lives if they devoted enough effort to it. Self-handicapping can become a serious matter of maladaptive behavior. For instance, individuals may regularly take drugs, including alcohol, before any important event in order to blame any negative outcomes on a performance-debilitating drug. Others may become chronic underachievers by always expending less than maximum effort because of personal doubts about their abilities.

Self-reported Handicap

Another related type of behavior is that of the **self-reported handicap**. This occurs when no actual inhibiting factor exists but, instead, the individual makes up an excuse to explain poor performance. For example, people sometimes use excuses that they "haven't played lately" or that "my muscles are really sore" when they do not do well in sports. A more serious occurrence of self-report handicapping is the person who chronically uses ill health as an excuse for not performing well. Hypochondriacs continually blame their failures on their lack of good health. Others may regularly report psychological symptoms, such as anxiety or job stress, which cause them not to perform adequately.

Realizing that clients may engage in self-handicapping and self-reported handicapping can be useful information for the therapeutic recreation specialist. When clients, for instance, do not give a task their best effort, the therapeutic recreation specialist may recognize the individual is threatened by the situation and is, therefore, entering into self-handicapping behavior in order to save face. The client may need additional support in order to try out the new behavior. Clients who use self-report handicapping also feel a threat to their self-esteem. Knowing the dynamics of self-report handicaps will help the therapeutic recreation specialist to understand clients' behaviors so he or she may assist clients to deal in a more adaptive way with the situation.

Learned Helplessness

The notion that we, as human beings, strive for control over ourselves and our environment is deeply rooted in our western culture (Grzdlak, 1985; Pender, 1987). As a matter of fact, the extent of discrepancy that exists between our perceived and desired levels of control may be seen as an indication of our degree of social adjustment (Grzdlak, 1985).

Both anecdotal material (Gatchel, 1980) and research reviews (e.g., Gergen & Gergen, 1986; Leary & Miller, 1986) have shown that experiencing a lack of control over adversive life situations produces a sense of uncontrollability. Repeated failure to effect outcomes that will allow one to escape adversive conditions can produce feelings of inadequacy, leading to the conclusion that no matter how much energy is expended, the situation is futile and the person is helpless to alter things (Iso-Ahola, 1980). The debilitating effect of such a perceived lack of control over events is termed **learned helplessness**. Feelings of helplessness lead to the development of apathy, depression, and withdrawal that, in extreme cases, may ultimately end in death due to perceived uncontrollability over a stressful environment (Gatchel, 1980).

A Case Study

Gergen and Gergen (1986, p. 352) have related the case of a woman hospitalized to receive psychiatric treatment who remained mute for almost ten years while living on a unit for patients with chronic mental illness known throughout the hospital as the "chronic hopeless" floor. Because of redecoration work on her unit, she and the other residents on her unit were moved to the first floor unit which had been occupied by "better" patients with "ground privileges" that permitted them the freedom to come and go as they desired.

Before the move, all patients being transferred were given complete medical examinations at which time the patient was judged to be in excellent health though she was still mute and withdrawn. To the great surprise of the staff, shortly after moving to the new unit the woman ceased to be mute and was socially responsive to the extent of being described as "gregarious." Unfortunately, the redecoration project was soon completed and she and the other patients were returned from the first floor to the "hopeless" floor. In a week's time, the woman collapsed and died. No pathology was revealed by an autopsy and it was suggested that perhaps she had died of despair. Perhaps the woman simply felt helpless to deal with her situation.

Helplessness and Control

Much of the initial research work on helplessness was accomplished by Martin Seligman and his colleagues (Seligman, 1980) who first studied dogs and their reaction to painful, uncontrollable shocks and later conducted studies with human subjects. With humans, Seligman's efforts have centered around the effect helplessness may have in bringing about depression.

One of the most cited works on helplessness was the classic study done by Langer and Rodin (1976). The study was completed in a nursing home, a setting in which many patients feel a lack of control over their environment. In the study, residents were given opportunities for personal responsibility (e.g., taking care of a plant) and for decision making (e.g., to decide which night of the week to view a movie). The sense of control gained from these relatively small opportunities to exercise control apparently had a markedly positive effect. In contrast to a comparison group, the residents who were given control over their environment were more alert, had higher levels of participation in activities, and exhibited a greater sense of general well-being.

The study demonstrated that residents of institutions do not have to be doomed to a life of helplessness but may benefit from opportunities to gain a sense of perceived control. In light of such findings, it is unfortunate that much of what occurs in institutions, hospitals, and other health care settings leads to feelings of helplessness. Too often interactions with health professionals foster feelings of helplessness in clients due to condescending behaviors, paternalistic approaches, and the mystification that surrounds many health care processes (Pender, 1987).

Helplessness and Therapy

Therapeutic recreation can represent the antitheses of the controlling environment often imposed on health care clients. Within therapeutic recreation, individuals are given opportunities to escape the normal routines of the health care facility and to feel in control of their environments. Clients in therapeutic recreation programs become involved in experiences in both mastering challenges and learning to endure frustration. In doing so, individuals learn that they are able to affect the world and deal with its consequences. They learn to accept personal responsibility for their actions through these experiences, from which they develop healthy self-regard (Iso-Ahola, 1980).

Howe-Murphy and Charboneau (1987) have provided a number of specific actions that leaders of therapeutic recreation groups may take to decrease helplessness and increase a sense of perceived control. These have been adapted from guidelines originated by Niles, Ellis, and Witt (1981) in their work on the Leisure Diagnostic Battery (LBD). The suggestions follow:

- In a group, mix "helpless" individuals with more competent individuals.
- Offer meaningful choices "within" activities.
- Provide the individual with choices "between activities" that are of equal attractiveness.
- Offer individual activities in which participants have equal possibility for success or failure.
- Increase the individual's skills and knowledge base through leisure education.
- Offer skills to be learned that are of specific interest to the individual.
- Reinforce an individual's abilities and efforts during his or her first encounter with an activity.
- Do not emphasize winning and losing in competitive activities.
- Offer an easy decision, then give details to initiate participation.

- Tell the individual in situations of failure that his or her failure was caused by a need for more effort or for redirected effort.
- Be aware that your own perception of an individual's freedom may not be the same as that person's own perception of freedom.
- Remind the participant in successful situations that perseverance and practice paid off! (p. 228)

Reactance

While helplessness is a common reaction to feeling that a situation is beyond control, sometimes individuals do not become helpless in the face of perceived loss of control but, instead, experience **reactance**. Thus, before closing this section on learned helplessness, some attention to the phenomenon of reactance seems to be demanded.

Reactance is the opposite of learned helplessness. Instead of giving up as people do when they become learned helpless, those exhibiting reactance become helpless while others exhibit reactance when their freedom of choice is threatened? Wortman and Brehm (1975) have hypothesized that individuals initially respond with reactance in order to overcome threats to freedom and control. If, however, they continually encounter failure in their efforts, they eventually respond with weaker reactions until the point that they become completely frustrated, depressed, and experience helplessness. Research findings by Roth and Kubal (1975) and Mikulincer (1988) have supported Wortman and Brehm's hypothesis.

It appears that when people first encounter difficulty they may exhibit reactance. If, however, repeated attempts to gain control over the situation fail, motivation is reduced and they begin to believe the situation is truly beyond their abilities to live with or change. At that point they experience helplessness and feelings of depression (Leary & Miller, 1986; Mikulincer, 1988).

The Self-Fulfilling Prophecy

Our prejudices can provide us with expectations that can set into motion self-fulfilling prophecies. For example, if Dave, the group leader, believes his group members "are unable to take care of themselves," he may treat them in a nurturing way. Such an approach only leads the group members to be dependent.

Thus Dave's original prejudice is confirmed (Gergen & Gergen, 1986). By acting in accord with his expectations, Dave "got what he expected." Perhaps he was able to inform his colleagues that, "I told you so!"

Sometimes the **self-fulfilling prophecy** is referred to as the *self-fulfilling expectation*. Others term it the *Pygmalion effect* after the Greek sculptor whose statue of a great beauty came alive due to his expectations (Gergen & Gergen, 1986). By whatever name, it remains a much studied phenomenon. The classic study on the self-fulfilling prophecy was done by Rosenthal and Jacobson, published in 1968. These researchers randomly identified elementary school children as "spurters" and informed their teachers that "reliable tests" had indicated these students (actually chosen at random) would show rapid intellectual gains during the school year.

The researchers thus established positive expectations for these children in the minds of the teachers. Did teacher expectations cause teachers to treat these students differently in a way that would lead to a self-fulfilling prophecy? Yes, it appeared so. Intelligence tests at the end of the school year indicated the "spurters" showed significant gains, not because they were actually more gifted but because their teachers expected them to do better. Observations of the teachers revealed that they were unwittingly responsible for the outcome by paying more attention to the "high achievers" and rewarding them for behaviors that were not rewarded in other children.

While there was a happy ending to the Rosenthal and Jacobson experiment, negative expectations can also come true as illustrated by Dave's leadership with the clients he encouraged to be dependent. Leaders of therapeutic recreation groups must be aware of possible prejudice, or preformed expectations, so they do not fall into the trap of the self-fulfilling prophecy. They also need to be aware that clients' self-expectations can play a role in the outcome of treatment or rehabilitation. If clients expect to improve, they will be more likely to do so. If they do not expect positive outcomes, improvement is far less likely (Sheras & Worchel, 1979).

Labeling

Leaders' transactions with clients can be influenced by the application of labels to clients. We usually associate labeling with the act of assigning a negative categorical term to an individual, often causing stigmatization. For instance, to label a client as "mentally ill" could result in having him or her perceived as an inadequate person possessing negative traits.

Rosenhan's Investigation

In what has perhaps become the best known study of labeling, Rosenhan (1973) investigated the effects of having people labeled as schizophrenic. He and his colleagues gained admission to psychiatric hospitals by exhibiting symptoms of schizophrenia, including complaints of vague auditory hallucinations. Once admitted, they dropped all pretenses of being schizophrenic. Staff, however, were not able to perceive the researchers' behavior as normal. The diagnostic label so strongly influenced staff members that whatever the researchers did was seen to reflect pathology. Eventually, the researchers were released but even so, they were still officially labeled as having schizophrenia that was "in remission."

Negative Labeling and Staff Reaction

Labeling a person, whether or not the label is reliable, can obviously affect others' responses to the labeled individual. Damaging effects can result if staff devalue the person due to a diagnostic label to which they have attached negative connotations. Staff, for instance, should never perceive the client as being "a deviant" or someone who is not equal to them. Such perceptions cause staff to be uncaring and act unprofessionally. This type of reaction by staff can lead the client to feel diminished and inadequate. This is, of course, very wrong. All clients are persons of worth and must be treated with dignity and respect.

Labeling and Therapy

Therapeutic recreation specialists also must never allow themselves to fall into the trap of perceiving individuals to represent the stereotype reflected by a diagnostic category. Stereotyping a client on the basis of the classification of a disorder or disability does not, of course, take the individual's uniqueness into account. It puts the focus on categorical differences instead of on the person. Thus, therapeutic recreation specialists must be on guard against the dangers of labeling clients.

Each client needs to be treated as a unique and worthwhile human being with individual limitations and abilities. This does not mean that diagnoses (a type of labeling) should be alleviated. Well-grounded diagnoses may serve valid legal and administrative purposes, enabling clients to receive care and agencies to organize services. Nevertheless, factual information regarding each client's abilities, needs, and desires—instead of a general label or diagnostic category—should form the basis for individual program planning.

Loneliness

Who suffers from loneliness? The truth is that all of us have been lonely at one time or another. In one study, more than 25 percent of the respondents admitted feeling "very lonely within the past few weeks" (Duck, 1986). Similar findings have been reported by Shultz (1988) who has cited figures to indicate one fourth of the population is lonely some time during any given month.

At-Risk Groups

If you are a university student away from home, you can no doubt relate to the topic of loneliness because students typically feel lonely when they begin their studies at a new school (Duck, 1986). At-risk groups for loneliness include adolescents, individuals who are dying, persons with chronic or socially unacceptable illnesses or body image problems, those who have undergone the loss of significant relationships, and people who have relocated geographically (Shultz, 1988, p. 397). It is important for the therapeutic recreation specialist to understand that loneliness and health problems are often closely associated. Loneliness can cause health problems and vice versa (Shultz, 1988). Hospitalization can bring on or intensify feelings of loneliness because people are removed from their normal environments and support systems (Shives, 1994).

Expectations

Most of us can define loneliness on some level because we have experienced it first hand. It is more than being alone, although isolation can be involved. "Loneliness occurs when one's network of intimate and social relationships is smaller or less satisfying than desired," according to Leary and Miller (1986,

p. 100). "The critical feature of loneliness," according to Duck (1986), "is a discrepancy between what we're doing and what we expect or hope to do" (p. 24). A lonely individual does not have his or her expectations for social relationships filled. Most of us would concur with Shultz (1988) that: "loneliness results from deficiencies in a person's social relationships; it is subjective and often not directly related to social isolation; and it causes unpleasant feelings" (p. 382).

The despair, dejection, and depression that may be felt by the lonely person are reflected in this quote from Perko and Kreigh (1988):

> The lonely individual perceives himself (or herself) as being deprived of intimate relationships with other human beings as well as not having an opportunity to share his thoughts, feelings, achievements, and life with significant others. It is a pervasive and painful experience that is perhaps more frightening than the feeling of anxiety. It is a state in which past relationships are almost entirely forgotten as well as one in which the future holds no promise. In essence, loneliness is experienced as an almost complete negation of being with an inability to feel, to care, or to love (p. 359).

Mood and Social Behavior

Transactions may be marked by a lack of caring for oneself or others. The lonely person may be moody, engage in self-deprecating acts, hold a morbid preoccupation with death, express suicidal ruminations or gestures, or experience social isolation and, perhaps, withdrawal from reality (Perko & Kreigh, 1988, p. 360).

The social behaviors of people who are lonely differ from others in three ways. The first difference is that lonely persons hold a negative outlook toward themselves and others. The second difference is that lonely individuals exhibit social-skills deficits. Finally, their social behavior is superficial. They act more inhibited and less intimate than others (Leary & Miller, 1986).

Loneliness and Therapy

All of these traits hold implications for the transactions of therapeutic recreation specialists with clients who suffer from feelings of loneliness. Because the client who is lonely may possess a negative outlook, the therapeutic recreation specialist needs to develop a therapeutic environment that reflects warmth and concern. To indicate a sense of caring, touch can be used in the form of patting the client on the shoulder, or laying a hand on the client's wrist or arm (Perko & Kreigh, 1988).

Lonely clients often have problems relating to others due to social skill deficiencies. The therapeutic recreation specialist can serve as a role model by modeling effective social skills when interacting with clients who are lonely. Further, the therapeutic recreation specialist can conduct social skills training or refer clients to social skills training groups.

People who are lonely report that they feel shy and awkward in social situations. They also take fewer social risks than others. Some are so self-focused that it keeps them from responding to others' needs and feelings. The therapeutic recreation specialist can help these individuals by providing opportunities through recreation activities to practice social skills. Another strategy is to help the client to make new relationships through participation in community organizations and activities.

Clients living at home may be encouraged to have an animal to provide companionship. Because clients are likely to suffer pain and hurt as they try out new social skills and gain confidence in their abilities, the therapeutic recreation specialist will need to remain supportive. At the same time, the therapeutic recreation specialist will need to slowly decrease clients' dependence (Shultz, 1988).

In summary, trust building is an important first step for the therapeutic recreation specialist to take with clients who are lonely. Creating a warm, caring atmosphere will allow these clients to become comfortable with you and themselves. Later, social skills training can be provided, along with opportunities to practice social skills and expand social contacts. While clients are building their skills and confidence in their abilities, the therapeutic recreation specialist needs to remain supportive, and slowly decrease client dependency.

Self-Efficacy

Self-referent thoughts play a central role in mediating behavioral change, according to Bandura's (1986) **self-efficacy** theory. Clients' personal evaluations of their abilities (i.e., their efficacy judgments) directly affect how they cope with their problems. "A person's efficacy expectancies describe that person's beliefs about his or her particular skills and capabilities, and they determine how the person reacts behaviorally, cognitively, and emotionally to problematic events," according to Leary and Miller (1986, p. 188).

Clients' expectations of themselves largely determine how willing they will be to deal with their problems, how much effort they will be willing to expend, and whether they will make a perseverant effort. Those who are self-doubters are likely to express little effort and will give up quickly if their initial efforts are not productive. Those with high efficacy expectations are apt to face their difficulties with determination, to exert maximum effort, and to persevere even when frustration is encountered.

Perceived Capabilities

The critical influence personal efficacy takes in people's lives was expressed by Bandura (1986) when he stated: "Among the different aspects of self-knowledge, perhaps none is more influential in people's everyday lives than conceptions of their personal efficacy" (p. 390). Bandura defined personal efficacy, or self-efficacy, as follows:

> Perceived self-efficacy is defined as people's judgments of their capabilities to organize and execute courses of action required to attain designated types of performances. It is concerned not with the skills one has but with judgments of what one can do with whatever skills one possesses (p. 391).

Response-Outcome Expectancy

Bandura went on to draw a distinction between personal efficacy judgments and response-outcome expectancy. Personal efficacy is the person's expectation that he or she can be successful in accomplishing a certain behavior or level of performance. It is the individual's subjective judgment that he or she can accomplish the sought end. Bandura gives the example of someone believing that he or she can high jump six feet.

The **response-outcome expectancy** deals with the consequence of the act, not the actual performance of the behavior. In Bandura's illustration the outcome expectancy for the high jumper might include anticipated applause, social recognition, trophies, and self-satisfaction.

Either one's expectations of personal competence or one's expectation of the consequences of performing an act can lead to dysfunctional behavior. For example, a young woman who is shy may avoid a social contact either because of feeling a lack of social competence or because of a belief that no matter how she performs in the interaction, the outcome will be rejection (Leary & Miller, 1986).

Too often, however, it seems that our clients believe performing a specific behavior will result in certain positive consequences, however, they will not attempt the behavior because they have self-doubts about their abilities to actually accomplish the act. Too often they avoid difficult tasks, put forth little effort, give up quickly when faced with frustration, dwell on what they perceive to be their personal deficiencies (which detracts attention from the demands of the task), decrease their expectations, and undergo feelings of stress and anxiety (Bandura, 1986, p. 395). This behavior is dysfunctional because it prevents them from: facing and taking on their problems and entering into challenging and enriching leisure activities that would allow them to develop their potentialities.

How do people gain the self-knowledge on which self-efficacy rests? Whether valid or invalid, efficacy judgments are based on four sources of information: performance, vicarious experiences, verbal persuasion, and physiological arousal (Bandura, 1986).

Performance. The most potent source on which efficacy expectations are built is the client's own performance accomplishments. In general, repeated successes increase perceived self-efficacy while continual failures decrease perceived self-efficacy. It should be added, however, that the individual's interpretation of his or her performance is a key. If successful performance is not viewed as a success by the individual, it will not have a positive impact on perceived self-efficacy. Making attributions to internal, stable, global, and particularly, controllable factors will most likely lead the client to positive beliefs about his or her abilities (Leary & Miller, 1986).

Vicarious experience. Although not as influential as mastery experiences, modeling can effect self-efficacy. We partly judge our capabilities by comparing ourselves to others. Observing others who are similar model successes provides information that raises judgments regarding our capacities. Seeing similar others fail lowers our self-expectations.

Verbal persuasion. Efforts at verbal persuasion do not always work because sometimes we do not believe what others tell us about our capabilities. The impact of persuasive efforts will likely be influenced by how credible the persuaders are seen as being. The more confident we are in those offering verbal persuasion, the more impact they will have.

Physiological arousal. Situations that increase feelings of anxiety and arousal to a high level are apt to be read as being problematic and create fear about our abilities. Moderate levels of arousal tend to facilitate performance and, thus, carry more positive expectations (Bandura, 1986).

Self-efficacy and Therapy

What can the therapeutic recreation specialist do with this background on self-efficacy during transactions with clients? Most evident is that knowledge of self-efficacy might be used to facilitate behavioral change by influencing clients' perceptions of personal efficacy. As previously noted, clients too often do not have confidence in their abilities to perform the behaviors of which we, as therapists, know they are capable. The therapeutic recreation specialist can assist the client to enhance his or her perception of personal efficacy through means of the four factors that influence self-efficacy.

Iso-Ahola (1984), in a discussion of leisure counseling and self-efficacy, and Savell (1986), in an article on therapeutic recreation programming and self-efficacy, have offered suggestions for assisting clients to enhance personal efficacy expectations. At the top of their lists is to encourage clients to participate in activities that allow mastery experiences and build a sense of personal accomplishment. In doing so, the initial exposure should result in a positive experience. Success in beginning endeavors will provide clients the courage to attempt something more challenging. Skill levels can be increased as client abilities and confidence grow.

When using vicarious experiences, the models should be similar to the clients and be observed to gain success through their persistence after encountering and overcoming difficulty. When the clients see others enjoy success despite difficulties, they will be encouraged to stick with difficult tasks. Verbal persuasion needs to come from a respected source. In a case cited by Iso-Ahola, wives of men who were postcoronary patients provided strong verbal persuasion. Savell has mentioned the use of discussions or exercises to allow clients to clarify their own thoughts so they may persuade themselves of their potentials. Physiological arousal may be managed through any of a number of stress reduction techniques discussed in Chapter 3, including relaxation techniques and biofeedback. Reducing clients' feelings of arousal can enhance self-efficacy.

As Leary and Miller (1986) have indicated, many therapeutic approaches utilize more than one of the four self-efficacy information sources. For example, the learning of relaxation techniques not only reduces arousal but provides for the mastery of a new skill. Savell (1986) has suggested that therapeutic recreation approaches should employ all four of the factors identified by Bandura.

Bandura's (1986) self-efficacy theory offers therapeutic recreation specialists insights into their clients' behaviors as well as practical means to assist clients to overcome difficulties. No doubt the theory will become widely applied in therapeutic recreation as practitioners become acquainted with it and related techniques.

Attributional Processes

Attribution theory has been termed the "primary paradigm in contemporary social psychology" (Shaw & Costanzo, 1982, p. 232). Although attribution theory began to enjoy popularity during the 1970s, it was first introduced by Fritz Heider (1944) in the mid-1940s (Shaw & Costanzo, 1982). Heider believed that people's perceptions of the causation of events had a great impact on their social behaviors (Gergen & Gergen, 1986).

Causes for Events

Shaw and Costanzo (1982) defined the processes of making attributions:

> Put most broadly, **attributional processes** are those processes governing a perceiver's attention to thought about and apprehension of perceived events. The events which serve as objects of perception might consist of the actions of social others, one's own actions, and/or environmentally produced effects. Attribution theory is typically concerned with the processes and schema invoked by the perceiver in assigning *causes* to these events (p. 232).

Attribution theory, therefore, involves the processes through which we try to infer causes for events from our observations. We engage in attributional processes to explain the events that occur in our lives. These explanations (or attributions) have significant psychological consequences. Our reactions to emotional events, our self-regard, our judgments of ourselves and others, and our expectations about the future are all subject to the influences of our causal attributions (Leary & Miller, 1986). We decide what other people are like based on our inferences from behaviors we observe and, most important for therapeutic recreation, we seek explanations for events that occur in our own lives. These self-attributions have important consequences on our subsequent behaviors and feelings.

Internal and External Attributions

Our attributions may be either internal or external. Making **internal attributions** places the cause of the events with us. Cause is perceived to be due to our personality dispositions, abilities, or the amount of effort expended. **External attributions** place the cause with the situation in which the event occurred. For instance, if we do well on an examination, we might likely attribute our success to internal causes, such as our intelligence or our preparation for the exam. If, however, we do poorly, we might make an external attribution by saying that the exam items were "ambiguous" (Leary & Miller, 1986).

The tendency to relate successes to internal causes and attribute failures to external causes is termed the **self-serving bias**. The tendency to blame others for unfortunate things that happen to them while ignoring situational causes is termed the **fundamental attributional error** (Gergen & Gergen, 1986).

In addition to internality (i.e., internal versus external causes), causes may be organized around three dimensions. These are stability, globality, and control. Causes may be perceived to be stable (long-term) or unstable, global (affecting many parts of our lives) or specific, and under our control or uncontrollable (Leary & Miller, 1986).

You may already be thinking that some of the phenomena previously discussed in this section of the chapter on transactions may be related to attributional processes. For instance, our self-esteem will likely be enhanced when we have success and we make internal, stable, global attributions and perceive the outcome to be under our control. Labeling ourselves or other persons (e.g., as "deviants" or "losers") may cause us to attribute all negative behaviors to personality dispositions, rather than to situations. The self-fulfilling prophecy can be explained by the labels we place on people that raise or lower our expectations of them, causing us to make original false perceptions true. Helplessness occurs when we perceive a sense of uncontrollability. Our feelings of self-efficacy may be directly affected by self-attributions (e.g., internal or external, stable or unstable, under our control or not within our control) when we interpret our performance.

Self-attributions and Therapy

Because of the importance of attributional processes, most approaches to psychotherapy use attributional analysis and seek to allow the client to reinterpret his or her problems. Making *reattributions* allows the client to generate explanations (attributions) for experiences that are not as threatening as those initially identified. For instance, the client comes to see something as being caused by a situation and not his or her personality. Another reattribution would be having the client view a negative event as an isolated incident rather than something consistent in his or her behaviors.

Some clients are plagued by chronic attributional patterns that cause problems for them. For example, persons who are chronically depressed magnify negative happenings and minimize successes. Those with low self-esteem often externalize successes and internalize failures. Such chronic patterns are not easily overcome, but with treatment clients can change their attributional styles. Changing self-blaming habits is apt to involve more than being supportive and allowing clients to gain successes. Learning to persist and try harder can be an important lesson in the face of adversity. If clients only are given opportunities for successes, they may give up quickly when faced with adversity. Above all, if clients can be led to see themselves as being capable of overcoming their problems, they may establish a sense of control and self-efficacy that will allow them to conquer their problems. In all approaches to therapy, it is critical that clients begin to perceive their problems to be changeable and controllable (Leary & Miller, 1986).

Therapeutic recreation can, of course, help clients gain confidence in their skills and abilities through providing opportunities for success. However, when rewarding successes, the therapeutic recreation leader must employ minimal rewards so an overjustification effect does not occur. The therapeutic recreation specialist needs to be on guard to let the individual retain as much internal control as possible.

Therapeutic recreation leaders can likewise help clients to learn to cope with outcomes that do not result in success and encourage clients not to give up, but to put forth additional effort or try new strategies. Finally, therapeutic recreation specialists can help clients to make reattributions as is often done in psychotherapy. For example, clients can come to believe that a skill they have had difficulty mastering is not really so important after all or that winning is not critical (since one-half of the teams lose every event!)

READING COMPREHENSION QUESTIONS

1.   What are purposes for having client records?
2.   How do source-oriented and problem-oriented records differ?
3.   What does SOAP stand for?
4.   Do you understand the guidelines for progress note writing? Can you apply them?
5.   What categories of behavior might you use in making observations for progress notes?
6.   Do you understand the principles for the teaching/learning process?
7.   Can you give examples of how you might apply one or more of these principles?
8.   Define counseling in your own words. What factors may be thought of as distinguishing leisure counseling from other types of counseling? Would you add any other factors of your own?
9.   What are the four orientations to leisure counseling proposed by McDowell?
10. Do you believe that leisure counseling is in an early stage in its development as a field?
11. Explain why the therapeutic recreation specialist should consider self-concept in client transactions.
12. By what means do people form self-concepts?

13. What is self-handicapping?
14. What is learned helplessness?
15. What are ways therapeutic recreation leaders can decrease helplessness?
16. What is reactance?
17. What are concerns related to labeling?
18. What is the Pygmalion effect?
19. How can therapeutic recreation leaders help lonely clients?
20. What is self-efficacy? How can therapeutic recreation leaders promote it?
21. How can therapeutic recreation leaders use information about attributional processes in transactions with clients?

Chapter Nine

CLINICAL SUPERVISION

CHAPTER PURPOSE

Clinical supervision is a term that has appeared in the literature of therapeutic recreation only recently. Today, however, the importance of clinical supervision is beginning to become recognized within the world of therapeutic recreation. Nevertheless, it is alarming that few therapeutic recreation specialists have received specific training in giving or receiving clinical supervision. This chapter presents an introduction to clinical supervision and information about the actual roles and functions of the supervisor and supervisee.

KEY TERMS

- Clinical supervision
- Skill development model of supervision
- Personal growth model of supervision
- Integrative model of supervision
- Dual relationship
- Informed consent

OBJECTIVES

- Comprehend the nature of clinical supervision.
- Understand the goals and rationale for clinical supervision.
- Recognize ethical considerations in clinical supervision.
- Recognize the roles and functions of supervisors and supervisees.
- Know stages experienced in clinical supervision.
- Know structures for conducting clinical supervision.
- Know methods and procedures for conducting clinical supervision.

THE PURPOSES OF CLINICAL SUPERVISION

Clinical supervision has two broad purposes. One is to facilitate the personal and professional development of the staff member receiving supervision. The second is improved client care and treatment through proper implementation of the agency's rehabilitation or treatment program (Austin, 1986).

The supervisor helps the supervisee to acquire and refine clinical practice skills and to grow as a professional. This supervision is an ongoing process that begins during initial field placements and never ends because even the master clinician always has more to learn. Accountability is the aim of the second purpose. It is the function of the clinical supervisor to assure that the therapeutic intents of the clinical program are accomplished. Supervisors make certain that the purposes and goals of the treatment or rehabilitation program are achieved. Nonetheless, it is not the role of the clinical supervisor to police the work of the supervisee. Clinical supervision involves a cooperative approach in which the supervisor and supervisee join together to achieve the ends of the clinical program.

A Dynamic Process

Clinical supervision then may be defined as a joint relationship in which the supervisor assists the supervisee to develop himself or herself in order to deliver the highest possible level of clinical service while promoting accountability in the agency's clinical program. It is a cooperative venture between the supervisor and supervisee to: improve the supervisee's abilities to perform as a clinician, with the goal of enabling the supervisee to function as independently as possible, and to insure the aims of the agency's clinical program are effectively completed. Williamson (1961) has offered perhaps the most complete definition of clinical supervision found in the literature:

> Supervision is a dynamic enabling process by which individual workers who have direct responsibility for carrying out some part of the agency's program plans, are helped to make the best use of knowledge and skills, and to improve their abilities so that they do their jobs more effectively and with increasing satisfaction to themselves and the agency (p. 19).

Four elements define the clinical supervision process according to Hart (1982):

1. Clinical supervision implies an ongoing relationship between the supervisor and supervisee. Such a continuing relationship is necessary because the supervisee is engaged in a developmental process in order to function at a higher level of clinical practice.
2. The clinical supervisor need not be the organizational supervisor. In fact, it may be argued that general organizational supervision and clinical supervision should remain separate functions.
3. Strategies and skills needed in the delivery of treatment or rehabilitation programs are the central concern during clinical supervision sessions. While the content of clinical supervision sessions may be wide ranging, it pertains to effective clinical practice behaviors.
4. The primary thrust of clinical supervision always is on the behavior of the supervisee as he or she interacts with clients and staff.

Skills related to the achievement of client objectives remain at the heart of clinical supervision. On occasion, however, clinical supervision involves issues related to teamwork or to maintaining positive relationships in working with other staff in order to conduct a successful clinical program.

Any clinician who works with clients can profit from receiving clinical supervision because all have the potential for continual development. Even master clinicians (i.e., those with advanced preparation and extensive supervised experience) can improve their clinical functioning. Therefore, supervisees can range from beginning students to practitioners with years of experience. Of course, the frequency and emphasis of supervision will vary according to the background of those being supervised. Supervising emerging therapists is likely to require supervisors to take on larger roles than they would with more experienced supervisees (Kaslow, 1986). No matter who the supervisee is, clinical supervision always involves: (1) a cooperative relationship or partnership between the supervisor and supervisee, and (2) an effort to improve the quality of the supervisee's practice (Austin, 1986).

THE STATUS OF CLINICAL SUPERVISION

Clinical supervision is an emerging area in therapeutic recreation that is just beginning to be recognized as a key element in successful clinical practice. Visits to clinical sites in recent years substantiate that the importance of clinical supervision has become acknowledged by a number of health care disciplines. It has been particularly accepted during the past 15 to 20 years as a critical aspect of clinical practice by clinical psychologists, psychiatrists, and psychiatric social workers.

This has lead Cherniss and Egnatios (1977) to the conclusion that mental health clinicians use clinical supervision more than other occupational groups to advance their professional development and that it appears to be the most significant factor influencing job satisfaction among these health care professionals. I have indicated elsewhere (Austin, 1986) that staff in settings other than mental health can likewise enjoy the benefits of enhanced professional development and job satisfaction that have been acknowledged to accompany clinical supervision programs.

The importance of clinical supervision is widely recognized by college and university faculty who train students for careers in therapeutic recreation, according to the results of a national survey by Gruver and Austin (1990). The overwhelming majority of faculty responding to the survey indicated it is essential to provide classroom instruction in clinical supervision to both undergraduate and graduate students. Almost 80% (79.1%) felt it is essential for undergraduates, while 92.7% felt it is essential for graduate students. Unfortunately, the same study revealed that only about 50% of the colleges and universities were actually preparing students to give and receive clinical supervision.

Why has clinical supervision remained a largely neglected area in therapeutic recreation until recently? There are a number of speculations that may be offered in response to this question. One possible reason for the lack of earlier interest by therapeutic recreation specialists in clinical supervision may be that practitioners did not take themselves seriously as clinicians. Simply providing recreation opportunities with clients does not require clinical supervision since clinical intents are not sought. Today, the clinical nature of therapeutic recreation is apparent within the field. The formation of the American Therapeutic Recreation Association and rapid growth in the literature of the profession related to clinical practice are reflective of a high level of clinical activity.

Another possible reason for the absence of interest in clinical supervision may simply have been a lack of information on the topic within the therapeutic recreation literature. Hopefully, coverage in textbooks such as this one and articles in professional journals will supply practitioners and educators with information on the topic. It may be that the term supervision conjured up negative feelings. Supervision may have been seen to be something to be feared. The view of the supervisor as one who looks over the employee's shoulder in order to judge his or her competence can create fear in the heart of the most dedicated staff member. Some refer to this type of supervision, where the supervisor sneaks around in order to snoop on staff, as "snoopervision." This type of snooping is, of course, not a part of clinical supervision, which represents a positive relationship between supervisor and supervisee. Clinical supervision does not involve being authoritative, catching supervisees doing something wrong, or keeping them "under thumb."

Clinical Supervision Versus Organizational Supervision

A distinction can be drawn between clinical supervision and organizational or administrative supervision. Clinical supervision focuses on skills and strategies needed to reach objectives with clients. In contrast, organizational or administrative supervision deals with overseeing, directing, and evaluating all staff work, as well as ensuring staff follow agency policies and procedures. The administrative supervisor stresses organizational effectiveness and efficiency in seeing that staff arrive at work on time, structure and meet their schedules, correctly order and check out supplies and equipment, and so forth (Austin, 1986; Bradley, 1989). Hart (1982) clearly stated the distinction between the two types of supervision when he wrote "administrative supervision is aimed at helping the supervisee as part of an organization, and clinical supervision focuses on the development of the supervisee as an interpersonally effective clinician" (p. 13).

It is my belief that organizational supervision and clinical supervision should be kept distinct and separate. The authoritative nature of organizational supervision (with administrative power) simply gets in the way of establishing the cooperative, helping relationship that must exist as a part of clinical supervision. In many respects, the process of clinical supervision parallels the therapist to client relationship. The supervisor must remain attentive to helping the supervisee meet his or her needs while maintaining a supportive atmosphere. The supervisee must feel free to be open and honest in his or her communications with the supervisor. While many agencies have supervisees receiving both their organizational and clinical supervision from the same individual, I would urge administrators to give every consideration to keeping the two types of supervision separate.

Clinical Supervision and Therapy

While several of the elements of psychotherapy are found in clinical supervision, clinical supervision should not be confused with therapy. Both therapy and clinical supervision involve a helper and someone receiving help. Both are characterized by fear, anxiety, and resistance to change. Both take place in a nonjudgmental environment (Kahn, 1979; O'Toll & Morofka, 1984).

Both, in short, are helping processes. But they differ in purpose and approach. The purpose of therapy is to resolve personal problems or inner conflicts. The purpose of clinical supervision is the improvement of clinical performance. The focus of therapy is on personal experiences and problems, while the focus of clinical supervision is work with clients. Change in therapy deals with the exploration and resolution of personal difficulties, while change in clinical supervision concerns behaviors, thoughts, or feelings that affect clients (Kahn, 1979; O'Toll & Morofka, 1984).

As noted by Platt-Koch (1986): "The supervisor should not probe any more deeply into personal conflicts than is necessary to support the therapist's (supervisee's) professional role" (p.10). If personal difficulties interfere to a large extent with working with clients, the supervisor should discuss the possibility of the supervisee seeking help from a trained psychotherapist.

THE MODELS OF SUPERVISION

Hart (1982) proposed three models of clinical supervision for counselors. These are the skill development model, the personal growth model, and the integrative model.

The **skill development model** utilizes a teacher-student relationship between the supervisor and supervisee while emphasizing knowledge of professional roles and methods. The supervisee establishes his or her professional identity while learning leadership roles such as leading groups, or administering client assessments. Supervisees acquire clinical skills that enable them to conduct therapy or rehabilitation programs. Examples of clinical skills include establishing client relationships, making diagnostic judgments, delivering interventions, and making referrals. Supervisees also learn to conceptualize aspects of client cases.

The **personal growth model** employs a relationship between the supervisor and supervisee that closely resembles a counselor-client relationship. The supervisor does not engage in deep psychotherapy, but does assist the supervisee to develop insight into self and affective sensitivity. One area under insight into self is that of understanding one's own needs so that personal needs remain in their proper place and do not take precedent over the needs of clients. A second area is learning to deal with "shocking" subjects such as child abuse, drug use, violence, and incest. A final area under insight into self is learning to deal with strong emotional reactions to situations (e.g., encountering hostility) or clients (e.g., countertransference) through discussions with the supervisor. Under affective sensitivity fall examination of the supervisee's interpersonal relationship patterns and how he or she affects others.

The third and final model is the **integrative model** which builds on the first two models. The integrative model employs a collaborative relationship between the supervisor and supervisee in order to integrate skill development and personal awareness into effective relationships with clients. This model is used with advanced students and experienced therapists. It utilizes a mutual effort between the supervisor and supervisee in which they share information regarding clinical practice and make and test hypotheses about client cases.

While untested in therapeutic recreation, Hart's models would seem to have application to clinical supervision within therapeutic recreation. Certainly, the skill development model is commonly employed in the training of student interns in therapeutic recreation. The personal growth model is perhaps less established in therapeutic recreation but has apparent implications for use with both interns and emerging professionals. The integrative model is undoubtedly least employed in therapeutic recreation. As the use of clinical supervision spreads in therapeutic recreation, however, greater utilization of the integrative model might be anticipated.

ROLES OF CLINICAL SUPERVISORS

Bradley (1989, pp. 302-307) has identified three roles for clinical supervisors. These roles closely parallel Hart's three models of supervision. The three roles for clinical supervisors proposed by Bradley are teacher, counselor, and consultant. Within the teacher role, the supervisor intends to instruct the supervisee in clinical practice skills.

The Teaching Role
Teaching activities include:

- Observing the supervisee in clinical practice;
- Identifying interventions to enhance the supervisee's performance;
- Applying interventions through demonstrations, modeling and other teaching techniques;
- Explaining rationales that underlie interventions and clinical strategies; and

- Interpreting important events that occur during clinical sessions.

The Counselor Role

Within the counselor role, the supervisor intends to facilitate the supervisee's self-growth as a clinician.   Specific activities include:

- Exploring the supervisee's feelings about clinical and supervisory sessions;
- Exploring the supervisee's feelings regarding specific techniques or interventions;
- Facilitating self exploration by the supervisee of worries or concerns regarding clinical sessions;
- Helping the supervisee evaluate personal competencies and areas for growth; and
- Providing opportunities for the supervisee to discuss their effect and their use of defenses.

The Consulting Role

Within the consultant role, the supervisor intends to allow the supervisee to exert control over the interaction and to encourage choice and responsibility on the part of the supervisee. Specific activities include:

- Offering alternative interventions or conceptualizations for the supervisee to consider;
- Encouraging brainstorming of strategies and interventions;
- Discussing client problems, motivations, etc.;
- Attempting to satisfy supervisee needs during clinical supervision sessions; and
- Allowing the supervisee to control and structure the supervision session.

Different roles are, of course, called for with various supervisees. For example, emerging supervisees (e.g., students and young staff) are likely to require the supervisor to take the teacher and counselor roles. More experienced supervisees (e.g., staff experienced in clinical practice) are apt to need the supervisor to fulfill the consultant role.

Clinical Supervisor Traits

Of course, there is no one set of characteristics that constitute the make up of an "ideal" clinical supervisor. Supervisees come with a variety of needs and different levels of development, and each has his or her individual personality. Therefore, the ideal supervisor will be the one that has the best match with the supervisee's needs, developmental level, and personality. There are nevertheless some core characteristics for clinical supervisors. A minimum qualification for the clinical supervisor is possessing the skills of a master clinician.

Becoming a master clinician involves gaining the professional competencies to perform at a high level and then polishing these skills during several years of experience. Generally, master clinicians hold a master's degree and have had a number of years of experience under a well-prepared clinical supervisor. Possessing such a background should bring with it the confidence and professional assurance needed in a supervisory position. In addition to feeling comfortable with his or her abilities, the clinical supervisor should have the respect of the colleagues and administrators with whom he or she works (Bradley, 1989).

Beyond being well prepared, self assured, and respected, what other characteristics should the clinical supervisor possess? A number of authors have addressed this question including Austin (1986), Bradley (1989), Fox (1983), Kaslow (1986), and Platt-Koch (1986). The discussion that follows is based on the comments of these authors.

Empathy and Caring

First, they must have a genuine concern for the growth and development of the students and fellow professionals that they supervise. Closely related is having the quality of being a caring and supportive person. Creating a supportive atmosphere is a hallmark of good supervision. Effective supervisors are empathetic, warm, and genuine. They give honest feedback and help supervisees work toward resolution of problems. They encourage exploration of new behaviors, involve supervisees in the supervisory process, and assist supervisees to move toward greater independence. In so doing, they build rapport and trust with their supervisees. The supportive function is one of the most important aspects of supervision (Holloway, 1995).

Openness

Successful supervisors are characterized as being nonthreatening, nonauthoritarian, tactful, understanding, accepting, and possessing a good sense of humor. They express confidence in the abilities of their supervisees and are not afraid to engage in self-disclosure with their supervisees if they feel it will be helpful. In general, they are not defensive but, instead, express a sense of openness. They are open to new ideas and are willing to examine their own feelings, thoughts and attitudes.

Knowledge

Additionally, effective clinical supervisors need to know how to use intervention or teaching techniques with supervisees. They are able not only to supply the right facts or information at the correct times, but they also motivate and inspire supervisees to try new behaviors and to challenge themselves. Finally, successful supervisors need to have the abilities of a good consultant to help supervisees to assess situations and themselves and to arrive at reasoned actions.

In summary, the effective clinical supervisor will possess many of the characteristics of any successful helping professional. In addition, the clinical supervisor must have a wealth of clinical experience on which to draw and a strong desire to enable students and staff to develop themselves professionally.

BENEFITS OF PROVIDING CLINICAL SUPERVISION

Page and Wosket (1994) and Williams (1995) have noted that clinical supervisors benefit from their responsibilities by developing personal awareness and new insights that can enhance their own clinical work. For instance, the supervisor can come to understand how the supervisee may have acted more therapeutically and then apply this discovery in his or her own clinical practice. Thus, by supervising the supervisee the clinical supervisor can re-examine his or her own performance at a distance, allowing an opportunity for self-reflection and personal growth. Page and Wosket have also mentioned that doing clinical supervision provides a change of pace for the supervisor by taking him or her away from often emotionally draining clinical work to the more intellectually stimulating area of clinical supervision.

THE ETHICAL CONCERNS
OF SUPERVISION

Nonmaleficence

The principle of **nonmaleficence** deals with ensuring that no harm is done. For clinical supervisors this involves being competent to assume a supervisory role (Page & Wosket, 1994). A fundamental question that each clinical supervisor must address is "Am I qualified to do clinical supervision?" Should an individual not yet possess the skills, knowledge, and clinical background to conduct clinical supervision, he or she would not be on sound ethical ground in accepting a supervisory assignment. The individual would be exceeding his or her abilities and, thus, be placing the supervisee in jeopardy (Bradley, 1989).

New therapeutic recreation specialists are understandably often anxious to do clinical supervision, particularly with student interns. It is commendable that new therapeutic recreation specialists wish to engage in helping relationships with students. However, before entering into supervisory responsibilities, a professional needs to complete a thorough self-assessment to determine if he or she possesses the necessary characteristics to do clinical supervision. Once a complete assessment has been conducted and it has been determined that an individual has the qualities needed to become an effective clinical supervisor, the person must gain the preparation required to conduct clinical supervision. This preparation may be gained through supervisory training provided by his or her agency, through workshops offered by professional societies, or through courses and other educational experiences conducted by colleges and universities.

Dual Relationships

A second area of ethical concern in clinical supervision is that of **dual relationships** between supervisor and supervisee. In the *Handbook of Counseling Supervision*, Borders & Leddick (1987) discussed three types of dual relationships: (1) The supervisor and supervisee are sexually involved; (2) the supervisor takes on the role of being the supervisee's therapist; and (3) there is a degree of closeness beyond the normal supervisory relationship (separate from sexual contact), that creates a danger of the development of a dual relationship.

Sexual Contact

The sexual contact issue is clear in terms of ethical considerations. As Bernard (1987) has stated: "There seems to be no defensible argument for the ethics of sexual involvement between supervisor and supervisee" (p. 53). Should the two persons who are in clinical supervision become sexually attracted to one another, a new supervisory arrangement should be established to insure the supervisee is supervised objectively. Of course, clinical supervisors should also take responsibility for seeing their supervisees are not sexually involved with clients.

Other Intimacy Concerns

The other two areas of dual relationship are less clear cut in terms of ethics. There are sometimes instances in which focusing on personal issues is appropriate during supervision when issues interfere with the supervisee's ability to serve clients. In these instances, it may be necessary for the supervisor to discuss the supervisee's personal issues. However, the supervisor should not engage in extended counseling. To determine exactly when further discussion is not appropriate involves judgment on the part of the supervisor.

The third area of dual relationships also involves judgment on the part of the supervisor. There is nothing wrong with becoming close friends with those with whom you share a great deal in common. However, the supervisor must constantly monitor his or her actions to be certain that a dual relationship has not evolved. There is an obvious problem with remaining objective should a relationship have developed beyond the supervisor-supervisee relationship. Should this occur, the supervisor needs to closely examine the situation to determine if an alternative supervisory arrangement should be made for the supervisee (Bernard, 1987; Bradley, 1989).

Issues of Informed Consent

By virtue of the clinical supervision, the supervisor is involved in an indirect relationship with the supervisee's clients. It is, therefore, incumbent on the supervisor or supervisee to inform clients of the supervisory arrangement and gain the clients' consent for this to take place if a student or trainee is to be engaged in clinical practice with them. This is called **informed consent.** Clients need to be led to understand that students and trainees are in time-limited assignments and be told the extent of their assignments. If any special arrangements are made to observe or evaluate the performance of the supervisee, clients participating in the session need to be informed. For example, if the supervisor is to attend an activity that he or she does not normally attend or if a special arrangement is made to videotape a session, these arrangements need to be discussed with clients. In general, clients need to be informed about any aspect of the supervisory relationship that could affect the clients' willingness to participate (Bernard, 1987; Bradley, 1989).

Confidentiality Concerns

The clinical supervisor has the ethical responsibility to see that communications between him or her and the supervisee are kept confidential. Therefore, particularly in the case of students, there needs to be an agreed-upon procedure in place so the supervisee will know if information is to be shared with a third party (such as a university faculty member). Similarly, clients need to know if confidential information about them will be shared with the clinical supervisor. The topic of confidentiality needs to be covered at the beginning of the supervisor-supervisee relationship and the supervisee-client relationship.

As may be ascertained from the discussion in this section on ethical concerns in clinical supervision, ethical issues are normally not simple matters. Ethical dilemmas are apt to occasionally arise even with the best planning. Knowing some of the key areas of ethical concern can, however, allow clinical supervisors and supervisees to anticipate ethical matters and deal with them before they become problematic.

SUPERVISORY RELATIONSHIPS

Three levels of clinical supervision have been proposed by Stoltenberg and Delworth (1987). In *Level 1*, supervisees are conceptualized as being relatively inexperienced and dependent on the supervisor but full of hope and motivation to become competent clinicians. Supervisees tend to be imitative, anxious, lack self awareness, engage in categorical thinking, and over accommodate to the supervisor who is perceived to be an "all-knowing" expert. A principle function of the supervisor is to provide the structure needed to keep the normal anxiety of the supervisee at a manageable level.

In *Level 2* supervisees are seen to be less imitative and more assertive while striving for greater independence, but suffer from a dependency-autonomy conflict. Supervisees' motivational levels fluctuate as they become more confused and less confident about the effectiveness of their interventions. The supervisor functions to help the supervisee deal with the dependency-autonomy conflict and become more independent in his or her clinical functioning.

In *Level 3* supervisees have an increased sense of personal identity and self-confidence. They have accepted themselves and are no longer defensive as they function relatively independently from the clinical supervisor. Their motivational levels are much more consistent as they are not as susceptible to pessimism or undue optimism. The function of the supervisor is largely consultation.

Loganbill, Hardy, and Delworth (1982) have indicated that the best suited supervisor is someone who has a higher level of competence and maturity and greater clinical experience than the supervisee. It is suggested that supervision from an individual with these characteristics will be more readily accepted than it would be from someone lacking the status afforded by possessing a higher level of competence, maturity, and experience. It is, therefore, important to complete an initial assessment of the supervisee to determine at which of the three levels (Level 1, Level 2 or Level 3) he or she is functioning. This assessment will help insure that a match can be made so that the supervisee receives supervision from someone who is functioning at a higher level.

Other variables that may influence the supervisory relationship are demographic factors, theoretical orientations, and personality dimensions. The impact of gender, sex-role attitudes, race, ethnic background, and social class are demographic variables that should be considered when matching supervisees with supervisors. Differences in theoretical orientations have been found to create conflict between supervisees and supervisors; therefore, consideration needs to be given to this aspect when assigning supervisees. Finally, personality clashes can interfere with the supervisor-supervisee relationship, so the personalities of individuals who might be placed together need to be taken into account.

While research has revealed no clear guidelines on matching supervisors and supervisees, it will be helpful for those determining the matches to give consideration to demographic factors, theoretical orientations, and personality dynamics when matching supervisors and supervisees and for supervisors to be aware of potential difficulties that may arise due to these variables so that if they do appear, they may be dealt with in a constructive and healthy manner (Borders & Leddick, 1987).

The Supervisory Alliance

Through the supervisory relationship the supervisee will grow from dependency to a relatively autonomous practitioner. By means of the helping relationship with his or her clinical supervisor, the supervisee will master and refine specific clinical skills, increase abilities to conceptualize client cases and concerns, become aware of the therapeutic use of self in the therapeutic process, and learn to translate theory into practice (Bradley, 1989). When viewed in these terms, the importance of the relationship between the supervisor and supervisee looms large indeed.

Pre-Assessment

Because of the critical nature of the clinical supervision process, a great deal of planning is required on the part of the supervisor to assure the relationship begins with as good a start as is possible. Before meeting with the supervisee, the supervisor will want to begin to assess the supervisee's clinical skills.

The supervisee may be asked to complete a self-assessment on a form provided by the agency or the supervisee may be requested to draft a statement to indicate strengths he or she may possess, areas of skill deficiency and areas of concern on which he or she wishes to focus (Borders & Leddick, 1987). Many additional means of assessment might be used as well. Among these are transcripts from which to assess the course preparation of the supervisee, the supervisee's resume, and communications from those familiar with the supervisee's developmental level. For example, a university faculty member could supply information as to the level on which the student supervisee would be functioning. Such information could be extremely useful when supervising graduate student interns whose backgrounds may vary widely.

Initial Supervisory Sessions

Another step toward orchestrating a solid supervisory relationship is a well conducted first session between the supervisor and supervisee. This meeting is an excellent opportunity for the two parties to discuss their expectations about the supervisory relationship. The initial session also sets the tone for the working relationship that will follow so it is important for the supervisor to begin to establish rapport and display an organized, reassuring approach with the supervisee. As Bradley (1989) has stipulated, the goals of the initial supervisory conference should be to establish clear understandings about the structure of clinical supervision and the nature of the supervisory relationship; and to create a supportive supervisor-supervisee relationship. Realistically, it may take several supervisory sessions to accomplish these goals. Therefore, it is more correct to discuss what will occur in initial supervisory sessions or the initial phase of supervision, rather than a single supervisory meeting.

What types of expectations need to be made clear regarding the structure of supervision and the nature of the supervisory relationship? Both Bradley (1989) and Borders and Leddick (1987) have provided a number of specific suggestions of items that should be covered during initial supervisory sessions. These include:

- Time required at the agency (if supervisee is completing practicum or internship).
- Supervisee's schedule including the frequency, length, and location of supervisory meetings.
- The structure or procedure that will be followed in supervisory sessions.
- The number and type of clients and programs with which the supervisee will be involved.
- How audiotapes, videotapes, case notes, and observations will be used in supervision.
- How the supervisee will be evaluated and the criteria to be employed in evaluation.

- Field site visit requirements and the organization and structure for the visits.
- Legal and ethical issues related to clinical practice.
- Procedures to be followed in case of emergency situation (e.g., suicide attempt).
- Plans for any group supervision.
- Establishment of the supervisee's learning goals, together with a plan to achieve the goals and measure outcomes.
- Review of expectations of the agency in terms of presentations, papers, or assignments.
- Review of expectations of college or university requirements, if the supervision, is provided as part of a practicum or internship.
- If the supervisor is providing administrative supervision as well as clinical supervision or if the supervisor must submit an evaluation of the student supervisee to a university, he or she needs to discuss problems inherent in the contradictory roles of clinical supervisor and evaluator.

Fox (1983, p. 39) has developed a set of questions to guide initial supervisory sessions between the supervisor and supervisee. While not as detailed as those items provided in the previous section, supervisors and supervisees may find Fox's questions useful to the process of clarifying expectations, particularly in regard to establishing learning goals for the supervisee and planning to achieve them. Fox's questions:

1. What do we expect from each other?
2. What can we give to each other?
3. Are our goals the same?
4. Can we achieve them?
5. How can we achieve them?
6. What constraints exist?
7. How will we know when we have achieved the goals?

In addition to establishing clear expectations about the supervision structure and the supervisory relationship, the supervisor wishes to establish a reassuring, supportive relationship with the supervisee during initial conferences. Time should be devoted in the first meeting for allowing the supervisee to describe his or her background. Areas that may be covered are types of previous experiences, familiarity with therapeutic recreation settings, influences on present philosophy of therapeutic recreation, reasons for becoming a therapeutic recreation specialist, and motivation for seeking the present growth experience. This process not only shows interest in the individual but provides information that will prove useful in the assessment of the supervisee. The supervisor should reciprocate by providing background information on himself or herself as it relates to the experiences of the supervisee. The supervisor should also demonstrate his or her qualifications for performing the role of clinical supervisor.

Issues of concern for the supervisee should also be dealt with during the initial phase of supervision. Time needs to be given to an exploration of the supervisee's expectations of supervision. Time also needs to be devoted to acknowledging and discussing the supervisee's fears regarding evaluation.

A supportive relationship will probably only begin to be formed during the initial supervisory session, or even during the initial phase of supervision. This point has been discussed by Bradley (1989) who has written:

> ....a supportive supervisor-supervisee relationship unfolds throughout the length of supervision and is reinforced by positively perceived supervisor behavior. Supervisees reportedly value supervisors who call them by name, use humor in the supervisory sessions, allow observations, share...experiences, help the supervisee develop strengths and a personal...style, and lead the supervisee to realize that developing new skills is an awkward process (p. 330).

In summary, as a result of initial supervisory sessions, the supervisor and supervisee will have formed the foundations for their working relationship and established clear expectations for the supervisory process. In doing so, they will have completed an assessment of the supervisee's clinical skills and knowledge as a basis for establishing learning goals for the supervisee. An important aspect to be considered when establishing clear expectations during the initial phase of supervision is the development of learning goals for the supervisee. Within the following section, the process of establishing learning goals and using them to guide the supervisory process is discussed.

SUPERVISION GOALS

Establishing learning goals for the supervisee can be helpful to both clarifying expectations and building the supervisor-supervisee relationship. First, working together on establishing the goals fosters a spirit of cooperation between the supervisor and supervisee. Second, the involvement of the supervisee increases the likelihood that he or she will be committed to accomplishing the goals. Third, goal achievement can be a positive motivational factor to inspire the supervisee. Fourth, the goal-setting process in clinical supervision serves as a model for the supervisee to follow in setting goals with clients. Finally, the formulation of a goals set provides structure to guide the clinical supervision process (Borders & Leddick, 1987).

When beginning the goal formulation process it may be necessary to discuss the purposes of establishing goals so that the supervisee comprehends the importance of goals to planning and evaluation. Sometimes the supervisee recognizes it is necessary to set goals, but does not understand the connection between each goal and actions required to reach a goal and ways to stipulate goal attainment (Bradley, 1989).

Because a great deal of information may be available as a result of the assessment, the supervisor needs to guard against being overwhelmed by the amount that the supervisee must learn. As with clients, goals need to be chosen that are realistic and achievable. The supervisor will probably have to guide the supervisee in selecting goals that coincide with the supervisee's needs and degree of readiness to master a specific skill or knowledge. Goals can be prioritized and sequenced so that they are manageable. It is also important to keep in mind that goals can be rewritten to reflect the supervisee's growth and additional information gained about the supervisee by the supervisor (Borders & Leddick, 1987).

Learning goals should each reflect an end result in a fashion similar to stipulating goals for clients. Therefore, each goal will be written as a behavior that the supervisee will display. As with the achievement of client goals, several enabling objectives may be used to break down goals into their component parts. Learning goals should conform to these characteristics, according to Fox (1983, p. 40):

- specific;
- explicit;
- feasible in regard to capacity, opportunity, and resources;
- realistic and attainable;
- seen in light of constraints;
- related to the task formulated;
- modifiable over time;
- measurable; and
- ordered into priority.

Fox (1983, pp. 46-48) outlined eight steps to be followed in developing a goal-oriented contract to direct the supervisory process. Whether or not a formal contractual agreement is drawn, the steps offer a helpful procedure to be used in the formulation of goals and the planning of learning activities to achieve goals and evaluation activities to assess outcomes. The supervisor and supervisee:

1. Generate baseline information.
2. Specify their focus and expectations.
3. Set priorities for goals.
4. Identify observable behavioral characteristics and describe how increased knowledge and skill will be exhibited by the supervisee.
5. Delineate their respective roles and explain their responsibilities.
6. Discuss the content of the supervisory program.
7. Agree on a time frame.
8. Specify criteria for a step-by-step evaluation of the achievement of goals and transferability into practice.

Baseline Information
In Fox's first step, the supervisor and supervisee generate baseline information that indicates the initial performance or knowledge level of the supervisee. Various approaches can be used in this assessment in addition to discussions between the supervisor and supervisee. These include the use of self-reports from the supervisee, role plays, observations, audiotapes, videotapes, and reports from other staff or faculty. Through such means of assessment, the supervisor and supervisee arrive at agreement on needs areas and baseline functioning in the areas.

Focus and Expectations

The supervisor and supervisee then specify their focus and expectations. Here they record what they ultimately hope to achieve. This step answers the question: What is to be accomplished and in what time frame? The supervisor and supervisee then proceed to set priorities for the goals.

Priorities

Goals are ordered in importance. Next the supervisor and supervisee identify observable behavioral characteristics, and describe how increased knowledge and skill will be exhibited by the supervisee. This critical step puts into concrete terms the evidence of achievement of each goal. This step answers the question: How will the worker show improved skills or knowledge?

Delineation

During the fifth step the supervisor and supervisee delineate their respective roles and explain their responsibilities. They decide who will do what. The question here is: What am I willing to offer or do?

Discussion

The supervisor and supervisee *discuss the content of the supervising program.* Specific learning strategies or interventions are identified.

Time Frame

In the next to last step, the supervisor and supervisee *agree on a time frame.* Questions to be answered include: How much time will it take to achieve the goals? How much time will be devoted to each meeting to accomplish the task? In what sequence will the goals be achieved?

Evaluation

The final step is that of *specifying criteria for a step-by-step evaluation of the achievement of goals and transferability into practice.* Methods for measuring change are agreed upon. This step answers the question: How will progress be measured?

While there are places of overlap within the steps proposed by Fox, the procedure offers guidelines that may be adopted in order to facilitate the work of the supervisor and supervisee. A supervisor may wish to modify Fox's procedure in order to fit his or her personal style or even develop his or her own approach using Fox's procedure as a model.

CLINICAL SUPERVISION STAGES

No studies have appeared in the therapeutic recreation literature on stages of development in clinical supervision. It may be assumed, however, that the progression of therapeutic recreation specialists would be similar to that experienced by counselors and therapists. A number of authors have delineated developmental stages through which counselors and therapists pass (e.g., Ard, 1973; Bradley, 1989; Borders & Leddick, 1987; Hogan, 1964; Loganbill, Hardy & Delworth, 1982; Stoltenberg, 1981). It is to these authors that we must turn for information on stages of development.

Initial Stage
All developmental theories identify an initial stage characterized by excitement, anxiety, and dependency. The supervisee is typically excited about the prospect of learning to apply therapeutic techniques, but anxious in regard to beginning a new relationship and learning new behaviors and information. At this stage the supervisee is highly dependent on the supervisor due to feelings of insecurity about his or her skills and knowledge. The supervisor needs to be accepting and supportive and to help the supervisee to anticipate and prepare for situations that could be anxiety provoking. In employing such an approach the supervisor assists the supervisee to feel supported as he or she works toward building clinical skills and greater independence.

Growth Stage
As the supervisee advances, he or she begins to exercise more independence and responsibility, but reverts to a state of dependency when crises occur. There exists conflict between wishing to function autonomously and the need to depend on the supervisor. The supervisee may disagree with the supervisor about clinical approaches. When it is discovered that the

supervisor is not omnipotent and all-knowing, anger, and disappointment often result.

This turbulent stage is likely to be a trying one for both the supervisee and the supervisor as the supervisee attempts to separate from the supervisor. The supervisor needs to recognize the confusion faced by the supervisee and to deal with the stage as one that is reflective of growth on the part of the supervisee. It is the role of the supervisor to remain nondefensive and supportive and to affirm the supervisee's competence without hampering the supervisee's growing level of independence.

The Maturity Stage

Eventually the supervisee comes to experience a greater sense of personal identity and self-confidence as he or she begins to mature and integrate learnings into his or her personal frame of reference. No longer defensive, the supervisee is able to accept himself or herself and experience an increased sense of freedom and creativity. The supervisee is able to engage in self-examination and to risk new behaviors. At this stage the supervisory relationship is open and collegial. Supervision is more consultative in nature so that peer supervision arrangements may be made for mutual problem solving and growth. Once this stage is achieved, the supervisee may become a supervisor for an individual in the initial developmental stage.

Knowledge of these developmental stages can be helpful to supervisors in understanding the dynamics of their interpersonal relationships with supervisees and to supervisees who are experiencing transitions from one stage to the next. By realizing the developmental level of the supervisee, the supervisor can react to the supervisee accordingly and determine an appropriate model of supervision to follow. The supervisee can understand his or her own developmental processes and be better prepared to react to them in a healthy fashion.

FACILITATION OF THE
LEARNING ENVIRONMENT

The supervisor has the task of arranging learning conditions that contain adequate structure and support to optimize the supervisee's learning. The amount of structure and support provided will vary according to the developmental level of the supervisee (Bradley, 1989). Topics covered in this section are how the developmental level of the supervisee affects the structure for learning, methods for supervisory interventions, and modalities for clinical supervision.

Developmental Level of Supervisee

As discussed earlier in the chapter, the supervisor may assume the role of teacher, counselor or consultant. The assumption of a particular role is largely dictated by the developmental level of the supervisee. Emerging professionals (i.e., students, new practitioners) generally need to focus their attention on achieving clinical practice skills so they are very task oriented and dependent on the supervisor who assumes the role of their teacher.

These supervisees, therefore, respond positively to structured teaching methods such as completing assigned readings, attending didactic presentations, observing senior therapists conduct sessions, doing role playing, listening to suggestions for appropriate client interventions, and discussing the connection between theory and practice. Due to their typically high levels of anxiety, they also appreciate receiving support and reassurance from their supervisors (Borders & Leddick, 1987).

It does need to be noted that not all persons who are in this early stage of development are young adults. Supervisees who are middle aged or older will likely experience the same anxiety that the young person experiences. Unlike their younger counterparts, however, they may have deeply ingrained habits and behavioral patterns which the supervisor must recognize. The supervisor must also recognize that adult learners may have been functioning with a relatively high degree of independence and autonomy. It may be difficult and threatening for them to relinquish their independent functioning and become dependent on the supervisor in order to learn new skills and knowledge.

Adult learners thus present a somewhat different challenge for the supervisor who may need to adjust his or her teaching approach to meet their unique characteristics (Bradley, 1989). For example, some of the teaching interventions normally employed with more advanced supervisees may be used occasionally with adult learners. Less directive approaches to teaching are typically preferred by supervisees who are experienced and have gained competence and confidence. They are apt to view the supervisor more as a resource person than an instructor and desire to enter into conversations with the supervisor regarding theoretical issues and case conceptualizations. Further, they are likely to take more responsibility for their learning than those who are less advanced and desire to enter into more of a peer-like relationship with the supervisor.

The more advanced supervisee is also likely to want the supervisor to be more confrontive about personal issues that may impact on his or her clinical work (Borders & Leddick, 1987). The supervisor's assessment of the developmental level of the supervisee will obviously be very helpful in determining the type of learning environment that will be optimal for his or her supervisee.

Methods for Supervisory Interventions

There are a number of interventions that supervisors may employ. Some of these have been mentioned, including reading assignments, didactic presentations, observations of senior staff, receiving suggestions for appropriate client interventions, and discussions of theory and practice. Other possible interventions are discussions of cases and activities, critiques of audiotapes and videotapes, role playing, conjoint interviewing, and co-leadership of individual or group sessions. In addition, supervisors may give specific instruction on cognitive skills, such as writing case recordings, or preparing individual program plans. Normally, following readings and didactic instruction, supervisors review the work of supervisees and then offer feedback (Borders & Leddick, 1987; Platt-Koch, 1986).

Modalities for Clinical Supervision

There are two primary modalities for conducting clinical supervision. The first, the individual conference, is the modality that perhaps most of us have as an image when thinking about clinical supervision. Individual supervisory sessions are regularly scheduled on a weekly or biweekly basis. They typically last about an hour.

The second modality is group meetings. They too are regularly scheduled, often on a biweekly basis when there is no individual conference. Within the group structure, supervisees often work together on a particular skill. The group method lends itself to teaching skills and may, therefore, be chosen as a means to instruct new supervisees who are learning clinical practice skills and techniques. The group meeting also is commonly used with more advanced supervisees who may do group processing. The main drawback with the group meeting is that it may be difficult to meet the diverse needs of supervisees with a group situation.

Some would add peer supervision as a third type of modality for clinical supervision. Within peer supervision, staff with advanced clinical practice skills meet with one another to provide clinical supervision. Such supervision may be completed in dyads or in small groups.

THE CLINICAL SUPERVISION EVALUATION

Both the supervisor and supervisee can benefit from formal evaluation sessions. For student interns, formal evaluations are typically held halfway through the experience (i.e., midterm) and at the conclusion of the experience (i.e., final evaluation). Any number of approaches can be used to structure the evaluation session. Evaluation instruments are commonly supplied by universities. Often, the supervisor completes an instrument on the supervisee and the supervisee is called upon to complete an evaluation of the supervisor. Generally, the supervisor first reviews his or her evaluation of the supervisee and then the student goes over his or her evaluation of the supervisor.

Another approach to evaluation is to review the supervisee's learning goals in an effort to determine progress in their attainment. This procedure helps the supervisee to see the gains he or she has made during the period of clinical supervision and to set goals for the future. The supervisor can serve as a model for the supervisee by engaging in self-evaluation, inviting feedback, and being open to criticism. The supervisee can be helpful to the supervisor by providing honest feedback that will assist the supervisor to adjust or modify his or her approach in the future.

Borders and Leddick (1987) reminded us of the close parallel between helping relationships between supervisors and supervisees and helping professionals and clients in discussing the final evaluation session as a termination session and a new beginning. They write:

The final supervision session is similar to the termination session with a client, in that it can be an important catalyst for change, not just the end.   Therapeutic termination sessions with clients have three functions: (a) summarizing progress toward goals, (b) discussing how changes will be maintained and identifying 'next steps' for continued growth, and (c) achieving a sense of closure in the relationship (p. 60).

SUMMARY

Clinical supervision is still a developing area in therapeutic recreation. Happily, its importance is beginning to become more recognized. All who work directly with clients from the newest student to the most seasoned senior staff member can profit from clinical supervision because all enjoy the potential to grow and no helping professionals ever reach the stage that they have all the answers. Within this chapter, an attempt has been made to explain clinical supervision and its potentially powerful impact on clinical practice. Hopefully, both future supervisors and supervisees will profit from the information offered in the chapter so that, ultimately, clients may benefit by receiving the highest level of clinical services that can be provided.

READING COMPREHENSION QUESTIONS

1.   Have those entering careers in therapeutic recreation received preparation for giving and receiving clinical supervision?
2.   Do university faculty value clinical supervision?
3.   Why has therapeutic recreation only recently embraced clinical supervision even though a number of helping professions have been using clinical supervision for several years?
4.   Can you define clinical supervision in your own words?
5.   What purposes does clinical supervision serve?
6.   How does clinical supervision differ from organizational supervision?
7.   What are similarities and differences between clinical supervision and therapy?

8.   Describe the three models of supervision proposed by Hart.
9.   Describe three roles for clinical supervisors.
10. What is a fundamental ethical question for any individual considering being a clinical supervisor?
11. What are dual relationships? Do you agree with the comments made about dual relationships in the chapter?
12. What is informed consent?
13. Why does confidentiality need to be discussed at the beginning of any helping relationship?
14. What are three levels of clinical supervision?
15. What are characteristics of the individual best suited to do clinical supervision?
16. Explain the nature and importance of the supervisor-supervisee relationship.
17. Why is the first supervisory session important?
18. What should be covered during initial supervisory sessions?
19. Why are learning goals important in clinical supervision?
20. What stages do supervisees pass through?
21. How does the supervisee's developmental level relate to the type of structure and support provided by the supervisor?
22. Name methods for supervisory interventions.
23. What are the two major modalities for doing clinical supervision?
24. What is peer supervision?

Chapter Ten

HEALTH AND SAFETY CONSIDERATIONS

Joan K. Austin, D.N.S., R.N.
David W. Dunn, M.D.
Martha J. Price, D.N.Sc., R.N.

CHAPTER PURPOSE

There are common physical occurrences or conditions that may threaten clients' health or physical safety. Diabetes mellitus, epilepsy, and long-term psychotropic drug use are examples of conditions that may affect a client's ability to participate safely in an activity. This chapter presents health and safety information to be considered when providing services for clients who have a seizure disorder, who are receiving medication for diabetes mellitus, or who are being treated with psychotropic drugs. Information is also provided regarding special mechanical aids upon which some clients must rely and which must be considered when providing therapeutic recreation services. Finally, information is presented on safety precautions when working with persons with HIV/AIDS.

Because diabetes mellitus is a chronic disease affecting approximately 5.2 million people in the United States (Olson, 1988), and because the treatment for diabetes mellitus can produce life-threatening side effects in the patient, basic information on diabetes mellitus and its management is necessary for the therapeutic recreation specialist. In addition, complications from the disease can cause conditions, such as blindness/visual impairment, loss of sensation, pain, and temperature changes, which will affect a client's ability to participate in specific activities. The first section of this chapter presents information on diabetes mellitus.

Another possible threat to clients' safety can occur during a seizure. Approximately one percent of the population suffers from recurrent seizures, or epilepsy (Hauser & Hesdorffer, 1990). Epilepsy sometimes occurs simultaneously with other conditions affecting the brain, such as mental retardation and cerebral palsy. Thus the therapeutic recreation specialist needs basic information regarding seizures, their usual treatment, and first-aid measures. Information regarding seizures is presented in the second section of the chapter.

Another section in the chapter is devoted to the client who takes psychotropic drugs for the treatment of mental health problems. Many therapeutic recreation specialists come into contact with these clients at mental health facilities. However, clients from any of the special populations may receive psychotropic drugs. Consequently, therapeutic recreation specialists who work with a variety of special populations will come into contact with clients receiving psychotropic drugs. Clients who receive these drugs may experience side effects that should be taken into consideration when recreation activities are planned and provided. Information on commonly prescribed psychotropic drugs includes desired effects, side effects, and possible implications for the practice of therapeutic recreation.

General guidelines for therapeutic recreation specialists to follow when working with clients who use mechanical aids such as braces, crutches, and wheelchairs also are presented. Clients who are elderly or who have common physical conditions such as arthritis, broken bones, spinal cord injuries, cerebral palsy, cancer, and muscular dystrophy often have physical limitations requiring mechanical aids, either temporarily or permanently. Therapeutic recreation specialists who work in hospital settings, nursing homes, rehabilitation centers, camps for children with physical disabilities, and institutions for persons who are severely retarded regularly serve clients with physical limitations. Information regarding possible safety hazards and implications for providing services are given. In addition, step-by-step guides for transferring clients from a wheelchair to a bed and from a bed to a wheelchair are provided. The final section provides safety guidelines for the therapeutic recreation specialist when working with clients with HIV/AIDS.

KEY TERMS

- Type I diabetes mellitus
- Hyperglycemia
- Partial seizures
- Desired effect
- Psychotropic drugs
- Tardive dyskinesia
- Type II diabetes mellitus
- Hypoglycemia
- Generalized seizures
- Side effect
- Antipsychotics
- HIV / AIDS

OBJECTIVES

- Appreciate the importance of client safety needs resulting from physical disorders, physical limitations, or effects of drugs.
- Know causes and first-aid treatment of side effects of glucose-lowering agents used to treat diabetes mellitus—insulin and oral hypoglycemic agents.
- Know first-aid treatment for different types of seizures.
- Describe desired effects and side effects of selected drugs (antiepileptic, antipsychotic, antidepressants, antimania agents, and antianxiety agents).
- Recognize safety considerations for clients who use mechanical aids during recreational activities.
- Recognize safety considerations for the therapeutic recreation specialist when transferring clients and when serving clients with HIV/AIDS.

Throughout the chapter the emphasis is on providing information for the therapeutic recreation specialist that will facilitate client and therapist safety. Common physical disorders and limitations that could result in client injury have been selected for presentation. The information is practical in nature and builds on information presented in introductory courses in therapeutic recreation and first-aid courses.

DIABETES MELLITUS

Diabetes mellitus is a metabolic syndrome arising from an absolute or relative lack of body insulin. Body (endogenous) insulin normally controls glucose levels in the body within a specific range. Normal fasting blood glucose (BG) is 70 to 115 mg/dl and after meals may rise but usually remains less than 140 mg/dl. Insulin facilitates glucose transport from the blood stream into cells, and insufficient insulin will cause the body to experience an elevated level of glucose in the blood stream. This physiological phenomenon is called *hyperglycemia*. Symptoms may include increased urination (as the body attempts to excrete the extra glucose), increased thirst (because of fluid loss through urination), weight loss (the calories from glucose are being lost in the urine), and fatigue. There are two major classifications of diabetes mellitus, Type I and Type II. Although both types are due to insufficient insulin and will produce hyperglycemia, the disease mechanisms are a bit different, as are treatment modes and potential complications.

Type I Diabetes Mellitus

In Type I diabetes mellitus there is little, if any, insulin being made by the body, thus the treatment requires daily replacement injections of insulin. Thus it is also known as *insulin dependent diabetes or IDDM*. Persons with Type I diabetes usually have a rapid onset of symptoms, over a period of days or weeks. These symptoms include those mentioned above and are often quite dramatic, as accompanied by weight loss, stomach pains, nausea and vomiting. If left untreated or not enough insulin is provided, the symptoms may continue, worsen and even progress into a physiological state of metabolic acidosis, coma and death. Approximately five percent of persons with diabetes have Type I, or what is called by some as *juvenile diabetes* because it most often occurs in children or young adults under 30. However, even people over 30 years of age may develop this type of diabetes. Treatment requires insulin injections and food intake sufficient to match the insulin schedule, as well as enough food for activity level and growth.

Type II Diabetes Mellitus

Type Il diabetes mellitus accounts for approximately 90 to 95% of all cases of diabetes. Typically, Type II is most often diagnosed in adults over 40, although a small percent of young adolescents or adults may be so classified. In Type II diabetes, the body makes insulin, but is unable to use it properly at the targeted cells (skeletal muscle, liver and fat cells), thus it is called *non-insulin dependent diabetes (NIDDM)*. In Type II, about 80% are overweight, and the symptoms of diabetes will occur gradually over years - fatigue, vision changes, increased urination and thirst. A person with this type of diabetes is at very high risk for heart attacks and strokes, so treatment is aimed at reducing cardiovascular risks—not smoking, blood pressure control, exercise, healthy diet in quality and quantity. For about 20%, diet and exercise may be sufficient to improve blood glucose control, but for others oral medications may be necessary. Until 1995, the pills available to treat this type of diabetes were limited to a category called "sulfonylureas." Now, additional drugs (oral agents) are becoming available that work in several different ways to help Type II diabetes be better controlled and to lower BG levels (See Table 10 -1). For some with Type Il, diet, exercise and pills will not be sufficient to control BG, and insulin treatment may be needed.

Side Effects of Glucose-Lowering Agents

Insulin and sulfonylureas have a direct lowering effect on blood glucose. Other oral diabetes medications have been designed to enhance the body's use of insulin and/or glucose, and so indirectly help to lower blood glucose. If medication is part of diabetes treatment, it is necessary to know the type of medication being used and that low blood glucose or **hypoglycemia** (a BG level of less than 70 mg/dl) is a possibility. There are signs and symptoms of low blood glucose —light sweating, shakiness, change in mood or thought patterns—and the person with diabetes should be informed about hypoglycemia and how to treat it.

The three main causes of hypoglycemia are:

- Too much of a diabetes medication and...
- Not enough food (such as not eating enough, skipping meals, delaying meals) or.....
- Physical activity without eating enough food before, during and after exercise

---

Hypoglycemia is also more likely to occur in those who keep their BG in tight control, but it is not necessarily a problem as long as symptoms are detected early and treated appropriately. Those with Type I diabetes of 10 or more years may experience a diminished awareness of hypoglycemia symptoms, and therefore frequent blood glucose monitoring (self-administered finger stick for a drop of blood that is placed into a glucose meter for a "reading") becomes very important. BG monitoring is encouraged before meals and whenever the person feels hypoglycemic or that blood glucose levels are out of range. This diminished awareness may also occur in those who aim to keep their blood glucose levels within a normal range ("tight control") at all times.

Those with Type II diabetes and taking sulfonylureas or combination therapies (i.e., sulfonylureas plus biguanide or insulin) may also experience hypoglycemia from the above noted causes. It is equally as serious a situation as in Type I, particularly when sulfonylurea drugs are used, because many of them are very long acting drugs. Older adults may be particularly vulnerable to this kind of hypoglycemia, and if it occurs they will not only need hypoglycemia treatment, but also continued observation for recurrence of the problem.

TABLE 10-1
AVAILABLE GLUCOSE-LOWERING AGENTS

Insulins (used for insulin replacement or to supplement endogenous insulin)

Note: action times noted are approximate and vary depending on insulin species source—animal or human—and individual absorption and metabolism

• *Short-acting*— called Regular Insulin
(usual onset 0. 5 - 2 hours; peak or maximum effect 2 - 4 hours, usual duration is 3 - 6 hours)

•*Intermediate acting* —called NPH or Lente
(usual onset is about 3 - 6 hours; peak or maximum effect 4 - 8 hours; usual duration 12 - 20 hours)

•*Long acting* — called Ultralente
(usual onset 6 to 10 hours; peak effect is minimal to none; usual duration 18 to 36 hours)

•Newer insulins are coming onto the market that are more rapid in onset and duration

Sulfonylureas (used primarily to stimulate the production of body's own insulin)

(Brand names: Orinase, Diabinese, Tolinase, Glucotrol, Glucotrol XL, Diabeta, Micronase, Glynase, Pres Tab)

Vary in onset and duration. With the exception of Orinase, which lasts 6 to 12 hours, these agents can last and be effective for up to 24 hours or longer. New generations continue to come onto the market.

TABLE 10-1 CONT.

Biguanides (used to improve insulin effectiveness at target cells and to suppress liver's secretion of stored glucose)

Metformin (Brand Name: Glucophage)

Onset of action, peak action, and duration are not applicable to this drug because it has its effect on blood glucose indirectly. Not likely to cause hypoglycemia. Should not be taken by those with kidney or liver dysfunction.

Alpha Glucocidase Inhibitor —used to slow the absorption of carbohydrate from the stomach and small intestine.

Acarbose (Brand Name: Precose)

Onset of action, peak action, and duration are not applicable to this drug because it has its effect on blood glucose indirectly.

Managing Hypoglycemia Reactions

Hypoglycemia may be mild, moderate, or severe. All three require immediate treatment; however, most individuals with diabetes who are managed on medications will have experienced hypoglycemia, will recognize the symptoms and seek treatment by eating foods that are quick-acting carbohydrates. Most will even carry glucose tablets, or LifeSavers, or other hard candies with them just in case hypoglycemia occurs. See Table 10-2 for amounts. For newly diagnosed or those new to the experience of hypoglycemia, there may be a tendency to over-treat with large candy bars, cake, or the like. Overtreatment will create a rapid and high rise in blood glucose that is equally undesirable.

TABLE 10-2
QUICK-ACTING CARBOHYDRATES USED IN HYPOGLYCEMIA TREATMENT

Approximate amount needed for one dose equal to 10 to 15 grams of carbohydrate.

- 4-6oz. of carbohydrate-containing liquids (e.g. unsweetened fruit juices, carbonated drinks)
- 5-6 LifeSavers candies
- 1 tablespoon of honey or Karo syrup
- 4 teaspoons or packets of granulated sugar or 6 1/2 inch sugar cubes (this might be more palatable in water, but can be eaten as is).
- 2 or 3 commercial glucose tablets

After administering a dose of quick-acting carbohydrate, symptoms should begin to improve. If not, then repeat the dose every 10 to 15 minutes until symptoms subside.

Moderate hypoglycemia will also respond to the above choices, but the treatment may need to be repeated after 10 to 15 minutes. If the person is confused, combative and unwilling to swallow, it may be necessary to give glucagon (a substance that must be given by injection and which stimulates the liver to release glucose).

Severe hypoglycemia occurs when the person has impaired consciousness or is unconscious and cannot swallow. The treatment needed is glucagon (injected intramuscularly or subcutaneously) or intravenous glucose.

Glucagon—Used to treat moderate or severe hypoglycemia is available in kits at local pharmacies. People who may be called upon to use this drug should be instructed beforehand in its preparation and administration.

How Activity or Exercise May Affect Blood Glucose

Exercise and activity is recommended at some level for all people regardless of whether or not they have diabetes. Exercise of moderate intensity and duration will improve how the body uses insulin, and therefore, cause *hypoglycemia*. If a person with diabetes who is managed on medications exercises, then he or she should make certain that sufficient food has been eaten to match when the medications are working. This matching will help avoid hypoglycemic episodes. Those who consistently exercise moderately or vigorously several times a week may experience an improved sensitivity to insulin that lasts for several hours after exercise. This may necessitate an adjustment (reduction) in insulin or sulfonylurea dose and should be discussed with the physician for appropriate management guidelines.

Exercise can also raise the blood glucose (hyperglycemia) of the individual whose diabetes is under-treated, meaning if there is too little insulin available to transport glucose into the muscle cells. The reason for this is that exercise is experienced by the body as a stress and will stimulate release of substances (cortisol, growth hormone, adrenaline) that trigger the body to secrete its own stores of glucose, known as *glycogen*. The body does this to assure that the muscles have a steady supply of glucose for energy needs. If blood glucose is high prior to exercise and there is insufficient insulin to transport glucose into the cell, then exercise will create an additional rise in blood glucose. It is preferred that the blood glucose be 250 mg/dl or less before moderate or vigorous exercise is undertaken. This target number may need to be modified for those with Type II diabetes who are undertaking exercise as part of weight loss and glucose reduction treatment, and physician guidelines would be helpful.

If the individual does do blood glucose monitoring, it would be ideal to have him/her test before, 30 minutes into, and immediately after exercise. Those with Type I participating in moderate to vigorous exercise should consume approximately 15 grams of carbohydrate for every 30 minutes of the activity. Those with Type II will likely need 15 grams of carbohydrate for every hour of continued activity. Encourage blood glucose monitoring for at least every 4 hours after vigorous exercise, to watch for possible hypoglycemia.

Other Exercise or Activity Safety Considerations

Because diabetes can cause complications involving nerves and blood vessels, it is important that individuals with diabetes be *medically evaluated before undertaking an exercise or activity program*. This is particularly true for those with Type II diabetes, for Type I's who have had diabetes for five or more years, for any person with diabetes who knows they have complications of diabetes (such as eye or kidney damage), or if the person has not participated in any activity or exercise for a long period of time.

Those with kidney or eye damage may need to participate in only low-impact activities that do not involve straining, lifting or jarring behaviors. Those who have nerve and muscle changes in their feet may need special foot protection or limited lower extremity impact activity, such as swimming. Too, they should be encouraged to examine their feet daily for sores, cuts, or blisters or any signs of infection.

Dietary Needs

The main problem in diabetes is that glucose (sugars) is not metabolized normally because there is either no insulin or the body does not use its own insulin well. Therefore, diet needs are primarily focused on making certain that the person has a healthy *(quality)* food intake each day in the amounts *(quantity)* needed for activity and growth, with limited amounts of foods that are simple sugars. For those who manage their diabetes with medications, there will be an additional issue of *timing* food to match the glucose-lowering medications. Timing, for those on diabetes medications, also pertains to not skipping meals or delaying meals beyond the time when meals are expected.

What this means is that people with diabetes have a wide variety of foods that they can choose from, even including some favorite foods and sweets. The guidelines are quality, quantity, and timing. Those who have had diabetes for some time and have been testing their blood glucose will often know which foods affect their blood glucose. Individuals may have specific other dietary restrictions, and these need to be determined beforehand - e.g. salt restriction, fats, proteins.

SEIZURES

Epilepsy is a disorder that is characterized by recurrent seizures. A seizure is believed to occur when a group of abnormal brain cells fire at the same time. Sometimes the abnormal firing or discharge spreads in the brain. Whatever the abnormal brain cells control in the body determines the nature of the seizure. For example, if the cells control movement of the right arm, the right arm could have repetitive movements.

Partial Seizures

There are many different types of seizures that can be classified into two large groups—partial and generalized. **Partial seizures** occur when the discharge from the abnormal brain cells remains in only one section of the brain. When the discharge involves most or all of the brain, a generalized seizure occurs.

Partial seizures can be broken down into two divisions— elementary and complex. Elementary partial seizures involve only one section of the brain and the person does not lose consciousness. An example would be the seizure described earlier where the client had repetitive jerking of one arm. Complex partial seizures involve parts of the brain that control thought processes. The person is not unconscious but experiences reduced consciousness. The person sometimes describes the seizure as being in a fog. One common complex partial seizure is called a psychomotor seizure. In a psychomotor seizure the person may make senseless movements such as walking around while pulling at his or her clothes, smacking his or her lips repeatedly, or speaking in an unintelligible manner. Complex partial seizures generally last a few minutes and are often followed by confusion and loss of memory during the seizure (Freeman, Vining & Pillas, 1990).

Generalized Seizures

In **generalized seizures** there is a loss of consciousness. If the loss is brief, the seizure is called a petit mal or absence seizure. The *absence seizure* generally lasts a few seconds and usually consists of staring or rolling back of the eyes. To an observer, the seizure may be seen as a brief lapse in activity. An absence seizure begins and ends abruptly.

Another type of generalized seizure is the *tonic/clonic* or what used to be called the grand mal seizure. Typically the person loses consciousness, stiffens all over, has jerking movements of the arms and legs, and has loss of urine. At the onset, the person temporarily stops breathing and the skin may become pale or bluish. The breathing resumes during the jerking (tonic and clonic) phase. Following the seizure the person is often sleepy and may have muscle soreness. The tonic/clonic seizure may be frightening to watch and generally seems to last longer than it does. The usual time is 2 to 3 minutes (Freeman, Vining, & Pillas, 1990).

Seizure First-Aid Treatment

Since there are different types of seizures, first-aid procedures vary. Some people have more than one type of seizure. It is necessary to find out what typically happens during the seizure, how long the seizures usually last, whether there is loss of consciousness, and whether there are any symptoms before the unconsciousness occurs.

The primary concern for the therapeutic recreation specialist is the safety of the client. Generally, no first-aid is necessary for any seizure except the tonic/clonic seizure. The lapses in the absence seizures are so short they are generally not dangerous. Normal safety precautions for crossing streets and bicycling should be sufficient. During psychomotor seizures, it may be necessary to guide the person if his or her reactions could result in danger. The Epilepsy Foundation of America suggests that an explanation be given to observers in order to help them understand that the person with epilepsy does not have control over his or her actions (*Epilepsy Parent and Family Networks Resource Materials*, 1989).

Tonic/clonic seizures may be unpleasant to watch and will often precipitate a feeling of needing to do something in the observer. The most important thing for the therapeutic recreation specialist is to keep calm. This is especially important if the seizure occurs around a large group of people because anxiety and panic could spread among the group. If the client is sitting or standing, ease the person to the floor and loosen any constricting clothing. Do not try to stop the seizure or try to revive the client. Once the seizure has started, it cannot be stopped. Do *not* under any circumstances try to force anything between clenched teeth.

People do not swallow their tongues during a seizure, and a great deal of damage can be done to the teeth and mouth (Freeman, Vining, & Pilas, 1990).

It is also helpful to clear the area around the person of any hard objects so he or she will not inadvertently inflict self-harm with the seizure movements. Turning the head to the side may help the release of saliva. It is not necessary to call an ambulance unless the seizure lasts for more than ten minutes, or if the client passes from one seizure to another without gaining consciousness (a condition called status epilepticus). Status epilepticus is rare, but does require immediate medical treatment. Status epilepticus in generalized tonic/clonic seizures is life-threatening (Dreifuss, 1988). After the seizure, someone should stay with the client until he or she is awake and no longer is confused.

Medical attention *is* necessary for a seizure in any client who is *not* known to have seizures, however, even if the seizure does not last very long and the client appears unharmed. The cause of the seizure may be an underlying medical problem (e.g. hypoglycemia, brain infection, and brain tumor) that may require further attention. Thus, the therapeutic recreation specialist should be knowledgeable of the client's medical history.

The therapeutic recreation specialist should be matter of fact about the seizure with both the person who had the seizure and those who watched it. It is important to get back to business as usual to decrease the possibility of embarrassment for the client who has had the seizure.

Activity Restrictions

Because therapeutic recreation often involves physical activity, the question regarding activity restriction is regularly encountered. There are no firm rules for the therapeutic recreation specialist to follow. Information from the client or the client's family regarding the nature and frequency of the seizures is an important consideration when decisions are made about the appropriateness of the activities. In addition, recommendations from the client's physician in regard to contact sports and swimming must be followed. It must be pointed out that there is risk in living, and the client should not be unduly restricted or overprotected. The therapeutic recreation specialist should weigh three factors—seizure control, seizure type, and the nature of the activity—when determining risk versus benefit for the client with epilepsy. Each will be covered separately.

With medication approximately 50 percent of people with epilepsy are seizure-free, and an additional 25 to 30 percent have fairly good seizure control. Only about 20 percent of the people with epilepsy fail to achieve significant seizure control from anticonvulsants. Persons with poorly controlled epilepsy experience daily seizures. Generally, normal safety precautions suffice for clients who enjoy good seizure control. The therapeutic recreation specialist should find out how often the client has been having seizures. Ask if the client is taking the anticonvulsant medication regularly because failure to do so can result in seizures.

The nature of the seizures also determines the need for activity restrictions. Some clients have seizures only during sleep (nocturnal seizures) and, consequently, need no restrictions. Seizures such as absence, elementary-partial, and complex-partial impose very few, if any restrictions on the client's activities. Instructions may have to be repeated for the client with absence or psychomotor seizures because he or she may miss hearing or seeing something during the seizures. In addition, activities such as bicycling should be confined to bike paths and parks that are away from busy streets. During swimming the therapeutic recreation specialist should make sure that the client swims with someone who is aware of the nature of the seizures and can get help if needed. Basic safety rules for everyone apply.

Tonic/clonic seizures, however, can subject the client to harm if they occur while swimming. A generalized tonic/clonic seizure often begins with a quick inhalation. If the client is under water, he or she could breathe in water. Swimming can be hazardous for clients with poorly controlled tonic/clonic seizures; they should be closely monitored. All personnel who are swimming with the client with epilepsy should be aware of the seizure disorder and know first-aid procedures.

When a seizure does occur during swimming, the client should be supported so his or her head is out of the water to reduce the chance of getting water in the lungs. As soon as possible, the client should be taken out of the water and examined immediately to determine if artificial respiration is necessary. Even if the client seems fully recovered, medical attention should be obtained to protect the safety of the client. Seizures in the water can be very dangerous and medical attention is essential to determine if there are any ill effects for the client (*The Child with Epilepsy At Camp*, 1981).

If a client strikes his or her head forcefully against a hard object during any seizure, the client may develop a head injury. Because symptoms of a head injury such as headache, sleepiness, confusion, and weakness may be similar to symptoms occurring normally after a seizure, medical attention should be obtained for the client.

Any activities that require continued attention such as climbing or horseback riding may also need to be avoided by the client with poorly controlled tonic/clonic seizures. If the client has regular seizures, a hard hat may provide needed protection during bicycling or horseback riding.

The therapeutic recreation specialist must assess each client with epilepsy and the activity individually. Guidance from medical personnel should be sought and followed. Regardless of the type, people who have been seizure-free for six months to two years usually have no restrictions and are given permission to drive an automobile.

ANTIEPILEPTIC DRUG THERAPY

The major treatment for seizures today is the long-term intake of antiepileptic drugs (AED). Other treatments have been tried with limited success. Since the 1920s a ketogenic diet consisting of food high in fat and low in carbohydrates has been used. Acupuncture and biofeedback are being used experimentally today to determine their potential for use. Neurosurgery is an option for some seizures that are difficult to control. The majority of people with epilepsy regularly take AEDs. Therefore, the therapeutic recreation specialist should be knowledgeable regarding the effects of the most common anticonvulsants.

The **desired effect** of an AED is to make the brain less apt to seize. The goal of AED therapy is to get a sufficient amount of drug into the bloodstream to reduce seizures. Occasionally clients take more than one drug daily to achieve optimal seizure control. In order to maintain the proper blood level, the AED must be taken at regular intervals. Provisions must be made by the therapeutic recreation specialist for the client to receive drugs during prolonged activities such as field trips and overnight camping. AEDs are taken orally unless the client is unable to do so because of illness such as nausea and vomiting. If the AED cannot be taken orally, provisions must be made for medical personnel to give the drug in another manner. If too many doses are omitted, the client will be at risk for seizures.

All drugs may cause effects in addition to the desired effect for which they are being prescribed. Unfortunately, AEDs have some of these **side effects**. It is important that the therapeutic recreation specialist be aware of possible side effects when assessing, planning, implementing, and evaluating activities for the client. Each client has to be assessed individually because not everyone experiences side effects and some may only experience them temporarily. The therapeutic recreation specialist must assess which side effects the client is experiencing. For example, a client who suffers from dizziness and an unsteady gait would have difficulty with an activity that required physical agility. In addition, the therapeutic recreation specialist may be the first to recognize a side effect, such as extreme drowsiness that may need medical attention.

The most commonly prescribed AEDs, along with their possible side effects are listed in Table 10-3. The table gives two names for each drug. The name that is listed first is the generic name. Each drug has only one generic name, which is never changed and is the same in all countries. The name that appears in parentheses is the trade name or the brand name. A drug can have many brand names. Except for phenobarbital, brand names are probably more familiar to you, since they are promoted by drug companies and are generally easier to pronounce. Generic names usually reflect the chemical makeup of the drug and are harder to pronounce and remember.

TABLE 10-3
ANTICONVULSANT DRUGS

Phenobarbital (Luminal, Mysoline)
Possible Side Effects: Sedation, lethargy, mental dullness, anemia, skin rash, and hyperactivity

Phenytoin (Dilantin)
Possible Side Effects: Unsteady gait, slurred speech, drowsiness, fatigue, gum swelling, skin rash, hair growth, stomach upsets, blood destruction, and double vision.

Carbamazepine (Tegretol)
Possible Side Effects: Sedation, unsteady gait, skin rash, anemia, and infections

Lamotrigine (Lamictal)
Possible Side Effects: Skin rash, lethargy, stomach upset, unsteady gait, and respiratory infections

Gabapentin (Neurontin)
Possible Side Effects: Sedation, lethargy, hyperactivity, irritability, dizziness, and headache

Valproic Acid (Depakene/Depakote)
Possible Side Effects: Loss of appetite, nausea and vomiting, decreased liver function, and unsteady gait

Source: Aicardi (1994); Dreifuss (1988)

It can be seen that the therapeutic recreation specialist must be familiar with first-aid and safety precautions for seizures and with possible side effects of AEDs in order to maintain client safety during recreation activities. The goal for therapy is seizure control with a minimum of side effects. With very difficult-to-control seizures, some clients are forced to tolerate side effects from more than one drug. The therapeutic recreation specialist should report side effects to the client, the client's family, or medical personnel. Sometimes drugs can be changed if a side effect is potentially harmful. Assessment of side effects should be made and the information used when planning, implementing, and evaluating client care.

PSYCHOTROPIC DRUGS

Many therapeutic recreation specialists provide services for clients who suffer from emotional disturbance or mental illness. In addition to other therapies such as psychotherapy and therapeutic recreation, most of these clients receive medication to reduce the symptoms of the mental illness. These drugs have an effect on the psychic function of the client and are known collectively as **psychotropic drugs.**

In this section basic information is presented on the four major classes of psychotropic drugs: antipsychotic, antidepressant, antimania, and antianxiety. It is important to realize that the information is about what usually happens when a client takes a drug regularly. The effects for any given individual may be different. Therefore, individual assessment for side effects must be completed before planning therapeutic recreation strategies.

Each class of drugs will be individually covered. Names of the common major drugs will be listed. Generic names will be presented first; brand names will appear in parentheses. The desired effects, possible side effects, and potential implication for the therapeutic recreation specialist are also given.

Antipsychotic Drugs

The first **antipsychotic drug,** chlorpromazine (Thorazine) was introduced in 1952. Since that time many antipsychotic drugs have been used in the treatment of psychotic patients. These drugs have revolutionized the treatment of schizophrenia and have been credited with dramatically reducing the number of patients in psychiatric institutions in the United States (Swonger & Constantine, 1976).

Uses

The major reason that antipsychotics are prescribed is to reduce the symptoms of schizophrenia so that patients can better take care of themselves and function in society. Today there are a large number of antipsychotics for the physician to choose from when treating psychotic patients. Table 10-4 lists generic names, brand names, and the desired effects of commonly used antipsychotic medications.

TABLE 10-4
ANTIPSYCHOTIC DRUGS

Name

Clozapine (Clozaril)
Chlorpromazine (Thorazine)
Thioridazine (Mellaril)
Mesoridazine (Serentil)
Trifluoperazine (Stelazine)
Perphenazine (Trilaforn)
Fluphenazine (Permitil, Prolixin)
Thiothixene (Navane)
Haloperidol (Haldol)
Primozide (ORAP)
Molindone (Moban, Lidone)
Risperidone (Risperdal)

Desired Effects

Major actions include the reduction of symptoms of schizophrenia (i.e., hallucinations, delusions, disordered thinking processes, and social withdrawal). There are also effects of reducing hyperactivity, emotional quieting, and decreased anxiety.

Sources: Schatzberg & Nemeroff (1995).

Unfortunately, antipsychotic drugs have a wide range of side effects. Table 10-5 contains the most common side effects of antipsychotic drugs. One of the earliest side effects is drowsiness. It is usually temporary and lasts only one or two weeks. Low blood pressure can also occur as a side effect. Symptoms of low blood pressure, which are dizziness and weakness, usually occur upon rising from a lying or sitting position to a standing position (Appleton, 1988). The therapeutic recreation specialist should avoid activities that require alertness and muscular coordination with these clients and watch these clients carefully to avoid falling.

TABLE 10-5
ANTIPSYCHOTIC DRUG SIDE EFFECTS

Extrapyramidal Side Effects (EPS)

- Motor restlessness where the client cannot stop moving (akathisia).
- Involuntary jerking and bizarre movements of muscles in the face, neck, tongue, eyes, arms, and legs.
- Tremors, muscle weakness, and fatigue.
- Parkinson-like symptoms such as rigidity, drooling, difficulty in speaking, slow movement, and an unusual gait when walking where the client has trouble slowing down.

Tardive Dyskinesia (TD)

- Abnormal mouth motion such as lip smacking, chewing, sucking, moving the tongue in and out of the mouth quickly, and pushing out the cheeks.
- Involuntary movements of the jaw, increased blinking, and spasms of muscles in the face, neck, back, eyes, arms, and legs.

TABLE 10-5 CONT.

Other Side Effects

- Drowsiness
- Low blood pressure
- Nausea
- Vomiting
- Rash
- Dry mouth
- Urinary retention
- Blood destruction
- Photosensitivity
  (especially with Thorazine)
- Edema
- Weight gain
- Feminizing effects
- Menstrual irregularities
- Blurred vision
- Constipation
- Seizures
- Skin discoloration
- Fever
- Drop in blood cell count
  (especially with Clozapine)

Sources: Appleton (1988); Newton et al. (1978); Schatzberg & Nemeroff (1995).

Extrapyramidal Side Effects (EPS)

Extrapyramidal side effects occur in up to 30 percent of all patients and have been found in 50 percent of older adults (Saxon & Etten, 1987). These side effects include Parkinson-like symptoms and can be so limiting for the client that a second drug (e.g., Cogentin, Artane, or Benadryl) is frequently given to counteract the EPS effects (Newton et al., 1978). Table 10-5 describes the most common extrapyramidal side effects. The most serious side effect, **tardive dyskinesia,** has been found to occur more often among older women with brain pathology. The therapeutic recreation specialist must be familiar with side effects of antipsychotic medications and should regularly assess each client to determine which, if any, side effect will affect the planning of recreation activities.

Knowledge of the potential side effects of antipsychotic drugs can guide the assessment of the client by the therapeutic recreation specialist. In addition, being aware that side effects may subside or be replaced by other side effects indicates the necessity of reassessment. When extrapyramidal symptoms (see Table 10-5) are present, activities that require physical agility such as bike riding, climbing, and gymnastics should be avoided. Even hiking down a steep hill can be potentially harmful for a client with a Parkinson-like gait. Supervision by personnel should be increased for those clients. Clients with tremors, muscle weakness, and fatigue may need to participate at a slower pace and have frequent opportunities for rest.

Some activities may not be particularly dangerous, but they subject the client to increased frustration. For example, activities that require good eye-hand coordination or clear vision can be frustrating. If the activity includes using needles or sewing with a sewing machine, the activity becomes potentially harmful. Aiming at a target, reading, and writing are potentially frustrating for clients who suffer from blurred vision or motor restlessness.

One side effect that occurs, especially with Thorazine, is photosensitivity, which means the skin becomes increasingly sensitive to burning by the sun. The therapeutic recreation specialist should check with medical personnel before the client is allowed to participate in an outside activity with maximum exposure to sunlight such as swimming. A sunscreen should be applied or, if possible, the medication could be changed to Mellaril, which does not cause photosensitivity (Bassuk & Schoononer, 1977). For activities in the sun, clients should wear sunglasses, protective clothing, and sunscreen lotion on exposed areas if they are receiving Thorazine.

Antidepressant Drugs

Several classes of drugs are available for the treatment of depressive disorders. These drugs can also be used for attention deficit hyperactivity disorder, enuresis (bedwetting), obsessive-compulsive disorders and anxiety disorders. The different drugs are probably equally effective, but vary in their side effects. See Table 10-6 for a list of common antidepressants. Most of the agents take about 3 weeks to become effective. They should relieve feelings of hopelessness, sadness, trouble sleeping, changes in appetite, decreased concentration, and guilt associated with depression.

Side Effects

The side effects of the tricyclic and heterocyclic agents are lethargy, dry mouth, blurred vision, constipation, weight gain, decreased blood pressure, and changes in heart rate and rhythm. The serotonin reuptake inhibitors cause upset stomach, headache, nervousness, or sleepiness. Bupropion can cause restlessness, insomnia, and rarely, seizures. All of these drugs can lead to mania in clients with bipolar (manic-depressive) disorder.

Antimania Drugs

Lithium is presently the primary drug used for the treatment of mania and the manic phase of manic-depression psychoses. Lithium is an element that is administered as a salt. Common brand names include Eskalith, Litlane, and Lethonate (Swonger & Constantine, 1976). Other drugs used are carbamazepine, Valproic Acid and Clonazepam.

Mania is a mood disorder characterized by a subjective feeling of elation. The person usually engages in endless activity and experiences a decreased need for sleep. Usually the person speaks quickly, as if under pressure to do so, and has flight of ideas where many unrelated topics are mentioned, one after another. Mania can progress to involve grandiose delusions, hallucinations, and paranoia (Bassuk & Schoononer, 1977). The exact mechanism by which lithium alleviates the symptoms of mania is unknown. However, studies reveal that long-term lithium therapy decreases the severity and frequency of manic episodes (Bassuk & Schoononer, 1977).

TABLE 10-6
ANTIDEPRESSANTS

Drug

Tricyclic antidepressants
  Imipramine (Tofranil)
  Desipramine (Norpramin)
  Amitriptyline (Elavil)
  Nortriptyline (Pamelor)
  Doxepin (Sinequan)
  Clomipramine (Anafranil)
Heterocyclic antidepressants
  Amoxapine (Asendin)
  Maprotiline (Ludiomil)
  Trazodone (Desyrel)
Dopamine reuptake blocker
  Bupropion (Wellbutrin)

Desired Effect

Relief of feelings such as hopelessness, sadness, helplessness, anxiety, worthlessness, and fatigue that are associated with depression.

Sources: Appleton (1988); Schatzberg & Nemeroff (1995).

Side Effects

Generally, the side effects are mild and are related to the level of lithium in the bloodstream. Early side effects include thirst, increased urine, decreased appetite, nausea, vomiting, diarrhea, and a fine tremor. These side effects usually do not persist with continued therapy. However, higher lithium levels in the blood can be very dangerous; symptoms include muscular weakness, blurred vision, drowsiness, and ringing in the ears. Excessively high levels can lead to convulsions, coma, and death (Newton et al., 1978). The therapeutic recreation specialist's recognition of the side effects can help ensure the clients' safety by encouraging the client to seek medical attention if higher-level symptoms occur.

Antianxiety Drugs

Antianxiety drugs or minor tranquilizers are used to treat clients who suffer from excessive anxiety and tension. They also are used for short-term therapy for insomnia. There are two major types that are prescribed and have similar desired effects— azapirone and benzodiazepines. The common drugs are listed in Table 10-7 along with their desired effects.

Although the drugs have similar desired effects, the benzodiazepines are the most commonly prescribed drugs for anxiety. Diazepam and Lorazepam given intravenously also are the treatment of choice for status epilepticus because of their anticonvulsant effect. In addition, Librium is used in the treatment of alcohol withdrawal (Swonger & Constantine, 1976; Bassuk & Schoononer, 1977; Newton et al., 1978).

Side Effects

The most common side effect of the benzodiazepines is drowsiness. Other side effects include dizziness, muscular incoordination, muscle weakness, skin rash, menstrual irregularities, and weight gain. Withdrawal reactions after prolonged use also have been found. Buspirone may cause dizziness, lethargy, upset stomach, and headache.

The therapeutic recreation specialist would need to assess the individual client for side effects such as drowsiness or dizziness before planning activities that require alertness and muscular agility. Side effects of the antianxiety drugs are usually temporary and generally do not limit the recreational activities of the client.

MECHANICAL AIDS

Many individuals have either permanent or temporary conditions that limit their physical mobility and require the use of mechanical aids. Mechanical aids are equipment such as braces, crutches, walkers, and wheelchairs, which assist clients in carrying out their activities of daily living. The use of mechanical aids allows the client to be as independent as possible. This section will present general guidelines for the therapeutic recreation specialist to follow when working with the client.

TABLE 10-7
ANTIANXIETY DRUGS

Drug

Azapirone

Buspirone (BuSpar)

Benzodiazepines

Chlordiazepoxide (Librium)
Diazepam (Valium)
Oxazepm (Serax)
Clorazepate (Tranxene)
Flurazepam (Dalmane)
Lorazepam (Ativan)
Prazepam (Centrax)
Triazolam (Halcion)
Temazepam (Restoril)
Halazepam (Paxipam)
Alprazolam (Xanax)
Clonazepam (Klonopin)

Desired Effect

Reduction of anxiety, relaxation of skeletal muscles, relief of symptoms of tension and insomnia, and anticonvulsant properties.

Sources: Newton et al. (1978); Appleton (1988), Schatzberg & Nemeroff (1995).

Safety for both the therapeutic recreation specialist and the client is the prime consideration. Every client differs in weight, disability, and size. Therefore, each client should be individually assessed in order to determine his or her abilities and need for assistance. The first general rule to follow if possible is *always consult with the client or the client's family regarding how much and what kind of assistance is needed.* Clients live with their mechanical aids and have safe and efficient routines that they follow. Even if a client has just recently developed the physical limitation, safe techniques have usually been taught to them by health care personnel prior to their participation in therapeutic recreation activities.

Braces, Crutches, and Walkers

Clients who use *braces, crutches,* or *walkers* have limited physical mobility and reduced weight-bearing ability in their legs. The therapeutic recreation specialist must assess each client's abilities prior to planning activities. Information should be sought from the chart, other medical and professional personnel, and the client. Assessment should include observation of the client to determine how well the client handles the mechanical aid in his or her activities of daily living. The therapeutic recreation specialist should assess how much balance the client has in various positions, whether one side of the body is weaker than the other, and how much physical endurance is present. The amount of physical endurance will affect how long the client can participate in more strenuous activities. If fatigue is present the client may be more apt to have an accident. In addition, clients who lack physical strength or mobility in both upper and lower extremities are less able to regain their balance or catch themselves if they begin to fall.

The therapeutic recreation specialist should conduct a physical inspection of the environment to insure client safety. Loose rugs, debris, and uneven or steep paths can make mobility more difficult for clients using mechanical aids. Paths that have sharp drops should be avoided.

The condition of the mechanical aid should also be observed. Equipment should be inspected to make sure that it is in safe condition and has no missing or loose pieces. Crutches and walkers should have secured rubber tips covering the base. Crutches should also have rubber covers over the shoulder piece and handpiece. Wheelchairs should have wheels that lock.

Clients may develop reddened or pressure areas from lack of circulation or irritation from the mechanical aid. The therapeutic recreation specialist, especially in long-term activities such as camping, is often responsible for assessment of skin. The client cannot always be relied on to know if pressure exists because of loss of feeling in the area. If any reddened or broken areas are observed, the therapeutic recreation specialist should call it to the attention of the client and/or medical personnel so proper measures can be taken to prevent further problems such as skin infection.

Clients who use braces, crutches, or walkers generally need minimal to moderate assistance. Ask the client or the client's family about the amount and type of assistance needed. Adequate assessment by the therapeutic recreation specialist should result in recreational activities in which the client can participate safely. Clients may need assistance with stairs, especially if the client uses a walker. The nature of the assistance depends on the type of physical disability, the length of time the client has had the limited mobility, and other conditions. For example, an elderly client suffering from a recent stroke may need maximum assistance with stairs and a child who has had leg braces for several years may need no assistance.

Before the therapeutic recreation specialist helps any client with a mechanical aid, the client should be told exactly what the therapeutic recreation specialist is trying to do. The use of a safety belt is especially helpful when clients are having problems maintaining balance.

When the client using crutches ascends stairs, the client should place the crutches under the unaffected side and grasp the banister with the free hand. The unaffected foot is lifted to the step above. Then, supporting the weight on the unaffected foot, the client pulls the crutches onto the step. The process is repeated until the client reaches the top of the stairs. To go down the stairs, the client again positions himself or herself so that the banister is on the affected side and both crutches are on the other. The client places the crutches on the step below and at the same time swings his or her affected foot out over the step. Supporting body weight with a hand on the banister and the crutches, the client steps down with the unaffected foot. The process is repeated until the bottom of the stairs is reached.

Catheters and Collection Bags

Clients who have loss of bladder function may have an indwelling urinary catheter and a collection bag. Urinary appliances are most common in the hospital setting. When working with the client, care should be taken to avoid pulling on the catheter because the pressure may irritate the bladder opening and predispose the client to an infection. It is imperative that the tubing and collection bag always remain *below* the level of the bladder. Lifting the appliance above the bladder will cause the urine to flow back into the bladder and possibly cause an infection.

Wheelchairs

When working with clients who are *wheelchair users*, ask them how the wheelchair works and what kind of assistance is needed, if any. Wheelchairs come in various styles. Armrests and footrests may be removable; some wheelchairs are self-propelled, depending on the needs of the clients. All wheelchairs should have brakes or locks on the wheels. Become familiar with the wheelchair before working with the client.

It is important to observe safety rules when transporting a client in a wheelchair. Safety precautions include locking the wheels of the wheelchair when it is not in motion. For example, the wheels should be locked when the client is getting in and out of the chair or when the client is being transported in the wheelchair inside a van. Always make sure that you have a good grasp on the handles of the wheelchair. Seat belts should be used to secure the client in the chair and avoid the possibility that the client can tumble forward at a sudden stop. When maneuvering over bumps and curbs, tilt the wheelchair back slightly by applying pressure on one of the tilting rods on the back of the chair. If you are pushing a wheelchair down a steep ramp, turn yourself and the chair around and proceed down the ramp backward. Your body will help control the speed of the wheelchair (National Easter Seal Society, 1980).

Wheelchair users who have full use of their arms may only need assistance when faced with an architectural barrier such as a flight of stairs. Except in the case of children, two people are usually needed to transport the client in the wheelchair up and down stairs. If the client is heavy three people may be needed. The wheelchair is taken up the stairs backward and down the stairs frontward. The people assisting should be positioned in front and back of the wheelchair. The chair should be balanced on the large wheels and lifted by the handgrips in back and the rods holding the footrests in front. The large wheels of the wheelchair are eased on the stairs one step at a time (National Easter Seal Society, 1980).

Some clients who are wheelchair users prefer to go it alone on the stairs. Generally, they fold up their chairs and move one step at a time by using their arms to lift their buttocks up and down the stairs taking their chair with them.

In some settings the therapeutic recreation specialist may be asked to assist a client from a bed to a wheelchair or chair. The therapeutic recreation specialist needs to utilize proper lifting and transferring techniques in order to protect the safety of both the client and himself or herself. It is easier to move a client if the person moving him or her stays close to the client's center of gravity. According to Owen (1980), improper lifting and bending account for more than half of all back injuries. Back injuries can be avoided if the legs rather than the back are used to lift or transfer clients. It is important for the therapeutic recreation specialist to maintain a straight back and bent knees when doing all lifting of clients.

There are many methods to use for transferring clients. One common method that might be used by the therapeutic recreation specialist to transfer a client safely from a wheelchair to a bed is presented in Table 10-8 and demonstrated in Figure 10-1.

Transferring the client from the bed to the wheelchair is usually easier since less lifting is required. Again, there are many methods. One common method to use is presented in Table 10-9 and demonstrated in Figure 10-2.

The same basic steps presented in Tables 10-8 and 10-9 can be used to transfer a client between chairs and between a wheelchair and a toilet. The distances between equipment should always be minimized. When transferring a client between chairs or between a wheelchair and a toilet, there should be about a 40-degree angle between the objects. If one side of the client's body is weaker than the other, the client should be moved toward the stronger side. The client will be able to assist more with the motion if he or she is moving toward the stronger side. The therapeutic recreation specialist should remember to keep his or her feet spread about shoulder width apart and to flex the knees.

Proper body positioning allows the muscle groups to work together and prevents injury to the therapeutic recreation specialist. Arm, shoulder, back, and stomach muscles should be used to pull. Lifting is done with the thigh and leg muscles (Owen, 1980). The safety needs of both the client and the therapeutic recreation specialist should be considered when the therapeutic recreation specialist transfers clients who have reduced physical mobility.

FIGURE 10-1
TRANSFERRING A CLIENT FROM A
WHEELCHAIR TO A BED

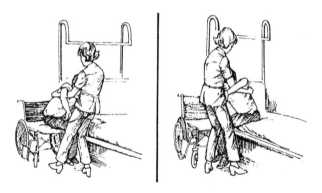

TABLE 10-8
TRANSFERRING CLIENT FROM A
WHEELCHAIR TO A BED

1. Minimize the distance between the wheelchair and the bed by placing the chair adjacent and parallel to the bed.
2. Lock the wheels on the wheelchair and the bed if the bed has wheels.
3. Raise the footrests and remove the armrest near the bed.
4. Stand in front of the client with your feet shoulder width apart. Your outside foot should be between the footrests.
5. Flex your knees.
6. Place your palms on either side of the client's rib cage.
7. Have the client put his or her arms on your elbows and hug your arms to assist.
8. Use your shoulder, arm, stomach, and back muscles to pull and your leg muscles to lift the client from the chair. Your knees should stabilize the client's knees.
9. Pivot your whole body to swing the client onto the bed.
10. Position the client in bed.

FIGURE 10-2
TRANSFERRING A CLIENT FROM A BED
TO A WHEELCHAIR

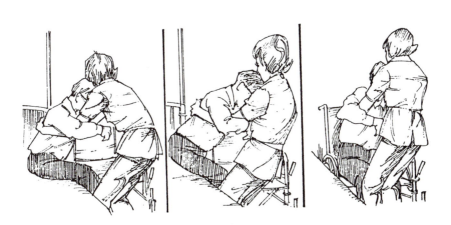

TABLE 10-9
TRANSFERRING A CLIENT FROM A BED TO A WHEELCHAIR

1. Minimize the distance between the wheelchair and the bed by placing the wheelchair adjacent and parallel to the bed.
2. Lock the wheels on the wheelchair and the bed if the bed has wheels.
3. Raise the footrests and remove the armrest near the bed.
4. Face the head of the bed. Spread your feet about shoulder width apart. Place one forearm under the knees of the client and place your other forearm under the client's shoulder.
5. Assist the client to the sitting position by pivoting the client on his or her buttocks and swinging his or her legs over the edge of the bed. The client should be sitting on the edge of the bed.
6. Stand in front of the client and block his or her knees with your own. Your feet should be spread shoulder width apart. The outside foot should be midway between and in front of the footrest.
7. Place your palms on either side of the client's rib cage.
8. Have the client put his or her arms on your elbows and hug your arms to assist.
9. Use your shoulder, arm, stomach, and back muscles to pull the client off the bed.
10. At the same time, pivot the client and lower the client into the chair flexing your knees.
11. Position the client securely onto the wheelchair.

HIV/AIDS

Acquired immunodeficiency syndrome (AIDS) is caused by a virus, referred to as the human immunodeficiency virus (HIV). When an antibody against the virus is found in the blood, it indicates the person has been infected by the virus. The immune system, which defends the body's health, is progressively weakened by the HIV. The disorder begins with no symptoms, progresses to AIDS-related complex (ARC) where persons have mild symptoms resembling the flu, and then progresses to full-blown AIDS. In full-blown AIDS, the symptoms are more severe and include enlarged lymph nodes, weight loss, recurrent fevers, neurologic abnormalities, and atypical cancers (Rote, 1990).

Because people can be infected with HIV many years before they have symptoms, it is important that the therapeutic recreation specialist be aware of how HIV is transmitted. HIV is not transmitted through casual contact, such as touching, hugging, using swimming pools or toilet seats, or sharing sports equipment (Grossman & Caroleo, 1996). HIV is transmitted through contact with contaminated body fluids. The concept of "Universal Precautions" is based on the assumption that all blood and body fluids with visible blood have the potential to cause infection (Center for Disease Control, 1987). If a therapeutic recreation specialist is engaged in an activity where a client's skin is broken, the client should be immediately separated from others to reduce the chance of contamination. The therapeutic recreation specialist should use latex, vinyl, or rubber gloves to avoid direct contact with blood while attending to the wound and wash hands after removing gloves. It is important to remember to have gloves and antiseptic towelettes available for activities where hand-washing facilities are not available.

SUMMARY

Providing therapeutic recreation services for clients from special populations requires knowing about the client's health and safety needs. Clients who have diabetic reactions or seizures may experience episodes that may threaten health and physical safety. Other clients who receive long-term drug therapy with psychotropic drugs may experience side effects that may affect their ability to participate in therapeutic recreation activities. Finally, clients who use mechanical aids may need assistance from the therapeutic recreation specialist. To assist the client safely and efficiently, the therapeutic recreation specialist must know proper transferring techniques and how to handle blood. This chapter has provided general information and basic guidelines for the therapeutic recreation specialist to utilize when working with clients.

READING COMPREHENSION QUESTIONS

1.   What are the main causes of hypoglycemia and hyperglycemia?
2.   What precautions should the therapeutic recreation specialist take when planning extended activities for clients with diabetes mellitus?
3.   What is the first-aid treatment for each type of seizure?
4.   What are the main factors to consider when planning activities for the client who is subject to tonic/clonic seizures?
5.   Which side effects of antiepileptic drugs and psychotropic drugs necessitate changes in activities due to safety considerations?
6.   What are the main safety considerations for clients who use mechanical aids?
7.   What are some basic principles to follow when lifting or transferring clients who have physical limitations?
8.   What precautions should be followed when coming into contact with blood?

REFERENCES

Adams, E.R., & McGuire, F. (1986). Is laughter the best medicine? A study of the effects of humor on perceived pain and affect. *Activities, Adaption, & Aging, 8* (3/4), 157-175.

Adler, T. (1989). Funnybone connected to cognition, physiology. *The APA Monitor, 20* (5), 16.

Aguilera, D. (1967). Relationships between physical contact and verbal interaction between nurses and patients. *Journal of Psychiatric Nursing, 5*, 5-21.

Aicardi, J. (1994). *Epilepsy in children* (2nd ed.). New York: Raven Press.

Alderman, R. B. (1974). *Psychological behavior in sport.* Philadelphia: W. B. Saunders Company.

American Diabetes Association, Inc. (1995). *Intensive diabetes management.* Clinical Education Series. Alexandria, VA.

American Diabetes Association, Inc. (1994). *Medical management of non-insulin dependent (type I) diabetes.* (2nd ed.). Clinical Education Series. Alexandria, VA.

American Diabetes Association, Inc. (1994). *Medical management of non-insulin dependent (type II) diabetes.* (3rd ed.). Clinical Education Series. Alexandria, VA.

Anderson, R. A. (1978). *Stress power!* New York: Human Sciences Press.

Appleton, W. S. (1988). *Practical clinical psychopharmacology* (3rd ed.). Baltimore, MD: Williams & Wilkins.

Ard, B. N. (1973). Providing clinical supervision for marriage counselors: A model for supervisor and supervisee. *The Family Coordinator, 22*, 91-97.

Ardell, B. (1977). *High-level wellness: An alternative to doctors, drugs, and disease.* Berkeley, CA: Ten Speed Press.

Austin, D.R. (1971). Catharsis theory: How valid is therapeutic recreation? *Therapeutic Recreation Journal, 5* (1), 30, 31, 44, 45.

Austin D. R., & Binkley, A. L. (1977). *A summary of the curriculum plan for the master of science in recreation: Option in therapeutic recreation.* Unpublished report. Department of Recreation and Park Administration. Bloomington, IN:Indiana University.

Austin, D. R., & Szymanski, D. J. (1985). Burnout or burnbright. *Camping Magazine, 57* (7), 26-28.

Austin, D. R. (1986). Clinical supervision in therapeutic recreation. *Journal of Expanding Horizons in Therapeutic Recreation, 1*, 7-13.

Austin, D. R., & Voelkl, J. E. (1986). Effects of social support and locus of control on camp staff burnout. *Camping Magazine, 58* (7), 18-21.

Austin, D. R. (1987). Therapeutic recreation. In A. Graefe & S. Parker (Eds.), *Recreation and leisure: An introductory handbook.* State College, PA: Venture Publishing.

Austin, D. R. (1989). Therapeutic recreation education: A call for reform. In D. M. Compton (Ed.), *Issues in therapeutic recreation: A profession in transition.* Champaign, IL: Sagamore Publishing.

Austin, D.R. (1996). Introduction and overview. In D.R. Austin & M.E. Crawford (Eds.). *Therapeutic Recreation: An Introduction* (2nd edition). Needham Heights, MA: Allyn & Bacon.

Avedon, E. M. (1974). *Therapeutic recreation service: An applied behavioral science approach.* Englewood Cliffs, NJ: Prentice-Hall, Inc.

Ayers, S., Colman, J. & DeSalvatore, G. (n.d.) *The parent-child activity group manual.* Storehan, MA: New England Memorial Hospital.

Bacon, S. (1983). *The conscious use of metaphor in Outward Bound.* Denver: Colorado Outward Bound School.

Ball, E. L. (1970). The meaning of therapeutic recreation. *Therapeutic Recreation Journal, 4* (1), 17,18.

Bandura, A. (1986). *Social foundations of thought and action: A social cognitive theory.* Englewood Cliffs, NJ: Prentice-Hall, Inc.

Barnes, E. K., Sack, A., & Shore, H. (1973). Guidelines to treatment approaches: Modalities and methods for use with the aged. *The Gerontologist, 13,* 515-522.

Baron, R.A., & Byrne, D. (1994). *Social psychology: Understanding human interaction* (7th ed.). Boston: Allyn and Bacon.

Bassuk, E. L., & Schoononer, S. C. (1977). *The practitioner's guide to psychoactive drugs.* New York: Plenum Publishing Co.

Beal, B. M., Bohlen, J. M., & Raudabaugh, J. N. (1976). *Leadership and dynamic group action.* Ames, IA: The Iowa State University Press.

Beaudouin, N.M., & Keller, M.J. (1994). Aquatic-Solutions: A continuum of services for individuals with physical disabilities in the community. *Therapeutic Recreation Journal, 28* (4), 193-202.

Beck, A.T. (1976). *Cognitive therapy and the emotional disorders.* New York: International Universities Press.

Beck, C.K., Rawlins, R.P., & Williams, S. R. (1988). *Mental health-psychiatric nursing: A holistic life-cycle approach.* St. Louis: The C.V. Mosby Company.

Beddall, T., & Kennedy, D.W. (1985). Attitudes of therapeutic recreators toward evaluation and client assessment. *Therapeutic Recreation Journal, 19* (1), 62-70.

Bedini, L.A., Williams, L., & Thompson, D. (1995). The relationship between burnout and role stress in therapeutic recreation specialists. *Therapeutic Recreation Journal, 29*(3), 163-174.

Belkin, G. S. (1988). *Introduction to counseling* (3rd ed.). Dubuque, IA: Wm. C. Brown Publishers.

Benfer, B. A., & Schroder, P.J. (1985). Nursing in the therapeutic milieu. *Bulletin of the Menninger Clinic, 49* (5), 451-465.

Benson, H. (1975). *The relaxation response.* New York: Avon Books.

Berger, B. G. (1987). Stress levels of swimmers. In W.P. Morgan & S. E. Goldston (Eds.), *Exercise and mental health.* New York: Hemisphere Publishing Corporation.

Berger, M., & Yule, W. (1987). Psychometric approaches. In J. Hogg & N. V. Raynes (Eds.), *Assessment in mental handicap*. Cambridge, MA: Brookline Books.

Berkowitz, L. (1972). *Social psychology*. Glenview, IL: Scott, Foresman and Company.

Berkowitz, L. (1978). Sports competition and aggression. In W. F. Staub (Ed.), *An analysis of athlete behavior*. Ithaca, NY: Movement Publications.

Bernard, J. M. (1987). Ethical and legal considerations for supervisors. In L. D. Borders & G. R. Leddick (Eds.), *Handbook of counseling supervision*. Alexandria, VA: Association for Counselor Education and Supervision.

Bernard, J.M., & Goodyear, R.K. (1992). *Fundamentals of clinical supervision*. Boston: Allyn and Bacon.

Berne, E. (1964). *Games people play: The psychology of human relationships*. New York: Grove Press, Inc.

Bernstein, D. A., & Borkovec, T. D. (1973). *Progressive relaxation training: A manual for the helping professions*. Champaign, IL: Research Press.

Bernstein, L., & Bertstein, R.S. (1985). *Interviewing: A guide for health professionals* (4th ed.). Norwalk, CT: Appleton-Century-Crofts.

Bertstein, D.A., & Carlson, C.R. (1993). Progressive relaxation: Abbreviated methods. In P.M. Lehrer & R.L. Woolfolk (Eds.), *Principles and practice of stress management* (2nd ed.). NY: The Guilford Press.

Birrell, J., & Henderson, M. (1986). *The psychological approach*. In C. Hume & I. Pullen (Eds.), *Rehabilitation in psychiatry*. New York: Churchill Livingstone.

Blackham, G. J. (1977). *Counseling:Theory, process and practice*. Belmont, CA: Wadsworth Publishing Company, Inc.

Blattner, B. (1981). *Holistic nursing*. Englewood Cliffs, NJ: Prentice-Hall, Inc.

Borden, G. A., & Stone, J. D. (1976). *Human communication: The process of relating*. Menlo Park, CA: Cummings Publishing Company.

Borders, L. D., & Leddick, G. R. (1987). *Handbook of counseling supervision*. Alexandria, VA: Association for Counselor Education and Supervision.

Bradley, L. J. (1989). *Counselor supervision: principles, process, and practice* (2nd ed.). Muncie, IN: Accelerated Development Inc. Publishers.

Brammer, L.M. (1988). *The helping relationship: Process and skills* (4th ed.). Englewood Cliffs, NJ: Prentice-Hall, Inc.

Brammer, L.M., Abrego, P.J., & Shostrom, E.L. (1993). *Therapeutic psychology: Fundamentals of counseling and psychotherapy* (6th ed.). Englewood Cliffs, NJ: Prentice-Hall, Inc.

Branden, N. (1985) *To see what I see and know what I know: A guide to self-discovery*. New York: Bantam Books.

Brill, N.I. (1995). *Working with people: The helping process* (5th ed.). White Plains, NY: Longman Publishers.

Brody, J. E. (1990). Personal health. *The New York Times*. January 25, 1990. Section B, p. 7.

Bullock, C. C. (1987). Recreation and special populations. In A. Graefe & S. Parker (Eds.), *Recreation: An introductory handbook*. State College, PA: Venture Publishing, Inc.

Bullock, C. C., Austin, D. R., & Lewko, J. H. (1980). Leadership behavior in therapeutic recreation settings. In G. Hitzhusen, J. Elliott, D. J. Szymanski, &

M. G. Thompson (Eds.), *Expanding horizons in therapeutic recreation* (Vol.7). Columbia, MO: University of Missouri.

Burlingame, j., & Blaschko, T. M. (1990). *Assessment tools for recreation therapy: Red book #1.* Ravensdale, WA: Idyll Arbor, Inc.

Butler, R. (1963). The life review: An interpretation of reminiscence in the aged. *Psychiatry, 26,* 65-76.

Cable, T.T., & Udd, E. (1988). Therapeutic benefits of a wildlife observation program. *Therapeutic Recreation Journal, 22*(4), 65-70.

Caldwell, L. L., Adolph, S., & Gilbert, A. (1989). Caution! Leisure counselors at work: Long-term effects of leisure counseling. *Therapeutic Recreation Journal, 23* (3), 41-49.

Campos, L., & McCormick,P. (1980). *Introduce yourself to transactional analysis: A TA primer.* (5th ed.). Stockton, CA: San Joaquin TA Institute.

Carkhuff, R. R. (1969a). *Helping & human relations: A primer for lay and professional helpers. Volume I: Selection and training.* New York: Holt, Rinehart and Winston, Inc.

Carkhuff, R. R. (1969b). *Helping & human relations: A primer for lay and professional helpers. Volume II: Practice and research.* New York: Holt, Rinehart and Winston, Inc.

Carrington, P. (1993). Modern forms of meditation. In P.M. Lehrer & R.L. Woolfolk (Eds.), *Principles and practices of stress management* (2nd ed.). New York: The Guilford Press.

Carson, R.C., Butcher, J.N., & Mineka, S. (1996). *Abnormal psychology and modern life* (10th ed.). New York: Harper Collins College.

Carter, M.J., Van Andel, G.E., & Robb, G.M. (1995). *Therapeutic recreation: A practical approach* (2nd ed.). Prospect Heights, IL: Waveland Press, Inc.

Cartledge, G., & Milburn, J.F. (1995). *Teaching social skills to children and youth* (3rd ed.). Boston: Allyn and Bacon.

Cartledge, G., & Milburn, J.F. (Eds.). (1986). *Teaching social skills to children* (2nd ed.). New York: Pergamon Press.

Cass, M.A. (1993). *Adventure therapy: Therapeutic applications of adventure programming.* Dubuque, IA: Kendall/Hunt Publishing Company.

Cassetta, R.A. (1993). Healing through caring touch. *The American Nurse,* July/August, p.18.

Cautela, J. R. (1977) *Behavior analysis forms for clinical intervention.* Champaign, IL: Research Press.

Cautela, J. R., & Groden, J. (1978). *Relaxation.* Champaign, IL: Research Press Company.

Center for Pet Therapy. (n.d.). *Center for pet therapy highlights third annual therapeutic recreation forum of New York State Recreation and Park Society.* New York: Center for Pet Therapy.

Centers for Disease Control. (1987). *Recommendations for prevention of HIV transmission in health-care centers.* MMWR, 36, suppl. 25.

Chakravorty, D., Trunnell, E.P., & Ellis, G.D. (1995). Ropes course participation and postactivity processing in transient depressed mood on hospitalized adult psychiatric patients. *Therapeutic Recreation Journal, 29* (2), 104-113.

Chapman, J. E., & Chapman, H. H. (1975). *Behavior and health care: A humanistic helping process.* St. Louis: The C.V. Mosby Company.

Chartier, M. R. (1976). Clarity of expression in interpersonal communication. In J. W. Peiffer & J. E. Jones (Eds.), *The 1976 annual handbook for group facilitators*. Iowa City, IA: University Associates.

Cherniss, C. (1980). *Professional burnout in human service organizations.* New York: Praeger Publishers.

Cherniss, C., & Engnatios, E. (1977). Styles of clinical supervision in community mental heath programs. *Journal of Consulting and Clinical Psychology, 45,* 1195-1196.

Chinn, P.L., & Kramer, M.K. (1995). *Theory and nursing: A systematic approach* (4th ed.). St. Louis: Mosby.

Clarke, W. (1967). Remotivation technique: A therapeutic modality. *Therapeutic Recreation Journal, 1* (1), 31, 35, 36.

Coats, B. (1989). *Runner's World training log.* Emmaus, PA: Rodale Press, Inc.

Cohen, R. G., & Lipkin, G. B. (1979). *Therapeutic group work for health professionals.* New York: Springer Publishing Company.

Cohen, S. S. (1987). *The magic of touch.* New York: Harper & Row, Publishers.

Colton, H. (1983). *Touch therapy.* New York: Zebra Books, Kensington Publishing Corp.

Combs, A. W. (1989) *A theory of therapy.* Newbury Park, CA: Sage Publications, Inc.

Combs, M. L., & Slaby, D. A. (1977). Social skills training with children. In B. B. Lahey & A. E. Kazdin (Eds.), *Advances in clinical child psychology, 1,* New York: Plenum Press.

Compton, D., Witt, P. A., & Sanchez, B. (1980). Leisure counseling. *Parks and Recreation, 15* (8), 23-27.

Connolly, M. L. (1977). Leisure counseling: A values clarification and assertive training approach. In A. Epperson, P. A. Witt & G. Hitzhusen (Eds.), *Leisure counseling: An aspect of leisure education.* Springfield, IL: Charles C. Thomas, Publishers.

Constable, J. F., & Russell, D. W. (1986). The effect of social support and the work environment upon burnout among nurses. *Journal of Human Stress, 12* (2), 20-26.

Coopersmith, S. (1967). *The antecedents of self-esteem.* San Francisco: W. H. Freeman and Company.

Corey, G. (1985). *Theory and practices of group counseling* (2nd ed.). Pacific Grove, CA: Brooks/Cole Publishing Company.

Corey, G. (1995). *Theory and practice of group counseling* (4th ed.). Pacific Grove, CA: Brooks/Cole Publishing Company.

Corey, S. C., & Corey, G. (1987). *Groups: Process and practice* (3rd ed.). Pacific Grove, CA: Brooks/Cole Publishing Company.

Cormier, W.H., & Cormier, S. (1991). *Interviewing strategies for helpers: Fundamental skills and cognitive behavioral interventions* (3rd ed.). Pacific Grove, CA: Brooks/Cole Publishing Company.

Cousins, N. (1979). *Anatomy of an illness.* New York: Bantam Books.

Cousins, N. (1983). *The healing heart.* New York: Avon Books.

Craighead, L.W., Craighead, W.E., Kazdin, A.E., & Mahoney, M.J. (1994). *Cognitive and behavioral interventions.* Boston: Allyn and Bacon.

Crawford, M. E., & Mendell, R. (1987). *Therapeutic recreation and adapted physical activities for mentally retarded individuals.* Englewood Cliffs, NJ: Prentice-Hall, Inc.

Critchley, D.L. (1995). Play therapy. In B.S. Johnson (Ed.). *Child, adolescent and family psychiatric nursing.* Philadelphia: J.B. Lippincott Company.

Crocker, J. W., & Wrobleski, M. (1975). Using recreational games in counseling. *Personnel and Guidance Journal, 53,* 453-458.

Dainow, S., & Bailey, C. (1988). *Developing skill with people: Training for person to person client contact.* New York: Wiley.

Damon, J., & May, R. (1986). The effects of pet facilitative therapy on patients and staff in an adult day care center. *Activities, Adaption, and Aging, 8* (3/4), 117-131.

Dattilo, J., & Mirenda, P. (1987). An application of a leisure preference assessment protocol for persons with severe handicaps. *Journal of the Association for Persons with Severe Handicaps, 12* (4), 306-311.

Dattilo, J., & Murphy, W. D. (1987). *Behavior modification in therapeutic recreation.* State College, PA: Venture Publishing.

Dattilo, J., & Murphy, W. D. (1987). Facilitating the challenge in adventure recreation for persons with disabilities. *Therapeutic Recreation Journal, 21* (3). 14-21.

David, D. (1990). Reminiscence, adaptation, and social context in old age. *International Journal of Aging and Human Development, 30*(3), 175-188.

Davis, P. (1995). *Aromatherapy: An a-z.* NY: Barnes & Noble Books.

Deci, E. L., & Ryan R.M. (1985). *Intrinsic motivation and self-determination in human behavior.* New York: Plenum Press.

Deig, L. (1989). *Reminiscence.* Unpublished paper. Bloomington, IN: Indiana University.

DeSalvatore, H.G. (1989). Therapeutic recreators as family therapists: Working with families on a children's psychiatric unit. *Therapeutic Recreation Journal, 23* (2), 23-29.

DeSalvatore, G., & Rosenman, D. (1986). The parent-child activity group: Therapeutic activities to use in parent-child interactions. *Child Care Quarterly, 15,* 211-222.

Diebert, A. N., & Harmon, A. J. (1977). *New tools for changing behavior.* Champaign, IL: Research Press.

Doman, G., Wilkinsin, R., Dimancescu, M.D., & Pelligra, R. (1993). The effect of intense multi-sensory stimulation on coma arousal and recovery. *Neuropsychological Rehabilitation, 3* (2), 203-212.

Dowing, G. (1972). *The message book.* New York: Bookworks/Random House.

Dreifuss, F. E. (1988). What is epilepsy? In H. Reisner (Ed.), *Children with epilepsy.* Kensington, MD: Woodbine House.

Duck, S. (1986). *Human relationships: An introduction to social psychology.* London: SAGE Publications.

Dunn, H. L. (1961). *High-level wellness.* Arlington, VA: R. W. Beatty.

Dunn, J. D. (1989). Guidelines for using published assessment procedures. *Therapeutic Recreation Journal, 23* (2), 59-69.

Dusay, J. M., & Dusay, K. M. (1984). Transactional analysis. In R. J. Corsini (Ed.) *Current psychotherapies* (3rd ed.). Itasca, IL: F. E. Peacock Publishers, Inc.

Dusek-Girdano, D. (1979). Stress reduction through physical activity. In D. Girdano & G. Everly (Eds.), *Controlling stress & tension: A holistic approach.* Englewood Cliffs, NJ: Prentice-Hall, Inc.

Edelwich, J., & Brodsky, A. (1980). *Burn-out: Stages of disillusionment in the helping professions.* New York: Human Science Press.

Edinberg, M. A. (1985). *Mental health practice with the elderly.* Englewood Cliffs, NJ: Prentice-Hall, Inc.

Egan, G. (1976). *Interpersonal living: A skills/contact approach to human-relations training in groups.* Monterey, CA: Brooks/Cole.

Egan, G. (1994). *Exercises in helping skills: A manual to accompany the skilled helper.* (5th ed.). Pacific Grove, CA: Brooks/Cole Publishing Company.

Egan, G. (1994). *The skilled helper: A problem-management approach to helping* (5th ed.). Pacific Grove, CA: Brooks/Cole Publishing Company.

Eisenberg, S & Delaney, D. J. (1986). *The counseling process* (2nd ed.). Chicago: Rand McNally College Publishing Company.

Eisenberg, S., & Patterson, L. E. (1977). *Helping clients with special concerns.* Chicago: Rand McNally College Publishing Company.

Ekberg, J. (1990). Senior fitness: Getting into the swim of things. *Parks & Recreation, 25* (2), 46-49.

Ellis, A. (1976). Rational-emotive therapy. In V. Binder, A. Binder, & B. Rimland (Eds.), *Modern therapies.* Englewood Cliffs, NJ: Prentice-Hall, Inc.

Ellis, A. (1984). Rational-emotive therapy. In R. J. Corsini (Ed.), *Current psychotherapies.* (3rd ed.). Itasca, IL: F. E. Peacock Publishers, Inc.

Ellis, G. D. (1987). A comparison of major assessment paradigms. Unpublished table. Salt Lake City, University of Utah.

Ellis, M.J. (1973). *Why people play.* Englewood Cliffs, NJ: Prentice-Hall, Inc.

Epilepsy school alert. (1974). Landover. MD: Epilepsy Foundation of America.

Epilepsy Foundation of America. (1975). *Basic statistics on the epilepsies.* Philadelpia: F. A. Davis Company.

Epstein, E. S., & Loos, V. E. (1989). Some irreverent thoughts on the limits of family therapy. *Journal of Family Psychology, 2,* 405-421.

Eubanks, R. E. (1976). Relationships: The manifestation of humanness. In G. A . Borden & J. D. Stone (Eds.)*Human communication: The process of relating.* Menlo Park, CA: Cummings Publishing Company.

Evans, D.R., Hearn, M.T., Uhlemann, M.R., & Ivey, A.E. (1993). *Essential interviewing: A programmed approach to effective communication* (4th ed.). Pacific Grove, CA: Brooks/Cole Publishing Company.

Ewert, A. (1987). Research in outdoor adventure: Overview and analysis. *The Bradford Papers Annual, 2,* 15-28.

Feil, N. (1993). *The validation breakthrough: Simple techniques for communicating with people with "Alzheimer's-type dementia."* Baltimore: Health Professionals Press.

Feldman, R.S. (1995). *Social psychology.* Englewood Cliffs, NJ: Prentice Hall.

Ferguson, D. D. (1983). Assessment interviewing techniques: A useful tool in developing individual program plans. *Therapeutic Recreation Journal, 17* (2), 16-22.

Ferrini, A. F., & Ferrini, R. L. (1989). *Health in the later years*. Dubuque, IA: Wm. C. Brown Publishers.

Fick, K.M. (1993). The influence of an animal on social interactions of nursing home residents in a group setting. *The American Journal of Occupational Therapy, 47*(6), 529-534.

Fidler, G. S., & Fidler, J. W. (1954). *Introduction to psychiatric occupational therapy*. New York: The MacMillan Company.

Field, C. (1989). *Reminiscing*. Unpublished paper. Bloomington, IN: Indiana University.

Fikes, C. R. (1976). A description of leisure counseling services in Texas community mental health and mental retardation centers. Unpublished master's thesis. Denton, TX: North Texas State University.

Fillingim, R.B., & Blumenthal, J.S. (1993). The use of aerobic exercise as a method of stress management. In P.M. Lehrer & R.L. Woolfolk (Eds.), *Principles and practice of stress management* (2nd ed.). NY: The Guilford Press.

Fine, A. H., & Fine, N. M. (1988). *Therapeutic recreation for exceptional children*. Springfield, IL: Charles C. Thomas Publisher.

Flynn, J. M., & Heffron, P. B. (1988). *Nursing: From concept to practice*. (2nd ed.). Norwalk, CT: Appleton & Lange.

Flynn, P. A. R. (1980). *Holistic health*. Bowie, MD: Robert J. Brady Co.

Fogle, B. (1984). *Pets and their people*. New York: Viking Press.

Folsom, J. C. (1968). Reality orientation for the elderly mental patient. *Journal of Geriatric Psychiatry, 1*, 291-307.

Ford, C.W. (1992). Where healing waters meet touch: Mind & emotion through the body. Barrytown, NY: Station Hill Press.

Ford, D. H., & Urban, H.B. (1963). *Systems of psychotherapy*. New York: John Wiley & Sons, Inc.

Fow, S.R. (1995). *Using photo therapy to promote healing and personal growth*. Educational session at the American Therapeutic Recreation Association Annual Conference, October 14, 1995, Louisville, Kentucky.

Fox, R. (1983). Contracting in supervision: A goal-directed process. *The Clinical Supervisor, 1* (1), 37-49.

Freeman, J.M., Vining, E.P.G., & Pillas, D.J. (1990). *Seizures and epilepsy in childhood: A guide for parents*. Baltimore, MD: Johns Hopkins University Press.

French, J., & Raven, B. (1959). The basis for social power. In D. C. Artwright (Ed.), *Studies in social power*. Ann Arbor, MI: Institution for Social Research.

Freudenberger, H. (1975). The staff burnout syndrome in alternative institutions. *Psychotherapy: Theory, research, and practice. 12*, 73-83.

Friedman, H. J. (1985). Horticulture in the treatment of recovering alcoholics. *Leisure Information Quarterly, 11* (3), 5,6+.

Friedman, M. M. (1992). *Family nursing: Theory and practice* (3rd ed.). Norwalk, CT: Appleton & Lange.

Fry, W.F. (1993). Introduction. In W.F. Fry & W.A. Salameh (Eds.), *Advances in humor and psychotherapy*. Sarasota, FL: Professional Resource Press.

Fry, W.F., & Salameh, W.A. (Eds.). (1993). *Advances in humor and psychotherapy*. Sarasota, FL: Professional Resource Press.

Frye, V., & Peters, M. (1972). *Therapeutic recreation: Its theory, philosophy and practice*. Harrisburg, PA: Stackpole Books.

Furstenburg, F. F., Rhodes, P. S., Powell, S. K., & Dunlop, T. (1984).The effectiveness of pet therapy on nursing home patients suffering with dementia. *Gerontologist, 24,* 245.

Gass, M.A. (1933). *Adventure therapy.* Dubuque, IA: Kendall-Hunt Publishers.

Gatchel, R. J. (1980). Perceived control: A review and evaluation of therapeutic implications. In A. Baum & J. E. Singer (Eds.), *Advances in environmental psychology: Volume 2. Applications of perceived control.* Hillsdale, NJ: Lawrence Erlbaum Associates, Publishers.

Gayle, J. (1989). *Reminiscence as a therapeutic intervention.* Unpublished paper. Bloomington, IN: Indiana University.

Gazda, G.M. (1982). Group psychotherapy and group counseling. In G.M. Gazda (Ed.), *Basic approaches to group psychotherapy and group counseling* (3rd ed.). Springfield, IL: Charles C. Thomas Publisher.

Geis, H. J. (1986). Why not prescribe a cat? *Prevention, 38* (10). 97-103.

Gergen, K. J. (1971). *The concept of self.* New York: Holt, Rinehart and Winston, Inc.

Gergen, K. J., & Gergen, M. M. (1986). *Social psychology.* (2nd ed.). New York: Springer Verlag.

Getchell, B. (1988), *The fitness book.* Indianapolis: Benchmark Press, Inc.

Gibson, J. L., Ivancevich, J., & Donnelly, J. H. (1988). *Organizations: Behavior, structure, processes* (6th ed.). Dallas: Business Publications, Inc.

Gilkey, W. A. (1986). *Biofeedback: Leaning to relax.* Bloomington, IN: South Central Community Mental Health Center, Inc.

Gillis, H.L., & Simpson, C. (1993). Project choices: Adventure-based residential drug treatment for court-referred youth. In M.A. Gass (Ed.). *Adventure therapy: Therapeutic applications of adventure programming.* Dubuque, IA: Kendall/ Hunt Publishing.

Girdano, D., & Everly, G. (1986). *Controlling stress & tension: A holistic approach* (2nd ed.). Englewood Cliffs, NJ: Prentice-Hall, Inc.

Girdano, D.A., Everylym G.S., & Dusek, D.E. (1993). *Controlling stress and tension: A holistic approach* (4th ed.). Englewood Cliffs, NJ: Prentice-Hall.

Glasser, W. (1965). *Reality therapy: A new approach to psychiatry.* New York: Harper and Row.

Glasser, W. (1976). Reality therapy, In V. Binder, A. Binder, & B. Rimland (Eds.), *Modern therapies.* Englewood Cliffs, NJ: Prentice-Hall, Inc.

Glasser, W. (1984). Reality therapy. In R. J. Corsini (Ed.), *Current psychotherapies* (3rd ed.). Itasca, IL: F. E. Peacock Publishers, Inc.

Gordon, C., & Gergen, K. J. (1968). *The self in social interaction.* New York: John Wiley & Sons.

Gordon, T. (1977). *Leader effectiveness training: L.E.T.* New York: Wyden Books.

Gray, D. E. (1975).The future of American society. In J. F. Murphy, the epilogue to *Recreation and leisure services.* Dubuque, IA: Wm. C. Brown Company, Publishers.

Greiner, D.S., & Demi, A.A. (1995). Family therapy. In B.S. Johnson (Ed.), *Child, adolescent & family psychiatric nursing.* Philadelphia: J.B. Lippincott Company.

Gronlund, N. E. (1985). *Stating behavioral objectives for classroom instruction.* (3rd ed.). London: The MacMillan Company.

Grossman, A.H., & Caroleo, O. (1986). Acquired immuno-deficiency syndrome (AIDS). In D.R. Austin & M.E. Crawford (Eds.), *Therapeutic recreation: An introduction,*2nd ed. Boston: Allyn & Bacon.

Growing confidence—Horticulture and stroke recovery. (1993). *Stroke Connection.* Golden Valley, MI: Courage Center.

Gruver, B. M., & Austin, D. R. (1990). The instructional status of clinical supervision in therapeutic recreation curricula. *Therapeutic Recreation Journal,* 24 (2), 18-24.

Grzdlak, J. L. (1985). Desire for control: Cognitive, emotional and behavioral consequences. In F. L. Denmark (Ed.), *Social/ecological psychology and the psychology of women.* New York: Elsevier Science Publishing Company, Inc.

Gunn, S. L. (1977). Leisure counseling: An analysis of play behavior and attitudes using transactional analysis and Gestalt awareness. In A. Epperson, P. A. Witt & G. Hitzhusen (Eds.), *Leisure counseling: An aspect of leisure education.* Springfield, IL: Charles C. Thomas, Publisher.

Gussen, J. (1967). The psychodynamics of leisure. In P. A. Martin (Ed.), *Leisure and mental health: A psychiatric viewpoint.* Washington, D.C.: American Psychiatric Association.

Gustafson, G. R., & Dorneden, M. A. (1988). Animal-assisted therapy: Its value in therapeutic recreation programming. *Leisure Information Quarterly, 15* (1), 4,5.

Haber, J., Leach-McMahon, A., Price-Hoskins, P., & Sideleau, B.F. (1992). *Comprehensive psychiatric nursing* (4th ed.). St. Louis: Mosby.

Hackney, H., & Cormier S. (1988). *Counseling strategies and interventions* (3rd ed.). Englewood Cliffs, NJ: Prentice-Hall, Inc.

Hales, D., & Hales, R.E. (1995). *Caring for the mind: The comprehensive guide to mental health.* New York: Bantam Books.

Hall, E. T. (1966). *The hidden dimension.* New York: Doubleday/Anchor.

Hamilton, E.J., & Austin, D.R. (1992). Future perspectives of therapeutic recreation. *Annual in Therapeutic Recreation, 3,* 72-79.

Hansen, J. C., Warner, R. W., & Smith E. M. (1980). *Group counseling: Theory and process* (2nd ed.). Chicago: Rand McNally College Publishing Company.

Harper, F. D. (1984). Jogotherapy: Jogging as psychotherapy. In M. L. Sachs & G. W. Buffone (Eds.), *Running as therapy: An integrated approach.* Lincoln, NE: University of Nebraska Press.

Harré, R., & Lamb, R. (Eds.) (1986). *The dictionary of personality and social psychology.* Cambridge, MA: The MIT Press.

Harris, E. (1981). Antidepressants: Old drugs, new uses. *American Journal of Nursing, 81* (7), 1308-1309.

Harris, T. A. (1976). Transactional analysis: An introduction. In V. Binder, A. Binder, & B. Rimland (Eds.), *Modern therapies.* Englewood Cliffs, NJ: Prentice-Hall, Inc.

Harrow, A. J. (1972). *A taxonomy of the psychomotor domain.* New York: David McKay Company, Inc.

Hart, G. M. (1982). *The process of clinical supervision.* Baltimore, MD: University Park Press.

Hauser, W.A., & Hesdorffer, D.C. (1990). *Epilepsy: Frequency, causes and consequences.* Landover, MD: Epilepsy Foundation of America.

Hawkin, M., & Ozuna, J. (1979). Practical aspects of anticonvulsant therapy. *American Journal of Nursing, 79* (6), 1062-1068.

Heider, F. (1944). Social perception and phenomenal causality. *Psychological Review, 51*, 358-374.

Henderson, S. (1980). A development in social psychiatry: The systematic study of social bonds. *The Journal of Nervous and Mental Disease, 168* (2), 63-69.

Hewitt, C. (1988). Training in social skills. In M. Willson (Ed.), *Occupational therapy in short-term psychiatry* (2nd ed.). New York: Churchill Livingstone.

Hewitt, J. (1985). *Teach yourself relaxation.* New York: Random House, Inc.

Heywood, L. A. (1978). Perceived recreative experience and relief of tension. *Journal of Leisure Research, 10*, 86-97.

Higginbotham, H. N., West, S. G. & Forsyth, D. R. (1988). *Psychotherapy and behavior change: Social, cultural, and methodological perspectives.* New York: Pergamon Press.

Hill, L., & Smith, N. (1985). *Self-care nursing.* Norwalk, CT: Appleton-Century-Crofts.

Hogan, R. A. (1964). Issues and approaches in supervision. *Psychotherapy: Theory, Research, and Practice, 1*, 139-141.

Hogg, J. & Raynes, N. V. (1987). Assessing people with mental handicap: An introduction. In J. Hoog & N. V. Raynes (Eds.). *Assessment in mental handicap.* Cambridge, MA: Brookline Books.

Hollin, C. R., & Trower, P. (Eds.). (1986). *Handbook of social skills training: Volume 2.* New York: Pergamon Press.

Holloway, E.L. (1995). *Clinical supervision: A systems approach.* Thousand Oaks, CA: SAGE Publications, Inc.

Hoozer, H. V., Ruther, L., & Craft, M. (1982). *Introduction to charting.* Philadelphia: J. B. Lippincott Company.

Horner, A.J. (1993). Occupational hazards and characterological vulnerability: The problem of "burnout." *The American Journal of Psychoanalysis, 53* (2), 137-142.

Howe, C. Z. (1984). Leisure assessment instrumentation in therapeutic recreation. *Therapeutic Recreation Journal, 18* (2), 14-24.

Howe-Murphy, R., & Charboneau, B.G. (1987). *Therapeutic recreation intervention: An ecological perspective.* Englewood Cliffs, NJ: Prentice-Hall, Inc.

Hultzman, J. T., Black, D. R., Seehafer, R. W., & Hovell, M. F. (1987). The Purdue stepped approach model: Application to leisure couseling service delivery. *Therapeutic Recreation Journal, 21* (4), 9-22.

Hunter, M.C., & Carlson, P. V. (1971). *Improving your child's behavior.* Glendale, CA: Bomar.

Huss, A. J. (1977). Touch with care or a caring touch? *The American Journal of Occupational Therapy, 31* (1), 11-18.

Hussian, R. A., & Davis, R. L. (1985). *Responsive care: Behavioral interventions with elderly persons.* Champaign, IL: Research Press.

Ismail, A. H., & Trachtman, L. E. (1973). Jogging the imagination. *Psychology Today, 6* (10), 78-82.

Iso-Ahola, S. E. (1980). Perceived control and responsibility as mediators of the effects of therapeutic recreation on the institutionalized aged. *Therapeutic Recreation Journal, 14*(1), 36-43.

Iso-Ahola, S. E. (1980). *The social psychology of leisure and recreation.* Dubuque, IA: Wm. C. Brown Company Publishers.

Iso-Ahola, S. E. (1984). Social psychological foundations of leisure and resultant implications for leisure counseling. In E. T. Dowd (Ed.), *Leisure counseling: Concepts and applications.* Springfield, IL: Charles C. Thomas.

Iso-Ahola, S. E. (1989). Motivation for leisure. In E. L. Jackson & T. L. Burton (Eds.), *Understanding leisure and recreation: Mapping the past, charting the future.* State College, PA: Venture Publishing, Inc.

Ivey, A.E., Ivey, M.B., & Simek-Morgan, L. (1993). *Counseling and psychotherapy: A multicultural perspective* (3rd ed.). Boston: Allyn and Bacon.

James, M., & Jongward, D. (1971). *Born to win: Transactional analysis with Gestalt experiments.* Reading, MA: Addison-Wesley Publishing Company.

Jessee, E. M. (1982). Pet therapy for the elderly. *Aging,* 331-332, 26-28.

Johnson B.S. (1995). *Child, adolescent & family psychiatric nursing.* Philadelphia: J.B. Lippincott Company.

Jones, J. J., & Pfeiffer, J. W. (Eds.). (1972). What to look for in groups. *The 1972 annual handbook for group facilitators.* Iowa City, IA: University Associates.

Jones, S. L., & Dimond, M. (1982). Family theory and family therapy models: Comparative review with implications for nursing practice. *Journal of Psychosocial Nursing and Mental Health Services, 20* (10), 12-19.

Kahn, E. M. (1979). The parallel process in social work: Treatment and supervision. *Social Casework, 60* (9), 520-528.

Kanfer, F.J., & Goldstein, A.P. (1991). Helping people change: A textbook of methods (4th ed.). NY: Pergamon Press.

Kaplan, H.I., & Sadock, B. (1995). *Comprehensive textbook of psychology/VI* (6th ed.). Baltimore, MD: Williams & Weilkins.

Karras, B. (1987). Music and reminiscence: For groups and individuals. In B. Karras (Ed.), *You bring out the music in me: Music in nursing homes.* New York: The Haworth Press.

Kaslow, F. W. (1986). Supervision, consultation and staff training— creative teaching/learning processes in the mental health profession. In F. W. Kaslow (Ed.), *Supervision and training: Models, dilemmas and challenges.* New York: The Haworth Press.

Kelley, H. H. (1950). The warm-cold variable in first impressions of persons. *Journal of Personality, 18,* 431-439.

Kelley, J. (Ed.). (1981). *Recreation programming for visually impaired children and youth.* New York: American Foundation for the Blind.

Kelly, J. R. (1982). *Leisure: An introduction.* Englewood Cliffs. NJ: Prentice-Hall, Inc.

Kibler, R. J., Barker, L. L., & Miles, D. T. (1970). *Behavioral objectives and instruction.* Boston: Allyn and Bacon, Inc.

Killen, K. H. (1977). *Management: A middle-management approach.* Boston: Houghton Mifflin Company.

King, I. M. (1971). *Toward a theory of nursing.* New York: John Wiley and Sons, Inc.

Knickerbocker, I. (1969). Leadership: A conception and some implications. In C. A. Gibb (Ed.). *Leadership.* Baltimore: Penguin Books.

Knowles, M., & Knowles, H. (1959). *Introduction to group dynamics.* New York: Associated Press.

Kongable, L.G., Buckwalter, K.C., & Stolley, J.M. (1989). The effects of pet therapy on the social behavior of institutionalzied Alzheimer's clients. *Archives of Psychiatric Nursing, 3*(4), 191-198.

Kovel, J. (1976) *A complete guide to therapy: From psychoanalysis to behavior modification.* New York: Pantheon Books.

Kraus, R. G., Carpenter, G. & Bates, B. J. (1981). *Recreation leadership and supervision: Guidelines for professional development* (2nd ed.). Dubuque, IA: Wm. C. Brown Publishers.

Kraus, R. (1983). *Therapeutic recreation service: Principles and practices* (3rd ed.). Philadelphia: W.B. Saunders company.

Krieger, D. (1979). *The therapeutic touch: How to use your hands to help or to heal.* Englewood Cliffs, NJ: Prentice-Hall Inc.

Kuhlman, T.L. (1993). Humor in stressful milieus. In W.F. Fry & W.A. Salameh (Eds.), *Advances in humor and psychotherapy.* Sarasota, FL: Professional Resource Press.

Kutner, B. (1971). The social psychology of disability. In W. S. Neff (Ed.), *Rehabilitation psychology.* Washington D.C.: American Psychological Association, Inc.

Lamport, N.K. Coffey, M.S., & Hersch, G.I. (1993). *Activity analysis handbook* (2nd ed.). Thorofare, NJ: SLACK Incorporated.

Lamson, A. (1986). *Guide for the beginning therapist.* (2nd ed.). New York: Human Sciences Press.

Langer, E. J., & Rodin, J. (1976). The effects of choice and enhanced personal responsibility for the aged: A field experiment in an institutional setting. *Journal of Personality and Social Psychology, 34,* 191-198.

Lawrence, D. B., & Harrison, L. (1983). *Massageworks.* New York: Putnam.

Lazarus, A. A. (1984). Multimodal therapy. In R. J. Corsini (Ed.), *Current Psychotherapies* (3rd ed.). Itasca, IL: F. E. Peacock Publishers, Inc.

Lazarus, A. A. (1989). *The practice of multimodal therapy.* Baltimore: The John Hopkins University Press.

Lazarus, A.A. (1992). The multimodal approach to the treatment of minor depression. *American Journal of Psychotherapy, 46* (1), 50-57.

Leary, M. R., & Miller, R. S. (1986). *Social psychology and dysfunctional behavior: Origins, diagnosis, and treatment.* New York: Springer-Verlag.

Lehrer, P.M. & Woolfolk, R.L. (Eds). (1993). *Principles and practice of stress management* (2nd edition). New York: Guilford Press.

Leitner, M. J., & Leitner, S. F. (1985). Recreation leadership principles. *Activities, Adaptation, & Aging, 7*(3/4), 25-41.

LeUnes, A. D., & Nation, J. R. (1989). *Sport psychology: An introduction.* Chicago: Nelson-Hall.

Levitt, S. (1988). Pet two poodles and call me in the morning. *50 Plus, 28* (7), 56-61.

Levy, J. (1982). Behavioral observation techniques in assessing change in therapeutic recreation/play settings. *Therapeutic Recreation Journal, 16* (1). 25-32.

Li, R. K. K. (1981). Activity therapy and leisure counseling for the schizophrenic population. *Therapeutic Recreation Journal, 15* (4), 44-49.

Lidell, L. (1984). *The book of massage.* New York: A Fireside Book.

Lindberg, J., Hunter, M., & Kruszewski, A. (1983). *Introduction to person-centered nursing.* New York: J. B. Lippincott Company.

Linden, W. (1993). The autogenic training method of J.H. Schultz. In P.M. Lehrer & R.L. Woolfolk (Eds.), *Principles and practices of stress management* (2nd ed.). New York: The Guilford Press.

Loganbill, C., Hardy, E., & Delworth, U. (1982). Supervision: A conceptual model. *The Counseling Psychologist. 10*, 3-42.

Long, G. L., Higgins, P. G., & Brady, D. (1988). *Psychosocial assessment: A pocket guide for data collection*. Norwalk, CT: Appleton & Lange.

Longo, D. C., & Williams, R. A. (1986). *Clinical practice in psychosocial nursing: Assessment and intervention*. (2nd ed.). New York: Appleton-Century-Crofts.

Luckmann, J., & Sorensen, K. C. (1980). *Medical-surgical nursing: A psychophysiologic approach*. (2nd ed.). Philadelphia: W.B. Saunders Company.

Luckner, J.L., & Nadler, R.S. (1995). Processing adventure experiences: It's the story that counts. *Therapeutic Recreation Journal, 29* (3), 175-183.

Luft, J. (1984). *Group processes—An introduction*. Mountain View, CA: Mayfield Publishing Company.

Lumsden, L. (1986). *The healing power of humor*. Bloomington, IN: South Central Community Mental Health Centers, Inc.

Lynch, J. (1989). Relax to the max. *Runner's World, 24* (3), 39, 40.

Macrae, J. (1993). *Therapeutic touch: A practical guide*. NY: Alfred A. Knopf.

Maddi, S.R. (1996). *Personality theories: A comparative analysis* (6th ed.). Pacific Grove, CA: Brooks/Cole Publishing Company.

Mager, F. (1962). *Preparing instructional objectives*. Belmont, CA: Fearson Press.

Maloff, C., & Wood, S. M. (1988). *Business and social etiquette with disabled people*. Springfield, IL: Charles C. Thomas Publishers.

Marcer, D. (1986). *Biofeedback and related therapies in clinical practice*. Rockville, MD: Aspen Publishers, Inc.

Marriner, A. (1983). *The nursing process: A scientific approach to nursing care* (3rd ed.). St. Louis: The C. V. Mosby Company.

Martens, R. (1975). *Social psychology and physical activity*. New York: Harper & Row, Publishers.

Maslach, C. (1982). *Burnout: The cost of caring*. Englewood Cliffs, NJ: Prentice-Hall, Inc.

Maslow, A. H. (1970). *Motivation and personality* (2nd ed.). New York: Harper & Row, Publishers.

Mason, L. J. (1985). *Guide to stress reduction*. Berkeley, CA: Celestial Arts.

Matson, K. (1977). *The psychology today omnibook of personal development*. New York: William Morrow and Company, Inc.

Maxwell-Hudson, C. (1988). *The complete book of massage*. New York: Random House.

Mayeroff, M. (1971). *On caring*. New York: Harper & Row, Publishers.

McBride, G. (1983). Teachers, stress, and burnout. In R. E. Schmid & L. M. Nagata (Eds.), *Contemporary issues in special education*. New York: McGraw-Hill Book Company.

McCandless, P., McCready, K.F., & Knight, L. (1985). A model animal therapy prorgram for mental health settings. *Therapeutic Recreation Journal, 19* (2), 55-63.

McDavid, J. W., & Harari, H. (1968). *Social psychology, individuals, groups, societies*. New York: Harper & Row, Publishers.

McDowell, C. F. (1974). Toward a healthy leisure mode: Leisure counseling. *Therapeutic Recreation Journal, 8* (3), 96-104.

McDowell, C. F. (1980). Leisure counseling issues: Reviews, overviews, & previews. In F. Humphrey, J. D. Kelley, & E. J. Hamilton (Eds.), *Facilitating leisure development for the disabled: A status report on leisure counseling*. College Park, MD: University of Maryland.

McDowell, C.F. (1984). Leisure: consciousness, well-being, and counseling. In E. T. Dowd (Ed.), *Leisure counseling: Concepts and applications*. Springfield, IL: Charles C. Thomas Publishers.

McFarland, K. M., & Wasli, E. L. (1986). *Nursing diagnosis and process in psychiatric nursing*. Philadelphia: J. B. Lippincott.

McGuire, F., Boyd, R., & Tedrick ,R.T. (1995). Preventing caregiver burnout. *Recreation Focus, 3*(1)4.

McKechnie, A. A., Wilson, F., Watson, N., & Scott, D. (1983). Anxiety states: A preliminary report on the value of connective tissue massage. *Journal of Psychosomatic Research, 27,* 125-129.

McKechnie, G. E. (n.d.) *Manual for the leisure activities blank*. Palo Alto, CA: Consulting Psychology Press.

McKechnie, G. E. (1974). Psychological foundations of leisure counseling: An empirical strategy. *Therapeutic Recreation Journal, 8* (1), 4-16.

Mead, G. H. (1934). *Mind, self, and society*. Chicago: University of Chicago Press.

Meador, B. D., & Rogers, C. R. (1984). Person-centered therapy. In R. Corsini (Ed.), *Current psychotherapies* (3rd ed.). Itasca, IL: F. E. Peacock Publishers, Inc.

Menninger, W. C. (1960). Recreation and mental health. *Recreation and psychiatry*. New York: National Recreation Association.

Meyer, M. W. (1962). The rationale of recreation as therapy. *Recreation in treatment centers (Vol. 1)*. Washington, D.C.: National Therapeutic Recreation Society, National Recreation and Park Association.

Mikulincer, M. (1988). Reactance and helplessness following exposure to unsolvable problems: The effects of attributional style. *Journal of Personality and Social Psychology, 54,* 679-686.

Miller, E. E. (1986). *Self imagery: Creating your own good health*. Berkeley, CA: Celestial Arts.

Miller, M. (1989). *Documentation in long-term care*. Alexandria, VA: National Therapeutic Recreation Society, National Recreation and Park Association.

Mirenda, J. J. (1973). Mirenda leisure interest finder. In A. Epperson, J. Mirenda, R. Overs, & G. T. Wilson, (Eds.), *Leisure Counseling Kit*. Washington, D. C.: American Alliance for Health, Physical Education, and Recreation.

Monroe, J.E. (1987). Family leisure programming. *Therapeutic Recreation Journal, 21* (3), 44-51.

Mosak, H., & Maniacci, M. (1993). An "Adlerian" approach to humor and psychotherapy. In W.F. Fry & W.A. Salameh (Eds.), *Advances in humor and psychotherapy*. Sarasota, FL: Professional Resource Press.

Mosey, A. C. (1973). *Activities therapy*. New York: Raven Press, Publishers.

Muller, B., & Armstrong, H. (1975). A further note on the "running treatment" for anxiety. *Psychotherapy: Theory, research, and practice, 12* (4), 385-367.

Munson, W. W., & Munson, D. G. (1986). Multimodal leisure counseling with older people. *Activities, Adaption & Aging, 9* (1), 1-15.

Murray, R.B., & Huelskotter, M.M.W. (1991). *Psychiatric/mental health nursing* (3rd ed.). Norwalk, CT: Appleton & Lange.

Murphy, J. F. (1975). *Recreation and leisure services.* Dubuque, IA: Wm. C. Brown Company, Publishers.

Murphy, J. F., Williams, J. G., Niepoth, E. W., & Brown, P. D. (1973). *Leisure service delivery system: A modern perspective.* Philadelphia: Lea & Febiger.

Murry, R.B., & Baier, M. (1993). Use of the therapeutic milieu in a community setting. *Journal of Psychosocial Nursing, 31* (10, 11-16.

Murry, R. B., & Huelskoetter, M. M. W. (1987). *Psychiatric/mental health nursing* (2nd ed.). Norwalk, CT: Appleton & Lange.

Myers, D.G. (1996). *Social psychology* (5th ed.). NY: The McGraw-Hill Companies, Inc.

Nadler, R.S., & Luckner, J.L. (1992). *Processing the adventure experience: Theory and practice.* Dubuque, IA: Kendall/Hunt Publishing Company.

Narrow, B. W., & Buschle, K. B. (1987). *Fundamentals of nursing practice* (2nd ed.). New York: John Wiley & Sons.

National Easter Seal Society. (1980). How to handle and push a wheelchair. In D. Austin and L. Powell (Eds.), *Resource guide: College instruction in recreation for individuals with handicapping conditions.* Bloomington: Indiana University.

Newton, M., Godbey, K. L., Newton, D. W., & Godbey, A. L. (1978). How you can improve the effectiveness of psychotropic drug therapy. *Nursing 78, 8* (7), 46-55.

Nicholi, A .M. (Ed.). (1988). *The new Harvard guide to psychiatry.* Cambridge, MA: The Belnap Press.

Nickerson, E. T., & O'Laughlin, K S. (1982). It's fun—but will it work?: The use of games as a therapeutic medium for children and adolescents. In E. T. Nickerson & K. O'Laughlin (Eds.), *Helping through action:Action-oriented therapies.* Amherst, MA: Human Resources Development Press.

Niles, S., Ellis, G., & Witt, P. A. (1981). Attribution scales: Control, competence, intrinsic motivation. In G. Ellis & P. A. Witt (Eds.), *The leisure diagnostic battery: Background conceptualization and structure.* Denton, TX: North Texas State University, Division of Recreation and Leisure Studies.

Nugent, E. (1995). Try to remember . . . Reminiscence as a nursing intervention. *Journal of Psychosocial Nursing, 33*(11), 7-11.

Okun, B. F. (1992). *Effective helping: Interviewing and counseling techniques* (4th ed.). Pacific Grove, CA: Brooks/Cole Publishing Company.

Olson, O. C. (1988). *Diagnosis and management of diabetes mellitus* (2nd ed.). New York: Raven Press.

Olsson, R. H., Shearer, T. W., & Halberg, K. J. (1988). The effectiveness of a computerized leisure assessment system for individuals with spinal cord injuries. *Journal of Expanding Horizons in Therapeutic Recreation, 3,* 35-40.

O'Morrow, G. S. (1971). The whys of recreation activities for psychiatric patients. *Therapeutic Recreation Journal, 5* (3), 97-103+.

O'Morrow, G. S. (1980). *Therapeutic recreation: A helping profession* (2nd ed.). Reston, VA: Reston Publishing Company, Inc.

O'Morrow, G. S., & Reynolds, R. P. (1989). *Therapeutic recreation: A helping profession* (3rd ed.). Englewood Cliffs, NJ: Prentice-Hall, Inc.

Ornstein, R., & Sobel, D. (1989). *Healthy pleasures*. New York: Addison-Wesley Publishing Company, Inc.

O'Toll, A. W., & Morofka, V. (1984). Designing a graduate program in psychiatric nursing. In S. Lego (Ed.), *The American handbook of psychiatric nursing*. Philadelphia: J. B. Lippincott Company.

Overs, R. P. (1970). A model for avocational counseling. *Journal of Health, Physical Education, and Recreation, 41* (2), 28-36.

Owen, B. D. (1980). How to avoid that aching back. *American Journal of Nursing, 80* (5), 894-897.

Page, S., & Wosket, V. (1994). *Supervising the counselor: A cyclical model*. New York: Routledge.

Palmer, L. L., & Sadler, R. R. (1979). *The effects of a running program on depression in rehabilitation clients*. Unpublished research report. Fisherville, VA: Research Utilization Laboratory, Woodrow Wilson Rehabilitation Center.

Panada, K. C., & Lynch, W. W. (1972). Effects of social reinforcement on the retarded child: A review of interpretation for classroom insruction. *Education and Training of the Mentally Retarded, 7*, 115.

Parke, R. D., & Sawin, D. B. (1975). *Aggression: Causes and controls*. Homewood, IL: Learning Systems Company.

Parker, R., Ellison, C., Kirby, T. & Short, M.J. (1975). The comprehensive evaluation in recreation therapy scale: A tool for patient evaluation. *Therapeutic Recreation Journal, 9* (4), 143-152.

Patrick, P. K. S. (1981). *Health care worker burnout: What it is, what to do about it*. Chicago: An Inquiry Book.

Pender, N. J. (1987). *Health promotion in nursing practice*. Norwalk, CT: Appleton-Century-Crofts.

Penner, D. (1989). *Eldercise*. Reston, VA: The American Alliance for Health, Physical Education, Recreation, & Dance.

Pep up your life: A fitness book for seniors. (n.d.). Washington D.C.: American Association of Retired Persons.

Perkins School for the Blind. (n.d.). *Horticulture program*. Watertown, MA.

Perko, J. E., & Kreigh, H. Z. (1988). *Psychiatric and mental health nursing* (3rd ed.). Norwalk, CT: Appleton & Lange.

Peterson, C. A. (1976). Activity analysis. In *Leisure activity participation and handicapped populations: Assessment of research needs*. Arlington, VA: National Recreation and Park Association.

Peterson, C. A., & Gunn, S. L. (1984). *Therapeutic recreation program design* (2nd ed.). Englewood Cliffs, NJ: Prentice-Hall, Inc.

Pfeiffer, E. F., & Galloway, J. A (1988). Type II diabetes mellitus and oral hypoglycemic agents. In J. A. Galloway, J. H. Potvin, and C. R. Shuman (Eds.), *Diabetes mellitus* (9th ed.). Indianapolis: Lilly Research Laboratories.

Platt-Koch, L. M. (1986). Clinical supervision for psychiatric nurses. *Journal of Psychosocial Nursing, 26* (1), 7-15.

Posthuma, B. W. (1989). *Small groups in therapy settings: Process and leadership*. Boston: Little, Brown and Company.

Potter, P. A., & Perry, A. G. (1987). *Basic nursing: Theory and practice*. St. Louis: The C. V. Mosby Company.

Price, M. J. (1983). Insulin and oral hypoglycemic agents. *Nursing Clinics of North America, 18* (4), 687-705.

Purtilo, R. (1984). *Health professional/patient interaction* (3rd ed.). Philadelphia: W. B. Saunders Company.

Quanty, M. B. (1976). Aggression catharsis: Experimental investigations and implications. In R G. Green & E. C. O'Neal (Eds.) *Perspectives on aggression.* New York: Academic Press.

Quattlebaum, M. S. (1969). Analyzing patients' behavior as an aid to disposition. *Hospital and Community Psychiatry, 20,* 241-242.

Rawson, H. E. (1978). Short-term residential therapeutic camping for behaviorally disordered children ages 6-12: An academic remediation and behavioral modification approach. *Therapeutic Recreation Journal, 12* (4), 17-23.

Reilly, D. E. (1978). *Teaching and evaluating the affective domain in nursing programs.* Thorofare, N. J: Charles B. Slack, Inc.

Reynolds R. P., & Arthur, M. H. (1982) Effects of peer modeling and cognitive self-guidance on the social play of emotionally disturbed children. *Therapeutic Recreation Journal, 16* (1), 33-40.

Richards, A., & Myers, A. (1987). Adventure challenge as a means of containment. *The Bradford Papers Annual, 2,* 45-53.

Ridenour, D. (1983). *Wellness: Building toward maximal health.* Bloomington, IN: South Central Community Mental Health Center.

Riehl, J. P., & Roy, C. (1980). *Conceptual models for nursing practice* (2nd ed.). New York: Appleton-Century-Crofts.

Ringness, T. A. (1975). *The affective domain in education.* Boston: Little, Brown and Company.

Robb, G. M. (Ed.) (1980). Outdoor and adventure programs: Complementing individual education programs and treatment plan objectives. *Practical Pointers, 4* (1), 1-23.

Robb, G. M., Leslie, J., & McGowan, M .L. (n. d.) *Sequential outdoor challenge activities.* Bloomington, IN: Indiana University.

Robb, S., Boyd, M., & Pristash, C.L. (1980). A wine bottle, plant, and puppy: Catalysis for social behavior. *Journal of Gerontological Nursing, 6*(12), 721-728.

Robb, S.S., Stegman, C.E., & Wolanin, M.O. (1986). No research versus research with compromised results: A study of validation therapy. *Nursing Research, 35* (2), 113-118.

Rogers, C. R. (1961). *On becoming a person: A therapist's view of psychotherapy.* Boston: Houghton Mifflin Company.

Rohnke, K. (1989). *Cowstails and cobras II.* Dubuque, IA: Kendall/Hunt Publishing Company.

Roland, C. C., Keene, T., Dubois, M., & Lentini, J. (1988). Experiential challenge program development in the mental health setting. *The Bradford Papers Annual, 3,* 66-77.

Roland, C .C., Summers, S., Friedman, M. J., Barton, G. M., & McCarthy, K. (1987). Creation of an experiential challenge program. *Therapeutic Recreation Journal, 21* (2), 54-63.

Rosenhan, D. L. (1973). On being sane in insane places. *Science, 179,* 250-258.

Rosenthal, R., & Jacobson, L. (1968). *Pygmalion in the classroom: Teacher expectation and pupils' intellectual development.* New York: Holt, Rinehart, & Winston.

Rosenthal, D., Teague, M., Retish, P., West, J., & Vessell, R. (1983). The relationship between work environment attributes and burnout. *Journal of Leisure Research, 15,* 125-135.

Rote, S. (1990). Alterations in immunity and inflammation. In K. L. McCance & S. Huether (Eds.), *Pathophysiology:The biologic basis for disease in adults and children* (Rothert & Daubert). St. Louis, MO: The C.V. Mosby Company.

Roth, S., & Kubal, L. (1975). The effects of noncontingent reinforcement on tasks of differing importance: Facilitation and learned helplessness effects. *Journal of Personality and Social Psychology, 32,* 680-691.

Rothert, E. A., & Daubert, J. R. (1981). *Horticulture therapy at a physical rehabilitation facility.* Glencoe, IL: Chicago Horticulture Society.

Rowe, C.J., and Mink, W.D. (1993). *An outline of psychiatry.* (10th ed.). Madison, WI, Brown and Benchmark.

Rucker, J. (1987). *The four-footed therapist.* Berkeley: Ten Speed Press.

Samuels, S. C. (1977). *Enhancing self-concept in early childhood.* New York: Human Sciences Press.

Sands, H., & Minters, F. C. (1977). *The epilepsy fact book.* Philadelphia: F. A. Davis Company.

Satir, V. (1972). *Peoplemaking.* Palo Alto, CA: Science and Behavioral Books, Inc.

Savell, K. (1986). Implications for therapeutic recreation leisure-efficacy: Theory and therapy programming. *Therapeutic Recreation Journal, 20* (1), 41-52.

Scanland, S.G., & Emershaw, L.E. (1993). Reality orientation and validation therapy: Dementia, depression, and functional status. *Journal of Gerontological Nursing, 19*(6), 7-11.

Scarf, M. (1980). The promiscuous woman. *Psychology Today, 14* (2), 78-87.

Schaefer, C. E., & Reid, S. E. (Eds.). (1986). *Game play: Therapeutic use of childhood games.* New York: John Wiley & Sons, Inc.

Schatzberg, A.F., & Nemeroff, C.B. (Eds.). (1995). *The American psychiatric press textbook of psychopharmacology.* Washington, D.C.: American Psychiatric Press, Inc.

Schimel, J.L. (1993). Reflections on the function of humor in psychotherapy, especially with adolescents. In W.F. Fry & W.A. Salameh (Eds.). *Advances in humor and psychotherapy.* Sarasota, FL: Professional Resource Press.

Schleien, S. J., & Wehman, P. (1986). Severely handicapped children: Social skills development through leisure skills programming. In G. Cartledge & J.F. Miburn (Eds.) *Teaching social skills to children* (2nd ed.). New York: Pergamon Press.

Schmokel, C. (1980). *An alternative to the Premack priniple.* Unpublished paper. Bloomington, IN: Indiana University.

Schmuck, R. A., & Schmuck, P. A. (1988). *Group processes in the classroom* (5th ed.). Dubuque, IA: Wm. C. Brown Company, Publishers.

Schoel, J., Prouty, D., & Radcliffe, P. (1988). *Islands of healing: A guide to adventure based counseling.* Hamilton, MA: Project Adventure, Inc.

Schofield, W. (1964). *Psychotherapy: The purchase of friendship.* Englewood Cliffs, NJ: Prentice-Hall, Inc.

Schul, B. D. (1975). *How to be an effective group leader.* Chicago: Nelson Hall.

Schulman, E. D. (1982). *Intervention in human services* (3rd ed.). St. Louis: The C. V. Mosby Company

Schultz, D. (1977). *Growth psychology: Models of the healthy personality.* New York: D. Van Nostrand Company.

Seligman, M. E. P. (1980). Fall into helplessness. In J. D. Samtic (Ed.), *Abnormal psychology: A perspective approach.* Wayne, NJ: Avery Publishing Group Inc.

Shank, J. W. (1985). Bioethical principles and the practice of therapeutic recreation in clinical settings. *Therapeutic Recreation Journal. 19* (4). 31-40.

Shank, J. W., & Kennedy, D. W. (1976). Recreation and leisure counseling: A review. *Rehabilitation Literature, 37* (9), 258-262.

Shannon, C., Wahl, P., Rhea, M., & Dyehouse, J. (1988). The nursing process. In C. K. Beck, R. P. Rawlins, & S. R. Williams (Eds.), *Mental health-psychiatric nursing: A holistic life-cycle approach* (2nd ed.). St. Louis: The C. V. Mosby Company.

Shaw, M.E., & Costanzo, P. R. (1982). *Theories of social psychology.* (2nd ed.). New York: McGraw-Hill Book Company.

Sheras, P.L., & Worchel, S. (1979). *Clinical psychology: A social psychological approach.* New York: Van Nostrand Reinhold Company.

Shinn, M., Rosario, M., Morch, H., & Chestnut, D.E. (1984). Coping with job stress and burnout in human services. *Journal of Personality and Social Psychology, 46,* 864-876.

Shives, L. R. (1994). *Basic concepts of psychiatric-mental health nursing* (3rd ed.). Philadelphia: J. B. Lippincott Company.

Shultz, C. (1988). Loneliness. In C. K. Beck, R. P. Rawlins & S. R. Williams (Eds.), *Mental health-psychiatric nursing.* St. Louis: The C. V. Mosby Company.

Simmons, J. A. (1976). *The nurse-client relationship in mental health nursing: Workbook guides to understanding and management.* (2nd ed.). Philadelphia: W. B. Saunders Company.

Simon, J. M. (1988). Therapeutic humor: Who's fooling who? *Journal of Psychosocial Nursing and Mental Health Services, 26* (4), 8-12.

Simon, S.B., Howe, L.W., & Kirschenbaum, H. (1995). *Values clarification.* New York: Warner Books, Inc.

Simon, S. B., & Olds, S. W. (1977). *Helping your children learn right from wrong: A guide to values clarification.* New York: McGraw-Hill Book Company.

Smith, J.C. (1993). *Understanding stress and coping.* New York: MacMillan.

Smith, R.W., Austin, D.R., & Kennedy, D.W. (1996). Inclusive and special recreation: *Opportunities for persons with disabilities* (3rd ed.). Madison, WI: Brown & Benchmark Publishers.

Smith, S. (1992). *Communications in nursing.* St. Louis: Mosby Year Book.

Smith, T. (1987). Foster families and adventure/challenge therapy. *The Bradford Papers Annual, 2,* 65-72.

Smith, T.E., Roland, C.C., Havens, M.D., & Hoyt, J.A. (1992). *The theory and practice of challenge education.* Dubuque, IA: Kendall/Hunt Publishing Company.

Sneegas, J.J. (1989). Social skills: An integral component of leisure participation and therapeutic recreation services. *Therapeutic Recreation Journal, 23* (2), 30-40.

Sohlberg, M.M., & Mateer, C.A. (1989). *Introduction to cognitive rehabilitation: Theory & practice.* New York: The Guilford Press.

Solomon, G. E., & Plum, F. (1976). *Clinical management of seizures: A guide for the physician.* Philadelphia: W B. Saunders Company.

Soltys, F.G., & Coats, L. (1995). The SolCos model: Facilitating reminiscence therapy. *Journal of Psychosocial Nursing, 33* (11), 21-26.

Sommer, R. (1969). *Personal space: The behavioral basis for design.* Englewood Cliffs, NJ: Prentice-Hall, Inc.

Stanley, J., & Kasson, I. (n.d.). *Guidelines for interviewing applicants and parents.* Trenton, NJ: Office on Community Recreation for Handicapped Persons, State of New Jersey Department of Community Affairs.

Steiner, C. M. (1974). *Scripts people live: Transactional analysis of life scripts.* New York: Grove Press, Inc.

Stephens, T. M. (1976). *Directive teaching of children with learning and behavioral handicaps* (2nd ed.). Columbus, OH: Charles E. Merrill Publishing Company.

Stephens, T.M. (1992). *Social skills in the classroom* (2nd ed.). Odessa, FL: Psychological Assessment Resources, Inc.

Stevens, B. J. (1979). *Nursing theory: Analysis, application, evaluation.* Boston: Little, Brown and Company.

Stevens, J.O. (1988). *Awareness: Exploring, experimenting, and experiencing.* London: Eden Grove Editions.

Stoltenberg, C. (1981). Approaching supervision from a developmental perspective: The counselor-complexity model. *Journal of Counseling Psychology, 28,* 59-65.

Stoltenberg, C., & Delworth, U. (1987). *Supervising counselors and therapists: A developmental approach.* San Francisco: Jossey-Bass.

Stone, W. L ., & Stone, C. G. (1952). *Recreation leadership.* New York: The Williams Frederick Press.

Storandt, M. (1983). *Counseling and therapy with older adults.* Boston: Little, Brown and Company.

Stoyva, J.M., & Budzynski, T.H. (1993). Biofeedback methods in the treatment of anxiety and stress disorders. In P.M. Lehrer & R.L. Woolfolk (Eds.), *Principles and practice of stress management* (2nd ed.). New York: The Guilford Press.

Stumbo, N. J. (1991). Selected assessment resources: A review of instruments and references. *Annual in Therapeutic Recreation, 2,* 8-24.

Sohlberg, M.N. & Mateer, C.A. (1989). *Introduction to cognitive rehabilitation: Theory & practice.* New York: The Guilford Press.

Soltys, F.G. & Coats, L. (1995). The SolCos model: Facilitating reminiscence therapy. *Journal of Psychosocial Nursing,* 33(11), 21-26.

Sugarman, D. (1988). Adventure education for people who have disabilities: A critical review. *The Bradford Papers Annual, 3,* 27-37.

Sundeen, S.J., Stuart, G.W., Rankin, E.A.D., & Cohen, S.A. (1994). *Nurse-client interaction: Implementing the nursing process* (5th ed.). St. Louis: Mosby.

Swackhamer, A. H. (1995). Alternatives: Complementary therapies: It's time to broaden our practice. *RN, 58*(1), 49-51.

Swonger, A. K., & Constantine, L. L. (1976). *Drugs and therapy.* Boston: Little, Brown and Company.

Sylvester, C. D. (1982). Exploring confidentiality in therapeutic recreation practice: An ethical responsibility in need of a response. *Therapeutic Recreation Journal, 16* (3), 25-34.

Sylvester, C. D. (1985). An analysis of selected ethical issues in therapeutic recreation. *Therapeutic Recreation Journal, 19* (4), 8-21.

Szymanski, D. J. (1989). *Hardiness and burnout in the staff of summer residence camps.* Unpublished dissertation. Bloomington, IN: Indiana University.

Tabourne, C.E.S. (1995). The life review program as an intervention for an older adult newly admitted to a nursing home facility: A case study. *Therapeutic Recreation Journal, 29* (3), 228-236.

Takata, N. (1974). Play as a prescription. In M. Reilly (Ed.). *Play as exploratory learning: Studies of curiosity behavior.* Beverly Hills, CA: Sage Publications.

Tamparo, C.D. & Lindh, W.Q. (1992). *Therapeutic communications for allied health professional.* Albany, NY: Delmar Publishers.

Taylor, C., Lillis, K. C., & LeMone, P. (1993). *Fundamentals of nursing* (2nd ed.). Philadelphia: J.B. Lippincott Company.

Teague, M.L., & MacNeil, R.D. (1992). *Aging and leisure: Vitality in later life* (2nd ed.). Dubuque, IA: Brown & Benchmark.

Thayer, S. (1988). Close encounters. *Psychology Today, 22* (3), 30-36.

The child with epilepsy at camp. (1981). Landover, MD: Epilepsy Foundation of America.

Thomas, P.S. (1994). Facility's TR department endorses aquatic therapy. *American Therapeutic Recreation Association Newsletter, 10*(4), 3.

Thornton, S., & Brotchie, J. (1987). Reminiscence: A critical review of the empirical literature. *British Journal of Clinical Psychology, 26,* 93-111.

Timberlake, W., & Allison, J. (1974). Response deprivation: An empirical approach to instrumental performance. *Psychological Review, 81,* 146-164.

Tinsley, H. E., & Tinsley, D. J. (1981). An analysis of leisure counseling models. *The Counseling Psychologist, 9,* 45-53.

Titlebaum, H. (1988). Relaxation. In Zahourek, R. P. (Ed.), *Relaxation & imagery: Tools for therapeutic communication and intervention.* Philadelphia: W. B. Saunders Company.

Toglia, J.P., & Golisz, K.M. (1990). *Cognitive rehabilitation: Group games and activities.* Tucson, AZ: Therapy Skill Builders.

Tubbs, S. L., & Moss, S. (1981). *Interpersonal communication* (2nd ed.). New York: Random House.

Unstress your life. (1987). Stanford, CT: Longmeadow Press.

Vernon, W. M. (1972). *Motivating children: Behavior modification in the classroom.* New York: Holt, Rinehart and Winston, Inc.

Voight, A. (1988). The use of ropes courses as a treatment modality for emotionally disturbed adolescents in hospitals. *Therapeutic Recreation Journal, 22* (2), 57-64.

Vortherms, R. (1991). Clinically improving communication through touch. *Journal of Gerontological Nursing, 17*(5), 6-10.

Wadle, K., Augsburg, B., & Martin, L. (1985). An evaluative study of a pet therapy program in the long term care psychiatric medical center. *Gerontologist, 25,* 135.

Waltzlawick, P., Beavin, J .H., & Jackson, D. D. (1967). *Pragmatics of human communication: A study of interactional patterns and paradoxes.* New York:W. W. Norton & Company, Inc.

Watson, J. B. (1913). Psychology as the behaviorist views it. *Psychological Review, 20,* 158-177.

Wehman, P., & Rettie, C. (1975). Increasing actions on play materials by severely retarded women through social reinforcement. *Therapeutic Recreation Journal, 9* (4), 173-178.

Wehman, P. (1977). Application of behavior modification techniques to play problems of the severely and profoundly retarded. *Therapeutic Recreation Journal, 11* (1), 16-21.

Wehman, P., & Schleien, S. J. (1980). Relevant assessment in leisure skill training programs. *Therapeutic Recreation Journal, 14* (4), 9-20.

Weiner, B. (Ed.). (1974). *Achievement and motivation and attribution theory.* Morristown, NJ: General Press.

Weiss, C. R. (1989). TR and reminiscing: The pursuit of elusive memory and the art of remembering. *Therapeutic Recreation Journal, 23* (3), 7-18.

Weiss, C. R., & Kronberg, J. (1986). Upgrading TR service to severely disoriented elderly. *Therapeutic Recreation Journal, 20* (1), 32-42.

Weiss, C. R., & Thurn, J. M. (1987). A mapping project to facilitate reminiscence in a long-term care facility. *Therapeutic Recreation Journal, 21* (2), 46-53.

West, O. (1990). *The magic of massage: A new and holistic approach.* Mamaroneck, NY: Hastings House Book Publishers.

Whitaker, D. S. (1985). *Using groups to help people.* New York: Routledge & Kegan Paul.

Whitcher, S. J., & Fisher, J. D. (1979). Multidimensional reaction to therapeutic touch in a hospital setting. *Journal of Personality and Social Psychology, 37,* 87-96.

Whitman, J.P., & Munson, W.W. (1992). Outcomes of adventure programs for adolescents in psychiatric treatment. *Annual in Therapeutic Recreation, 3,* 44-57.

Whitmer, R.W. (1982). *Whitmer's guide to total wellness.* New York: Doubleday & Company, Inc.

Wilberding, J.Z. (1992). Values clarification. In G.M. Bulechek & J.C. McCoskey (Eds.), *Nursing interventions: Essential nursing treatments* (2nd ed.). Philadelphia: W.B. Saunders Company.

Wilkinson, J., & Canter, S. (1982). *Social skills training manual.* New York: John Wiley & Sons.

Williams, A. (1995). *Visual & active supervision: Roles, focus, technique.* New York: W.W. Norton & Company.

Williamson, M. (1961). *Supervision—new patterns and processes.* New York: Associated Press.

Willson, M. (1987). *Occupational therapy in long-term psychiatry.* (2nd ed.). New York: Churchill Livingstone.

Willson, M. (1988). *Occupational therapy in short-term psychiatry.* (2nd ed.). New York: Churchill Livingstone.

Wilson, S.L., & McMillan, T.M. (1993). A review of the evidence for the effectiveness of sensory stimulation treatment for coma and vegetative states. *Neuropsychological Rehabilitation, 3*(2), 149-160.

Wilson, S.L., Powell, G.E., Elliot, K., & Thwaites, H. (1993). Evaluation of sensory stimulation as a treatment for prolonged coma—seven single experimental case studies. *Neuropsychological Rehabilitation, 3*(2), 191-201.

Winn,W.A. (1982). Physical challenge approaches to psychotherapy. In E. T. Nickerson & K. S. O'Laughlin (Eds.), *Helping through action-oriented therapies.* Amherst, MA: Human Resource Development Press.

Winslow, B. (1989). *NTRS training & education committee survey.* Unpublished report. Northridge, CA.

Witman, J. P. (1987). The efficacy of adventure programming in the development of cooperation and trust with adolescence in treatment. *Therapeutic Recreation Journal, 21* (3), 22-29.

Witman, J. P., & Lee, L. L. (1988). Social skills training for adults in psychiatric treatment: A program model. *Journal of Expanding Horizons in Therapeutic Recreation, 3,* 18-28.

Witt, P. A., & Ellis, G. D. (1987). *The leisure diagnostic battery users manual.* State College, PA: Venture Publishing, Inc.

Witman, J.P., & Munson, W.W. (1992). Outcomes of adventure programs for adolescents in psychiatric treatment. *Annual in Therapeutic Recreation, 3,* 44-57.

Wolfe, R. A., & Riddick, C. C. (1984). Effects of leisure counseling on adult psychiatric outpatients. *Therapeutic Recreation Journal, 18* (3), 30-37.

Woods, M. L. (1971). Development of a pay for recreation procedure in a token economy. *Mental Retardation, 2* (1), 54-57.

Woollams, S., Brown, M., & Huige, K. (1976). *Transactional analysis in brief.* Ann Arbor, MI: Huron Valley Institute.

Wortman, C. B., & Brehm, J. W. (1975). Responses to uncontrollable outcomes: An integration of reactance theory and the learned helplessness model. In L. Berkowitz (Ed.), *Advances in experimental social psychology.* (Vol. 8.). New York: Academic Press.

Wubbolding, R. E. (1988). Reality therapy: A method made for the recreation therapist. *ATRA Newsletter, 4* (6), 6,7.

Wubbolding, R. E. (1988). *Using reality therapy.* New York: Harper & Row.

Yalom, I.D. (1985) *The theory and practice of group psychotherapy.* (3rd edition). New York: Basic Books.

Yan, J.H. (1995). The health and fitness benefits of tai chi. *The Journal of Physical Education, Recreation & Dance, 66*(9), 61-63.

Yorukoglu, A. (1993). Favorite jokes and their use in psychotherapy with children and parents. In W.F. Fry & W.A. Salameh (Eds.), *Advances in humor and psychotherapy.* Sarasota, FL: Professional Resource Press.

Yura, H., & Walsh, M. B. (1988). *The nursing process* (5th ed.). Norwalk, CT: Appleton & Lange.

Yurcicin, S. (1995). Aquatics and the ATC. *Rehab Management, 8*(3), 50.

Zahourek, R. P. (1988). Imagery. In Zahourek, R. P. (Ed.), *Relaxation & imagery: Tools for therapeutic communication and intervention.* Philadelphia: W. B. Saunders Company.

INDEX

AUTHOR INDEX